D1547381

# Fascism in Film

MARCIA LANDY

# FASCISM IN FILM

## The Italian Commercial Cinema, 1931-1943

PRINCETON UNIVERSITY PRESS | PRINCETON, NEW JERSEY

Copyright © 1986 by Princeton University Press

Published by Princeton University Press, 41 William Street,
Princeton, New Jersey 08540

In the United Kingdom: Princeton University Press, Guildford, Surrey

All Rights Reserved

Library of Congress Cataloging in Publication Data will be found
on the last printed page of this book

ISBN 0-691-05471-1

This book has been composed in Linotron Palatino

Clothbound editions of Princeton University Press books are printed
on acid-free paper, and binding materials are chosen for strength
and durability

Printed in the United States of America by Princeton University
Press, Princeton, New Jersey

# CONTENTS

*(following page 146)*

1. Luciano De Ambrosis (Prico) in *I bambini ci guardano*, Vittorio De Sica, 1944 (Museum of Modern Art, Stills Archive)

2. Maria Denis (Dorina) and Adriano Rimoldi (Mario) in *Addio giovinezza!*, Ferdinando Maria Poggioli, 1940 (*Antologia del cinema italiano, il film sonoro, dal 1929 al 1943*)

3. Isa Miranda (Gaby) in *La signora di tutti*, Max Ophuls, 1934 (*Antologia del cinema italiano, il film sonoro, dal 1929 al 1943*)

4. Assia Noris (Arlette) in *Batticuore*, Mario Camerini, 1939 (Museum of Modern Art, Stills Archive)

5. Raffaele Viviani (Marchese Fusaro) in *La tavola dei poveri*, Alessandro Blasetti, 1932 (*Antologia del cinema italiano, il film sonoro, dal 1929 al 1943*)

6. Edoardo De Filippo (The Governor) and Leda Gloria (Carmela) in *Il cappello a tre punte*, Mario Camerini, 1935 (*Antologia del cinema italiano, il film sonoro, dal 1929 al 1943*)

7. Annibale Ninchi (Scipio) in *Scipione l'Africano*, Carmine Gallone, 1937 (Museum of Modern Art, Stills Archive)

8. Giuseppe Gulino (Carmeliddu) in *1860*, Alessandro Blasetti, 1934 (Museum of Modern Art, Stills Archive)

9. Vittorio De Sica (Gianni-Max) in *Il signor Max*, Mario Camerini, 1937 (Museum of Modern Art, Stills Archive)

10. Adriana Benetti (Maria) and Gino Cervi (Paolo) in *Quattro passi fra le nuvole*, Alessandro Blasetti, 1942 (Museum of Modern Art, Stills Archive)

11. Isa Miranda (Marina) in *Malombra*, Mario Soldati, 1942 (Museum of Modern Art, Stills Archive)

12. Clara Calamai (Giovanna) and Massimo Girotti (Gino) in *Ossessione*, Luchino Visconti, 1943 (Museum of Modern Art, Stills Archive)

THE commercial films produced in Italy from 1931 to 1943 are a way to unlock the hearts and minds of people under fascism, to find out how ideas and images predating fascism came to roost in fascism and how attitudes prevalent under fascism persisted beyond that era. These films are also a reservoir of contradictions, and an examination of their pretexts and subtexts, their overt and covert attitudes, exposes structures of opposition to as well as support for the state apparatuses. Why then have these films not been screened or examined? Why have scholars taken no great interest in them? Histories of Italian and world film have conspicuously omitted discussion of the films of this era except to refer briefly to them as propaganda, as "telefoni bianchi" (white telephone) films, as escapist entertainment, as frivolous.

Recent critical work has challenged these commonly held views of Italian commercial cinema of the fascist years and paved the way for new readings of films produced during the "Ventennio." In 1974, a conference on Italian neorealism held in Pesaro, Italy, climaxed in a call to reevaluate the origins of the postwar Italian cinema. The conference led to a retrospective in 1975 where films of the fascist era were screened. Though it had been traditional for film scholars and critics to isolate certain film texts as "anticipations" of neorealism (e.g., *I bambini ci guardano* [The Children Are Watching Us] and *Quattro passi fra le nuvole* [A Walk among the Clouds]), no one had previously looked for neorealism's antecedents. In 1976, another conference was held at Ancona, Italy, which afforded the opportunity for an initial reappraisal of the films produced from 1931 to 1943.

Since 1976, studies have appeared primarily in Italy covering many different aspects of film production under fascism, studies of censorship, distribution, financing, the role of the Church, the status of intellectuals in the cinema, the star system, the role of criticism and of film theory during that era, and the relations between the prefascist and fascist cinema. These studies stress relations to the Hollywood cinema, particularly in the nature and role of the genre film. Critics have documented Soviet influences as well as later influences from the French cinema. Additional films have been uncovered. A variety of genres—adventure films, historical dramas, comedies, melodramas, and musicals—have surfaced. Dominant directors of the period have been discussed, especially Alessandro Blasetti and Mario Camerini, and, more recently, Ferdinando Maria Poggioli. Theoretical and critical writings on the cinema have also been examined. Today, the task of the scholar and critic is made vastly simpler by these pioneering efforts.

Of the approximately 700 films produced during the fascist regime, about 300 to 350 remain, many only in negative. Other than the films at the Centro Sperimentale in Rome and the archives in Milan, these films can be located in the United States at the Library of Congress and the Museum of Modern Art in New York, and in the film archives in London, Berlin, Prague, and Budapest.

My study of the Italian cinema is based on a number of resources. First, more than one hundred of these films were made available to me at the Centro Sperimentale di Cinematografia in Rome, the film section of the Library of Congress, and the Museum of Modern Art. The pioneering work of Ted Perry in the United States and works of such Italian critics as Adriano Aprà and Patrizia Pistagnesi, Francesco Savio, Roberto Campari, Lino Micciché, but especially the studies by Gian Piero Brunetta on the history of Italian cinema, have provided documentation, a background against which to examine these films. Such studies of fascism as Nicos Poulantzas's *Fascism and Dictatorship*, Gaetano Salvemini's *The Origins of Fascism in Italy*, Ernesto Laclau's *Politics and Ideology in Marxist Theory*, Togliatti's *Lectures on Fascism*, Renzo De Felice's biography of Mussolini, Victoria de Grazia's *The Culture of Consent*: *Mass Organization of Leisure in Fascist Italy*, Adrian Lyttelton's *The Seizure of Power*: *Fascism in Italy 1919-1929*, and the writings of Edward Tannenbaum, Philip V.

Cannistraro, and George Mosse, among others, provided me
with a basis to link film production to the history of the era.
   To the institutions where I screened films—the Centro Sperimentale di Cinematografia, the film sections of the Library
of Congress and of the Museum of Modern Art, to the staffs
that assisted me, and to all the critics and historians, I can
only repay them with my esteem. I am grateful to the Museum
of Modern Art for permission to use photographs from the
Stills Archive and for allowing me to reproduce frame en-
largements from their *Antologia del cinema italiano, il film sonoro.*
I also want to thank the University of Pittsburgh, which
granted me a leave from my duties in film studies to pursue
this work, provided me with a travel grant, funds for screen-
ing the films, and additional funds to defray typing expenses,
and to Ruth Ann Schulte for transforming handwritten text
into typed copy. I want to express my gratitude and appreciation to my colleagues, Lucy Fischer, Dana Polan, Maridina
Salvatori, and to Victoria de Grazia for their careful and patient reading and commenting on various versions of the man-
uscript. I am most indebted to Stanley Shostak, colleague and
collaborator on many film projects, for his challenging criticism and for his encouragement. I assume full responsibility
for the final text as I do for the translations from the Italian.

*Pittsburgh*
*February 1985*

# Fascism in Film

# Remembrance of Things Past

Most film critics and filmgoers have formed an impression of the Italian commercial cinema from such silent films as *Quo Vadis* and from postwar neorealist films. A long period in the production of Italian feature films from the beginnings of sound to the end of World War II has not had any impact on our understanding of Italian cinema. I am well aware in writing about the films produced in Italy from 1931 to 1942 that most of my readers will have seen few, if any, of these films and may be inclined to dismiss them as propaganda. My book is intended to address this oversight and change some of these impressions.

The postwar Italian cinema is identified with the movement known as "neorealism," whose major project was the de-mystification of the ideology and practices of fascism. Such familiar films as *Open City, Paisan, Bicycle Thieves*, and *Shoe Shine* confronted the effects of fascism. In their content, they explored authoritarianism; bureaucracy and power; violence; consensus and conformity; the oppression of workers, and passive obedience to tradition, the law, and the state. In their style, they sought to develop a film language that was critical of the formalism, hermeticism, and escapism which they felt characterized the cultural practices under fascism. The neorealist cinema sought to create a language to embody its critique and to communicate a sense of new cultural imperatives. Neorealism, as the name suggests, "reclaimed the territory of reality, and in that reclamation denied the claims of past filmmaking while announcing itself as a beginning for filmmaking to come."[1] Filmmakers sought a way of structuring cinema through the use of real images and events. The desired

[1] Robert Philip Kolker, *The Altering Eye: Contemporary International Cinema* (Oxford: Oxford University Press, 1983), p. 17.

style was improvisational, journalistic, and colloquial. The cinema was to be more sociological than overtly political, stressing hunger, poverty, domestic relations, and social class.

In their zeal to regenerate Italian cultural practices, the neorealists created their own myths. The most blatant myth was the myth of "newness," of "beginning." Although the neorealists sought to examine the nature of fascism, they obscured their own beginnings in the fascist era. For example, before 1945, films had indeed been made on location; the use of nonprofessional actors was not uncommon; and the reclamation of reality had already begun.[2] In their rejection of what had gone before, the neorealist filmmakers and critics eliminated an important resource for understanding the very issues they claimed to study, namely, the ways in which fascism was able to gain support and adherents.

The preceding cinema became the "skeleton in the closet," as Lino Miccichè has described it,[3] thereby creating a lacuna in the history of Italian cinema. If history is a reminder of necessity, the forgetting of this history does not make it disappear,[4] nor does it in any way ensure that it will not recur. By underrating the "Italian cinema which was rebuilding itself

[2] Gian Piero Brunetta, *Cinema italiano tra le due guerre: Fascismo e politica cinematografica* (Milan: Mursia, 1975), pp. 91-98. See also Pierre Leprohon, *The Italian Cinema* (New York: Praeger, 1972), pp. 79-84; Peter Bondanella, *Italian Cinema: From Neorealism to the Present* (New York: Frederick Ungar, 1983), pp. 23-25; Franco Venturini, "Origins of Neo-Realism," in *Springtime in Italy: A Reader on Neo-Realism*, ed. David Overbey (Hamden, Conn.: Archon Books, 1978), pp. 169-97; Mira Liehm, *Passion and Defiance: Film in Italy: From 1942 to the Present* (Berkeley and Los Angeles: University of California Press, 1984), pp. 12-16. Gian Piero Brunetta discusses Nino Martoglio's *Sperduti nel buio* (Lost in the Darkness, 1914) and *Teresa Raquin* (1915) as exemplary texts of the Neapolitan school of filmmaking which utilized the external locale of Naples. In discussions of the development of neorealism, these films have been cited as harbingers of the realist aesthetic. *Storia del cinema italiano 1895-1945* (Rome: Riuniti, 1979), p. 166.

[3] Lino Miccichè, "Il cadavere nell' armadio," in *Cinema italiano sotto il fascismo*, ed. Riccardo Redi (Venice: Marsilio, 1979), pp. 9-18.

[4] Fredric Jameson, *The Political Unconscious: Narrative as a Socially Symbolic Act* (Ithaca: Cornell University Press, 1981), pp. 100-101.

around classical genres like the comedy and melodrama," the neorealist aesthetic also underrated the role of popular cinema in the formation of ideology.[5] Adriano Aprà and Patrizia Pistagnesi have suggested that "the suppression of the 1929-43 cinema on the part of traditional critics was always more of a conspiracy of silence than an ideologically motivated refutation; it hid a diffidence, not so much toward the fascism of these films as toward their character as spectacles, and, in the final analysis, toward film as the product of a collective imagination."[6] My examination of the cinema of the thirties and early forties proceeds on the assumption that these films have a great deal to teach about the discourse of fascism and how the subject was situated within it.

According to Aprà and Pistagnesi, when the films of the Ventennio were viewed at the Ancona retrospective, the critics were surprised that they "hold up so well with time, that the *average* quality (typical of the film industry) was so high, and above all that from these films is extracted an image of Italian reality—with all the mediations of a cinema tied to the classical rules of the spectacle—different and above all more complex than the simplifications of traditional histories . . . had led one to believe."[7]

The "reality" alluded to by Aprà and Pistagnesi refers to the diverse ways these films, like their Hollywood counterparts, found to "give the audience what it wants," rather than specializing in a programmatic approach.[8] While it is the case that films such as *Lo squadrone bianco, Alcazar, Scipione l'Africano, Vecchia guardia*, and *Camicia nera* reveal the familiar and public face of fascism with its emphasis on national destiny,

---

[5] Adriano Aprà and Patrizia Pistagnesi, *Notes on the Unknown Italian Cinema* (New York: Museum of Modern Art, 1978), p. 2.

[6] Ibid., p. 4.

[7] Ibid.

[8] The "repressive tolerance of the fascist regime," notes Edward R. Tannenbaum, "was actually more insidious and corrupting than the overt inhumanity of the Nazis. The latter is not likely to reappear as a danger; the former might." *Fascism in Italy: Society and Culture 1922-1945* (London: Allen Lane, 1972), p. 4.

power, conquest, sacrifice, hero worship, and the objectification of the masses, along the lines of Susan Sontag's discussion of "fascinating fascism,"[9] the Italian films have important links to the Hollywood adventure films and historical dramas in their subordination of message to entertainment.

The films are instructive about the subtle ways in which people's needs and desires were managed. The cinema of the era was, in fact, a family cinema. The narratives and their imagery were built on the foundation of sexual difference, on an ahistorical discourse (even where they appear most historical) that arises from biological categories: young and old people, men and women, nature. Natural conflicts were pitted against social conflicts in an attempt to repress and redirect concrete historical and economic considerations. The films play on fears of chaos, irresolution, and the unknown. They offer a vision of a world where anxieties are mastered. The desire for change is gratified through the appearance of change.

But the films are not mute about their strategies. Even where the narratives seem to be most exemplary of ideology talking to itself, they expose themselves. When they are working hardest to create a sense of shared attitudes and community, they appear to parody the very things they endorse. In certain instances, especially in the comedies and melodramas, the films appear almost consciously to express opposition, though this opposition must be read as ambiguous, if not contradictory. In any case, in order to be successful, the cinema had to make contact with the experiences of its audience, and this entailed the creation of a popular cinema based on commonly shared images.

A close examination of the history and nature of film production in Italy during the fascist years forces a revision of the idea that under fascism every aspect of life was controlled by the dominant state apparatus and that this control always manifested itself in overtly coercive fashion. Even under fas-

[9] Susan Sontag, "Fascinating Fascism," in *Movies and Methods*, ed. Bill Nichols (Berkeley: University of California Press, 1976), pp. 31-43.

cism, consent was necessary.[10] Although it is true that in the early twenties, the fascist movement had no clear and positive program and it was, as Angelo Tasca has claimed, *"not organizing but disorganizing* the masses."[11] By the middle twenties the regime began to address the development of strategies for wooing the masses, strategies that were "not so different from those faced elsewhere in Europe by liberal-democratic regimes in the process of stabilizing their rule."[12] As Victoria de Grazia cautions, though the Italian fascist regime sought to develop organizations and policies designed to promote consensus, its form of creating consent must be differentiated from those of liberal democratic governments, since under fascism "force was both the premise and the constant threat."[13] Nonetheless, as a study of the commercial films demonstrates, the regime sought increasingly to appeal to all classes, to create a sense of collective social endeavor, to make the "new order" attractive through the development of cultural forms aimed at penetrating all forms of social life: the family, the workplace, and even leisure activities.[14] The fascist cultural "revolution" envisioned the transformation of the daily interior life of the worker.[15]

The regime was slow in developing the commercial cinema as an apparatus that could serve these ends. Only gradually did the notion of cinema as a vehicle for creating a "popular culture" emerge, and with it the development of narratives, themes, and images geared to a vision of a new and modern

---

[10] According to Adrian Lyttelton, "Mussolini gave frequent assurances that literature and the arts should remain free and not subject to political control." *The Seizure of Power: Fascism in Italy 1919-1929* (New York: Charles Scribner's Sons, 1973), p. 380.

[11] Angelo Tasca, *The Rise of Italian Fascism, 1919-1922* (New York: Howard Fertig, 1966), p. 25.

[12] Victoria de Grazia, *The Culture of Consent: Mass Organization of Leisure in Fascist Italy* (Cambridge: Cambridge University Press, 1981), p. 3.

[13] Ibid., p. 23.

[14] Anna Panicali, "L'intellettuale fascista," in *Cinema italiano sotta il fascismo*, ed. Redi, pp. 29-50.

[15] Renzo De Felice, *Fascism: An Informal Introduction to Its Theory and Practice*, ed. Michael Ledeen (New Brunswick: Transaction Books, 1976), p. 55.

society, a society in the throes of industrialization and modernization. This struggle for change manifested itself in the contradictory and ambiguous visions of "reality" that emerge in the films of the thirties and early forties, contradictions and ambiguities not far removed from internal ideological conflicts of culture and politics under fascism.[16] It has been a critical disservice merely to dismiss the film production of the thirties as escapist and to accord exclusive attention to those texts that seem overtly monumental and, hence, "fascist" or to those that signal the emergence of the neorealist aesthetic.

This study argues that these "escapist" films, admittedly less popular with Italian audiences than their Hollywood counterparts of the era, deserve attention because in them one finds images, attitudes, and values that can help to alter, expand, and redefine the nature of fascist ideology. The image of the fictional world that emerges from a study of these films is a profoundly eclectic one, touching on central aspects of everyday reality—the nature of sexual roles, the family, work, the physical environment, the conflict between rural and urban values. For the most part, the films strive to reconcile class and sexual differences, to reaffirm the importance of the family, and to exalt a sense of national identity couched in a progressive rhetoric, one that uses history to legitimate tradition or change, but, in so doing, the films, stylized and artificial as they may seem, reveal conflicts and offer the

[16] See de Grazia, *The Culture of Consent*; Tannenbaum, *Fascism in Italy*; George L. Mosse, *Masses and Man: Nationalist and Fascist Perceptions of Reality* (New York: Howard Fertig, 1980). Philip V. Cannistraro, *La fabbrica del consenso: Fascismo e mass media* (Roma-Bari: Laterza, 1975); Palmiro Togliatti, *Lectures on Fascism* (New York: International Publishers, 1973); Tasca, *The Rise of Italian Fascism*; Gaetano Salvemini, *The Origins of Fascism in Italy* (New York: Harper and Row, 1973); Giovanni Mira and Luigi Salvatorelli, *Storia d'Italia nel periodo fascista*, 2 vols. (Turin: Einaudi, 1970); Nicos Poulantzas, *Fascism and Dictatorship: The Third International and the Problem of Fascism* (London: NLB, 1974); Ernesto Laclau, *Politics and Ideology in Marxist Theory* (London: NLB, 1977); De Felice, *Fascism*; Renzo De Felice, *Mussolini il fascista*, vol. 1: *La conquista del potere 1921-1925* (Turin: Einaudi, 1966) and Mihaly Vajda, *Fascism as Mass Movement* (New York: St. Martin Press, 1976).

viewer a sense of the nature and the irreconcilability of these conflicts.

At the beginning of the fascist era, the film industry was in disarray. The development, in fact the rebuilding, of the Italian film industry was a formidable task, as formidable as the problems of capitalization and modernization in other sectors of industry the regime attempted to revamp.[17] At one time, Italy had been a pioneer in the production of feature films and was therefore not bereft of expertise, interest, and a sense of direction. In the early silent era, Italian films not only had great domestic currency but were influential and lucrative export items. According to Jack C. Ellis, "the Italians' inclinations were toward historical and religious spectacles set in their own glorious past."[18] These films, moreover, had an impact on early American film production. D. W. Griffith, in particular, emulated the form and style of some of these historical epics. However, in the early twenties, due to a combination of economic and social factors, the industry experienced devastating financial decline. Among the factors contributing to this decline were disorganized forms of production, industrial improvisation to "plug the holes," production costs rising to staggering heights, an almost complete lack of foreign markets, arrested development both technologically and creatively, and, above all, competition from the Hollywood cinema.[19] The problems went far deeper than economic underdevelopment. As James Hay has suggested, "Italy's lack of technology was not as responsible for the demise of the industry during the twenties as were the insipid thematics of the movies, coupled with the growing attractiveness of American images."[20]

The old historical epic form and style no longer attracted audiences. Nonetheless, Italian filmmakers continued to

[17] Tannenbaum, *Fascism in Italy*, pp. 100-120.

[18] Jack C. Ellis, *A History of Film* (Englewood Cliffs, N.J.: Prentice-Hall, Inc., 1979), p. 52.

[19] Brunetta, *Cinema italiano tra le due guerre*, pp. 15-28.

[20] James Hay, *Popular Film Culture in Fascist Italy* (Bloomington: University of Indiana Press, 1986).

mount archaic and expensive productions in an attempt to regain the success of such films as *The Last Days of Pompei, Cabiria*, and *Quo Vadis*. The Italian star system (*Il divisimo*) intensified financial losses, since stars continued to demand exorbitant salaries for films that had little likelihood of making a profit.[21] If the industry was to survive it had to confront its obsolescent practices and meet the challenges of cultural economic change either through new private initiatives or with the assistance of the government. Initially the government was reticent. According to Philip V. Cannistraro, the first intervention of the regime was administrative rather than financial.[22] In the early twenties, the government reaffirmed the 1913 censorship guidelines prohibiting films that offended private morality and public decency; contained scenes that were violent, cruel, repugnant, or perverse; disturbed the public order; or damaged the authority or prestige of public officials. No new and explicit rules were laid down to politicize the cinema in the interests of promoting fascist ideals.[23] Mussolini created a commission to oversee the implementation of the censor's guidelines. No major changes occurred until 1934 when the regime began to act more aggressively to spread fascist ideas and the office of censorship was moved to the Ministry of Press and Propaganda.[24]

In 1924, the regime created Instituto LUCE (L'Unione Cinematografica Educativa), which was to produce documentaries and newsreels and to screen and censor foreign newsreels.[25] In the course of a few years, LUCE succeeded in managing public information in monopolistic fashion. Through the *cinegiornali*, the newsreels, the regime imposed itself in a significant way on the arena of mass communication.

[21] Brunetta, *Cinema italiano tra le due guerre*, p. 19.

[22] Cannistraro, *La fabbrica del consenso*, pp. 274-80.

[23] Ibid., p. 274.

[24] Ibid., p. 275. See also *The New York Times Encyclopedia of Film*, vol. 3 (New York: Times Press, 1984).

[25] Brunetta, *Storia del cinema italiano 1895-1945*, pp. 236-39. See also Elaine Mancini, *The Free Years of the Italian Film Industry 1930-1935* (Ann Arbor, Mich.: University Microfilms, 1981).

LUCE was designed as the propaganda arm of the regime and as such received financial support.

In the sector of commercial film production, the picture was quite different. The situation was, to echo Edward Tannenbaum, "scandalous." Commercial film producers received no assistance from the regime: "The Italian market was dominated by American productions which conquered the world during the era of silent film, while the Italian industry all but died for want of capital and up-to-date methods and themes."[26]

The only significant attempt to revivify and restructure the ailing industry came from private initiative, particularly through the efforts of Stefano Pittaluga. In 1925, he convened a congress of film producers, businessmen, and distributors which articulated a series of proposals for the improvement of production and distribution. In the following year, Pittaluga assumed control of the UCI (Unione Cinematografica Italiana). He absorbed smaller companies, centralized operations, modernized the technology and production methods, and attempted to rationalize the relationship of foreign to domestic products without drastically curtailing imports. Ultimately, his company, the Società Anonima Stefano Pittaluga, became the Cines-Pittaluga Company that, according to Peter Bondanella, "would eventually form the basis of the Ente Nazionale Industrie Cinematografiche (ENIC) which the government formed in 1935 to direct the entire industry."[27] Moreover, the government gave Pittaluga the franchise to distribute LUCE films, an action that signified an initial movement of cooperation between the regime and private enterprise. Pittaluga's policies provided the future direction for the industry and were maintained after his death in 1931 under the leadership of Emilio Cecchi, head of the Cines studio (later Cinecittà), and Luigi Freddi, who assumed the position of director general of cinematography in 1934.

In 1931, the regime again intervened with a series of pro-

[26] Tannenbaum, *Fascism in Italy*, p. 269.
[27] Bondanella, *Italian Cinema*, p. 12.

tectionist measures designed to stem the overwhelming competition from Hollywood and to enhance Italian production.
A quota system was initiated, which stipulated that for every
ten films programmed in theaters, there must be one Italian
film. Furthermore, foreign films that were not dubbed in Italian were prohibited. In 1934, the government attempted to
institute the practice of taxing foreign films produced in Italy
and rechanneling the funds to Italian producers. In this same
year, the regime began to offer prizes for films that were
deemed to be of high artistic quality, and the appointment of
Luigi Freddi as director general of cinematography initiated
what became known as the "Freddi era," associated with the
"white telephone" films.[28] Freddi's approach was characterized by measures aimed at modernization of the industry
along Hollywood lines and a production policy that favored
entertainment over propaganda. His attitude toward cinema
was shared by Giuseppe Bottai, the minister of culture, who
asserted:

The government has wanted to aid the industry in a specific activity
which is to resist foreign industry, and to bring to our market some
films of plot, variety, and imagination, which constitute a powerful
attraction to the public. I go rarely to the cinema, but I have always
believed that the public is invariably bored when the cinema wants
to educate it. The public wants to be entertained, and it is precisely
on this terrain that we wish today to aid the Italian cinema.[29]

Supporting this position, Freddi prophesied: "Today the cer-
tainty is born that in a very short time, the Italian fascist will
have his say in the cinematic arena. It will be a word that will
serve the hour in which we live."[30]

Freddi played a significant role in redesigning the structure
of the Italian cinema. Recognizing the need for more experimentation, more professionalism, better scripts and acting,

[28] Adriano Aprà, "Linee di politica cinematografica da Blasetti a Freddi,"
in Cinema italiano sotto il fascismo, ed. Redi, pp. 107-115.

[29] Brunetta, Storia del cinema italiano, p. 308. See Vittorio Mussolini, "In
cerca della formula," Cinema 2 (10 February 1937), pp. 34-41.

[30] Massimo Mida and Lorenzo Quaglietti, Dai telefoni bianchi al neorealismo
(Rome-Bari: Laterza, 1980), p. 20.

and film education, he laid the groundwork for the development of a popular cinema. Bottai's and Freddi's pronouncements corroborate the heavily commercial orientation of both the government and private industry at this time, the fact that the development of a popular cinema was motivated more by economic than by ideological considerations. The films that received government prizes were not necessarily those that exalted fascism but rather those that demonstrated box-office appeal. Indoctrination and propaganda took a back seat to profit. Threaded through Freddi's discussion are references to the importance of competition, professional excellence, international acclaim, the concrete problem of increasing public attendance at films, reducing imports, especially from the United States, and proper forms of protection for national film products while at the same time satisfying the demand for films. As part of the effort to modernize the industry, representatives of the Italian industry visited European capitals in order to glean methods for enhancing Italian production. They also visited the United States to study the American film industry. Joint production companies were formed with French, German, and Hungarian companies, and American filmmakers such as Frank Capra were invited to Italy prior to the outbreak of the war to share their expertise with Italian directors and producers.

The creation of the Centro Sperimentale di Cinematografia in 1935 was intended to improve the quality of film production. The Centro was conceived of as a cultural resource, containing a school, library, and cinematheque. The institution sponsored the publication of a journal and of books on the cinema. Under the leadership of Luigi Chiarini, such directors as Alessandro Blasetti and writers as Umberto Barbaro worked and taught. According to Chiarini, the aims of the Centro were to raise the technical and cultural level of filmmaking through experimentation in film production methods and the development of appropriate film theory and criticism.[31] Toward the latter half of the thirties, the Centro became a locus for nonfascist intellectuals who articulated new

---

[31] Brunetta, *Storia del cinema italiano*, pp. 317-19.

trends in filmmaking, trends that were to become associated
later with antifascism and with the neorealist aesthetic. Massimo Mida, Giuseppe De Santis, Luigi Zampa, Mario Alicata,
and Cesare Zavattini were representative of the critics who
called for new directions. Although Chiarini himself sub-
scribed to fascist ideals he demonstrated extraordinary openness to experimentation and even toleration of oppositional
tendencies.[32]

The near-doubling of Italian film production during the next
five years was also enhanced by the intervention of the IRI
(Istituto per la ricostruzione industriale), a state-created organization for the investment of funds in the private sector
whereby loans and subsidies were granted to film producers
and distributors. As an incentive to promote film production,
the government offered awards to certain films. Such films
as *Squadrone bianco* (White Squadron) and *Scipione l'africano*
(Scipio Africanus) received funding on the grounds that they
fostered fascist ideals and had wide box-office appeal. The
regime's investment climbed from 18 million lire in 1934 to
71 million by 1937.[33] As a consequence of the greater state
and private cooperation, operations in the film industry became more streamlined, and films that presented new images
of contemporary social life began to appear.

By 1938, the nature and status of Italian commercial film
production had changed. More films were being made. The
feature films had improved both technically and stylistically,
and box-office receipts were on the increase. The regime had
by now committed itself more fully to the film industry. Mussolini inaugurated the newly built Cinecittà, modeled along
the lines of Hollywood as a facility that could support a full
cycle of film production. Moreover, the threat by the regime
to close off American imports was finally materialized. The
German-Italian alliance and the 1938 Alfieri law succeeded in
drastically reducing American films.[34] Furthermore, in an ef-

[32] See Luigi Chiarini, *Cinematografo* (Rome: Cremonese, 1935) and *Cinque
capitoli sul film* (Rome: Italian Editions, 1941).

[33] Brunetta, *Storia del cinema italiano*, p. 293.

[34] Cannistraro, *La fabbrica del consenso*, pp. 396-97.

fort at centralization in 1941, the government attempted through legislation to limit production companies. The object was to eliminate inferior productions and to reduce credit to film companies, thus effectively leaving the way open for the larger, more profitable producers. The regime and the film industry did not want to limit the number of films produced, but rather to stabilize the continuing crises in the film industry through greater centralization. Nonetheless, in 1940, eighty-three films were produced by forty-seven companies, and in the following year eighty-nine were produced by fifty-four companies.[35] Moreover, new theaters were opened in 1940 in rural areas and films were needed to supply these theaters.[36]

The critical writings in the thirties corroborate changes in direction. The dominant journals were *Lo schermo, Bianco e nero, Critica fascista, Intercine,* and *Cinema.* In these journals, in the contemporary histories of film, and in the film criticism of the time, one can trace the vicissitudes of fascism. For example, in the early years, writers were concerned to emphasize the role that film could play in relation to the growth of fascism. Articles and reviews addressed the nature and roles of the Hollywood cinema, particularly the work of such directors as Frank Capra. It is not surprising that the American film should receive attention, given its popularity with Italian audiences and given the Italian film industry's struggle to regenerate itself along American lines. What is surprising, however, is the influence of the Soviet style of filmmaking (Blasetti's *1860* is a notable example).[37] This tendency emanated most conspicuously from the "fascists of the left" whose interest was in a vision of fascism as a new and revolutionary movement. Soviet montage in the films of the era was not indicative of adherence to Marxist theory and practice but a recognition of the effectiveness of montage in the treatment of "epic" subjects, of historical events, and of mass action. The Soviet influence was never as dominant as the American

---

[35] Brunetta, *Storia del cinema italiano,* p. 298.
[36] Ibid.
[37] Brunetta, *Cinema italiano tra le due guerre,* pp. 67-73.

or even the Hungarian. The practice of assimilating foreign models and styles was always regarded with some caution, for fear of overwhelming Italian cultural concerns, but the incorporation of foreign techniques was ultimately to produce films with an apparent Italian content, films that, to quote Freddi, constituted "art for the people."

Toward the end of the thirties, critics such as Umberto Barbaro, Luchino Visconti, Giuseppe De Santis, and Carlo Lizzani encouraged dialogues about "realism," reacting against the "artificiality" of the cinema of genres.[38] The journal articles on scripting, acting, and especially the reviews of foreign and Italian films were the media through which re- action against existing film production grew. In the years from 1941 to 1943, this discourse became more insistent. Films that displayed realist tendencies were discussed and identified as models. The appearance of Luchino Visconti's *Ossessione* in 1942 was part of this tendency. Visconti himself had written articles about Giovanni Verga in the journal, *Cinema*, the dom- inant forum associated with these ideas. In the pages of *Ci- nema*, articles on Verga, American fiction, the films of Jean Renoir, and Italian films revealed the growing predilection for the realist mode. The essays registered negative reactions against the films of evasion.

The critics and filmmakers associated with *Cinema* are evi- dence of oppositional tendencies at work in the film industry in the later years of fascism. The dialogue over realism was, in part, an attempt to make contact with prefascist literary and ideological movements and to develop new cultural models for the future based on European and American writ- ers and filmmakers. The critical essays in *Cinema* demonstrate changes in attitudes toward film and social reality in the late 1930s and early 1940s. They also reveal that the rejection of the genre cinema was based on style as well as content.

[38] Mida and Quaglietti, *Dai telefoni bianchi al neorealismo*, pp. 183-270. For example, while a critic like De Santis might feel ambivalent about some of Poggioli's work, he praised Blasetti's *Quattro passi fra le nuvole*, *L'uomo dalla croce* by Rossellini, and such works of De Sica's as *Un garibaldino al convento* and *Teresa Venerdì* as being more open, less hermetic.

An analysis of the genre films offers an insight into the workings of mass culture, how subjects are situated within ideological formations and how these processes are effected within the text and in relation to the audiences.[39] According to Thomas Schatz, the genre film should be considered "not only as some filmmaker's artistic expression, but further as the cooperation between artists and audience in celebrating their collective values and ideals. In fact, many qualities traditionally viewed as artistic shortcomings—the psychologically static hero, for instance, or the predictability of the plot—assume a significantly different value when examined as components of a genre's ritualistic narrative system."[40] One of the primary characteristics of the cinema of genres is its formulaic nature. The narratives are dependent on a predictable progression, moving from conflict, through elaboration of conflict, to resolution. The context of the genre film is not a historical society (though the film will be embedded in some historical context), but an idealized community. This community will be presented in formulaic fashion, identified through the characters who are representatives of the community, through a use of space and place in indeterminate fashion, and through "certain dramatic conflicts that we associate wth specific patterns of action and character relationships."[41] The actors in the conflicts are not individualized but linked to a fixed iconography, their actions more often related to magical and mythic agencies than to logic.

Because these narratives belong to the realm of the folk tale or romance, they appear to be dissociated from their cultural and social milieu and have been accordingly judged as escapist, but their origins in popular storytelling, their relationship to collective forms of representation, their very formulaic and stylized qualities, their basis of appeal to mass audiences, suggest that these works, in their style and content, have

[39] Sergio Grmek Germani, "Introduzione a una ricerca sui generi," in *Cinema italiano sotto il fascismo*, ed. Redi, pp. 81-98.

[40] Thomas Schatz, *Hollywood Genres: Formulas, Filmmaking, and the Studio System* (New York: Random House, 1981), p. 15.

[41] Ibid., p. 21.

profound roots in shared cultural attitudes. In their unchanging and changing aspects, the genre films address cultural consensus, if not modes of subversion to consent, and, hence, provide a vehicle for identifying and understanding how ideology functions.

These genre films, in spite of or perhaps because of their conventions and rules, yield information about the ways in which real needs are transformed into the created needs, about the way desire is managed. Their "escapist" dimension can be analyzed in more complex terms as the consequence of myth, fantasy, and necessity, accessible to the critic through a reading of the films' motifs, conventions, and cinematic language. Moreover, as can be seen in the development of the film genres through the thirties and early forties, these films are not mere reproductions of each other and of unchanging attitudes. The Italian melodramas, for example, reveal a sensitivity to changing attitudes, and finally even subtle opposition to the "heroic" and "revolutionary" discourse associated with the early phases of fascist ideology.

Ideology is not a mere cloak for reality, a form of false consciousness that disappears when material reality changes. The reduction of ideology to a category of false consciousness misrepresents the substantial role that images, attitudes, and beliefs play in maintaining social conditions and, therefore, hampers the possibility of critically evaluating the importance of cultural formations in sustaining social reality. Conversely, the assumption that ideology is all-encompassing negates the possibility that any social action is possible.

Ideology is a force for legitimating existing societies, their institutions and way of life. When ideology is widely accepted as describing "the way things are," it can be considered as hegemonic, as having a dominant position in a society.[42] Traditionally, ideological practices have been linked to official political rhetoric, to the practices of the state, but they per-

---

[42] Antonio Gramsci, *Selections from the Prison Notebooks*, ed. Quentin Hoare and Geoffrey Nowell-Smith (New York: International Publishers, 1978), pp. 260-261. See also Raymond Williams, *Marxism and Literature* (Oxford: Oxford University Press, 1977), pp. 108-136.

meate areas of everyday existence seemingly most remote from the public sphere.[43] Ideology seems to be most effective where it appears least obvious, least coercive, least ideological, and more as a natural process that enables people to function and to survive. A submission to the status quo must, therefore, be accounted for in terms of a "more general process of representation through which individuals are recruited into a social order. . . . The places or positions represented and the sense of self represented by the dominant social order must appear to be desirable; we must want to be recognized in that place, in that image we take to be our-selves."[44] The popular Italian cinema of the Ventennio, especially those feature films described as escapist, therefore have much to communicate about fascist culture. Rather than being removed from Italian reality, they are a good indication of how that reality was constructed.

My approach to an analysis of the films' ideological discourse is dependent on recent work in genre theory. In my analysis of the films, I explore the various strategies employed as part of the textual system of genre narratives from the role of the director and the stars to the conventions and rules associated with genres. For example, directors were, as in the Hollywood cinema, associated with certain genres and from their works audiences could expect a definable style tied to predictable thematic preoccupations. Mario Camerini (1895- ) made a few films during the silent era and the postwar period, but his most distinctive and popular work was done between 1929 and 1943. He is associated predominantly with romantic comedies. Another filmmaker whose films span the silent era to the present, Alessandro Blasetti (1900- ), made historical films, adventure films, and melodramas. Carmine Gallone (1886-1973) was known for his spectaculars. Having directed the famous *Scipione l'africano*, the ultimate in films that sought to connect contemporary fascism to the Roman

---

[43] Bill Nichols, *Ideology and the Image: Social Representation in the Cinema and Other Media* (Bloomington: Indiana University Press, 1981), p. 2.
[44] Ibid.

past, he also applied his flair for spectacle toward directing films that featured operas and opera singers.

One of the most neglected and interesting directors of melodrama, Ferdinando Maria Poggioli (1897-1945), directed such films as *Gelosia* (Jealousy) and *Sorelle Materassi* (The Materassi Sisters). Augusto Genina (1892-1957), another of the "epic" filmmakers of the period, also directed documentaries, war films, and melodramas. His *L'assedio dell' Alcazar* (The Siege of the Alcazar), made in a high rhetorical style, was designed to celebrate the Falangist cause during the Spanish Civil War. Raffaele Matarazzo (1909-1966), Mario Soldati (1906- ), Renato Castellani (1913- ), and Luigi Chiarini (1900-1975) were all identified with the movement known as "calligraphism," films that utilized earlier literary texts, melodramas especially, and were presented in a highly stylized manner.

Vittorio De Sica (1901-1974) began his film career as an actor. He starred in many of Mario Camerini's comedies. In the early forties he began directing, with a penchant for romantic comedy and melodrama, influenced perhaps by Camerini, his mentor. Amleto Palermi (1889-1941) directed melodramas such as *La peccatrice* (The Sinner), *Cavalleria rusticana*, and *Napoli d'altri tempi* (Naples of Other Times).

While the director endows the genre conventions with a particular signature in style and theme, the star occupies an equally important position as the embodiment of the particular conflicts and fantasies represented, and Italian films increasingly became star vehicles. But though the sound film created new star images, these actresses never had the same charisma and appeal of such silent divas as Lydia Borelli. Furthermore, Italian stars were never as popular with audiences as Hollywood stars. Audiences continued to elevate such figures as Charles Chaplin, Greta Garbo, Fred Astaire, and Deanna Durbin. The physical appearance of certain Italian stars and the kinds of roles they play often resemble Hollywood types and stereotypes.[45]

[45] Roberto Campari, *Hollywood-Cinecittà: Il racconto che cambia* (Milan: Feltrinelli, 1980), pp. 128-65.

Luisa Ferida was the incarnation of fiery passion, often cast as outlaw, peasant, or wronged lover. Osvaldo Valenti, who often performed with her, was the suave villain, false counselor, traitor, or usurper, in Blasetti's films in particular. Isa Miranda, the Italian version of Marlene Dietrich, played a variety of roles but most often that of the seductress as in Max Ophul's *La signora di tutti* (Everyone's Woman). She could also play a more sedate role as devoted daughter, wife, and mother as she did in *Passaporto rosso* (Red Passport). In contrast to Isa Miranda's cold, unattainable, and oppressed women, Assia Noris's roles were light, witty, and playful. Often forced for a time to fend for herself until she finds a proper mate, she was competent and eventually triumphant. Elsa Merlini was associated with musicals and comedies, playing the ambitious secretary or the clever wife.

Fosco Giachetti, veteran of such films as *Squadrone bianco* (White Squadron), *Vecchia guardia* (The Old Guard), *L'assedio dell' Alcazar* (The Siege of the Alcazar), and *Scipione l'africano*, was the exemplar of the fascist hero, but he was also popular in melodramas, having acted in such films as Mattòli's *Luce nelle tenebre* (Light in Darkness) and Castellani's *Un colpo di pistola* (A Pistol Shot). His character was moral, serious, disciplined; in short, he was the ideal "man's man." Though he was capable of deep attachments, his first commitment was to public duty. De Sica himself described the character parts he played for Camerini in the following manner: "The characters in Camerini, in this case, bourgeois or petty bourgeois, were delicate with a certain grace."[46] De Sica played roles with "light irony, melancholy even" whether as the desperate millionaire ready to give away his money or as the taxi driver acting like a millionaire.

An analysis of the role of the "star" and of the types of roles available provides valuable insight about genre representation, but this book is not a formalist analysis of genres. While according prominence to the role of genre, I situate my discussion of these narratives in the context of the films' treat-

---

[46] Francesco Savio, *Cinecittà anni trenta*, 3 vols. (Rome: Bulzoni, 1979), 2:486.

ment of generational and gender conflict. The first section of the book, "Generation and Gender," explores the representation of youth, of men, and of women in a variety of genres— musicals, adventure films, comedies, historical films, and melodramas. My rationale for an analysis of generational and gender representation is twofold: to identify the dominance of such a biological discourse under fascism and also to demonstrate how such a discourse is a force in the presentation of "the way things are."

Given the prominence of the fascist rhetoric devoted to youth, the first chapter, "The Children Are Watching Us," examines the various representations of young people and explores the reality and fiction of youth as a signifier of new cultural and aesthetic directions. In the early thirties young people, particularly young men, are fired with enthusiasm and, as in Alessandro Blasetti's *Vecchia guardia* (1935), ready to bring the "revolution" into existence and destroy the old moribund institutions. They are willing to endure hardship, personal sacrifice, and even death. Often young people are portrayed in the context of schools and orphanages where they battle to liberate themselves from sterile and repressive conditions. Children are the agents in uniting the family, sometimes at the expense of their own lives. In the films of the forties, however, children are used to dramatize the breakdown of domestic life, though they may be powerless to avert disaster, as in De Sica's *I bambini ci guardano*. Generational conflict seems to be a continuous motif, often standing in for or replacing class conflict.

The second chapter examines representations of women with particular attention to patterns of courtship, love and eroticism, work and domesticity, conflicts between career and marriage, and the common image of woman as "entertainer." The women's roles in the films offer an insight into a range of available female archetypes. Women are portrayed as seductresses, fallen women, entertainers, aspiring white-collar workers, long-suffering wives and mothers, obedient daughters, and unequal comrades in the enterprise of war and imperialism. The common bond uniting these diversified images of women is service, and, whether they succeed or fail, their object in life is to enhance the male and the family. In the melodramas, their role becomes central as they are shown to represent the failure of conventional social and interpersonal structures. Sexuality becomes the dominant signifier of repressed and distorted relationships. In Visconti's *Ossessione*, a pointed critique of the positioning of the subject in fascist ideology, the woman's sexuality becomes the vehicle for the male's enslavement to eroticism and exposes the ways this eroticism is manipulated in order to legitimate family and property.

In the third chapter, I probe the dominant images of men in the films of the thirties in the context of a quasi-religious pattern of conversion. The men, whether aristocrats, entrepreneurs, soldiers, professional men, workers, adventurers, or opportunists, are portrayed in the context of competition with other men, vocation, service and sacrifice, or domestication. The conversion motif portrays men struggling against lack of direction, passivity, loss of identity, dissipation, or falsely motivated desire. The men undergo a series of frustrations and trials until they are reconciled to a "virile," active, and self-assured image of themselves and of social responsibility. Soldiers find their identity in a contemplation of death and transfiguration through war and national goals; aristocrats (as in Blasetti's films), in patriarchal responsibility to their subjects; workers, in work and in the gratifications of family. Conversely, the films of the early forties cast a dark light on these objectives, dramatizing the dissolution of the personality, the destructiveness of competition, the failure of "normal" familial and sexual relationships, the threatening image of impotence, and the ubiquitousness of violence and aggressive images of male domination. The world of these films bears striking similarity to the themes and images of *film noir*.

In the second section of the book, "Genres," I turn to the historical film, comedy, and melodrama to explore the ways in which the uses of history, the role of work and leisure, and the presentation of the family are encoded in the films

of the era as well as the ways in which the films reveal changing attitudes over the course of the thirties and early forties.
In Chapter Four, I examine how the historical film adapts a
diversity of themes and attitudes that relate to the public and
the private spheres, accounting for the popularity of historical
subjects, settings, and costume dramas. Films set in Roman
times were made, but by far the more prominent periods
portrayed were the Renaissance and Risorgimento, particularly the latter.

The films used history as thinly veiled allegories for the
present, as political parables, as moral exempla, as presentations of the "great man" view of history, and as spectacle.
The historical drama offers variations on the theme of past
glory and splendor to be emulated in the present, the struggle
to legitimize nationalism, the continuity between past and
present, the exaltation of militarism, and the emphasis on the
need for struggle and victory. Historical treatments united
pedagogy and entertainment, concealing didacticism in spectacle, but in some films, the historical and costume drama
might also encode a subtle critique of the status quo not acceptable to the regime or in particular the censors. Such popular actors as Gino Cervi, Osvaldo Valenti, Luisa Ferida, and
Amedeo Nazzari were associated with these films, and while
not as expensively mounted as the earlier historical epics or
as Hollywood films, the films began to bear a resemblance to
their more polished Hollywood models. Blasetti, in particular,
was able to enhance the genre, through reliance on narrative
structures drawn from fairy tale, romance, and history, as
well as from the Hollywood film. Lavish historical settings,
glamorous characters, rapidly edited scenes of combat done
in the style of Soviet montage, large casts, and beleaguered
but victorious heroes are characteristic of such films and carriers of the films' ideological discourses.

Chapter Five unites a discussion of comedy with the particular representations of class relations and the roles of work
and leisure in order to integrate the issue of generational and
sexual conflicts to the broader social context represented
within the fictional world. Although the comedies do not

directly confront political issues, many of the films, particularly those of Camerini, do provide in their strategies of evasion an oblique presentation of social and political contradictions. These films are highly informative about fascist ideology in its most subtle and pervasive aspects. For example, Camerini's films portray the struggles of "little" people to survive. His clerks, taxi drivers, and salespersons are at first lured by the seductions of upward mobility, wealth, and power, but the characters gradually learn the falsity of these aspirations and return to their own class and to the comforts of home, work, and personal enhancement. The films speak to the discontents and aspirations of workers, offering compensation for economic and class limitations through their romantic and comic structures. The visual style, the presence of stars such as Vittorio De Sica and Assia Noris, and the skillful handling of narrative, works, like the Hollywood film, to bind the audience to empty desire and illusory pleasure, made to appear inevitable and attractive. Images of tourism, play, sports, and entertainment are inserted as a way of dramatizing the pleasures of a modest and collective existence. The style of the films announces that the film as artifact also seeks to communicate the same spirit to its audiences. When work itself is actually portrayed, as in Ruttmann's film *Acciaio* (Steel), the emphasis is on the equation between labor, machinery, and natural imagery in order to naturalize industry and productivity.

Of the genres produced, the melodramas especially reveal the Italian cinema's growth in stylistic and technical competence, and the concluding chapter investigates the ways in which such films as *Ossessione, Gelosia, Sorelle Materassi, Morte civile*, and *Malombra* dramatize the breakdown of family ties and interpersonal relationships, the failure of self-discipline, and the fragility of conformity. They portray a world that is hostile, violent, hypocritical, unyielding, unredeemed and unredeemable, where privilege, status, and authority are corrupt. The treatment of obsession, unrequited love, madness, confused identity, impotence, isolation, and thwarted desire is central, and the films pursue these issues often without the requisite happy ending. The melodramas' psychological treatment of class and sexual concerns provides the most tantalizing evidence for the contradictory aspects of fascist ideology. The films appear, on the one hand, to be critical of the status quo; their gloomy and dark style, a negative comment on the times. On the other hand, in their emphasis on family, they can also be read as reiterating, in a new way, old obsessions and discontents. Nonetheless, as we shall see, they provide the most complex stylistic and psychological form for examining the Italian cinema of genres and for evaluating the transformations in style and ideology.

Throughout these genres certain themes and images recur: the conflicts between rural and urban life, between traditional and modern attitudes. Often, rural life is presented in sentimental and idealized terms. Blasetti's *Terra madre*, Palermi's *La peccatrice*, Matarazzo's *Treno popolare*, and Trenker's *Condottieri* elevate the simple lives of workers and peasants, the healing and productive powers of peasant life, and contrast the beauty of the countryside to the decadence of city life. Even the epic *Scipione l'africano* highlights the role of the peasantry as the backbone of Roman productivity and conquest. However, not all films denigrate urban life. Such films as *Carnevale di Venezia, Palio, Napoli d'altri tempi, Una donna tra due mondi*, and *Napoli che non muore* treat the city as a character, an important force in molding the lives, aspirations, and choices of the characters, for better or worse.

The lure of empire and heroic action is exemplified in such films as *Il grande appello* and *Squadrone bianco*, where the exoticism of Africa symbolizes adventure and the rewards of travel and conquest. Images of the desert, dramatic skies, mountains, are frequent, as are images of technology—machinery, trains, ships, planes, and communications equipment. The war films, in particular, feature such images in abundance. Ritual enactments, covering every aspect of social life—weddings, funerals, political gatherings, processions, feasts, and religious and secular festivals, enhancing the aura of conversion, dedication, celebration, and the continuity of traditions and customs, are present in all genres.

My discussion of the films emphasizes the frequent elements of self-reflexivity. Many of the films, but especially the comedies and musicals, call attention to their status as film, whether the filmmaker is as self-conscious as Camerini in *Batticuore* where his central character goes into the cinema and looks at a film that mirrors her own situation and dialogue, or whether the film features a surrogate form of entertainment as in *Carnevale di Venezia*, using self-referential modes to form a bond with the audience in the creation of entertainment. The self-referentiality—as in the Hollywood cinema or as in the avant-garde text—serves to distance the audience, if only momentarily, from the diegesis and to make the spectators aware that what they are seeing is, after all, "merely a fiction." In the case of commercial cinema, in contrast to modernist texts, the self-reflexivity works contradictorily toward the end of canceling differences rather than distancing the spectator for critical purposes.[47] The emphasis on "performance" in the commercial cinema creates a bond between producers and consumers, putting the audiences in a privileged position, flattering it, and then absorbing it by giving it equal status with the performers. The incorporation of the audience into the production provides a significant strategy for erasing differences and conflicts between actor and spectator and for generating identification. By examining the film's emphasis on "performance," it is possible to gain a deeper insight into the texts' "interactions" with and designs on the audience.

What emerges from an examination of these films of the thirties and forties, therefore, is not a picture of life under fascism, any more than an examination of Hollywood films of the same era provide an accurate representation of life in the United States. Rather, the films provide a mosaic of myths involving the family, work, social involvement, youthful heroism, sacrifice, dreams of empire, sexual conflict, romance

[47] Jane Feuer, *The Hollywood Musical* (London: British Film Institute, 1982), pp. 35-47. See also Dana Polan, "Brecht and the Politics of Self-Reflexive Cinema," *Jump Cut* 17 April 1978), pp. 29-32.

and leisure, and, most particularly, of strategies, often used self-consciously, to naturalize experience, to create a sense of the "way things are." The narrative structures, the generic and cinematic conventions, the iconography, and the self-referential elements of these films should be understood as constituting a fusion of the imaginary and "real" conditions of existence rather than as directly reflecting social conditions, or, conversely, as being totally fantastic. It is precisely their fusion of social and psychological conflicts with the elements of myth that constitutes their ideological discourse. These films go beyond the more obvious and public modes of political propaganda to make contact with their audiences and with their immediate lives.

This is not predominantly a study of the public dramas of the fascist era nor their expression in the cinema of the time. The position of the charismatic leader, the authoritarian personality, the imagery of public pageants and spectacles, the epics of war and imperialism, have been abundantly discussed in relation to fascist culture. My readings of the films, which single out the issues of sexual conflict, generational differences, the position of the family, the contradictory uses of history, rural and urban myths, and portraits of work and leisure as the dominant concerns of the narrative films, address the less spectacular but more immediate and familiar ways the films make contact with the lived and imaginary aspects of the world of the audience. The very familiarity of these concerns creates a sense of continuity with a past that appears to transcend politics, but through which politics and ideology can move often without the awareness of the audience. My study explores equally the films of the thirties as well as the "prefigurations" of the neorealist aesthetic. Moreover, while the films of key directors of the era such as Camerini, Blasetti, Poggioli, Soldati, and Castellani receive extensive attention, the works of other less prominent directors such as Chiarini are also explored. The early films of De Sica, Rossellini, and Visconti made prior to 1945 are thematically and stylistically relevant to an understanding of the film production of that era and are discussed in this context.

The feature films themselves will be the focal point of my study. I do not include any discussion of the news and documentary films produced by LUCE on the grounds that these are more congenial to a study of the mass media and the public sphere of political action. Nor do I discuss the silent cinema. These films, though important, have their own identity and style, and are, properly, the object of another study. The transformation of the Italian cinema occurs with the coming of sound, and the films produced constitute a homogeneous body of production. Above all, this study seeks to interrogate, on the one hand, the assumption that ideology is totally monolithic and hegemonic, and on the other, that it is negligible and easily dismissed as false consciousness. A reading of these films provides an opportunity for locating a type of politics less spectacular than the usual formulations of "fascinating fascism," but closer to everyday politics exemplified in the domestic sphere and in sexual politics.

# Generation and Gender

# CHAPTER ONE

# The Children Are Watching Us

R EPRESENTATIONS of young people are integral to the Italian cinema, spanning the prewar and postwar eras. Though the emphasis on youth can be linked to fascist ideology, it can also profitably be connected to the cinema of genres, which favors youth in its choice of "stars" and narratives that abolish time and history. In this sense, fascist ideology is erased even where the films appear to be most aligned with the ideals of the movement and the regime. As we shall see in this chapter, stories about young people in film are indeed related to fascist ideology, but they also expose unresolved conflicts as the imagery of youth fuses with older, more traditional ideological structures.

Under fascism, the elevation of youth was in part rhetorical and symbolic, in part, pragmatic. The fascist movement sought to communicate an image of itself as dynamic, new, and revolutionary, committed to social, political, and cultural rejuvenation. In a practical vein, the regime created organizations such as "Fascist University Groups, or GUF, *balilla* for little boys, Young Italian units for girls, and Wolf Club Circles for the smallest 'new Italians.' "[1] These organizations were, as Victoria de Grazia has indicated, "truly mass organizations, not only because of their several million members, but because they intentionally grouped people by sex, by social group, by age, and by activity to prevent any autonomous expression of class identity or class alliance."[2]

Renzo De Felice discusses this emphasis on mass organization as a major feature of the revolutionary aspect of fascism:

[1] Victoria de Grazia, *The Culture of Consent: Mass Organization of Leisure in Fascist Italy* (Cambridge: Cambridge University Press, 1981), p. 16.
[2] Ibid.

The fascist regime has a central element that distinguishes it from reactionary and conservative regimes: The mobilization and active participation of the masses. That this participation later takes on a demagogical form is another matter; the principle is one of active participation, not exclusion. This is one of the revolutionary elements. Another revolutionary element is that Italian fascism wanted to achieve the transformation of society and the individual in a direction that had never been attempted or realized in the past.[3]

De Felice's discussion challenges conventional notions of fascism as reactionary. This is not to say that he sees the fascist regime as revolutionary in the Marxist sense, as representing the dictatorship of the proletariat, the redistribution of wealth, and the abolition of the state, but that he sees fascism as seeking to modernize society rather than as sustaining conservative forms. Mass organization was thus an important element in mobilizing support, appealing to students, especially to youth, and, through youth, creating an image of progress, opportunity, and common interests.[4] Looking at fascism from a revolutionary perspective, particularly viewing it not only as an economic and political revolution but also as a cultural revolution, helps to identify its goals, its character, and its strategies.

The role of artists and young people in the "new culture" was to create such a revolutionary discourse, and film became increasingly important to this enterprise. The regime's emphasis on youth finds its counterpart in the films of the era that seek to portray appealing images of young people. In its quest for an appropriate film language, the Italian film industry acknowledged the superiority of the Hollywood film in capturing the "myth of youth," which transcended the literal use of young people and came to signify, more broadly, attitudes of energy, pugnaciousness, freshness, and health.[5]

[3] Renzo De Felice, *Fascism: An Informal Introduction to Its Theory and Practice*, ed. Michael Ledeen (New Brunswick, N.J.: Transaction Books, 1976), p. 55.

[4] George L. Mosse, *Masses and Man: Nationalist and Fascist Perceptions of Reality* (New York: Howard Fertig, 1980), pp. 169-70, 242.

[5] Gian Piero Brunetta, *Cinema Italiano tra le due guerre: Fascismo e politica cinematografia* (Milan: Mursia, 1975), p. 68. See also Hortense Powdermaker,

The popularity of such figures as Jackie Coogan, Shirley Temple, Judy Garland, such films as *The Adventures of Tom Sawyer* testified to the cinematic potential of the child. The films of Chaplin, Hawks, Ford, and Capra, so popular with Italian audiences, were part of a broader myth of America as young and vital.

The Italian films that feature young people strive to capture the image of youthful innocence, resourcefulness, naturalness, and pragmatism. Young people are the vehicles for exposing unjust familial restraints, moribund social institutions, and uncreative "materialism." These youthful figures dramatize the necessity for change, the demands of nature versus culture, the restraints of "civilization," and the virtues of industriousness. They chastise their elders and generate guilt over existing conditions. Above all, they are a magical force for social transformation.

Young people are present in a variety of film genres: comedies, adventure films, melodramas, and musicals, struggling to define themselves against traditional attitudes and behavior. They are shown as neglected, abandoned, redeemed, as the vanguard of a new political consciousness, and as the hope of the future. Significantly, this practice does not cease after the war as one can see in such neorealist films as *Roma, città aperta* (Rome, Open City), *Sciuscià* (Shoe Shine), and *Ladri di biciclette* (Bicycle Thieves). The children in the postwar films, too, reproach the adults for indifference, lack of commitment, disloyalty, the breakdown of family relations, the corruption of cohesive political structures, and the general loss of community vitality. The youths' heroic lives or deaths are the means of revitalizing the community and forging new alliances.

While the featuring of young people in the films of the era converged with the fascist regime's practical efforts to mo-

---

*Hollywood, The Dream Factory: An Anthropologist Looks at the Movie-Makers* (New York: Little, Brown, 1950), p. 229. On the impact of American mythology and literature in Italy in the 1930s and 1940s, see Mira Liehm, *Passion and Defiance: Film in Italy from 1942 to the Present* (Berkeley and Los Angeles: University of California Press, 1984), pp. 34-38.

bilize youth and to portray youthful zeal, in reality the situation was more ambiguous and problematic.[6] For example, youth organizations did, indeed, express disaffection with liberal and traditional attitudes and values, but, as Edward R. Tannenbaum asserts, this opposition remained solely on the level of verbalization:

Ostensibly the feeling of community generated by the youth groups was opposed to traditional bourgeois values; in some ways it was a calculated substitute for the values of family and privacy. For the most part young Italians enjoyed getting together in their uniforms, shouting slogans and sharing the prescribed patriotic ritual. The ONB and the GIL [Opera Nazionale Balilla and Gioventù Italiana del Littorio, youth organizations] trained them to respond to the new, popular culture, as opposed to the older bourgeois culture. In effect, however, Fascist Italy was merely catching up with the more modernized countries, particularly the USA, in using its youth organizations and activities to foster feelings of togetherness and enthusiasm—similar to pre-Second-World-War American rallies and organized heckling in connection with 'the big game'—in which verbal assaults were made on the outward manifestations of traditional bourgeois values without endangering their content.[7]

Adrian Lyttelton affirms this position. He finds that "on the one hand, the youth organizations represented an instrument of pressure and surveillance which helped to intimidate the teachers and secure their conformity; on the other, they kept alive resentment against the party and the political ideology which it embodied."[8] The films encode similar contradictory attitudes. One can detect elements of surveillance even in the style and texture of the films as they emphasize looking, but one can also recognize a mistrust and critique of all authority, which intensifies in the films of the early forties.

The young people in the films of the 1930s are often positioned as oppositional figures; their actions portrayed in the

[6] Edward R. Tannenbaum, *Fascism in Italy: Society and Culture 1922-1945* (London: Allen Lane, 1972), p. 186.

[7] Ibid., p. 143.

[8] Adrian Lyttelton, *The Seizure of Power: Fascism in Italy 1919-1929* (New York: Charles Scribner's Sons, 1973), p. 410.

language of generational conflict. Yet, while they appear in the vanguard of new values and attitudes, they often articulate the traditional values of nationalism, male comradeship, the importance of competence, virility, leadership, and personal sacrifice. For the young man, the arena of action is the social sphere as he submerges personal desire in the public good; for the young woman, successful competition for the man and the rewards of family service to him and to the family are central.

## Young Adventurers

In the films that portray war and political struggle, boys and young men are presented as figures of redemption, innocent and wholesome, righteously crusading for a world purged of decadence and corruption. The son's redemption of the father is a basic narrative paradigm, and the imagery of health and disease quite common. A typical example of this type of film is Mario Camerini's 1936 film, *Il grande appello* (The Great Call). The film opens with the rubric: "The scenes in Africa were shot entirely in the territory of the Empire with the cooperation of the Ministry of Press and Propaganda, of the Colonies, of War, and of Aeronautics." Made to glorify the war in Ethiopia, the film seems exceptional in the work of Camerini whose predilection was for romantic comedy. Yet, on closer viewing, the film is typical of Camerini's approach, for it is less an epic, a spectacle, and more a treatment of the familial relations. The narrative fuses public and private sectors through identification of the family with the interests of the nation, effected primarily through conflict and reconciliation between the father and son.

The film is set in Italy and in North Africa. In Genoa, a dying woman seeks to send messages to her son and her estranged husband in Ethiopia. The mother becomes the intermediary in the drama of sacrifice and reconciliation. In Djibouti, the father, Bertani, manages the Hotel Orient, a center of international intrigue. Bertani is indifferent to the Italian aspirations in the area, has no sense of commitment to his country's war, preferring to profit by selling arms to

the enemy Ethiopians. Furthermore, Bertani is involved in a
sordid relationship with a Spanish woman who is his ally in
the enterprise of smuggling weapons to the enemies of Italy.

When he receives news of his son, Enrico, Bertani decides
to find him. The young Enrico is a radio operator, totally
committed to his work. On-location shots show industrious
Italians. The dominant images are of movement, collectivity,
and affectionate male relationships, in contrast to the "degeneracy of the Ethiopians, Frenchmen, and Spaniards." A
series of oppositions defines the film's conflicts and chart its
ultimate direction: Djibouti and Addis Ababa, foreigner and
Italian, profit and purpose, individualism and collectivity,
renegade father and honorable son.

Bertani locates Enrico in Addis Ababa. From his perspective, the camera isolates scenes of group solidarity, men singing, exchanging personal histories, working energetically and
willingly. Bertani invites Enrico to live with him in Djibouti,
but Enrico, self-righteously and passionately, explains that he
cannot do this; his patriotism forbids it. The editing contrasts
the obese, unkempt father and the youthful, clean-cut young
man. The conflict between the father and son is prologue to
the scenes of actual fighting as the Italians rally to respond
to a surprise attack by the natives, many of them falling in
the melee. Enrico is seriously wounded. Bertani goes to the
hospital where Enrico has been taken and learns that his son
must have an operation. He tries to talk to Enrico, but his son
rejects him.

In Djibouti, where the Ethiopians at the hotel are celebrating their victory, Bertani's mistress is plotting to smuggle
more ammunition to the enemy. Bertani no longer wants to
be part of this enterprise, but his accomplices coerce him into
further cooperation. One of the smugglers threatens him with
death if he does not participate, but Bertani is determined to
redeem himself in the eyes of his son.

The film culminates in scenes of battle. Bertani, dressed in
native garb, turns on his accomplices and shoots them but he
is shot. Against the background of Italian men and equipment, he is filmed in close-up looking up to a sky filled with

Italian planes as he utters his last word, "Italia," and dies. Thus, the film presents the conversion and redemption of the father, first through the agency of the dying mother who brings father and son together and, especially, through the young man, the son, who symbolizes a new life, the life of total subordination of personal interests to the nation. The conversion strategies involve the drama of corruption, guilt, and penance, transposing religious symbolism onto the drama of war and conquest and endowing the action with a spiritual aura. The role of the son's wounding and potential martyrdom are traced to the father's opportunism, obsession with profit, and family disloyalty, even more specifically by providing the weapons that have wounded his son. The generational conflict is inscribed as a strategy to quell opposition by deflecting attention from the actual motives for the war.

The portrayal of the misguided natives, used as tools by the exploitative Europeans, the equation of sexual licentiousness and greed, provides the legitimation for the struggle. It is a war against immorality, social disintegration, and selfish accumulation. The natives themselves are presented as in need of proper guidance to protect them from adventurers who are responsible for their moral deterioration. But above all, the film's total effect relies on the affective strategies generated by the father-son conflict at the film's center, and especially on the orchestration of images associated with organization and disorganization, innocence and degeneracy, and self-aggrandizement and martyrdom. As is so often the case in such films, the son who redeems the father replaces the conventional romance as the center of narrative interest.

According to Aprà and Pistagnesi, "This film, in the intention of its creators, wanted to show fascism in anti-heroic fashion, as a drama of the conscience, as Oedipal conflict, and it succeeded well enough to the point that it raised the ire of some zealous bureaucrats."[9] In fact the film's discourse blends well with the indirect political discourse so congenial

---

[9] Adriano Aprà and Patrizia Pistagnesi, *I favolosi anni trenta 1929-1944* (Milan: Electa, 1979), p. 81.

to American (and British) audiences of the time. The person-
alization of the theme of imperialism by means of the familial
and generational conflict overshadows if not suppresses the
film's imperial thematics.

One of the most popular and prominent directors of the
era, one whose career spans the silent, prewar, and postwar
cinema, Alessandro Blasetti was known for his historical epic
films celebrating heroic figures and heroic enterprises. His
career captures the major tendencies, contradictions, and
changing styles and politics of the Italian cinema of the Ventennio.[10] His films of the thirties seem to constitute a strange
mixture of Hollywood narrative codes and Soviet montage,
of psychological concerns wedded to overt political themes
and strategies. To him, *Vecchia guardia* seemed to be one of
the earliest expressions of neorealism. Certainly the film is
cast in the mold of the social problem film of the thirties,
replete with description and prescription. The characters also
seem to follow Hollywood models of romance and community
service. The role of the young hero in the film, Mario, as
agent of transformation, is also familiar.

*Vecchia guardia* is an encomium to the *squadristi*, the vigi-
lantes of the fascist cause.[11] The martyr of the film is little
Mario who wants more than anything else to help the fascists
defend honest people against the machinations of the socialists. He sacrifices his life to create a society where there will
no longer be strikes and strikers to obstruct institutions from
doing their proper work of serving the community. Dr. Cardini, the head of the psychiatric hospital, is distraught as he
struggles to do what is necessary to help his sick patients.
The strikers are portrayed as uninterested in their work, as
pawns in the hands of socialists, and as more concerned with
their economic well-being than with the helpless patients in
the hospital. The mayor and other town officials are presented
as inefficient and impotent, the socialists as lazy, belligerent,

[10] Ibid., pp. 76-77.

[11] Philip V. Cannistraro, in *La fabbrica del consenso: Fascismo e mass media*
(Rome-Bari: Laterza, 1975), finds *Vecchia guardia* to be "the most effective film
ever realized on a strictly fascist subject," p. 288.

and rabble-rousing. On the other hand, the fascists have a genuine concern for the people and their needs, serving the crucial function of supplanting the defunct social institutions.

Roberto, the leader of the fascist squad, both a model son to Dr. Cardini and a model brother of little Mario, is a man of action, indefatigable in his quest to purify the community, to rid it of its bad leadership for the mental health of all. The strategies he uses to accomplish his goals are collective attacks on recalcitrant members of the community, especially night raids, and open defiance of civil laws that his group consider antithetical to their political objectives. In appearance, Roberto (Mino Doro) is clean-cut, close-shaven, elegant in his black uniform, and intense and virile. His sidekick Marconi is, as in the swashbuckling films of the late 1930s, an Alan Hale character, rough, awkward, boisterous but gentle toward animals, children, and neighbors in need.[12] He is presented as comical, acting swiftly but in good humor against socialist leaders. One of his "pranks" is having the local barber, Aristide, shave half of the socialist Branchetti's beard as the camera pans spectators laughing, especially young spectators, while Branchetti rages vainly. Marconi's act of giving the striker-radicals a dose of castor oil is also presented as amusing, a form of justified revenge on them for their resistance to doing what is in the community's best interest.

The mayor and the school superintendent are presented as pompous windbags, totally indifferent to solving the political conflicts in the town. After they announce a temporary closing of the school, the fascists openly defy the authorities by opening the building and teaching classes themselves. The romantic female lead in the film is a teacher who refuses to obey the authorities by continuing to teach her classes. Her dedication to Roberto and to the political cause is great and the film portrays Maria and Roberto's increasing emotional involvement with each other. Maria's devotion to Roberto is expressed in her commitment to his politics, her subordinat-

---

[12] Roberto Campari, *Hollywood-Cinecittà: Il racconto che cambia* (Milan: Feltrinelli, 1980), pp. 128-65.

ing herself to Roberto and the *squadristi*. Her love for Roberto and for fascism are intertwined.

Mario, however, is the fulcrum of the action, the vital center of the film's meaning and rhetorical strategies. He is young and precocious, profoundly interested in mechanics and technology. He repairs sewing machines and clocks, and is in the process of building a clock for the sitting room. The image of the clock becomes a symbol for youth after Mario's death, and for the new time created by fascism (like the fascist calendar). Mario is a magical-religious figure. He can tame the mentally ill, calming an escaped patient when all others fail to control the man. His desire to fight alongside the older men leads to his death, and his martyrdom becomes a rallying point for both fascists and nonfascists in the community. His sacrifice is the motive for the ritualistic procession at the end, symbolic of the March on Rome: "Today no one stays at home. Mario is with us." With superimpositions of Mario, the film ends with the marching men. The processional culminates with the call to Rome (*a Roma*) and the epilogue reads, "Together they marched with *il Duce*."

In addition to functioning as the symbolic center of the film, bringing together attitudes of loyalty and devotion to the cause with the meaningfulness of sacrifice, heroism, and community, Mario also functions as an observer, the audience within the film in concert with the audience outside the film. Through his eyes, the audience views the action and distinguishes trustworthy from untrustworthy characters and actions. He is the guarantor of the good intentions of the squad members. His purity of motive functions to neutralize any critical response to the fascist actions, and the motif of family unity fuses with the motif of collectivity.

Another aspect of the fusion of private and public spheres so characteristic of the genre film emerges in the representation of the father. His role as guardian of the mental health of the community, his siring of two fascist heroes, and his conversion to fascism emphasize several attitudes basic to the film: the idea of conversion to fascism as necessary and inevitable, the conception of resistance to existing institutions as healthy because of the degeneracy of these institutions, and the idea of a "rebirth" in fascism. More concretely, Dr. Cardini, as the father of Roberto and Mario, represents the class interests of the bourgeoisie as do the teacher, the chemist, and the nuns at the hospital, and it is they who support the squad members and isolate the troublemakers. The workers are converted after the death of Mario. The socially disruptive elements are all healed of their "illnesses." The film also orchestrates other pervasive Blasetti motifs: generational conflict and rural and urban conflicts. This rural setting is "purified" of its disrupting urban components, that is, alienated workers, strikes, agitators, and bureaucrats. The generational and class conflict is "resolved" in the death of Mario, which unites old and young.

The camera uses low-angle shots to elevate the heroic characters, and through medium and long shots, Blasetti creates tableaux of the historic events alluded to in the prologue: "This film aims to exalt Italian squadrism and to re-create unforgettable moments in its history. The story takes place in a small town in central Italy in October 1922, the eve of the March on Rome." Blasetti's merging of historical events and fiction works to transform history into myth. His treatment of landscape enhances his efforts at universalizing the events. The many shots of the rural countryside with a background of sky and clouds attempt to create the sense of the naturalness of the human conflicts. The music, the drums, the singing, and the sound of marching feet enclose the film, enhancing its rhetorical treatment of the events and characters, revealing the film's attempts at making affective contact with the audience to catalyze it into action.

Youth becomes the ground on which this message is dramatized; it is the link to naturalness, purity of motive, and the future. It signifies the redemption of the past. Moreover, while the film exposes class conflict, it elevates the idea, through the symbol of youth, of the redemption from class conflict, the means whereby classes are unified in the idea of the "people," of the community.

The classical children's adventure film is best exemplified

by Flavio Calzavara's *Piccoli naufraghi* (1939) (or *Piccoli avven-turieri* as it was also titled). Calzavara was a director known for his adaptations of literary works and for nineteenth-century costume dramas; however, *Piccoli naufraghi* is inspired by contemporary events, namely, the Ethiopian campaign, and involves young boys who are bored with school and in search of adventure. The familiar components of the children's adventure genre—the runaway, the sea or land journey, shipwreck, life on a desert island, treasure, dramatic escape, and return—are portrayed in Calzavara's film.

The film is dedicated to youth as the opening titles reveal: "In the spring of the XIV[th] year, we salute our navy which with the most ardent youth continues to work toward the conquest of Empire." Documentary footage introduces images of young men boarding a ship headed for Ethiopia and of a young father as he kisses his child farewell. In a classroom, a teacher lectures young boys on the parts of speech as they, sprawled at their desks in boredom, surreptitiously pass around a photograph of a battle scene (Marco Bellocchio's 1972 *Nel nome del padre* reproduces a similar classroom scene in its exploration of the resurgence of fascism and in its development of the equation between repressive educational conditions, the restlessness and cynicism of youth, and its attraction to fascism.) Calzavara's film celebrates war as a response to the sterility of existing instruction. Even the teacher wants to escape and fight in Ethiopia. His wish is granted. The news of the teacher's impending departure activates the boys and a group of them make plans to stowaway on a ship bound for Ethiopia. In the only domestic scene in the film, one that involves a woman, a boy is shown being badgered by his mother. The family, too, is presented as oppressive and a legitimate motive for the boy's escape from school and home to the excitement of combat in exotic places.

Aboard the ship, the young boys create an atmosphere of summer camp. Their discovery by the crew is handled indulgently, and the captain, who seems stern at first, reveals himself to be a benevolent paternal figure who treats the boys with tenderness and concern. The boys are fed, given bedding, and permitted to spend their leisure time singing patriotic songs. The young black servant boy, Simba, is delighted to serve people of his own age.

This idyll is shattered by a shipwreck, which provides the opportunity for the young adventurers to strike out on their island escapades. At the moment of collision, they seize the lifeboats and head out to sea. After much hardship, they locate an island and carry their wounded teacher ashore. His dying words are an exhortation to the children to be courageous. The boys struggle to create shelter and feed themselves. Simba saves the day as he finds a fish and assumes the role of cook for the other boys. Unlike Peter Brook's *Lord of the Flies* (1963), this film stresses the cooperativeness, ingenuity, and solidarity of the youths, as they create their version of Utopia in the midst of adversity. Calzavara lingers on their ingenious strategies for survival. Their rescue comes in the form of a pirate ship that arrives to unload contraband goods which turn out to be war materiel headed for Ethiopia. The pirates are not eager to save the boys, and they impress them into the work of unloading the ship. Fortunately, one of the pirates is not devoid of patriotism. With his help, the boys take over the ship and steer for home. To the strains of victorious music, the ship departs, leaving the other pirate-traitors stranded on the island.

*Piccoli naufraghi* seems consonant with the goals of Cinema GUF, the organization devoted to appealing to fascist youth, to expressing fascist ideals to and through young people.[13] The film employs a familiar practice of the adventure film in its denigration of daily life in school and at home, associating institutions with repression, and using the classical idea of a return to nature as the means of recovering integrity, vitality, and manhood. Under primitive conditions, the youths are tested and triumph. Even more significantly, the film makes a parallel between the conditions of survival in nature and survival in war. War is re-created as adventure and the in-

[13] Gian Piero Brunetta, *Storia del cinema italiano 1895-1945* (Rome: Riuniti, 1979), pp. 341-59.

evitable survival of the hardiest. The emphasis on escape, on
starting anew, on action rather than contemplation, on social
and psychological reconstruction makes the film's celebration
of war seem innocent. The style of the film, too, appears
guileless in its insertion of music and dances, in its portrayal
of innocent young boys constantly confronted by danger as
they band together bravely to contend with the elements. The
use of the young black boy, Simba, symbolizes the childlike
Africans, dependent on and cooperative with the benevolent,
high-minded young Italians. The film also distinguishes the
benevolence of the dedicated authorities, the teacher and the
ship's captain, from the "pirates" at home and abroad.

## School Days

A fair number of Italian films of this era are set in schools,
girls' schools in particular.[14] The school functions as more than
mere setting or background for theme, action, and character.
By focusing on institutions for young people, these films consciously treat issues of generational conflict, discipline and
lack of discipline, repression and subordination. The role of
the school is not always the same in the films of the thirties
and forties. In some instances, as in *Piccoli naufraghi*, the
school is presented as a stifling institution. The children are
forced to submit to irrelevant instruction while the real arena
for learning is found in social action. The school is thus quickly
abandoned in the film for the life of action and adventure. In
such films, there appears to be a parallel between fascism's
negative attitudes toward reflection and intellectualism and
its positive attitudes toward practical activity. On the other
hand, a film such as Poggioli's *Addio giovinezza!* portrays the
school as idyllic, the arena of license and play, in contrast to
the burden of adult responsibility. Alessandrini's *Seconda B*'s
presentation of school life falls somewhere between these two
attitudes.

[14] This is not surprising considering the emphasis placed by the regime on
educational reform, and on organizing the lives of young people in school
and after school. See Tannenbaum, *Fascism in Italy*, pp. 171-208.

The German film, Leontine Sagan's *Mädchen in Uniform* (Girls in Uniform, 1931) was influential for Italian filmmakers in spite of its oppositional treatment of Prussian militarism, of sexual repression of and among women, and of authoritarianism. For example, Goffredo Alessandrini acknowledged his debt to Sagan's film for his own *Seconda B*, also set in a girls' school, focusing on problems of authority and permissiveness, the relationships between teachers and students, and the restlessness and near-destructive consequences of the young women's behavior.

The school is a place of confinement for bored and rich young women. The central figures in the film are Professor Monti (Sergio Tofano), a repressed, impressionable, struggling male teacher who is badly in need of direction and support; Signora Vanni, a matronly female teacher, who avidly desires to provide that support; and Marta, a problem student, mischief-maker, manipulator, and seducer. Despite the institutional setting and the presence of the older and younger women, the film revolves around the male professor as the object of desire of the two women who compete for him. The older woman becomes the focal point for issues of control and discipline, the younger of permissiveness. Through the agency of Marta, the film criticizes permissiveness, making it appear wanton and destructive, and through the agency of Signora Vanni discipline is made to appear desirable. The professor is the beneficiary of the conflict as he acquires manhood, authority, and competence. His transformation is measured through his changing appearance and gesture.

Signora Vanni is Monti's companion and his advocate with the administration. She also teaches him how to dress and how to behave in class. Marta is the young subverter, coming between Vanni and Monti as she uses her father's wealth and influence first to woo him to her house. Later, in assisting him with his work of cataloguing specimens (he is a teacher of natural history), she plays a cruel seductive trick on him as her student colleagues observe them from a prearranged hiding place. This game costs Monti his job as well as alienating him from Vanni.

The film's structuring of oppositions extends to the kinds of teaching portrayed. Vanni is the gym teacher and in her classes, the young girls are taught self-discipline through exercising and learning to follow instructions. Monti's natural history classes are unruly. He cannot control the students, who refuse to listen, to answer questions, and to follow directions. His use of stuffed specimens inspires the mischievousness of the girls and, more fundamentally, serves as a metaphor for his own condition. Furthermore, Maria Denis, who plays Marta, is portrayed as young and beautiful, radiating energy and narcissism, whereas Dina Perbellini, who plays Vanni, looks matronly. In the editing, the image of one woman is frequently followed by an immediate dissolve to the other as if signalling the professor's inability to distinguish and choose. Vanni triumphs, however, as Monti repents his folly and returns to her, chastened, ready now to complete his education as a respectable university professor and resume his relationship with her. Marta's manipulations are exposed and she apologizes to Signora Vanni for her insubordination.

The film develops the imagery of surveillance. Early in the film, the audience is positioned behind Monti as he gapes at Vanni and the young women doing their calesthenics. Signora Vanni is often in the position of a voyeur surveying Monti from various perspectives and at various times as he is alone, in class, or with Marta. The doorman and the maid are the eyes and ears of the school as they gossip about the students and teachers. Looking becomes an index to lack of control, on the one hand, and mastery, on the other.

The treatment of the girls in the school, other than Marta, differs from Sagan's sympathetic treatment. Alessandrini makes no attempt to develop relationships among them beyond Marta's exploitative use of them. The head of the school and the other teachers are, for the most part, caricatures of authoritarianism, subservience, inquisitiveness, and officiousness. The workers in the school are comic types who serve mainly to expose the folly of the teachers. Marta's father is the stock portly businessman, ambitious and ready to assert his power and authority. Vanni and Monti, on the other hand, come to exemplify the virtues of service, order, stability, and respectability. In these two characters, the film works to effect reconciliations between sexuality and work, dominance and subordination, authority and license. The young people in this film are "disciplined" into conformity and productivity like their responsible elders. The "rewards" are inclusion rather than ostracism, and, of course, romance.

Another school film, concerned with similar conflicts but taking a more detached and critical perspective, is Ferdinando Maria Poggioli's *Addio giovinezza!* The film focuses on the relationships among the students rather than between teachers and students. Based on a play by Sandro Camasio and Nino Oxilia, the text was a popular one for filmmakers and audiences. Before the Poggioli sound film of 1940, the film had been made twice without sound, in 1913 and 1927. *Addio giovinezza!* draws on some popular narrative motifs: the carnival nature of student life, love and renunciation, the "last fling," Don Juanism, and the rites of passage from youth to maturity. The image of male camaraderie so common to films of the time is here playfully presented. Student life appears joyful, a time of physical, sexual, and mental exuberance. The central figure, Mario, is an attractive Don Juan incarnation who falls in and out of love, his conquests gained easily, his greatest obstacle how to keep the women happy and out of each other's way and his male peers friendly and not envious. His first serious problem presents itself upon his graduation, the necessity of moving into the world of family responsibility and work.

Throughout the film, the spectator is made conscious of spectacle and performance, though the spectacle is not of the public character of the historic and epic films but rather of the rituals of civil life. The drinking parties, theatrical presentations, academic processions, and graduation ceremonies are woven into the film, inviting the audience within and without the film to become part of the performance, to lose themselves in the "performances." The actual stage performance presented by the students, in particular, becomes an opportunity to participate in the carnival atmosphere where the drama is the selection of the most beautiful woman. Beauty is thus the supreme value, and the appreciation of it, the film's ultimate concern. This aspect of theater is juxtaposed against the performance of work and family responsibility. The act of looking, the experience of aesthetic pleasure, offers the audience the opportunity to indulge vicariously in this pleasure while it lasts.

The women in the film, Dorina, played by Maria Denis, and Elena, played by Clara Calamai, are the contenders for Mario's attention. Again, as with *Seconda B*, the women compete for the man. They also serve as instruments for moving the men through their education and transformation into serious and professional workers. Each woman represents a different class. Dorina is a worker; Elena is a member of the leisured class. Mario, however, comes from sturdy rural stock, and upon graduation he will become a doctor, thus fulfilling the expectations of his parents. Elena renounces Mario, and Mario renounces Dorina. Neither woman belongs in his new life. Dorina, in particular, articulates in her farewell scene with Mario the difference in their class positions. Youth has permitted a flexibility in relationships and action, but with the farewell to youth such flexibility no longer pertains.

The film is structured around the final recognition and acceptance of differences. Its very carnival atmosphere guarantees that youthful experiences are transitory. The compensation for the loss of youth and pleasure resides in the enshrinement of these pleasures in memory. The film itself serves this function in capitalizing on the youth and nostalgia that permeate the film. Dorina is the agent for the nostalgia. She is the incarnation of youth and Mario's renunciation of her is, like the final image of the gate that closes between them, the sign of the separation of classes and life styles.

*Addio giovinezza!* is an important film for several reasons. On the technical level, the film displays a high level of professionalism in its handling of narrative continuity, in its use of spectacle, in its style of film acting, in its uses of iconography, and in its play with spectator involvement. In the six years between *Seconda B* and this film, filmmakers had thrown off the theatrical elements of the first sound films and had learned to move within the medium of the sound film and to explore the Hollywood strategies of representation. In its playing self-consciously with the power of the image and of performance, the film seems on one level of perception to be exploring its own potential. The nostalgia and aestheticism seem to identify it as a film of evasion, a retreat into fantasy. At the same time, however, it reveals more poignantly than *Seconda B* unresolved conflicts between work and play, youth and maturity. Mario's rite of passage is effected through objectifying Dorina, taking the freely offered fruits of the seamstress' labor, the sampler, in exchange for her person. Youth is thus portrayed as the locus of class, economic, and sexual conflict. Maturity is based on deprivation.

Presenting a less puritan vision of the rewards of renunciation, Vittorio De Sica's 1940 film, *Maddalena zero in condotta* (Maddalena, Zero in Conduct), a popular film at the time, is a comedy set in a young girls' school that plays with oppositions between repressive and authoritarian institutions and those who subvert authority. Structured around the classroom and the home, the classroom episodes stress the attempts of the teachers to impose discipline and the young women's energetic attempts to disrupt and frustrate institutionalization. For the most part, the teachers are caricatured in the portly male professor who is intent on asserting his dominance, the severe female principal, who is responsible for maintaining order and continuity, and the inept male gym teacher who cannot perform the exercises he sets for his students. The young female teacher of commercial writing, Signorina Malgari, like her students, is oppressed by this environment. The students are portrayed as unruly, seizing every opportunity to play tricks on the teachers and on the teacher's pet.

Maddalena, the ringleader in insubordination, succeeds in disrupting the normal functioning of academic life and, in the process, of liberating the oppressed Signorina Malgari. Taking

advantage of the teacher's absence from the classroom, she
and her colleagues rummage through the teacher's papers
where Maddalena finds a love letter inserted into a book on
commercial correspondence, written by Signorina Malgari to
an imaginary person. Maddalena reads it and mails it to Hartman, the author of the book. The letter arrives in Vienna
where it is delivered to the firm of Hartman. The letter is
brought first to an old man, then to a middle-aged man, and
finally to a young man, each representing a different generation of the Hartman family. De Sica plays all three roles.
This metamorphosis highlights the film's concern with generational differences and the emphasis on youth. While the
grandfather and father reject the letter, the son decides to be
adventurous and locate the writer. With a companion, he
travels to Rome and to the Audax School where, after much
confusion, the two men become romantically involved with
Maddalena and the teacher.

The scenes in Malgari's house and Maddalena's are the
setting for the courtship sequences, while the school setting
becomes the locus for elaborate scenes of investigation, mis-
identification, and confessional. The final sequences in the
film reveal order restored as a new teacher appears to assume
Malgari's position and the cycle of repetition asserts itself.

De Sica gently satirizes the institution of the school and
provides a fantasy of liberation from its strictures cast in the
mold of romantic comedy. Sexual fantasy provides the escape
from dreary routine and repression. The letter that brings an
imaginary love object to life who is willing to drop his business
affairs to seek romance is the signifier for the film itself as the
vehicle for transforming the oppressive structure of quotidian
existence. The young female students' attempts to resist banality are linked to the film's similar attempts to transform
the immediate surroundings by evoking and invoking liberatory fantasies. Like *Addio giovinezza!*, Maddalena portrays
youth as energetic, adventurous, and rebellious in contrast
to the staid, pompous, and incompetent older generation,
but, unlike the Poggioli film, *Maddalena zero in condotta* is not
based on renunciation and an acceptance of the world of work

and responsibility. The tricks the students play on their teachers can be read as the film's playful agenda, though its "subversive" alignment with the young people seems consonant with the film's critique of repressive institutions. The comic resolution is the restoration of social relations through love.

De Sica's *Teresa Venerdì* (1941) takes place in a girls' orphanage rather than a school. Using Hollywood images and character types, the film makes the young girl, Teresa, the agent of social change. Stephen Harvey, commenting on this film, finds that

> . . . the characters . . . are all seemingly based on contemporary Hollywood prototypes. The wishful ingenue heroine is strongly reminiscent of the American Anne Shirley, and De Sica resembles Cary Grant at his most antic; Magnani's other woman, a coarse and pretentious golddigger, is blood kin to Gypsy Rose Lee who struggled vainly to entice Tony Martin away from Alice Faye in all the thirties Fox musicals. Flanking these characters are such archetypes as the whimsically incompetent butler, the giddy heiress, the scatterbrained mother and vulgar parvenu father.[15]

Similar to the Hollywood ethos, *Teresa Venerdì* holds out the possibility of upward mobility through merit.

In classic narrative fashion, the young orphan becomes the instrument of the rake's transformation. Teresa (played by Adriana Benetti), innocent, unspoiled, altruistic, and self-sacrificing, is able to reclaim the roué doctor played by De Sica. Dr. Pietro Vignalli is a disappointment to his father. He squanders his money, plays around with women, and refuses to take his profession seriously. Again, we have a film that, in spite of its title, makes the man's transformation the central issue. He is the object of the young women's competition and the good woman wins him.

The doctor meets Teresa at the orphanage where, as a result of his father's arrangements, he has become the institution's physician. As in De Sica's other films (and in Camerini's, his mentor), there are sentimental scenes involving children. The

---

[15] Steven Harvey, *"Teresa Venerdì"* (New York: Museum of Modern Art, 1978), mimeographed, p. 2.

children's obedience, gratitude, humor, and bravery are high-lighted, and Teresa herself is the paragon of virtue. Of course, there is also the troublemaker who tries to create difficulties for Teresa with the doctor, but her plans fail. At first the physician balks at his responsibility for the children, but gradually Teresa's beauty and competence involve him in spite of himself, though he is pulled in several directions.

The denouement occurs when Teresa, having run away from the orphanage, comes to the doctor's house for protection. Conflicted over her presence but drawn to her, Vignalli reluctantly reports her presence to the headmistress. Teresa returns to the orphanage but Vignalli finally comes and takes her away with him. An exchange has occurred. Teresa has "saved" him from Lolita (Anna Magnani), a chanteuse, and from financial ruin, and he in turn "saves" her by taking her out of the orphanage and giving her a home. Significantly, her redemption of him corresponds to his father's wishes, and it was his father who found him the position in the orphanage that enabled him to meet Teresa. Thus, Pietro's acceptance of conformity is consonant with the father's expectations of the son. In a sense, too, Pietro becomes the orphan's, Teresa's, father.

The element of performance is important in this film as an index to "proper" social roles. We learn that Teresa's parents were artists, and she herself performs for the younger children. In one scene, she recites the part of Juliet to her eager and admiring audience. Lolita, too, is a performer, and she is shown singing with a band. Lili, the spoiled young heiress whom Pietro rejects, is addicted to role-playing, though her audience is limited to her family and Pietro. In a sense, then, Pietro chooses the best performer, whose role-playing accords with socially desirable attitudes. Teresa's role, like Juliet's, is chaste, devoted, dependent, and self-sacrificing, whereas the other two women are portrayed as self-indulgent and self-aggrandizing.

In renouncing the rich heiress, Pietro chooses service over wealth and Teresa's removal of Lolita (confirmed by Pietro) seems to signify a choice of familial responsibility, of parenthood over sexuality. What does Teresa gain? She gains a home, a parent, and the opportunity to continue to nurse and parent others, especially Pietro. Like De Sica's later films, the film's rhetoric turns on sentiment developed through the images of youth and innocence, which are at first threatened but later affirmed. Sexual and class conflict are suppressed or ignored.

As in *Seconda B*, the antibourgeois element is present only to elevate the sturdier working-class values that are universalized in psychological fashion; merit, responsibility, loyalty, family integrity, and benevolent authority. In many ways, De Sica's film reproduces the Camerini formulae: wealth is corrupting; businessmen are vulgar and to be ignored; happiness is with your own kind; inflated aspirations lead to difficulties. The film's formal qualities depend on certain conventions, too, that can be found in Mario Camerini's films and in the Hollywood cinema. The film's unity is dependent on a fairly tight editing of sequences that use locale and character contrast for thematic purposes. Characters are not highly individuated. Comic elements are introduced by means of ironic contrasts and physical gesture. In all its aspects, the film seems geared to appeal to a broad audience and to reinforce familial sentiments.

Though Raffaello Matarazzo's film *Il birichino di papà* (1943) moves between the family and the school, and seems to share similar strategies and concerns with these other films, it finally takes a different direction. Matarazzo, a popular filmmaker in the 1950s, produced melodramas and some comedies in the 1940s. A comedy, *Il birichino di papà* focuses on the heroine, and the conflict that opens the film concerns the question of her resistance to femininity. Nicoletta refuses to grow up, refuses to conform to the behavior assigned to young women. The opening shots of the film follow her as she madly races a carriage. The editing moves at a frantic pace to indicate her energy and wildness. These scenes serve proleptically to develop her antipathy to restraint. Her father, sympathetic to her struggles (the mother is absent), resists the efforts of others to control her until the Marchioness, the future mother-

in-law of Nicoletta's sister, Livia, insists on having Nicoletta
sent to a school where she can be disciplined and learn to
submit to her final destiny. The father is fiercely protective
of his daughter but he is overwhelmed by the pressures and
acquiesces. Nicoletta, too, succumbs.

In school she becomes impossible. She refuses to submit to
routine and takes every opportunity to subvert institutional
practices. She fails in all her courses, answers questions
wrong in class, and makes fun of her teachers. Her most
blatant act of defiance occurs during a school performance to
which parents are invited. As the young girls are performing
ring dances with hoops and scarves for an admiring audience,
the performance is disrupted by the loud sound of Nicoletta's
voice as she perches on a window ledge, singing "I can't stand
your face."

Concerned for Livia, Nicoletta runs away from school to
help her sister, whose marriage is foundering. Roberto and
his sister find Livia too provincial in comparison to their own
aristocratic friends, and take every opportunity to remind her
of her inadequacies. When Nicoletta arrives at the house, she
finds Roberto closeted with another woman. Enraged, she
forces Livia to leave, but ultimately, Nicoletta effects a reconciliation between Livia and Roberto. As her reward, she
receives the assurance that she need not return to school.

The film is a musical but not of the backstage variety.
Though Nicoletta sings, she is not an entertainer seeking to
make her way in the world of theater. Her singing (and she
is the only singer in the film) functions as a way of highlighting her exuberance and spontaneity, her difference from
others. Her singing also functions as a form of license, rele-
gating her antisocial attitudes to the level of exceptionality
and play. Played by Chiaretta Gelli, Nicoletta is an unusual
heroine. As Ted Perry describes her, she is a character "of
great vitality and fierce independence."[16] Her eruption into

[16] Ted Perry, "Before Neorealism" (New York: Museum of Modern Art,
1978), mimeographed, p. 4. See also Ted Perry, "The Road to Neorealism,"
*Film Comment* 14 (November/December 1978), p. 9.

song at crucial moments seems to communicate qualities that might in dialogue be considered subversive and problematic.

Viewing the film is an exercise in physical endurance since the pace of the editing and acting is frenetic, overwhelming the viewer with its speed and intensity. *Il birichino di papà* operates within the archetypal forms of comedy and of certain forms of the Hollywood musical. The heroine is the means of transforming repressive social relations within bounds. As an agent of change she struggles against the moribund aristocratic figures who seek to control her own and her sister's life. She seeks to disrupt the restraining atmosphere of the school, and she violently resists the hypocrisy and constraints of domestic life. In contrast, her sister is the consummate victim of class and domestic oppression, and Nicoletta like a knight-errant seeks to free Livia. Nicoletta herself does not succumb to the pressures of family or institutional life. The dominant image associated with her is movement, particularly escape, though the final moments of the film stress her role as the mediatory figure, reconciling conflict and transforming hostile forces within the family. As an agent of change, she is associated with the country, with animals, with birth, and with open spaces. Her relationship to her father is one of mutuality, not authority, and her physical appearance seems androgynous.

Nicoletta opposes the Marchioness, her family, and the bureaucrats at the school, aligning herself with her father, with a destitute lawyer, with workers, and with her oppressed sister. The young woman, as in classical comedy, becomes the means of uniting the conflicting elements, serving to mediate between classes and between the sexes. Although she does not transform the school, she disrupts its operations as she disrupts the family. The film clearly poses sexual and class conflicts even while it moves to reconcile them.

## Children in the Family

A significant number of films portray the child as an intermediary who reconciles differences in the family. In some instances, the existence of the child is sufficient to discipline the parents to accept domestic or social responsibility. In others, the child's sacrifice effects reconciliation. In films of the early forties, however, the child does not save the family but functions as a critic of domestic relations.

In Mario Soldati's *Piccolo mondo antico* (Small Antique World), a costume melodrama characteristic of Soldati, the birth of the daughter is the source of the family conflict, her death the source of reconciliation. The family conflict erupts from a class conflict between aristocrat and bourgeois. The Marchesa opposes her son's marriage to the daughter of a humble functionary and she disinherits him, refusing even to see her granddaughter. In addition, she seeks actively to obstruct her son Franco's political work in behalf of the unification of Italy.

This costume drama, based on a famous novel by Antonio Fogazzaro, combines romance, intrigue, politics, and war. The romantic elements involve the relationship between Franco and Luisa, who defy convention and elope. Their relationship runs the gamut from intense involvement with each other, marital conflict over Franco's politics, separation as Franco moves to the city to engage in political struggle, rupture over the death of Ombretta, their child, to final reconciliation as Franco goes off to fight for Italy.

The film is set in the context of nationalist struggle of mid-nineteenth century Italy. Working for Cavour, Franco and his colleagues are intimidated by the authorities who seek to expose their secret political activities. Subject to harassment and the threat of imprisonment, Franco continues to write pro-nationalist propaganda and to participate in political demonstrations. He tries to convince Luisa of the importance of these activities but she views them as threatening to family life. She blames Franco for the tragic death of their child, Ombretta, which takes place while he is absent from home with his political work. The drowning accident occurs while Luisa herself has left the house to ask the Marquise for assistance.

The child's presence is central to the film although she is not endowed with any individuality. Rather, she is the stereotypic innocent: naive, playful, curious, obedient, and precocious, sensitive to familial discord, and vulnerable to disaster. Her death mediates the conflict between familial security and political commitment, for it is through her that the parents are reconciled. Like Mario's death in *Vecchia guardia*, her death is translated as the necessary massacre of the innocents that is required to unify and mobilize the community. Her suffering as a mother serves to prepare Luisa for a greater political sacrifice for which she was earlier unprepared. As she watches the men go off to war, she is shown in close-up as a maternal figure, embracing with her look all the young and idealistic men who are embarking on a heroic adventure.

The film plays with the familiar motifs of patriotism, nationalism, noble sacrifice, and family loyalty. For his efforts, Franco is rewarded in several ways. His mother finally reinstates his patrimony and inheritance; he is vindicated for his political activism in the successful mobilization of his political energies; and he is reunited with his wife. The real villains of the piece, the aristocratic Marchesa and her allies, are shamed into compliance. The Marchesa's "conversion" takes place after Ombretta's death when in a dream she is confronted with her guilt. The film sets up an opposition between the brittle, cold, stilted, and artificial opulent world inhabited by the aristocracy and the warm, friendly, though chaotic world of Franco and his colleagues, where conversation, art, and politics merge.

Romantic images pervade the film, operating to elevate the action and to involve the spectator affectively. Franco is a musician and the image of him at the piano as well as the use of romantic music provide a positive milieu whereby the politics by association are endowed with the aura of creativity, energy, and adventure. The paintings on the walls of natural landscapes as well as the images of nature, especially sea, mountains, and sky, against which the action takes place also lend themselves to the idealization of political action. The iconography of the characters, Massimo Serato as Franco, Alida Valli as Luisa, and the child, reinforces the sense of purity, innocence, and heroism. The use of images in the film to dramatize these conflicts is evident in the objects placed in Franco's house, the pictures of Italian heroes, the political leaflets, the draped flags, and the political posters. The subordinate characters are cast, it appears, with the notion of enhancing the conflicts between the dedicated and well-meaning political figures and the forces of obstruction. The loyal, absent-minded professor, totally devoted to Franco and the political struggle, is juxtaposed against the decadent aristocrats. His seriocomic role serves to legitimate the behavior of Franco and his colleagues.

The film ostensibly seeks to ennoble political struggle and, particularly, struggle of a nationalistic variety, using past history to animate the present. At the same time, the requirements of the melodrama seem to move in two directions. On the one hand, the psychological pressures of melodrama move to transform the political problems posed in the narrative into the domestic arena, particularly with the pathos of the child's death. On the other hand, these same issues also serve as pressure points in the film, points of conflict and contradiction that have no coherent relation to the resolution. The displacement of the marital conflict onto the war, the channeling of the personal conflict into the political, and the conversion of mourning and sacrifice into legitimized aggression are central to the film's work and apparent on closer scrutiny.

Less overtly political, Ferdinando Maria Poggioli's *La morte civile* (Civil Death), is based on a novel by Paolo Giacometti and concerns the relationship between a mother and child. The major conflict in the film involves the "healing" of the community. The focus is less on the child as a leading character and more on her role as a potential sacrificial victim and as a cause of contention between adults. When the film begins, Rosalia's husband is taken to prison for murder. In order to support herself and the child, Rosalia accepts a position as housekeeper and governess with Dr. Palmieri. Sympathetic to her dilemma, he offers to pass off the child as his, and she presents herself as her own child's governess.

Dr. Palmieri, in contrast to Corrado, the husband, is respectable, generous, and hard-working. His offer to help Rosalia is based on the desire to mitigate his own loneliness. Unfortunately, some of the townspeople are not as generous, finding the relationship between Rosalia and Dr. Palmieri a subject of gossip and criticism. The doctor also must contend with the backward attitudes of members of the community toward his medical practices. A young child, Carletto, suffering from a high fever and inflammation, is treated by Dr. Palmieri. The distraught father does not want to send Carletto to a hospital and begs Palmieri to treat the child at home. Palmieri acquiesces but the townspeople are outraged, complaining that the doctor has violated sanitation laws. A delegation goes to the mayor to complain that Palmieri is guilty of criminal negligence and also of moral laxity.

Palmieri and Rosalia are identified with the care and nurture of children, and with self-sacrifice; the husband, Corrado, with self-indulgence. Corrado escapes from prison and seeks his wife and child. He arrives during a religious ceremony, and in an extended sequence of pilgrimage, Poggioli inserts the spectator into the line of worshippers which Corrado has joined first and Rosalia joins later. The procession terminates in the church. In a dramatic moment, as the priest at the altar turns and holds up a reliquary cross, Rosalia recognizes Corrado in the mass of people. Fearful for her child, she seeks to keep Ada from Corrado; however, he comes to Palmieri's house and attempts to discover the identity of the child which Rosalia insists is Palmieri's. Corrado urges Rosalia to go away with him. She tells him that she is happy with Palmieri and wants to stay. Palmieri informs Corrado that the child is Corrado's, that after Corrado's imprisonment he had felt obligated to help Rosalia. He appeals to Corrado to think of the child's needs, for Corrado cannot offer Ada a proper environment.

In a heavily laden emotional scene, Corrado describes his life in prison where he felt like a dead man convicted by society, experiencing "civil death." Moved, Rosalia agrees to leave with him if he will allow the child to remain with Palmieri. Corrado asks only that he be allowed to see his child once more. The child and the man confront each other in a scene designed to produce maximum sympathy from the viewer, as he says goodbye to the child. When Rosalia learns that Corrado is gone, conscience-stricken, she tries to find him but arrives too late. He has jumped into a rocky ravine and is dead. As Rosalia remains by him, crying, a religious procession passes by in the distance.

*La morte civile*, like so many of Poggioli's films, is framed in a religious context. The actual journey of the main characters is identified as a pilgrimage, linked to the religious procession that climaxes the film. The film presents a society in conflict, division in the family, division among members of the community that threatens the future of its children. Little Carletto's health hangs on the trustworthiness and dedication of Dr. Palmieri who must quell the disruptive and antagonistic elements in the town. Rosalia's child, who grows up in an environment of instability, violence, and murder, is threatened by the return of her father who is a primary representative of this way of life. Though presented as a victim, Corrado's "civil death" is the result of self-indulgence, his inability to discipline himself and to control his passion. The film begins with murder and ends with a suicide, framed in images of violence. In contrast to Corrado's flamboyance, moodiness, and self-preoccupation is Rosalia's self-abnegation and her commitment to service. The imagery of Rosalia as madonna, as painted by Corrado and as represented through the film's iconography, fuses with the other religious imagery in the film to provide the antidote to the disruptive and chaotic world she confronts.

The children in the film are the inspiration for devotion to duty, providing the adults with the opportunity for conversion to self-effacing action. The film seems to equate passion with disease and ultimately with confinement and death. The artist, Corrado, is the carrier, the initiator of the disease, whereas Palmieri is the true physician, committed to the mitigation of suffering. Rosalia is the link, the intermediary between the two men, the wife of Corrado and the wife-to-be of Palmieri. The child, too, loses one father but gains another. Her double identity is revealed in the two names she receives as Corrado's child and later as Palmieri's. As in so many films of the period, the motif of conversion, of transformation into a new identity, is central.

The leading characters in the film are professional men, physician and artist, and the competence and stability of the physician is contrasted with the erratic genius of the artist, the good father to the bad father. The bad father is eliminated, so the good father may emerge. The film elevates the virtues of competence, commitment to service, responsibility, and benevolent authority. The religious symbolism in the film seems to reinforce a traditional image of familial piety. Yet the film's style subverts its ostensible content. In its melodramatic excess, in its contrived "resolution," the film appears more critical than pious and prescriptive, more preoccupied with civil dissolution than conformity. Health and wholesomeness seem to belong more to the world of childish fantasy than to the "real" world.

Poggioli's *Sissignora* (1941) does not involve overt political issues any more than his *La morte civile*. The politics in his films stays within the conventions of family melodrama, focusing on private forms of conflict.[17] The film provides, however, a complex insight into immediate and internalized contradictions as articulated and experienced under fascism. Though this film does not focus on the child in the narrative development, the young woman and the child are central agents in the transformational strategies of the narrative, serving to rationalize the action and point of view.

A young woman, Cristina (Maria Denis), displaced from the country to the city, finds a job through a Catholic employment agency with two hard-to-please sisters (Emma and Irma Gramatica). Cristina is subjected to their arbitrary whims, unable to satisfy their demand for mechanical obedience. The title of the film, "Yes, Madam," derives not only

---

[17] Giuseppe De Santis, "Sissignora," in *Dai telefoni bianchi al neorealismo* (Rome-Bari: Laterza, 1980), pp. 250-51.

from the sisters' demand of complete subordination from the maid, but from the broader representation in the film of the pressures on Cristina to conform to other peoples' demands. Cristina is dismissed by the Rabbiani sisters when they learn that their nephew has fallen in love with her and entertains the notion of marriage. Completely enamored of him, she spurns the affections of a man of her own class. Cristina's next position is at the home of a bankrupt *commendatore* who must let her go when he finds that he cannot pay her wages. She finds employment as a nursemaid. Her employer, a widow, more concerned with amusing her indifferent lover than with her child's health, ignores the child. He develops a serious illness that Cristina, in her zeal to nurse him, catches and from which she almost dies.

Throughout the film, Poggioli stresses the plight of illegitimate and unwanted children as well as abused and neglected working-class women. At the employment agency, Cristina meets other women in her same situation, who are struggling to survive independently but who are either exploited by men or by their employers. One of her friends takes her to an orphanage to visit her own illegitimate child. A contrast is set up between this woman's devotion to the child she cannot maintain and Mrs. Valdata, the wealthy woman who, though she can financially support her child, has little interest in his well-being. Little Giorgio is not homeless as are so many characters in the film, but he shares with them, including Cristina, the experience of being neglected, a sacrificial victim to petty personal desires and, in particular, to status and respectability. For the Rabbiani sisters, respectability takes precedence over affection, and for Mrs. Valdata, personal gratification takes precedence over familial responsibility.

Taking her own responsibilities seriously, Cristina forms a bond with Giorgio, treating him with care and attention as if he were her own child. Her personal life deteriorates as she realizes that she and her sailor lover, Vittorio, can never marry. Worn out from nursing the child and having succumbed to the disease herself, she is no longer able to function. Emilio (Elio Marcuzzo), a fellow worker from the same village as Cristina, arrives in time to have her taken to the hospital where she can be treated. In a tearful scene between Cristina and Giorgio, the woman and the child part from each other.

*Sissignora* offers no happy ending. Though it has all the classic ingredients of comedy—the beautiful young woman who falls in love with a person of another class, a love that is reciprocated, a heroine who is a hard-working, generous, and self-sufficient person who appears to have the possibility of escaping her situation—the film is a classic melodrama. Cristina's situation is presented as one of almost complete hopelessness. The dominant image in the film is of the illegitimacy and indifference of social and domestic institutions. The foundling home, the Catholic agency, and the family are all places that purport to care for dependent individuals but, in fact, are indifferent to their needs for affection and self-esteem. Those who occupy positions of authority and responsibility are bureaucratic, arbitrary, or totally unconcerned about the people they serve. The absence of father figures is striking in the film: the nuns at the agency supervise the lives of their young female clients; the Rabbiani sisters are bereft of husbands; Mrs. Valdata is a widow. The men in the film, the bankrupt commander, Vittorio, Mrs. Valdata's lover, and Emilio, are unable to act, victims themselves or indifferent to the needs of others. The disintegration of affective ties between men and women, adults and children is almost complete, except for the supportive personal relations between the working women and children. The class conflict in this film seems to center in the clash between bourgeoisie and workers. The style of the film is similar to *film noir*: chiaroscuro lighting, the framing of individuals in doorways, the use of disorienting angles, the alienating city environment, the emphasis on enclosed, claustrophobic places, and thematically the focus on corrupt, malign forces that obstruct and destroy individuals.[18]

[18] J. L. Place and L. S. Peterson, "Some Visual Motifs in *Film Noir*," in *Movies and Methods*, edited by Bill Nichols (Berkeley: University of California Press, 1976), pp. 325-38.

The presence of children throughout the film, their vulnerability and helplessness, serves as the dominant vehicle to reinforce the critique of public and private institutional practices in the film and to generate sympathy for the victims. In short, Poggioli's film, while playing with his usual concerns with the importance of service and family loyalty, also offers a critique of class, sexual, and interpersonal relations. His handling of narrative structure and theme differs from the overtly political treatment of children and family in *Vecchia guardia*.

Vittorio De Sica's *I bambini ci guardano* (The Children Are Watching Us, 1944), often cited as one of the important pre-neorealist texts,[19] uses a young boy to involve the audience in the film's judgments on a moribund society. While sharing stylistic characteristics with the neorealist film, it can be understood more appropriately within the context of the other melodramas of the later years of the Ventennio. The film is drawn from a novel, *Prico*, by Cesare Giulio Viola, who worked on the film script with De Sica, Adolfo Franci, Margherita Maglione, Gherardo Gherardi and Cesare Zavattini, one of the architects of neorealism. De Sica's *Bicycle Thieves* and *Shoe Shine* also feature young chldren.

The plot of *I bambini ci guardano* is simple. A young child is the victim of marital conflict between his parents. Prico's father, a petty-bourgeois bureaucrat, is jealous of his wife. Having discovered that she is having an affair with another man, he insists that she leave the child. He takes Prico to his own mother's house but she is unable and unwilling to care for him. Prico becomes ill and the father takes him home where, after a visit from the mother, the father relents and a reconciliation is effected by the couple. At vacation time, the family goes to a seaside resort where the wife (Isa Pola) tries to enjoy herself despite the constant surveillance of her husband, who seeks to guard her from potential seducers. Prico has a semblance of family life until the time arrives for his father to

[19] Peter Bondanella, *Italian Cinema: From Neorealism to the Present* (New York: Frederick Ungar, 1983), p. 53.

return to work in the city, leaving his wife and child to remain on holiday a while longer. The mother's former lover arrives, and they resume their relationship. Prico is again neglected. He tries to run away, attempting to return home, but he has no money and is sent away by the ticket agent at the railway station. Dejected, he walks along the railroad tracks. He is almost hit by a train, frightened by a railway worker, lost on the beach, and eventually found by the police who return him to his mother.

At home again, Prico refuses to tell his father what has happened, fearing to betray his mother. After a letter from the mother, indicating that she is not planning to ever return home, the father makes arrangements to send Prico to a boarding school. The father outfits the boy, takes him to the school, and when he returns home, commits suicide. The final sequences of the film involve the housekeeper's visit to the school to inform Prico of his father's death. The mother arrives too, but he ignores her, only acknowledging the housekeeper's presence.

The film is unrelenting in its movement from one disaster to the next. From the very beginning, Prico's resentment against his mother is made obvious. She takes him to the park ostensibly for him to play but she also uses this as an opportunity to meet her lover. Prico watches his mother as she greets the man, and the child sullenly refuses to have anything to do with him. His playtime is spoiled as he stands alone at a distance watching the two. Life at home is not any more satisfactory. The father, preoccupied with his obligations at work and with his dissatisfactions at home, is unable to talk to the child. The housekeeper, Agnese, is kind to the child but unable to compensate for his loneliness and sense of injury. While the women in the film are associated with experiences of violence, rejection, and abandonment, the father emerges as the nurturant figure. The film plays with the reversal of traditional male and female roles. Ultimately the father is associated with home and tending for the child, in a society where such care is expected from the woman. The mother is the philanderer, the one who runs off with a lover, who is restless and unable to assume responsibility for the child.

Prico is presented as a sensitive child, forced prematurely to confront conflict. He is not shown as interested in sports but in puppet shows and magic. He lives in a world of women: Agnese (the housekeeper), his mother, his grandmother, and Paolina, but his encounters with them are disillusioning, as he is torn between anger and loyalty. He is compelled to maintain secrecy to protect his mother which creates conflict between him and his father. The father's suicide marks the complete disintegration of the family. Prico's only friend now is a priest, Father Michele, whom Prico has learned to trust. The final shots in the film show Prico walking slowly away from the women, Agnese and his mother, toward the priest standing in the doorway. In a long take, the camera films Prico as he joins the man and the scene fades.

As with *Shoe Shine*, De Sica's use of the child as the film's central figure and focus is highly rhetorical. The adult world as mirrored through the child's look is harsh, alienated, and ungenerous, but the problems stem not from economic but from psychic deprivation. The critique of the family, of immediate and extended members, seems to be the film's central concern. The child, along with the audience who inhabits his perspective, becomes the judge of the domestic failure. Like other melodramas made during the war years, the film examines the disintegration of the family. The father's weakness, the mother's restlessness, the child's vulnerability call into question images of authority, respectability, loyalty, and the efficacy of hard work, and the film seems to reproach their absence.

In its evasion of overt politics, the film seems most political. Like Visconti's *Ossessione*, the politics of the time are here seen in private, not public, fashion, as if acknowledging that the reproduction of social relations takes place in the immediate arena of the neighborhood and the family. *I bambini ci guardano* can be seen as a nostalgic text, lamenting the loss of social bonds. It can also be seen as a critical text, exposing the fundaments of fascist ideology: heroic male sacrifice, female service and subordination, and youthful enthusiasm, by portraying the breakdown of these "values." The image of the child thus functions, as it does in *Shoe Shine*, as a safe strategy for an innocent unmasking of political structures. The implied prescriptions—love and responsibility—are almost irrelevant to the excess of negative affect generated by the narrative.

## Summary

These films are united by their tendency to position young people as intermediaries and as agents of transformation. The objects of change are teachers and parents, educational institutions and the family. Authority figures are presented as tyrannical and moribund at worst, ineffectual at best. These young people redeem reprobate but potentially salvageable adults. Young males such as the boys in *Piccoli naufraghi* or the son in *Il grande appello* are pitiless in their rejection of the status quo. They appear to be figures of opposition to traditional values. The adults are often the beneficiaries of youth's vitality, rebelliousness, and engagement.

The portrayal of generational conflict so common to these films converges with their tendency to present all conflict in biological terms. Differences in age, sexual difference, the image of nature itself posit a basis for social struggle and, hence, for reconciliation. Furthermore, a strain of anti-intellectualism accompanies the zeal for change. Learning is portrayed as pedantic and trivial, whereas action is exalted, especially action in the political arena and war. The image of the clock in *Vecchia guardia* serves as a reminder of the immediate imperative for action and the futility of a moderate and reflective approach to change. The countless satiric representations of the classroom situation become the occasion for youths' assumption of control or at least escape.

The treatment of youth is developed along the lines of sexual difference. Both young men and women balk at institutional constraints, but the young men escape into the broader arena of public action, whereas the young women escape to the family. Industriousness and competence are two qualities essential to the young male adventurers. Young women possess the qualities of cleverness. Even at their most rebellious, young girls such as Nicoletta in *Il birichino di papà* act in the interest of family. In the films that portray militant struggle or adventure, young women are excluded or are peripheral. They seek romance and marriage for themselves or are agents for the awakening of romance in others.

The image of surveillance appears in many of the representations of young people. They constitute an audience within the film, and their spectatorship is related to the film's alignment with youth. The young scrutinize their elders and find them wanting, the most extreme example of this being De Sica's *I bambini ci guardano* where the looking is specifically linked to the parental conflict and the young child's direct or indirect reproach. The look appears to constitute another form of control, a mechanism for engendering guilt, and a strategy whereby the narrative can rationalize the conversion of the adults to more socially acceptable behavior. In *La morte civile* the behavior of the adults is shaped by the child and the family is reconstituted, whereas in *I bambini ci guardano* and *Sissignora* the children reproach the adults, but their look does not have the power to produce a magical transformation.

The films featuring young girls and the films where the child appears as critic seem ambiguous on the position of the family. On the one hand, they portray parental figures in critical fashion. On the other, they situate the family as an alternative to repressive institutions. While the films appear to expose the indifference and the rationalizations of the adults, they also appear to be nostalgic for the protection of the home.

The "revolutionary" image of youth thus appears quite contradictory in the final analysis. The "new culture" recuperates the family, validates sexual difference, realigns hierarchical relations purged of undesirable elements, and dramatizes war as a prime force for renovating social institutions. The presence of young people, however, injects a new element in the reshuffling of social relations and actions. Portrayed as catalysts, rebels, critics, and voyeurs, the young people add a subtle, affective, and rhetorically coercive element to the narratives. The youthful perspective increases the capacity of the external spectator for identification, but also restricts the vision to the young people's perspectives and judgments.

Though these films ostensibly share a more or less common ideology, subtle differences are discernible, differences arising from specific generic conventions, the style and outlook of individual directors, and the time the film was made. For example, the comedies "resolve" their conflicts, whereas the melodramas do not, for the most part. Moreover, the comedies usually create an opposition between the community and the family, while the melodramas specialize in domestic conflict and feature psychological problems more prominently. Blasetti's films incline more to the public arena, whereas the De Sica films incline toward the portrayal of personal and domestic conflict. Finally, the florid rhetorical treatment of the thirties and such films as *Vecchia guardia* gives way increasingly to the darker, more ambiguous treatments of the early forties as characterized in the Poggioli films and in De Sica's work. The issue of generational conflict remains continuous as does the emphasis on young people, though the forties films can be read as questioning the power of youth to produce change in the face of indifference, violence, and the inability of the family to mitigate or contain social conflict.

# CHAPTER TWO

# Women, Penitents, and Performers

O N Christmas Day 1933, in Palazzo Venezia, Mussolini celebrated the First "Mother and Child Day." Laura Fermi describes how he publicly honored ninety-three women, one from each province in Italy, for their reproductive fecundity. Only later did he acknowledge "the part fathers played in the production of children and honored not the most prolific mothers but the most prolific couples."[1] At another ceremony in Pontina, the Ceremony of the Wedding Rings, women, among whom was Queen Elena, threw their rings into a burning crucible to symbolize their support for and identification with the regime's objectives. Such festivities were cultivated by the state as a means of political display and of mass entertainment. The displays involving women dramatized women's service to the state, their place in the family, and their reproductive function.

In a less spectacular vein, the regime encouraged women's organizations such as the Fasci Femminili and the women's sections of the Dopolavoro, the organization concerned with the development of after-work or leisure activities. These groups stressed, even for working women, that woman's primary obligation was to the family as wife and mother. Apparently, women were not totally acquiescent to this segregation and definition of their social role, for, as Victoria de Grazia reports, the women expressed a preference for the same after-work activities as men, for sports, movies, and theater as opposed to classes in the domestic arts.[2] Nonethe-

---

[1] Laura Fermi, *Mussolini* (Chicago: University of Chicago Press, 1961), pp. 295-96. See also Tomaso Sillani, *What is Fascism and Why* (London: Bern Limited, 1931), pp. 201-208.

[2] Victoria de Grazia, *The Culture of Consent: Mass Organization of Leisure in Fascist Italy* (Cambridge: Cambridge University Press, 1981), pp. 41-43.

less, women were encouraged, if not coerced, into traditional behavior and activities.

The feature films of the time do not reproduce the public spectacles, nor do they appear overtly to propagandize. The ring ceremonies, the female death squadrons, and the demographic campaigns are absent. Rather, the representations of women are couched in the unexceptional language of domesticity, sacrifice, and service, in a more "universal" language of female iconography, gesture, psychology, and conflict.[3] By reproducing classical women's narratives, the films present themselves as innocent of political coercion. The narratives draw their sustenance from familiar plots, ways of ordering events, modes of closure, and realization of character with deep roots in cultural images, particularly myths of women. The films are conceived of and perceived as entertainment, and the filmic codes operate to conceal rather than to expose social meanings.

The mainstream cinema as practiced through the Hollywood model engages the viewer. The audience can "identify" with the story and with the characters. The boundary between film and audience blurs, and the process of immersion is pleasurable. Spectacle becomes supreme and, as Dana Polan argues, "blocks, ignores, shuts out other forms of cognition."[4] Such a view of the filmic experience suggests that form takes precedence over content, that the image itself as spectacle and as substitute for "reality" has a power lacking in actual social interactions. Moreover, the act of looking takes on greater significance, for, like the voyeurism to which it is likened, the gaze is not innocent but touches deep psychic and cultural attitudes.

In this context, woman's image is particularly important as a force in creating spectacle, as an object of fascination even for women themselves, and as a source of perceptions about the self and the world. Even more, woman can be regarded

[3] Maria-Antonietta Macciocchi, "Female Sexuality in Fascist Ideology," *Feminist Review* 1 (1979), pp. 67-82.

[4] Dana Polan, "Above All Else To Make You See: Cinema and the Ideology of Spectacle," *Boundary 2* 11 (Fall/Winter 1982/83), p. 37.

as a synecdoche for the film itself. Both women and film are objects to be looked at, sources of pleasure, but the woman is doubly scrutinized, within the film and by the audience in the movie house. Moreover, she is, within the diegesis, largely passive—to be looked at and to be acted upon. Even within the very form and style of the film, women's position can be seen as one of containment. She is held in her place by law and custom and by cultural forms as well.

In cinema, Annette Kuhn says that "the woman's image is typically fetishized by means of lingering close-ups, which constitute woman as spectacle, and also by means of the glamorous costumes, make-up, lighting, and setting."[5] Hence, in order to deconstruct the film experience, the act of looking must itself be analyzed, of men looking at women, women looking at men or at themselves, and the spectator looking at the film. In this fashion, spectatorship can be regarded as political. The films discussed in this chapter are self-conscious about their status as entertainment, and the figure of the woman as entertainer is significant whether the woman is actually an entertainer or not.

In addition to being structured by the act of looking, woman's representation is also controlled by the narratives themselves, which code sexual relations in the language of romance, eroticism, and seduction. A critical viewer will notice that though women may be identified as the titular centers of the film and as central to the development of the narrative, they are in fact only a "pseudo-center."[6] They represent anything but themselves as women. They are surrogates for the director, impersonators of men, and objects of surveillance.

[5] Annette Kuhn, *Women's Pictures: Feminism and the Cinema* (London: Routledge and Kegan Paul, 1982), p. 61. See also Kaja Silverman, *The Subject of Semiotics* (New York: Oxford University Press, 1983), pp. 126-193.

[6] Claire Johnston, "Myths of Women in the Cinema," in *Women and the Cinema*, ed. Karyn Kay and Gerald Perry (New York: E. P. Dutton, 1977), p. 411. See also Laura Mulvey, "Visual Pleasure and the Narrative Cinema," *Screen* 16 (Autumn 1975), pp. 6-18; David N. Rodowick, "The Difficulty of Difference," *Wide Angle* 5 (1982), pp. 4-15; Michael Renov, "From Fetishism to Subject: The Containment of Sexual Difference in Hollywood's Wartime Cinema," *Wide Angle* 5 (1982), pp. 16-27.

Many narratives involving women serve to enact a disciplinary process on the female, couched not as discipline but as
redemption. According to Annette Kuhn:

> There seems, therefore, to be a tendency on the part of the classic
> Hollywood narrative to recuperate women. . . . this recuperation
> manifests itself thematically in a limited number of ways: a woman
> character may be restored to the family by falling in love, by 'getting
> her man,' by getting married, or otherwise accepting a 'normative
> female role.' If not, she may be directly punished for her narrative
> and social transgression by exclusion, outlawing, or even death.[7]

Most of the films that portray women reveal an affinity with
what Maria-Antonietta Macciocchi has identified as the fascist
attempt to imprison women "in the 'iron ring' of an eternal
'mother image' right to the point of self-extinction." Macciocchi
strongly emphasizes that "the eternal plague of fascism is
spread through an epidemic of familialism," which "requires
women to lose their autonomy."[8] Yet this "epidemic" is not
only obvious in the Italian cinema of this era but in the Hollywood cinema too, in such "woman's" films as *Stella Dallas*
(King Vidor, 1937), and *Dark Victory* (1939). The line between
fascist and nonfascist ideology often blurs in the films. While
many of the Italian films discussed in this chapter do not
unambiguously glorify the woman's entrapment, they do
make it obvious that domestic accommodation is achieved at
the expense of the woman's autonomy. Patrizia Pistagnesi's
study of the family romance in films of the fascist era works
on the assumption that the feature films can most profitably
be seen as dependent on the classic narrative, its structures,
conventions, and codes in which the representation of the
woman is an index to ideology and politics.[9]

[7] Kuhn, *Women's Pictures*, pp. 34-35.

[8] Macciocchi, "Female Sexuality in Fascist Ideology," pp. 69, 73.

[9] Patrizia Pistagnesi, "La scene familiare nel cinema fascista," in *Cinema italiano sotto il fascismo*, ed. Riccardo Redi (Venice: Marsilio, 1979), pp. 99-104. See also Janet Walker, "Feminist Critical Practice: Female Discourse in *Mildred Pierce*," *Film Reader 5* (1982), pp. 164-72; Julia Lesage, "Feminist Film Criti-cism: Theory and Practice," *Women and Film* 1 (1974), pp. 12-19; Judith Mayne, "Visibility and Feminist Criticism," *Film Reader 5* (1982), pp. 120-24.

Since the Italian cinema moved increasingly to adopt techniques from the popular Hollywood cinema, it is possible to identify the representations of women as multiple facets of the relationship between cinema and ideology rather than a mere reproduction of fascist myth and ritual. Certain films do indeed elevate the idea of the woman of service, the suffering madonna, the recuperated prostitute who returns to the mother, the domesticated entertainer, but the narratives can be viewed more profitably as consciously, or in spite of themselves, offering a critique of these familiar representations of woman. Although representations of women are closely bound to cultural myths, they are also sensitive to changing social conditions. Ideology is both a clarification and distortion of real-world experience, and it cannot be totally static.

Representations of women and acting styles in the Italian silent cinema can be traced to the nineteenth-century Italian theater, to lyric opera, to Pre-Raphaelite art, and especially to the literary work of Gabriele D'Annunzio. The fascination of such art lay in its power to rise above the daily struggle in its disregard for the quotidian existence and for the common individual, and in its ability to make contact with collective desire. The world of the diva was rooted in sensuality, in beauty, and in the conflict between desire and forms of domination. The diva was an exceptional figure, most commonly a woman, who was the incarnation of desire. She suffered greatly and engendered suffering in others. Lyda Borelli and Francesca Bertini were important divas during the silent cinema. A sample of some of their films' titles should provide an index to the quasi-sacred, erotic roles they played. Borelli starred in such films as *La donna nuda* (The Nude Woman, 1912), *Il bosco sacro* (The Sacred Wood, 1915), and *La leggenda di Santa Barbara* (The Legend of St. Barbara, 1918). Bertini acted in *Idillio tragico* (Tragic Idyll, 1912), *La signora delle camelie* (The Lady of the Camelias, 1915), and *La contessa Sara* (Countess Sara, 1920).

The grand style of gesture, the emphasis on the body and on physiognomy of the diva, was suited to the silent cinematic apparatus and to the quest of the early Italian filmmakers to find ways to create a visual language that could capture the imagination of mass audiences. Moreover, the emphasis on personality, on the power of the image to transcend the immediate and commonplace, and on the generation of fantasy converges with social and political developments.

Gian Piero Brunetta discusses how:

The diva is not only a body, a look, an ensemble of characteristic and repetitive gestures; she is also at the same time the most emblematic incarnation of a world over which she exercises absolute power. The woman-diva, thanks to her fascination, to her sexual power, dominates and can destroy a world which possesses economic and political power. In this sufficiently diffuse motive resides certainly one of the elements of major identification for the bourgeois public which found, other than the pleasure of vision, a sort of compensation that repaid their own frustrations and sense of inferiority.[10]

The passing of the Italian diva coincided with the coming of the First World War, the public rejection of the epic spectacles, the competition with the Hollywood film that offered new and more vital images of men and women as well as more varied forms of narration, and the industry's inability to meet the exorbitant salaries demanded by the stars at a time of economic precariousness for the industry.

The diva of the silent cinema had not relied on physical beauty and youthful appearance in order to beguile audiences. The source of her appeal derived from her stature, the plasticity of physiognomy, the theatrical gesture and body language, and the symbolic properties of her role within the narrative. As the Italian cinema began to change, female roles diversified and physical beauty became an important element, a necessary commodity in the selling of the film. The female types that augmented the image of the fatal mysterious woman were the passionate natural woman, the fragile and difficult daughter of the bourgeoisie, the romantic and carnal

[10] Gian Piero Brunetta, *Storia del cinema italiano 1895-1945* (Rome: Riuniti, 1979), p. 78.

female, the young saucy ingenue, the sophisticated worldly woman, and the vigilant wife.[11] While such diversification is evident, the fact remains that these seemingly different types polarized themselves around oppositions between the public and private spheres, between carnality and spirituality, and between the virtues of service as opposed to self-indulgence.

The Hollywood imprint can be detected in the changing iconography of the actresses in the 1930s and '40s, derived from such diverse stars as Marlene Dietrich, Greta Garbo, Bette Davis, Joan Crawford, Hedy Lamarr, and Jean Arthur. Even more significantly, the narrative forms were modified to reveal more varied and down-to-earth images of service and domestication. The diva was demoted to the shopgirl, the wife, the mother, the spurned love object, the repentant sinner, and the selfless entertainer. The romance, the comedy, and the melodrama became the major forms of the "woman's film," that is, of films centering on women's issues and appealing to women viewers.

The films in this chapter present women as entertainers, penitent sinners, wives, and mothers. They portray women who have chosen careers, women who are forced to lead independent lives, women who are socially deviant, women who are in search of or sought by men, and women who struggle to escape domesticity but eventually return to the family. The dominant dilemma for women is the choice between marriage and a career or between two kinds of men, exploiters or providers. Rarely do the women combine work and career and rarely do they marry upward. The dominant virtues associated with these women are family loyalty, self-sacrifice, domestic responsibility, class loyalty, devotion to children, and industriousness.

[11] See Guido Aristarco, "Le cinema italien pendant le regime fasciste," in *Fascisme et resistance dans le cinema italien 1922-1968*, ed. Jean A. Gili (Paris: Lettres modernes Menard, 1970), p. 21. See also "Dive: Maschere e miti del cinema," *Cinema 1* (10 September 1936), p. 183; and Mira Liehm's discussion of the femme fatale in the early Italian cinema in *Passion and Defiance: Film in Italy from 1942 to the Present* (Berkeley and Los Angeles: University of California Press, 1984), pp. 19-21.

## A Woman between Two Worlds

The choice between marriage and career is an identifying feature of the "woman's film." The presence of such a conflict usually announces a benign or severe form of discipline on the female.[12] Either the woman will be made to sacrifice personal happiness for the rigorous isolation of work, or she will renounce work for domesticity. The Hollywood cinema, in its musicals and romantic comedies, often blurs this conflict through linking love and work, mate and co-worker. Such a reconciliation is rarely the case in the films described in this chapter. A good number of films that involve the woman as entertainer emphasize a more traditional perspective, portraying the psychological impoverishment of a career and the plenitude of family. Moreover, the disciplining of the female is also enacted on her as an object to be perpetually scrutinized. She is doomed to look at others but never to attain her desires.

The "modern" conflict between domesticity and work is dramatized in Gustav Machaty's film, *Ballerine*, based in Giuseppe Adami's novel, *Fanny, ballerina della Scala*, about a young dancer who has a promising career. The film opens reflexively with a shot of a young woman and man at Paestum, where he is photographing her among the ancient Greek ruins. He urges her to stay, but she protests that she must get to a rehearsal. The conflict between love and career is introduced against this background of classical beauty, a remnant of the past. When the ballerina arrives at the theater, Rochetti, the ballet master, announces that he will substitute her for the star in spite of the objections of others, delivering a speech about classical ballet and the importance of discipline and control. However, Fanny's near-stardom is truncated when Rochetti collapses and dies. When the news of Rochetti's death is announced, Mario Verandi, a newspaperman on his way to America, offers to cover the story and becomes romantically involved with Fanny. He learns of her deep at-

[12] John Ellis, *Visible Fictions: Cinema: Television:Video* (London: Routledge and Kegan Paul, 1982), p. 67.

tachment to Rochetti, who had been like a father to her. Now she is only one of a number of unemployed aspiring dancers. The film sets up a contrast to Fanny in the character of a singer who does not share Fanny's dedication to art. She prefers to live lavishly supported by an American business-man whose commercial affairs have brought him to Italy. In spite of the warnings of friends, the woman gives up her work and becomes totally dependent on him, ignoring the words of a friendly cleaning woman who tells her that she was like her, but "ended up cleaning other people's rooms." This parallel plot is anticipatory of Fanny's abandonment later.

Fanny finds work with Madame Alexa, a dedicated director who sees potential in Fanny and hires her as a prima ballerina. After a romantic evening at the opera where Fanny and Mario see *La traviata*, Mario tells Fanny of his love for her. Madame Alexa, who sees them after the performance, is shocked to learn from Mario that Fanny has agreed to marry him. She confronts Mario with the question, "What about Fanny's ca-reer?" and Mario responds that Fanny will give up her career to be his wife. Madame Alexa urges Fanny not to abandon her dancing, which has been an important part of her life since childhood. "You are an artist." Fanny remains deeply involved in her work, praised for and exhilarated by her crea-tivity, but Mario angrily tells her: "How different we are from each other. Ambition devours you. All you want is applause." She, in turn, accuses him of being a "vulgar bourgeois." On the eve of the performance, Fanny receives a farewell note from Mario, and, desperate, she decides that she will go with him "where she belongs." Seeing him in the wings, she thinks he is waiting for her, but learns that he still intends to leave. He is merely covering the performance. She is now ready to perform. The audience responds wildly, and this sequence is followed by a montage of images of Fanny's whirlwind per-formances at different theaters, indicating the passage of time and her success as an entertainer. The final sequences of the film are at San Carlo. Fanny's dancing is superimposed with a musical score and then the scene cuts to a high-angle shot of the dance ensemble in different choreographed patterns.

*Ballerine* ends with a solitary image of the woman bereft of a private life, abandoned by the man, and forced into isolation. The ultimate effect of the film is to convey by means of the visual imagery the idea of accomplishment gained at the expense of personal life. Since the film has set up the opposition between discipline and happiness, and since it has associated discipline with work and happiness with love and sexuality, its elimination of the latter alternative negates any notion of compromise. Moreover, the presentation of dance as based on renunciation and discipline is portrayed finally as depersonalizing, even Prussian. (The film is, after all, a German-Italian production.)[13] The Busby Berkeley mechanical images of the dance sequences intercut with isolated images of Fanny seem to reinforce this idea. The linking of Fanny to Rochetti, the dead father surrogate, and to Madame Alexa, the hard-driving, phallic woman, suggests that Fanny's world is the male domain, that Mario's insistence on removing Fanny from this sphere and into the domestic sphere is a conflict over authority and control of Fanny's life and identity.

In outlook, the film appears critical of bourgeois ideas of family and domesticity, a critique of love and marriage, yet it seems at the same time to enact other bourgeois attitudes, presenting a Germanic elevation of renunciation, subordination to duty, and disciplined performance. If Mario's expectations of domesticity with Fanny and exclusive attachment to the husband are labelled bourgeois by Fanny, the alternative is equally bourgeois, where behavior is subordinated totally to work performance. There is no place for personal satisfaction. The female's traditional role of service to the family is transferred from the husband to another authority. In short, Fanny fulfills Rochetti's injunctions to her to be a great artist at the expense of her personal life.

The nature of spectatorship in the film seems to reinforce

[13] On the connection between Italian and other Axis films, see Aristarco, "Le Cinema italien," p. 26.

the film's narrative strategy of recuperation. The self-reflexive dimensions in *Ballerine* involve photography, various forms of performance, singing and ballet, the presentation of on-stage and behind-the-scenes action, and the presence of audience within the film. Women are the objects of scrutiny and the look is associated with images of women's isolation or depersonalization, a form of punishment for their submitting to this way of life. In many ways, Fanny appears a reproach to the independent woman, a warning to her of the rigors of single life. She is a counterpart to certain male characters in such films as *Squadrone bianco* where existence is determined by austere father figures and life is governed by performance. As a commentary on itself, the film turns art into another form of hard work, subordinating the players and the audience, disciplining them to be worthy performers and worthy spectators, revealing the cost of such an exercise but making it appear inevitable.

The woman in *Una donna tra due mondi* (A Woman between Two Worlds, 1936), directed by Goffredo Alessandrini, is a pianist. However, the familiar conflict between career and family is subordinated to a conflict between potential husbands. The two worlds of the film title, therefore, signify two male worlds, one of wealth and leisure, the other of romance and hard work. The woman's role as an entertainer is a pretext for situating her properly within the male world of achievement. An international production, the film is based on a German novel by Ludwig von Wohl entitled *The White Woman of the Maharajah*, and bears the imprint of its German source in its overstated insistence on the woman's subjection. The popular Isa Miranda plays the "white woman," Mira Salviati. The film is built, as the title suggests, around a series of oppositions: discipline and idleness, white and nonwhite people, workers and aristocracy, sexuality and sublimation. *Una donna* opens with a view of the world of wealth and intrigue, focusing on Miss Daisy Elkins, a blonde, vain American woman who is for the moment the playmate of the maharajah. The maharajah, her bored lover, has been exiled from his country by the British and is involved in numerous political intrigues.

In contrast to the foreigners, the group of Italian musicians is presented as dedicated to their art, as comradely, and as poor but honest. Mira, the pianist in the group, is in love with the violinist, Stefano. She is filmed in the position of a spectator, an audience surrogate, as she gazes at him with total devotion. He is totally immersed in his work and impatient with mediocrity. He is enraged at having to perform for unappreciative guests. The group is dismissed when the maharajah complains about their practicing, but are immediately rehired when he sees Mira and invites them to perform for him. Stefano plays brilliantly as Mira is again filmed observing him intensely. The element of spectatorship and performance are central to the film, serving to develop the dichotomy between appropriate and inappropriate involvement with individuals and the social group. Mira is portrayed as misunderstanding her relationship to Stefano as she seeks to make herself the object of his regard and "misunderstands," like the audience within and without the film, the nature of his commitment to "excellence."

When the maharajah sends her flowers, she and Stefano quarrel. A colleague tells her that Stefano is disturbed by the nobleman's attentions to her, but she responds petulantly that Stefano does not care for her. In a stormy scene, she tells Stefano that he should know that she loves him. He, however, tells her that she is not serious about her work and that her piano playing is no good. She leaves him angrily, confiding to one of the other musicians: "I have a right to have someone be kind to me." Stefano replaces her with a new pianist, and she attempts to leave the city. She is intercepted by the maharajah's physician, Dr. Leyburn, and she accepts the invitation to stay at the nobleman's estate. As she explains to the doctor: "The maharajah is good to me. A woman has to feel that she is loved." When the maharajah proposes marriage to her, she accepts, though his colleagues are uneasy about the relationship. Moreover, the information emerges that the maharajah's wife died at his hands when he discovered her unfaithfulness.

At a reception planned by the maharajah, Mira is dressed Indian-style, standing in front of a picture that appears to be of her, but is actually the maharajah's dead wife, signifying that Mira is in danger of losing her identity. When she realizes that the maharajah, now free to return home, plans to take her with him, she dissolves the engagement and leaves, going instead to find Stefano. The two are reunited and the final image of the film shows the musicians together once again, walking arm in arm. The group is expanded to include Mimi, Daisy's maid, who has abandoned her mistress and has joined the musicians.

Thus the film reuintes members of the same nationality, class, and race and establishes that collectivity, camaraderie, and devotion to creativity is superior to wealth and power. Music, especially Stefano's performance on the violin, is the dominant vehicle for establishing bonds of solidarity; it is associated with industriousness, self-esteem, wholesomeness, and especially wholesome relationships. In opposition, the foreigners in the film are associated with intrigue, manipulation, and particularly with reflected reality. The film's primary setting, the hotel, a conventional setting for films of intrigue, is a signifier of the alienation and emptiness of modern urban, cosmopolitan existence, exemplified too by its "foreign" inhabitants. It serves to create a contrast to the dedicated community exemplified by the Italian performers.

The characters are associated with images of mirrors, photographs, and paintings, suggesting self-preoccupation and self-division. Moreover, the title of the film offers a clue to the film's structure. The world of the Italians is opposed to that of the foreigners; the two women, Mira and Daisy, are contrasted. Mira and the dead Indian woman are juxtaposed, and the oppositions transmit the themes of Western superiority over Eastern decadence, Italian creativity over English and American sterility, work over leisure, happy poverty over stultifying wealth. The model figure is Stefano whose dedication to music takes precedence over sentimental attachment to Mira. His superior talent absolves him from his harsh treatment of her in the name of excellence and self-discipline. Her subordination to him finally is the mark of her "growth." Given the two worlds portrayed, her rejection of the romantic but indulgent attitude of the maharajah positions her properly within the world of work, discipline, and renunciation.

The role of performance is central to the film. Long sequences are devoted to Stefano's violin playing with Mira as the dominant spectator. She, however, is irrelevant as a performer. Stefano denigrates her playing. If she is a picture brought to life for the maharajah, an object to be scrutinized, she is the admiring spectator for Stefano. In either case, the role relegated to her appears "between two worlds," as object of admiration for the man, or as admiring the male object. Objectification, subordination, and exclusion are inevitable. What the film reveals, while it elevates her choice of Stefano, is the similarity of these two worlds. Though the film is not self-conscious about its alternatives, it nonetheless reveals the impossibility of the "choice," the film's coercive strategy in forcing the female into proper submission.

The values associated with the artists, in spite of the film's attempt to create a sense of bohemian freedom and joyful unconventionality, appear consonant with the fascist contradictions surrounding notions of collectivity, loyalty, subordination of the self, and conformity. Underlying the elevation of creativity is coercion; underlying the assumption of spontaneity is discipline and control; underlying the idea of collective interaction among struggling equals is the idea of submission to the figure with authority. The criterion of performance centers in the promotion of productivity as an end in itself. In a sense, Mira stands as a surrogate for the audience, disciplined into respectful attention. The image of the woman functions thus as intermediary in yet another way, as a bridge between the extremes of nonconformity and coercive involvement, while at the same time exposing the film's coercive strategies.

Mario Soldati's *Dora Nelson* (1939) recapitulates the motif of the woman as entertainer for the purpose of ultimately elevating the woman as dutiful wife and potential mother by means of the device of the double. In *Dora Nelson*, the metaphor of cinema is expressly developed, it would seem, for the purpose of likening marriage and spectacle, and regarding marriage as the successful adoption of a female role. The classic elements in the narrative are the theater–life opposition, the problems of dual identity, and the rags-to-riches plot. The film begins with a group of gypsy performers, complete with violin music. A couple of bemedalled officers greet one another and the "princess" arrives, but she suddenly breaks down and has hysterics, and it becomes clear that the audience is watching the filming of a movie. Cameras become visible as the "princess" (Assia Noris) has an argument with the director and walks off the set.

At the studio, the director learns that there is a woman who looks like his leading lady. Desperate to finish the film, he agrees to a look-alike substitute. Pierina, a shopgirl (played also by Assia Noris), is selected for the part, and, at the studio, goes through different stages of being prepared for the filming. She emerges looking "perfect" for the part. No one can discern the difference between the "impostor" and the real star, though the producer worries about the ruse. While the impostor seeks to fulfill the prerequisites of her role in the film within the film, the real Dora abandons her family for an affair with a prince. She tyrannizes her husband and daughter as she tyrannizes workers on the set, accusing them of being "bourgeois." The husband, Giovanni, a wealthy businessman, asks Pierina to impersonate his wife for a few days for the sake of the family, and she agrees.

The house is elegant. Giovanni takes Pierina on a tour, showing her the family portraits, and prompting her on her role as mistress of the estate. At an engagement party for the daughter, the false Dora entertains the guests and charms them, much to Giovanni's approval. However, when Pierina learns that the woman she is playing is a "bad" woman, she threatens to leave. She is restrained by a relative who, thinking that the couple has had a quarrel, urges them to kiss and make up. Realizing that she has fallen in love, Pierina remains. The real Dora is swindled by the prince, who is also an impostor, and she learns from the social page of the newspaper that her substitute on the set is playing her role at home. Angrily, Dora returns to her husband—but too late. A newspaper clipping announces: "The strange case of the dead revived . . . the first husband of Dora Nelson, believed dead in a train crash, has returned after eight years. The marriage of Dora Nelson and the noted industrialist Giovanni Ferrari has been annulled. . . ." Another newspaper clipping announces that he has remarried.

Pierina, the submissive worker, by virtue of her pliability, her true familial sentiments, and her fidelity, is rewarded. She gains a wealthy husband and is rescued from a life of obscurity. The two women played by the same actress portray the opposition between an irresponsible attitude toward conjugal responsibility and one that entails subordination to the husband, being of service to others, and inhabiting the domestic role credibly. The real Dora impersonates being a wife, while Pierina inhabits the role. As an entertainer, Dora is presented as capricious, arbitrary, and even immoral. The film criticizes Dora's lax attitudes toward family, linking them to viciousness and even antisocial behavior.

The device of doubling is common in the genre film. In some instances, the figure of the double is represented by means of twinning as in *The Corsican Brothers*, *The Man in the Iron Mask*, and *Cobra Woman*. Doubling can also be developed through the use of siblings, or the idea of look-alikes who are not necessarily related by blood. Doubling involves, as Lucy Fischer has shown, an opposition between positive and negative values, one side representing antisocial and the other side conformist attitudes.[14] The conflict produces the repression of one and the emergence of the other. A demystification of the representation of the female would thus involve an understanding of the process of splitting and polarizing the

[14] Lucy Fischer, "The Two-Faced Women: The 'Double' in Women's Melodrama of the 1940's," *Cinema Journal* 23 (Fall 1983), pp. 24-43. See also J. P. Telotte, "The Doubles of Fantasy and the Space of Desire," *Film Criticism* 6 (Fall 1982), pp. 56-68.

female character. In *Dora Nelson* the "bad" Dora is punished
for her promiscuity, and the "good" Dora takes her place.
And the "magical transformation" is enacted through the sub-
stitution of one performer for another.

The emphasis on role-playing is linked to the idea of social
performance. By means of the two Doras, the film attempts
to distinguish between "authentic" behavior and impersonation, implying that anyone can be a public performer but the
real test of role-playing involves playing the right role, which
in this case seems to be the role of wife and mother. The
reflexive elements in the film, the film within a film, the role
of the director, the behind-the-scenes shots of actors preparing for the performance, call attention to entertainment, but
rather than affirming the success of the performer and the
liberatory aspects of entertainment, *Dora Nelson* mocks itself.
Substituting the "real thing" for the artifact, the alternative
to the "film" is the family, made to look more spectacular
than "film" with its images of wealth and splendor, and its
attentive, adoring, and needy husband, waiting for the right
woman to fill the role. Thus, the self referential elements work
to affirm the actual film, which transfers its conceptions of
cinema into the domestic arena.

Through developing a mother-and-daughter relationship,
Amleto Palermi's *Il carnevale di Venezia* (Carnival in Venice,
1940) portrays a woman's total devotion to her daughter to
the point of self-abnegation. Like the mother in Rouben Mamoulian's *Applause*, she subordinates her own career to her
daughter's; however, the daughter's "career" does not turn
out to be a musical one but rather marriage to a nobleman.
In contrast to Hollywood musicals, the film does not reconcile
talent, success, and domesticity,[15] but rather the subordination of personal creativity to work and domesticity.

Montini, a musical conductor, is disappointed that his talented daughter, an opera singer, played by Toti del Monte,
is wasted as an employee in a tobacco factory. Moreover,
Ninetta's daughter, Tonina, instead of engaging in serious

---

[15] Jane Feuer, *The Hollywood Musical* (London: British Film Institute, 1982).

study at the music conservatory in an effort to become an opera singer herself, is having an affair with a young noble-man, Count Sagredo. A baker, Marchetto, passing by the conservatory after the students have left, picks up a shawl that he recognizes as Tonina's, bringing the shawl to Ninetta who assumes that Marchetto is the young man who is se-ducing her daughter. When confronted by her mother who asks her if she has been seeing Marchetto, Tonina, unwilling to reveal her real lover, "confesses" that she indeed has been with Marchetto. The consequence of her confession is her betrothal to the baker. On the evening of a Venetian festival called the Feast of the Savior, Tonina disappears to join the Count and his friends.

As the title of the film indicates, the festive setting is integral to the film's meaning. In many of the comedies and musicals such as *Il carnevale di Venezia*, festivals are part of the setting, if not an integral part of the film's point of view, signifying social solidarity.[16] The festival scenes allow the filmmaker to capitalize on the spectacle of Venice at night and on Italian social life as being celebrational and joyful. At the festival, the only discordant note is Ninetta herself, who, upset over the daughter's departure, sits morosely at a table as her father conducts the orchestra. Urged by her father, Ninetta sings a lullaby which Tonina hears and recognizes. The music moves Tonina, and she returns home. She arrives to find her mother praying before the madonna, and the mother and daughter are reconciled.

Tonina resumes her singing lessons, determined to be an obedient daughter. Now she is obsessed with the idea of success, but frustrated at her limitations. She does not account to her mother for her sudden ambition, but we learn from Paolo that he has a plan, namely to introduce a new opera singer at a ballet that he and his friends are organizing. Con-trary to the many films that portray the aristocracy as decadent and self-indulgent, this film reveals them as attractive and responsible. Paolo's concern for Tonina appears to be genu-

---

[16] De Grazia, *The Culture of Consent*, p. 215.

ine. Eager to advance her career, he plans her debut for the carnival, and she energetically practices opera arias. The practice sessions, however, involve Ninetta's singing and Tonina's listening in frustration, aware that she cannot compete with her mother.

Marchetto, in a rage at having been duped by Tonina and her family, demands financial compensation for emotional damages as well as expenses incurred for an engagement party. The resolution to the financial dilemma appears in the person of Paolo, who comes to ask Montini for permission to allow Tonina to perform. Montini tells him that the mother is better than the daughter, but Paolo insists in presenting Tonina as the "nightingale of San Marco." Ninetta, however, is amenable, seeing the debut as an opportunity for her daughter, and Montini relents when he realizes that the money for the performance will enable him to settle accounts with Marchetto. Ninetta also learns that Paolo is in love with her daughter.

The final sequences of the film return again to the carnival. Inside the performance room, Montini nervously complains that Tonina is not ready for the debut, and he shouts last-minute instructions until Ninetta orders him to leave as the crowds gather in the streets to hear the "nightingale." Tonina reveals to her mother that she has lost her voice, and Ninetta substitutes for her daughter. The audience is wildly enthusiastic. Only Montini recognizes the singer's identity. Paolo and his friends rush into the studio and engulf Tonina with praise. Tonina tries to reveal the truth but he dismisses what she has to say. Ninetta sits alone at the piano as her father enters and tells her, "Poor child. I alone understand that it was you who sang." Her response is, "But he'll marry her," as she leans against her father in a gesture of resignation.

Though the film has certain classic elements of the musical—romance, spectacle, the struggle to succeed in the world of entertainment, a seeming self-reflexivity about performance and spectatorship, and an emphasis on spectacle—the film downplays the triumph of spectacle in the triumph of the domestic drama and the subordination of women's creativity.[17] Unlike Victor Savile's *Evergreen* (1934), modeled after the Hollywood musical, where the heroine impersonates her mother and is forced to confess and be absolved for her crime of fraud, *Il carnevale* suppresses the confession within the film. Moreover, in the Savile film, the heroine, Harriet Green, Jr., is able to throw off her past and establish her own identity as a performer, whereas Tonina and her mother remain fused through the conspiracy. Similarly, Mamoulian's *Applause* (1929) portrays conflict between a mother and daughter in relation to performance, but it is the daughter who substitutes for the mother. Ninetta's creativity is unrecognized except by her father and is the instrument for resolving her daughter's social and domestic status. Tonina, with her mother's help, using her mother's voice, is now able to settle down and assume her place as a wife. That Tonina's marriage is based on a fraud is irrelevant and the film makes no effort to clarify the imposture. Since it concerns itself solely with the motif of self-sacrifice on the mother's part, the film makes no pretense of resolving the problems created for the daughter.

From the beginning, Ninetta's great talent is placed in the service of work, at the tobacco factory, at the festival, and finally to enhance her daughter's position. Her relationship to her father is ambiguous. Directed by him, serving him, and, finally, bonded with him through the secret the two share about Tonina's "success," Ninetta seems robbed of any personal identity. In fact, the daughter's appropriation of her voice is the further sign of the mother's being silenced. The final image in the film of a silent Ninetta leaning against her father for support reinforces her total subordination.

The compensation for her sacrifice, the utilization of her gift for others, is hardly a matter of concern. It is tied to the assumed value of service to the family and the presumed satisfaction of entertaining others without reward. The element of carnival is central to an understanding of the film's relation to itself. Spectacle, the idea of social life as festive,

[17] Christian Viviani, "Who Is without Sin? The Maternal Melodrama in American Film 1930-39," *Wide Angle* 4 (1980), pp. 4-17.

should compensate for individual inadequacy, should provide the vehicle for forgetting, for erasing, conflict. Yet it has
the reverse effect on the film as in all the musical scenes;
individual conflict and dissatisfaction are apparent. Ninetta's
performance in the factory ends in a conflict with one of the
workers. At the Feast of the Savior, while the audience enjoys
itself, Ninetta struggles with her pain over the disappearance
of her daughter, and at the carnival, she is set apart from
others, unrecognized for her contribution.

Thus, if the film wishes to establish the attractiveness of
sacrifice, the meaningfulness of sacrifice, the personal rewards for talent, the transformative nature of performance,
and the power of collectivity, it subverts itself. Instead, it
exposes their fraudulence. It exposes how the women are
trapped, used by others, in order to maintain the outward
trappings of social performance at the cost of voiding themselves. The mother's voice is taken away and the daughter
who cannot possess the voice must exploit this fraud in order
to merge with her aristocratic lover. The internal audience too
is defrauded, since they are denied the knowledge of the real
singer. The external audience, however, shares the secret with
the family. Working with what the audience knows, the filmmaker gratifies the audience's expectations. Moreover, the
film's strategies, its silences in particular, seem to argue for
its working on shared assumptions, articulated and implied.
Playing with the seemingly self-evident role of the subordination of the private to the public, of individual action to
collective submission, of self-expression to the negation of
self, the narrative positions the woman as the agent of these
transformations.

The idea of confession, central to so many Hollywood films,
especially musicals, where the audience within the film witness the exposure of disguises, deceptions, and impersona-
tions, is conspicuously absent in *Il carnevale di Venezia*. Fraudulence is necessary to legitimize the subordination of personal
gratification to action, and of conflict to the domestic and,
hence, public good. The continuity of the public sphere can
only be maintained by suppressing the truth, by not con-

fessing, by keeping the secret of impersonation intact. The image of carnival in this film, like the conventional festive vision of comedy but more transparently, takes on the unintentional connotation of coercion, since the celebration itself provides a further incentive for the suppression of truth.

The disciplining of the female performer is reenacted in Renato Castellani's 1942 film, *Zazà*, which dramatizes the familiar conflict for women between conventional family life and independent existence. Castellani, a prominent director of the period, was acclaimed for the high level of technical proficiency displayed in his films, the tautness of narrative structure, the superb *mise-en-scène*, the careful attention to environment and detail, and, above all, the complex handling of sexual relations. The title character of *Zazà* is similar to the character of Helen Faraday, played by Marlene Dietrich in Von Sternberg's *Blonde Venus* (1932). Isa Miranda, whose star image was often likened to Dietrich's, portrays Zazà. Like the Dietrich character, Zazà is an entertainer, the object of men's admiration, a potential danger to other women, a source of disruption, and, therefore, an object of punishment.[18]

*Zazà* opens with a man asleep on a train. He awakens at a stop, runs off to get refreshments and misses the train. In the restaurant, he meets a journalist, and from him learns about a singer in the town (St. Etienne). He decides to go to the performance. Zazà, a coquette, is the star attraction, and Dufresne (Antonio Centa) is attracted to her. Dufresne goes backstage to see her, and, ambivalent about becoming involved with her, leaves. At the station again, he waits for a train but finally decides to return to the theater. He arrives in time to observe Zazà performing, singing of love, arousing her male audience to admiration and involvement. He spends the night with her, and the following morning, Zazà vows her eternal love to him. Her longing for conventional family life is conveyed by means of a shot of her looking out the window and observing a family together in their apartment. Dufresne,

---

[18] E. Ann Kaplan, *Women and Film: Both Sides of the Camera* (New York: Methuen, 1983), pp. 50-51.

however, does not tell her that he is already married. Zazà takes him to the train station and tries to extract a promise from him about his return, but he is evasive. As she says farewell to him, she presses a key into his hand. The initial shot of the film on the train is repeated as Dufresne sleeps. When he awakens, he opens the window and throws the key away. He returns home, carrying flowers. The interior is lavish, befitting his status as a successful engineer. He calls his wife, but his servant tells him that his wife is away with the child. He returns to Zazà, and they plan to take a trip together. Again, the image of a train is seen but this time the couple is together.

They go to a hotel where Dufresne had stayed many years ago, and where Zazà is mistaken for his wife. In haste, Dufresne leaves Zazà and returns home. Alone in the room, she views a wedding party from her window. As earlier, her views of domestic bliss are presented from a position of Zazà's looking enviously at others. She comes downstairs as the wedded couple enters and joins them for drinks. The contrast is reinforced between her isolation and their wedded bliss. Dufresne returns and apologizes for ruining their holiday, but from her manager-friend Zazà learns that her lover is married. Enraged, she determines to seek revenge.

Dressed in black, Zazà goes with Natalia, her maid, to Dufresne's house to reveal everything. When she arrives, she assumes a foreign identity and asks to see Dufresne's wife. The woman is out, but Zazà insists that she can wait. While in the sitting room, a child enters. She asks Zazà questions about herself, whether she is married and has children. She shows a religious book to Zazà and then goes to the piano to play a song for her. Zazà cries and loses her appetite for revenge. She gets up to leave but on the way out confronts the wife who has just returned. Zazà tells her that she has made a mistake, compliments the woman on her gracious child, and leaves.

The earlier image of Zazà's glamorous life has now dissipated and she is seen as abandoned in love and excluded from conventional pleasures. Finally, Dufresne decides to renounce everything for her, but she sends him back to his wife. She informs him of her visit to his house, reassuring him that she has betrayed nothing. As she renounces him with firmness, her face is submerged in shadow. Her face can be seen from outside above the curtain in close-up as she watches his image getting more remote.

The film plays with themes familiar to Castellani and also to the time. The inevitable conjunction of women as nurturant figures is reinforced, and two images of women are reconciled in Zazà. On the one hand Zazà, the entertainer and coquette, is punished for her sensual and indulgent life.[19] Her punishment is to be forever excluded from the family circle. Having been an object of desire, the focal point of men's gaze, she is now doomed to look out at others and to be "unfulfilled." On the other hand, her "redemption" resides in her final act of renunciation when she abandons her anger and intended revenge and restores her lover to his wife and child, choosing a life of loneliness to one of self-indulgence.

Zazà, like Madame Bovary, stands at her window watching others, consumed by unfulfilled desire. In public life she is the center of attention, the object of men's desire, while her private life increasingly becomes isolated and sterile. Her only compensation, like Paolo's in Blasetti's *Quattro passi fra le nuvole*, is the knowledge of having served others by being a preserver of the family. In this way she, too, acts as a vicarious nurture figure. Moreover, Castellani seems to suggest that if direct gratification is not possible, the satisfaction of honorable service and resignation is. Balanced, therefore, against the successes of the theater which are ephemeral and the bohemian life associated with it which is arbitrary and precarious, the private and personal virtues of authenticity, self-discipline, and self-sacrifice are portrayed as ennobling though painful.

The engineer's life is linked to train travel, to moving between the home and theater, attempting to accommodate to both worlds, with Zazà as intermediary. The permanent sep-

[19] Ibid., pp. 53-54.

aration of the two truncates his mobile existence, restoring him to his "rightful place" by his wife and child's side in spite of himself. Women are thereby united—the wife, the child, Zazà, and Natalia, Zazà's maid—in preserving the health of society and saving men from themselves. Unlike other films that feature entertainers, this one ends at Zazà's apartment and with her alone rather than returning to her admiring public.

Zazà's desperate and obsessive attachment to her lover is central, and she extricates herself from unbridled sensuality, rage, and the desire for revenge. The images of domestic life that seem so idyllic to her and to the newlyweds are presented for the external audience finally as linked to duty, proper regard for children, and male stability. The virtues of heroic action are not in evidence as Castellani focuses on individual accommodation to service and the woman's socially supportive role in maintaining family life.

The element of spectatorship, however, is central to the narrative "resolution," for the film develops the women's dual positioning as the object of the gaze and as spectators. In the final analysis, the woman is observed by the filmic audience as isolated and pinioned passively to the window, framed by the film. Though the narrative casts Zazà's act in the noble context of service, the final image, an image of confinement, reveals her filmic and social exclusion.

## Endangered Wives

The figure of the watchful wife attuned to the vagaries of a wandering husband has its roots in the comedy of manners and in light opera. Its darker side is represented in grand opera and melodrama. The figure of the jealous husband has even more ancient roots. Both figures appear in the numerous films involving domestic conflict and reconciliation. Underlying these treatments are the now familiar motifs of marriage as performance, of the actor's roles as involving impersonation and disguise, and of the conflict between the home and the world external to it. These films pose the necessity of continuity, and the role of the family as an instrument of production and reproduction. The presentation of women in the films interacts with fascist ideology in such a way as to elevate the women as producers of children, as supporters and sustainers of the community and of the political collectivity.

The idea of secrets and disguises is important in Max Neufeld's film, *Una moglie in pericolo* (A Wife in Danger). Secrecy is necessary to maintain the family in this frothy comedy of manners, a good example of the "white telephone" style of filmmaking. The film opens (and closes) on a domestic scene. Mary, the wife, is ensconced in bed listening to the phonograph, and Pietro, her husband, is working at his desk. But conflict begins to surface. He gets up and turns off the distracting phonograph and returns to work. Restless, she interrupts his work with questions about what to wear to a ball. On his desk, she finds tickets to a ball which place them in Box 13, and she complains about how "Father never wanted thirteen at the table." He gives up his writing and goes to bed, where he attempts to read a book, but Mary interrupts him again by asking, "What are you reading?" He responds that he is reading a book about a wife who gets into trouble, and she responds with assurance, "A good wife never gets into trouble." With this prologue, the comedy sets out to explore whether and how a wife can be unfaithful.

The potential source of the "danger" to their marriage is Giorgio, a Don Juan figure, who collects from women tokens of his amorous exploits. The other Lothario figure in the film is Mary's father, who chases women with much less success than Giorgio. Giorgio receives gifts from his women; the father lavishes gifts on them. The paths of Giorgio and Pietro converge in the men's work; both work at the Foreign Office. Peitro has a desk job and Giorgio is appropriately a diplomatic courier. An assignment, it turns out, that will keep Pietro late at the office, prohibits him from attending the party.

Mary, on hearing the news, tries to get her father to take her but he declines, saying he has a headache and will go to bed. He is, however, planning secretly to go to the affair, and the maid comments to Mary that "All men are cheats." Mary decides to go to the ball with the maid. Since it is a masked affair, she does not fear detection. She provides the maid with a dress and takes one of her aunt's for herself. Her husband gives Giorgio his ticket. At the ball, Giorgio attempts to seduce Mary. She escapes momentarily, but he follows her, appearing at her doorstep. He manages to insinuate himself into the house and, determined not to leave, he feigns illness. Mary arranges to exchange clothes with the maid whom she sends to Giorgio in her place. Giorgio calls Pietro and brags to him that he met a beautiful woman in whose house he now is. Pietro chides him, "You are an incorrigible Don Giovanni," but ironically, he wishes him luck. While Mary goes to bed, Lina, the maid, wearing the mistress's dress and perfume (Black Narcissus), plays with Giorgio as a clock plays an aria from *Don Giovanni*. When Giorgio leaves, he drops a fan into the shrubbery on the balcony and almost gets caught by a policeman who takes him for a thief.

Giorgio is nearly exposed when he comes to the house to share the celebration of Pietro and Mary's anniversary. He gives Pietro a blow-by-blow account of his recent conquest. The game almost explodes when he reveals that this is the house where he had been the previous night. However, when he sees the aunt, wearing the incriminating dress, he (and Pietro) is convinced that the mystery woman was the aunt and not Mary. Pietro and Mary have a laugh at his expense and the "secret" is safe. As they dance, she asks him how the novel, *A Woman in Danger*, ends, and he tells her: "The husband and wife separate." The moral of the tale, says Pietro, is "It's better not to confess." Teasing him, Mary asserts that she will confess—that she loves him, and thus marriage is safe.

The family constellation in the film involves an absent mother, an inept aunt who stands in as a mother surrogate, an unreliable father, and a childlike daughter whose dominant occupation is to maintain the fiction of an ideal marriage, and a son-in-law, Pietro, who is redeemed from being a cuckold. He emerges with his wife's complicity as a hard-working, sincere, and responsible man. Giorgio, the irrepressible Don

Juan, is chastened for his exploits. Lina, the maid, the real object of Giorgio's seduction, is never exposed nor does she expose the impostor. Not only does she clean the house but she cleans up the family's sexual affairs. The film makes no pretense of elevating her status, or of rewarding her in any way. In short, her service and loyalty to the family has no limits. Pietro and Mary's marriage is safe thanks to Lina's excellent qualities as clean-up artist and guardian of family secrets, revealing too that domestic positions are based on the capacity to maintain secrecy.

The politics of the film thus center in the drama of "diplomacy" and "intrigue." Pietro and Giorgio's formal occupation as diplomats is relevant to the progress of the film, though the real diplomats turn out to be the women who keep the men pacified. The primary politics are domestic though the domestic politics can be read back into the public sphere. The ostensible self-reflexivity of the film resides in the parallel between the book read by Pietro and the film itself. The meaning of the resolution of the film is read against the resolution in the book. The book is closer to reality but the reality is transformed into the fiction of the film. The family life of the couple is identified with a fiction and their lives are portrayed as devoted to maintaining the fiction. Confession would only rupture the fiction.

The centrality of disguises, role-playing, and allusions to Mozart's *Don Giovanni* as well as to the book signal the public register of the domestic drama, the assertion that "impersonation" is necessary to continuity, specifically in the fixed position of class and sex, and that the "secret" will be kept about the ways in which diplomacy, intrigue, and deception are central to social continuity. The secret of the maid's instrumentalization can only be kept if the idea of confession is eliminated. Thus, everyone knows but no one will tell.

The motif of the Don Juan figure restrained by a resourceful woman is reiterated somewhat differently in Mario Mattòli's 1938 film, *La dama bianca* (The Woman in White). The film stars Elsa Merlini, playing a more sophisticated role than her 1931 perfromance in *Segretaria privata*. She plays opposite

Nino Besozzi, the wandering, lecherous husband, who needs
constantly to be reminded of his marital obligations. Marina
seeks to lure her husband, a lawyer, away from his office and
his "clients," who are mainly women. Armed with the excuse
of health and with the complicity of a doctor, Marina takes
her husband Giulio to a mountain resort. When they arrive
at the resort, Giulio is already looking for excuses to leave,
to escape his wife.

Many shots in the film are devoted to scenery, views of
mountains, sky, and other natural beauties. The scenic shots
are not merely filler or establishing shots, but signal a particular attitude toward the filmic events, namely, the positioning
of the spectator in the role of tourist as well as of tourism as
a panacea for marital ennui, wandering attention, and the
banality of daily life. The setting in the hotel and the fashions
conjure up 1938 elegance, Italian style,[20] though on a far less
lavish scale than a Hollywood film of the same era. Landscape
and setting also function like spectacle in the musical as a
disruption in the narrative, as a form of compensation, the
compensation of entertainment through looking. Also, the
purity of the rural environment becomes a signifier for the
"natural" domestic environment.

Marina confesses, to the dismay of an older woman at the
hotel, that she and her husband have no children, that they
sleep in separate rooms, and that they have a "modern" marriage. Thus, the problematic of the film—how to solidify domestic ties—unfolds as Giulio machinates to be called back to
the city and Marina machinates to keep her husband in the
country. The couple learns from one of the guests that a
mysterious woman in white comes to his room each night,
and Giulio's interest is aroused. The idea appeals to Marina
and she appears in his room dressed as the woman in white,
covered with a white veil. The following morning he looks
more contented than he has been since their arrival. Confu-

[20] Adriano Aprà and Patrizia Pistagnesi, *I favolosi anni trenta: Cinema italiano
1929-1944* (Milano: Electa, 1979).

sion arises, however, when he learns that the same woman has visited another guest.

The group of tourists take a trip to a nearby waterfall and grotto and, in between shots of the landscape, the men argue about the identity of the woman in white. Giulio takes Signor Savelli, the claimant to the woman's attention, for a hair-raising ride through the mountains in the hope of forcing Savelli to reveal the woman in white's identity. When they finally return to the hotel, still confused about which man the woman has visited, they discover a carnival-like atmosphere where all the women are dressed in white dresses and covered in white veils, and all the men are dressed in black. The husband, enraged, prepares to leave. The mystery is finally solved when Savelli's woman in white reveals herself to him and when Marina reenacts her seduction of her husband which does, in fact, pacify him.

The essence of the "mystery" is, after all, the wife's challenge to keep her husband entertained, to seduce him anew, to keep him enthralled. And the carnival atmosphere at the end with the reproduction of many women in white replicates this task for all of the women. The conjunction of games, carnivals, tourism, and forms of diversion applies equally to the role of the audience which must be seduced through these strategies much as Giulio must be seduced. And the role of the women is to legitimize these activities.

Palermi's *Napoli che non muore* (Naples Never Dies, 1939) portrays a woman's unsuccessful struggle against incorporation into the family. Unlike *Una moglie in pericolo* and *La dama bianca*, which accept role-playing as essential to marriage, *Napoli che non muore* seeks to authenticate familial relations and, hence, focuses on the woman's conversion. The film, a French-Italian co-production, was made in the studios at Cinecittà, and the cast includes such well-known actors of the time as Paola Barbara, Fosco Giacchetti, and Bella Starace Sainati. Marie Glory plays the female lead, the Frenchwoman, Anne Dumesnil.

Naples was a favorite setting, as can be seen by such films as *Ballerine*, *Napoli d'altri tempi* (Naples in Other Times), *Napoli*

*verde-blu* (Blue-Green Naples), *Una donna tra due mondi* (A
Woman between Two Worlds), and *Napoli che non muore*. In
Palermi's film, the city is not a mere backdrop for the action
but comes to signify the opposition between the public and
the private spheres, romantic and everyday existence. The
film introduces the metaphor of the city with a view of Naples
at night as seen from the sea, and Tito Schipa's voice is heard
singing a romantic Neapolitan lyric. Gradually, the viewers
learn that they have been sharing a privileged view of the
bay from the perspective of the ship on which a young Frenchwoman, Anne, is a guest of Italian friends.

The yacht arrives and the captain introduces an acquaintance, Mario (Fosco Giachetti) to Anne. Mario offers to be her
guide through Naples and environs. The next sequences provide a celebration of Italian landscape, architecture, and mon-
uments as well as of local customs and festivals similar to
those seen in such films as *Il carnevale di Venezia* (Carnival in
Venice) and *La dama bianca* (The Woman in White). Anne, an
orphan, finds herself responding ecstatically to the place and
expressing her happiness and sense of belonging to Mario.
Her romance with Naples merges with her growing love for
him. The two become engaged and he invites her home to
meet his family. Mario's home is lavish, supervised by his
widowed mother (Bella Starace Sainati). She, with the assistance of her daughter-in-law Teresa (Paola Barbara), a model
of the domesticated woman, instructs the servants on preparations for the affair. The servants are portrayed as completely and happily integrated into the family. Anne and
Mario marry. The wedding and the honeymoon are telescoped into the images of a card announcing the marriage
and a succession of shots of a ship, a train, train wheels, and
a clock. The action returns to the house, and to the enactment
of domestic routines. Mario returns to the office. Anne, however, is at loose ends, wandering about the house, observing
others busy with their domestic work. Though everyone tries
to interest her in family affairs, she claims her primary attachment is to Mario and to getting to know Naples better.

In order to fill her time, Anne begins to go out, taking Teresa with her to the horse races, boat races, and to card parties, much to the consternation of Mario's mother, who expresses her concern over Anne's "strange" behavior. A confrontation develops between Anne and the family after Anne, on a whim, joins a boat race and wins. Pietro berates Teresa for neglecting the family, while Anne intervenes to assume responsibility for having taken Teresa out of the house. An argument between Mario and Anne develops in which Anne complains to him that everything seems different now, not like the Naples she knew. She wants a house of her own, to be separated from the family, but Mario, unsympathetic, responds that her behavior is outrageous. Moreover, he does not want to leave home and he berates her for not settling down. In the dining room, Mario's mother laments that Anne is not the right wife for her son. Teresa, now restored to her domestic role, worries about what will happen to Mario.

Mario enters his club where the men from the boat race are talking about Anne, and he angrily strikes one of the men for defaming his wife. He returns home to find Anne absent. When she arrives at the house, he berates her for her indifference to the family. The family is in a state of chaos as they worry about Mario's future. While they argue, Teresa and Pietro's child toddles out of the room and climbs the stairs to Anne's room. She greets him gruffly, reproaching him for bothering her. As he backs out of the door, he slips and falls down the stairs. The mother and Teresa rush to rescue him as Pietro and Mario argue over Anne's culpability. Anne slips away from the house as the family conducts a vigil over the unconscious child, and she goes to a music professor's house. A sudden dizziness overwhelms her. The professor brings Anne "home" and announces her pregnancy. Under a painting of the madonna, Mario tells her that the Naples she desired is really here in the house.

The dominant concern thus appears to be the assimilation of the deviant woman into the family and into the role of nurturant figure.[21] The final image of the holy family is set

[21] Pistagnesi, "La scena familiare," pp. 99-104.

against the images of the city, a romanticized urban environment, associated with modernity and antiquity, sophistica-
tion, leisure, and sexuality. Anne, the Frenchwoman, responds to this aspect of city life, but as a woman and as a
foreigner, she is clearly out of place, for the woman's world
is restricted to the house and domesticity. The mother is the
dominating presence; her presence as a role model and a
preserver of the family is clearly portrayed. In spatial terms,
the house, especially the kitchen, dining room, and bedroom,
are the parameters of female life and the image of the madonna and child, associated initially with Teresa and her child,
become increasingly central. Woman's work is opposed to
leisure and Anne's "error," for which she does penance, is
her attempted avoidance of childbearing and domestic service.

In spite of the film's lavish portrayal of upper-class life, the
world of wealth is not denigrated as in the Camerini films.
The images of luxury, consumption, and visual spectacle are
legitimated by means of family piety. The woman's role serves
to dramatize a number of transformations: 1) from the public
to domestic sphere; 2) from leisure to work; 3) from independence to family assimilation; 4) from alien individual to
community identification; 5) from French "libertinism" to Italian respectability; and 6) from childish irresponsibility to adult
seriousness. The vehicles of her conversion are biology and
guilt. Her pregnancy brings her into the family and her guilt
over her treatment of Teresa's child humbles her. The film
seeks to make domestic life an attractive and natural solution
for women, but it also portrays the disciplinary strategies
necessary in order to effect this domestication.

The role of the music professor, while modest in scope, is
important as an agent of conversion. He brings Anne "home"
after her rupture with the family and is thus instrumental in
healing the reconciliation. He is the bridge between the public
and private spheres. The function of music in the film, its
connection to the life of Naples, to its romanticism and mystery as well as to its presence within the home as a signifi-
cation of family unity, reinforces the motif of the internali-

zation of Italian culture along the lines of domestication. Therefore it is appropriate that he be the one to bring Anne back, finally, to the family.

The domestic issues posed by the film, and particularly the film's presentation of women, evokes parallels with the fascist rituals that elevate the role of women in reproduction and in the family. Palermi's film portrays with these attitudes, but Anne's "conversion" exposes the strategies and contradictions of the woman's subordination to production and reproduction, and the ways she is physically and psychically repressed.

## The Mother in Us All

The figure of the mother is not intrinsically dramatic, but the ways in which she is represented in the films provides drama, if not melodrama. The single woman frequently has a child out of wedlock. She is not punished for her "transgression" as she might be in a Hollywood film but for her isolation from the family, and the narrative works to find her a proper husband or return her to her parental home. Her "sin," like her sister's, the entertainer's, is to have ventured into the public sphere, and the world of men.

In Camerini's 1933 film, *T'amerò sempre* (I'll Love You Always; remade in 1943 with Alida Valli in the leading role), the dominant issue is not the conflict between career and marriage but between deviance and respectability. Marriage becomes the "solution" to Adriana's (Elsa di Giorgio) sordid and struggling existence. The film begins in an actual maternity ward where Camerini shows rows of babies tended by nurses before they are presented to their mothers. Shots of the infants being weighed, bathed, powdered, and swaddled are part of the documentary footage, which is edited so as to convey the sense of a production line, a vision of regimentation. The sequence seems to set the film's critical tone of institutional treatment of the young and the need for personal care and nurture within the family. In contrasting shots, family members are shown greeting the various mothers and embracing babies, while Adriana is being subjected to admonitions by an aristocratic woman who informs her that she should not expect to make any personal demands on the child's father. As consolation she tells Adriana that she is young and in time will forget the Count and leaves Adriana crying and clutching her infant as others in the neighboring beds look on sympathetically.

By means of a superimposition, the scene flashes back to a courtyard in front of an apartment house where Adriana as a small girl plays alone, while another child passes, scolded by its mother for talking to Adriana. Adriana's mother, a prostitute, has no time for her daughter. Left to her own devices, Adriana overhears her mother and one of the male visitors arguing. Frightened, she runs to her mother's room and finds her crumpled on the floor. Her mother dead, she is brought to an orphanage. The time she spends in the institution is telescoped. The incidents selected, for example, involve the girls' interest in sexuality. They are shown voyeuristically observing young women as they stroll and kiss their young men. The new object of voyeurism becomes Adriana herself, who now has a lover, a young Count, the man by whom Adriana has her child. The scene returns to the present as the Count's sister, who had visited Adriana, coldly describes to the Count how she visited Adriana in the hospital and told her not to bother the family: "Naturally, she cried. They all do."

Adriana settles with her child in her own apartment. She has a new job at a beauty salon, "Oscar's." The clients are pampered rich women, imperious and affected. Adriana strikes up a friendship with the firm's accountant, Fabbrini (Nino Besozzi), a shy man whose demeanor contrasts sharply with Oscar's and with the clients and their husbands. After work, he invites Adriana to go to a film with him and his sister, but Adriana refuses, unwilling to take time away from her child.

The Count reappears at the salon, and Adriana hides in Fabbrini's office, though she does not explain her actions to the accountant. In gratitude for his cooperation, she accepts Fabbrini's invitation to come to his house for a family celebration that evening. The celebration is a true family affair replete with solicitous mother, kindly father, congenial children, aunts, uncles, picture albums, joking, dancing, and food. The family is impressed with Adriana, and Fabbrini proposes marriage, but Adriana refuses his offer. The Count offers a different proposal: to support her and the child so that he can visit her regularly. Enraged, she rejects his offer. The climax comes at work when the Count confronts Adriana and harasses her. Fabbrini overhears them, and learns about the child. He defends Adriana against the Count, telling her that he could not tolerate her being treated in such an abusive manner. She accepts his offer of marriage and the invitation to live in his mother's house with her child.

*T'amerò sempre* works rhetorically to generate sympathy for abandoned women and children. Adriana enlists sympathy first as an abused child, later as the victim of the Count's seduction and manipulation. The film, like so many of Camerini's films, emphasizes class conflict, especially between the aristocracy and the workers. The decadent values of the upper class contrast sharply with the generosity, affection, and honesty of the workers.

The film's narrative strategies are heavily dependent on melodramatic conventions—the abused orphan, neglected and sent to an orphanage, the young woman at the mercy of the aristocratic seducer, her struggle to survive in a world inhabited by self-interested, exploitative members of the upper class, and the loyal young man who rescues her from this hostile environment. Adriana is associated with the virtues of family loyalty, responsibility, self-sufficiency, caring for others, and the simple pleasures of companionship. The film is structured around a series of oppositions. Adriana and the Count's sister, Oscar's customers and Fabbrini's family and friends, the Count and Fabbrini, aristocrat and worker, home and business. The affective appeal of *T'amerò sempre* lies in its melodramatic focus on the wronged woman, undefended and in need of support, on abused and neglected children, and on the polarization of victims and aggressors. The "resolution" to the conflict lies in the woman's incorporation into the family and into her own class milieu, among people who can appreciate and defend her.

Her independence, which has created her problems, is renounced for the security of domesticity. With Fabbrini's mother, Adriana, a worthy mother herself, has now found her proper place and redeemed her own victimized mother (also a woman alone). She is now protected by the umbrella of respectability that was denied her as a child. By finding people more like herself, she is saved from the cruel treatment of the upper classes. Safety resides in the home and with members of the same class.

Camerini's *Come le foglie* (Like the Leaves), made in 1934, supports Patrizia Pistagnesi's views on the importance of the family in the Italian cinema. The film portrays the struggles of a young woman to overcome the decadent upper-class parasitism of her family. Isa Miranda is the star. In the same year she also starred in Max Ophuls's *La signora di tutti* (A Woman for Everyone), another film about a fallen woman who relives her reprobate life through flashbacks. Nennele, the heroine of the film, is aligned with her father. She takes the place of the reprobate mother and becomes herself a proper wife and eventual mother in contrast to her greedy and promiscuous mother, Giulia (Mimi Aylmer). Giulia is obsessed about lack of money in her desire to maintain a lavish lifestyle. The son (Cesare Bettarini) is a playboy. The setting is properly luxurious and the atmosphere serves to convey indulgence and seductive intrigues, the trademarks of the wealthy class as presented in films.

While his family lives beyond its means, the father, Signor Rosani (Ernesto Sabbatini), confronts bankruptcy. Rosani is determined to sell all of his holdings in order to repay what he owes. The men seek to dissuade him but he is determined to do the noble gesture, though the men call him mad, and tell him there is no reason for him to be so honest.

When the wife, Giulia, learns of the news of the bankruptcy, that even the villa in which they live is no longer theirs, she becomes hysterical. However, the party planned for the evening is not cancelled. Guests begin to arrive, among whom is Massimo (Nino Besozzi). Deeply involved with his work, he is contrasted to Tommy, who is concerned only with gambling and tennis. The Duchess, whom Giulia is trying to impress, arrives, and Giulia cannot even be courteous to Massimo, so eager is she to court nobility. Thus the film has introduced a social-climbing mother, a ne'er-do-well son, harassed employees, a desperate father, and a daughter who vainly tries to salvage a desperate situation. The bourgeoisie are shown as being given to self-indulgence, seduction, and display.

*Come le foglie* is devoted to a study of how each of the family members responds to these new financial and social vicissitudes. Tommy is annoyed at having to live without servants. He becomes more heavily involved in gambling; Nennele finds work as an English tutor, though she complains of her lack of preparation for teaching. An important turning point for her comes when she sees an accident on the construction site where one of the workers falls from a dam. As a consequence, she confronts the triviality of her past. Tommy, however, is not similarly affected. On his way to interview for a job, he is spattered with mud and cancels the interview. Giulia, too, cannot change her ways. She takes up with an Englishman to amuse herself. Knowing Signor Rosani's disappointment with Tommy, Massimo attempts to compensate for the son. He finds Tommy a position as a secretary to an engineer but while on the job, Tommy gets a phone call from Madame Orlo, an old friend who belongs to Tommy's world of shady activities, and leaves his post. When Massimo learns that Tommy has deserted his work for Madame Orlo, he chastises him and lectures him on responsibility, but Tommy lashes out at Massimo, telling him that he is not like Massimo. Tommy decides to marry Madame Orlo who seduces him with money for gambling. Nennele tries unsuccessfully to dissuade him. The brother and sister have been walking in the woods. As Tommy turns and leaves, the camera cuts to an image of leaves blowing on the ground, the symbol of the scattering of the family. When Nennele returns home, she discovers that her mother has made plans to visit her Englishman for the night. Massimo arrives and Nennele tells him about the disintegration of her family. She feels that her mother and brother have brought shame to the Rosani family.

Massimo proposes marriage to Nennele, but she refuses, saying that she will not accept charity. Desperate, she attempts suicide, but her father dissuades her. The two embrace and beg each other for forgiveness. The headlights of a car can be seen in the dark as the father and daughter stand at the entrance to the house awaiting Massimo. The last shot of the film is of Rosani looking on benevolently at the lovers. The father has gained a new son and Nennele has compensated for her mother. Moreover, Nennele and Massimo become the support for the father who has failed to be a proper authority in the family. The father is saved by the efforts of the daughter.

Massimo and Nennele are symbolic of the new man and woman. He is dedicated to work and to family, as she is. Their loyalty to the father is also important. The class issue is central to the film. Ted Perry notes, "*Come Le Foglie* (1934) exposes the deterioration of a petit bourgeois family. The daughter's maturity is directly tied to escaping from that bourgeois atmosphere, in learning to break with her father and in finding her own self and her own sexual identity."[22] Yet the "break" is with the mother, not the father, and Nennele's discovery of sexual identity is through him and Massimo, the son who will eventually become the father. Moreover, the escape from bourgeois attitudes is not really an escape so much as a transformation from one set of bourgeois attitudes to another, one more consonant with the ideology of alignment between bourgeois and working-class interests based on work, the role of the family as an instrument in production, and the reproduction of attitudes such as loyalty, domesticity, community, and discipline. Private life, sexuality, and idleness are associated with decadence and death, "like the leaves."

[22] Ted Perry, "Before Neorealism" (New York: Museum of Modern Art, 1978), mimeographed, pp. 5-6.

As the title suggests, Palermi's film, *La peccatrice* (The Sinful Woman, 1942) portrays one of the vast array of erring women that reappear in the narrative and dramatic arts, women who must go mad, die, or become respectable. The style of the film has qualities in common with *film noir* in its use of the constant juxtaposition of areas of light and dark.[23] The faces are shrouded. Most of the sequences are night scenes and the characters are often seen with shadows falling across their faces. The composition of the shots relies on unbalanced perspectives of the characters and events as well as the use of mirrors, mirror reflections, framing devices. The characters are positioned in corners, against walls, and in enclosed spaces. The element of voyeurism, of surveying and being surveyed, is prominent and the general effect is to convey a sense of an unstable environment. The motifs associated with the city include the physical threat of urban life, the precariousness of the single woman's position, and the fragility of domestic relationships. The exceptions to this sinister environment are the brightly lit, tableaulike scenes shot in the countryside and in Maria's mother's house, which seem to create an alternative to the city life.

The film alternates between past and present. In the present, Maria (Paola Barbara), the "sinful woman," is employed in a bar-brothel. She neglects her work to tend a sick friend. The young woman, Anna, is delirious, and begs for her mother, crying out, "I have sinned." Maria tries to comfort her, but is called away by the manager who has no sympathy for his employees and insists on Maria's performing her duties. During the night, as Maria lies in bed, the scene flashes back to the past, when she was involved with her first lover, Alberto. Unemployed and pregnant, she begs Alberto to take her away. He is indifferent to her plight. Nonetheless, she decides to leave home and join him. At her home, her mother, played by Bella Starace Sainati, sits weeping and saying her

---

[23] J. L. Place and S. L. Peterson, "Some Visual Motifs in *Film Noir*," in *Movies and Methods*, ed. Bill Nichols (Berkeley: University of California Press, 1976), pp. 325-38.

rosary beads for her wayward daughter, but Maria leaves her
for Alberto only to learn from his landlady, who vilifies Maria,
that Alberto has left town.

The dark, dreary environment changes to a brightly lit children's hospital where Maria works. Maria holds an infant,
looking like a madonna with child. The sense of her isolation
is underscored as the mail is delivered and there is none for
her. Maria, whose own baby has died, has been caring for
these sick or abandoned infants. She is called to the office
where a farmer, Andreas (Camillo Pilotto), stands holding a
sick infant. He informs Maria and the head nurse that the
child cannot be cared for on the farm and that he would like
it to be tended in the hospital until well, and Maria nurses
the child.

The farmer and his wife return in a few months to claim
their little Tonino, and Maria hands over the infant sadly.
Andreas expresses his gratitude to her for the improved
health of the child and invites her to live with his family on
the farm where she can care for Tonino. He tells her that life
is simple but good in the country, and she agrees to go. While
on the farm, Maria meets a young man who is interested in
developing a relationship with her. Maria, however, is im-
mune to him. One evening he bursts into her room and,
overcome by passion, attempts to kiss her. Angry at her un-
responsiveness, he insults her, accusing her of being a sinful
woman. Maria makes up her mind to leave. She does not tell
the farmer and his wife her real motive for going, only that
she wants to work in the city. She meets Pietro (Vittorio De
Sica), and they decide to live together. Their idyll is interrupted by the arrival of Signor Ottavi who has come for money
that Pietro owes him. When Ottavi sees Maria, he is attracted
to her. Maria learns from Ottavi that Pietro is not coming
back. Now events are brought into the present, for the flashback has been the background to Maria's working in the club
for Ottavi. Her friend Anna has been taken away to a hospital.
On her way to visit Anna, Maria is intercepted by Ottavi,
who roughs her up. He takes her to a sleazy hotel. At the
hotel she confronts him and tells him that he has ruined Anna.

The hotel room is dark and the blinds from the windows cast shadows that look like prison bars. Ottavi takes her purse and with it all her money. She finds Pietro again who helps her get a job at a laundry. The scenes at the laundry are authentic, shot on location, and laundry workers are shown on the job.

The owner and his wife are uneasy about Maria, and eventually the police come to look for her. Maria has no choice but to escape again. Her life is portrayed as a series of trials at the hands of hostile or indifferent men. By chance, Maria meets Andreas at a small outdoor restaurant and he invites her to return to the farm, a proposition she accepts. This sequence of the film takes an idealized turn. The setting is pastoral, interlaced with scenes of peasants working happily, singing as they do the haying. Everything in the country is light, spacious, and open in contrast to the sordidness, the cramped and hostile environment of the city. In Blasetti-like scenes of the countryside, Maria is presented as a nurturing figure. The young man who had been hostile to her earlier has now been converted to love and admiration. But Maria decides to go home to her mother.

Pietro, who has been looking for Maria, finally learns of her whereabouts and comes to the farm to get her, only to discover that she has returned home. Her first visit on her return to the city is to the restaurant where she had gone with Alberto. She observes him, sitting in the same corner, self-absorbed as he eats. Lamely, he says that this is the first time he has been to the restaurant since his return to the city. She is silent as the camera cuts to her hand clutching a knife then releasing it. She refuses his offer to pay for her coffee, and exits. As she emerges from the restaurant, the lighting is chiaroscuro, and the camera tracks her as she walks across a bridge. The scene alternates between Maria's anxious mother and Maria who slowly approaches the house. The reunion is extended as the perspective shifts from high- to low-angle shots, from daughter to mother. The music intensifies as the two cry and embrace.

The film exploits voyeurism as it develops the "inside" view of the sinful woman's life. The bordello, the parade of lovers, the underworld connection, and the motif of seduction and betrayal are designed to generate audience involvement. *La peccatrice* capitalizes on spectatorship. Maria "observes" her own past; men ogle her constantly: Alberto, who scrutinizes her as she prays in the church; Paolo, who watches her as she dances with Pietro; Ottavi, who devours Maria lecherously with his look as did the worker on the farm. The only escape from this scrutiny is at home with her mother.

The film does not end with marriage. Maria's escape from the men in her life is a retreat to the home and identification with mother. Throughout the film Maria has been associated with maternal ways, as a nurse at the children's hospital, as nursemaid to Tonino on the farm, and as a nurse to the ailing Anna who herself seeks reconciliation with her mother. Moreover, life on the farm links her to the earth and is the pivotal moment in her decision to return home and to her mother. Anna's last word in the film is "mother" as they embrace. The religious and pastoral elements in the film fuse to reinforce her abandonment of a dissolute life and her restoration to a proper sense of nurture expunged of sexuality. The images of maternity are contradictory. On the one hand, they reproach the harsh world associated with the men in Maria's life, much as the scenes of the country reproach the rapacious and acquisitive scenes of urban life. Through Maria, and Anna to a lesser extent, the film displays a sympathy toward the exploited urban proletariat and toward exploited women in particular.

On the other hand, the image of Maria as nurturant figure also seems to posit a nostalgic and escapist view of social relations, a retreat from sexual conflict in the idea of beginning again and in the idealization of the madonna. Yet *La peccatrice* does seem to stand in a critical relation to those films that elevate sacrifice, the intact family, and marriage. The film affirms Ted Perry's observations on the Italian films of the early 1940s. He finds that they "are less strident, less opinionated, and less willing to impose anything upon their viewer. They are willing to confront and present the inconsistencies and contradictions of life."[24] *La peccatrice* does not legitimize existing class and social relations. The women in the film, particularly Maria, are economically and sexually oppressed. The men are presented as manipulative and inadequate. The idealization of motherhood and rural life seem more fantastic than realizable, overwhelmed by the dominant portrayal of the sordid urban environment.[25] The shots of Maria's mother, the rural landscape, and the scenes in church seem loosely stitched into the film's fabric, satisfying certain conventional aspects of closure. But these scenes seem finally unrelated to the problems posed by the film. The overwhelming atmosphere of the film is dark and oppressive, leaning more toward a critique of than a prescription for prevailing attitudes.

## Summary

These films featuring women, whether single, independent women or married women, share certain common strategies, motifs, and themes. In some, obedience and service to the father is central, with transference of allegiance to the husband. Where the image of the mother or the mother-surrogate is dominant, the emphasis is on the bond between the mother and the daughter as a guarantor of nonpromiscuous relations. Everywhere is inscribed the subordination of the woman: to parental figures, to children, and, where overtly political, to the cause of fascism. The suppression of woman's voice, symbolically or literally, as in *Il carnevale di Venezia*, is evident. Where the subject is entertainment, the women are either isolated or transformed into the spectators or bearers of creativity. Even in the early comedies of Camerini where the women seem to have a more independent position, they are intermediaries in the process of social transformation, though they are portrayed less as icons of service and as more actively creative and capable of opposition and resistance. Whether

[24] Perry, "Before Neorealism," p. 11.
[25] Janey Place, "Women in *Film Noir*," in *Women in Film Noir*, ed. E. Ann Kaplan (London: British Film Institute, 1980), pp. 35-54.

bourgeois or working-class women, the instrumentalization of women is the rule. The interesting aspects of the films, however, is the way they play with their audiences, yielding information about the ways in which they create complicity.

A significant aspect of women's portrayal from a class perspective involves departures from their Hollywood models; upward mobility is deemphasized, though evident in some films. The tendency is rather to position women doubly, in the traditional domestic sphere and also within their class origins. The rich heiress who endows the struggling young worker; the millionaire who raises the talented and poor young woman, the young woman who "makes it" on talent, are rare phenomena. Women thus become also the signifiers of unity and the bridges between public and private spheres, between classes, and between generations.

The presence of impersonation, disguises, doubling, and secrecy provides the way to read these films against the grain. While the films position women in traditional fashion as biological creatures, wives, mothers, daughters, servants, and fetish objects, they expose the deception, self-reduction, and secrecy necessary to domesticate the women. The aspect of a double life entails a constant sense of theater, of role-playing necessary to "keep the show going." There is no emphasis on authenticity. The role-playing stresses ingenuity and cleverness in the triumph of artifice. The wife must always perform, must always be watched and watchful very much like her sister the entertainer, only the wives and mothers perform at home.

In the case of the entertainers and the "sinners," the films enact another process, a "looping" whereby women are returned to the "source," to their families and hence are isolated from society. Home signifies retreat or safety after corrupting encounters with men in the public sphere and with an alienating social environment. The "resolution" thus may signify a "rebirth" or a form of social death. In any case, the ending of these films is highly ambiguous, and does not reinstate the conventional romance and marriage pattern.

With the films made after 1940, especially the melodramas,

the viewer can witness more apparent strategies of subversion of the women's role that challenge the conciliatory strategies of the family romance. In these films, thwarted women and tormented men occupy dominant positions. The darker side of family is exposed in these films, which become explorations of competition, aggression, jealousy, and obsession. The melodramas portray sexual and class conflict in highly critical fashion.

# CHAPTER THREE

# A Man for All Seasons

ALTHOUGH much has been written in recent years about women and the cinema, there has been less analysis of the representation of men. Similarly, the position of women in the Italian cinema has received more attention than the position of men. Studies of women's representation trace the ways the female subject is inscribed in the text and also the way that very inscription provides a basis for deconstructing the position of the female. Male representation invites a comparable analysis of its genealogy, its various expressions, and its effects. The representation of men, no less than that of women, provides an index to the politics and style of the Italian cinema during the fascist years.

Certainly, fascist ideology strongly addressed men's position in society. The idea of the "new man" was an important aspect of fascist rhetoric. The idea of the fascist hero was a consequence of the misreading of Nietzsche on the superman, of the aesthetics and aims of futurism, and of the mystique of nationalism. He was, like fascism itself, a collage of conflicting images and attitudes. The fascist myth of the hero bore slight resemblance to Nietzsche's conception of the superman who rejected the old morality and institutions, and was a harbinger of a new era, an expression of potential as yet unrealized. But the fascist "new man," rather than being "beyond good and evil," was squarely rooted in the traditional values of renunciation, sacrifice, and service, values associated with Christian morality. Moreover, according to George Mosse,

. . . the new man continued a stereotype that had its roots in nineteenth-century nationalism. This was based upon an ideal of male strength and beauty, upon an aggressive virility, an *élan vital*, which we have attributed to the pilot who dominated the skies. The new fascist man was supposed to be the very opposite of muddleheaded and talkative intellectuals, of the exhausted old men of the dying bourgeois order. The antibourgeois rhetoric and imagery was strong here, yet symbolized by an old type, who himself represented bourgeois respectability, order, and domination.[1]

For a time, the man of the hour was Gabriele D'Annunzio. Later it was Benito Mussolini. D'Annunzio was never as popular with the masses as Mussolini who was the object of widespread adulation. Mussolini's supporters were not restricted to one particular segment of society, though his strongest advocates were those individuals with upwardly mobile aspirations, an attitude most commonly associated with the petty bourgeois class. However, as Edward Tannenbaum has cautioned, petty bourgeois attitudes of conformity, respectability, the longing for social betterment can also be found among the more "affluent peasants and workers, members of the middle and upper bourgeoisie whose status seems threatened."[2] For those individuals, the new man was an amalgam of their own aspirations, desires, and fears. In this respect, Mussolini, the embodiment of contradictory attitudes, was an appropriate hero for them.

His popularity was great among both men and women. Even children were moved to enthusiasm by *il Duce*. Speculating on the source of Mussolini's appeal, writers have cited his showmanship, his rhetorical flair, his "virile" stance, and his sexual exploits.[3] There is no doubt that Mussolini's self-fashioning was calculated to produce an impact on his audiences. He was a mixture of Roman Caesar and Renaissance *condottiere*, Friedrich Nietzsche and Gabriele D'Annunzio, Casanova and paterfamilias, dictator and socialist man of the people.[4] Above all, he was a performer.

His precursor, D'Annunzio, was a different type of per-

---

[1] George L. Mosse, *Masses and Man: Nationalist and Fascist Perceptions of Reality* (New York: Howard Fertig, 1980), p. 240.

[2] Edward R. Tannenbaum, *Fascism in Italy: Society and Culture 1922-1945* (London: Allen Lane, 1972), p. 249.

[3] Laura Fermi, *Mussolini* (Chicago: University of Chicago Press, 1961), pp. 147-49.

[4] Luigi Barzini, *The Italians* (New York: Atheneum), p. 146.

former. According to Luigi Barzini, D'Annunzio "lived like a
Renaissance prince . . . a voluptuary surrounded by borzois,
a gaudy clutter of antiques, brocades, rare Oriental perfumes
and flamboyant but inexpensive jewelry; dressed like a London clubman; preferably slept with duchesses, world-famous
actresses, and mad Russian ladies; wrote exquisitely wrought
prose and poetry; rode to hounds."[5] His taking of Fiume was
regarded by nationalists as a spectacular act of political and
military derring-do. Mussolini did, in certain respects, model
himself after D'Annunzio, especially in relation to the lavish
public gesture, though he never slavishly imitated D'Annunzio's *fin de siècle* posture of decadence.

D'Annunzio's life was like the spectacle films such as *Cabiria*, to which he lent his name. The spectacle of the silent
cinema is characterized by melodramatic excess, replete with
casts of thousands, larger-than-life heroes, fascinating mysterious women, and extraordinary feats of physical prowess.
Its effect was, as Vernon Jarratt has said, dizzying.[6] The sound
cinema did not really abandon the spectacle, but the form
was domesticated. The cinema of the thirties and forties produced far more films with less grandiose visions of life, history, and heroes. Just as the images of women took on new
characteristics, so too the images of men diversified to include
a broader range of archetypes, attitudes, and social classes.
Mussolini's public image, more than D'Annunzio's, became
the prototype of the male heroic figure of the 1930s; it also
became the structuring absence in those films of the late thirties and early forties that portray the disintegration of the
male authority figure.

The cinematic representations of men were not mere reflections of Mussolini, his precursors, and his followers, nor
were they schematic reproductions of the "new man." Images
converge at significant points with fascist ideology but, as is
the case with women's representation, the portrayals of men,

[5] Ibid., p. 88.
[6] Vernon Jarratt, *The Italian Cinema* (New York: Macmillan, 1951), pp. 15-
19.

especially in the genre films, are deeply rooted in cultural myths that cannot simply be labeled as fascist. More importantly, a deconstruction of the films reveals the strategies that underlie the postures and performances of the male figures, what they had to renounce and repress in order to be accommodated to the narratives of public action and domestic life. Furthermore, when examined chronologically, the images of men in the cinema over the twenty-year period of fascism undergo significant changes, more so even than the films involving women.

The films feature Don Juan and Lothario figures, husbands and single men who cannot, without help, confine themselves to one woman. Frequently such men are bankers, industrialists, and aristocrats. There are also the young men who fall in love beyond their station and must learn renunciation. The typical severe father figure also contends with the undisciplined young man until the young man is "educated." Such films seem particularly characteristic of the early thirties.

Another dominant presentation of men in the films involves the drama of conversion, which features a young man who goes through the symbolic stages of disillusionment and loss until he reconstructs a new identity, is "born again" into leadership, creativity, and service. This narrative pattern seems most often linked to the war and adventure films, though not exclusively. The portrayals of the Don Juan figure and the "new man," while differing in their character treatments, settings, and images, are united in their reaffirmation of traditional values and narrative patterns.

The films after 1938 feature more obviously "reprobate" figures—tyrants and gigolos—complex male figures who seem to offer a deconstructed version of the "new man," and seem most broadly critical of existing social relations.

## Husbands and Lovers

The "white telephone" films are a legacy of the comedy of manners. The lavish settings, the evocation of a world of wealth and luxury, and the presence of characters whose greatest problem is marital infidelity are the identifying features of such films.[7] On the surface, these narratives would seem to merit the disapprobation heaped upon them of being frivolous and inconsequential. On closer inspection, the seemingly trivial characters and situations are an index to familiar bourgeois myths and attitudes. The dominant conflicts are marital imcompatibility, sexual identity, and submission to conformity.

The melodramas and historical films of the 1930s reiterate similar themes and motifs. The men in the films are often Don Juan figures struggling to escape the protective and possessive clutches of women. They seek adventure to mitigate boredom, boredom in the family and boredom in their occupations. Frequently they are wealthy or aristocratic, and a reading of the film communicates the idea that the rich also have problems. The satiric and critical elements are not always immediately evident. Wives are portrayed as manipulative, suspicious of their husbands' every movement and threatening to expose their vagaries, or in the dramas, the women assume the position of figures of nurture and guidance, returning the men to a sense of responsibility. Ultimately, the men are disciplined to accept conjugal roles, or at least the appearance of domestic conformity.

Men of a lower social class—shopkeepers, clerks, workers, or even struggling artists—are disciplined in yet another fashion. They are "educated" to accept their own social position. For example, the young man falls in love with a wealthy or aristocratic woman only to learn that she is unavailable. She is coerced by her family to marry within her own social class and to suppress her romantic inclinations. Or she is presented as frivolous and therefore an inappropriate mate for the young man. He learns to relinquish her and find another woman or sublimation in his work.

In the majority of men's portrayals, the male position is one of renunciation, of reduced expectations, or adoption of new goals. Sexuality is repressed. Social appearances are pre-

---

[7] Adriano Aprà and Patrizia Pistagnesi, *Notes on the Unknown Italian Cinema* (New York: Museum of Modern Art, 1978), p. 3.

served. Rich and poor men alike are controlled by severe social and economic limitations that preclude a successful fusion of wealth, career, and romantic attachments. The popularity of the Don Juan figure can be traced to several sources. Most obviously, sexual conflict is a dominant feature of both comedy and melodrama, the traditional battle of the sexes. In the prefascist culture of the twenties and thirties, for the middle and upper classes at least, sexual liberation was a burning issue; however, the cinema of the thirties is puritanical. The family also plays an important role. Hence the Don Juan figure, a figure of desire and of transgression, seems an appropriate image to communicate conformity and resistance to codes of sexual morality and domestic responsibility.

In Blasetti's *Terra madre* (1931) a misguided nobleman learns to accept "responsibility for the welfare of the workers living on his land."[8] Significantly, the agent of Marco's restoration to the land and to his people is a woman. Associated with the land and with fertility, she is a reincarnation of the film's title, the "earth mother." Through her combined exhortation, castigation, and seduction, she brings the young nobleman to a sense of duty. Thus, Blasetti's portrayal of the leader seeks to fuse the homely virtue of family with service to the community. By presenting the male figure as vulnerable and by situating his struggles in the personal arena, the film reduces the distance between the audience and the hero.

The film, which takes place for the most part in the country, equates urban life with decadence. Blasetti's treatment of the rural environment bears affinity to the *strapaese* movement, which was "naturist and cosmopolitan."[9] Blasetti seems to follow the lead of fascist ideology which elevates agrarain above urban existence. His protagonists are closely tied to the

[8] Ted Perry, "Before Neorealism" (New York: Museum of Modern Art, 1978), mimeographed, p. 7.

[9] Tannenbaum, *Fascism in Italy*, p. 306. For a discussion of the myths of "strapaese" and "stracittà," rural versus urban ideology, see Alessandrini's comments on the film in Francesco Savio, *Cinecittà anni trenta*, 3 vols. (Rome: Bulzoni, 1979), 1:24-25. See also James Hay, *Popular Film Culture in Fascist Italy* (Bloomington: Indiana University Press, 1986), p. 179.

natural environment. Unlike the extreme sexual abstinence of the public man of action, the male figures, like the Don Juan figures, manifest at least the outward appearance of achieving sexual gratification.

Marco (Sandro Salvini), a Sicilian landowner, returns to his home in Sicily with his fiancée, Daisy (Isa Pola), a "modern" woman. He returns with the idea of selling his ancestral lands for commercial development. The peasants who greet him on his arrival are portrayed as trusting, expectant children delighted to have the *padrone* back again and unaware that he has planned to forsake them and his heritage.

Blasetti typecasts his characters: the wise old man in the community (much like the old man in Dovzhenko's *Earth*), the fat, faithful serving woman, the loyal superintendent of the estate, and the earthy mothers with their numerous children. Life on the estate centers on ritualized activities: planting, harvesting, festivals, and traditional ceremonies. The peasants are portrayed as circumscribed by work, family gatherings, and service to the master. The events are often filmed in dynamic fashion as in Soviet montage, shot diagonally and rhythmically, from different angles.[10] Pastoral images are juxtaposed to images of the urban group associated with Marco, filmed through a haze of cigarette smoke, draped lazily in chairs, playing cards and games of seduction, and separated spatially from the peasants.

Marco meets Emilia (Leda Gloria), the daughter of his superintendent who, not recognizing him, accuses the master of abandoning his people and the land. Indifferent to her pleas, if not to her, he turns over the estate to a new agent and manager and leaves for the city in order to gratify Daisy, who finds life in the country intolerable. When Marco leaves, the new manager hounds the peasants out of their homes. As a consequence of his negligence, a fire breaks out that threatens to engulf the estate. Marco, carousing with Daisy

[10] Vito Zagarrio, "Il modello sovietico: Tra piano culturale e piano economico," in *Cinema italiano sotto il fascismo*, ed. Riccardo Redi (Venice: Marsilio, 1979), pp. 185-89.

and her fashionable set, learns about the disaster and, recognizing that his relationship with Daisy is inconsequential, decides to return to Sicily and to the estate. In an act of heroism, he saves a child trapped in a raging fire. He also struggles physically with the manager and orders him to leave, telling the people that "this land is mine and shall remain mine." He marries Emilia and together they run the estate. The benevolent *padrone*, the industrious workers, the mother, and children, the family, and the land are linked together at the film's close.

Marco has been transformed from an indifferent, though not cruel, scion of privilege who unwittingly causes great harm to his people, to a true master, savior of women, children, the old, the infirm, and the peasants. The true hero recognizes and acknowledges his responsibility, which is his by virtue of his noble birth and his position as proprietor of the land master over the peasants. His responsibility is legitimized by the film's appeal to nature. "Mother Earth" sanctions property and patriarchy. The images of the land and the peasants' lives are fused so as to convey the naturalness, hence rightness, of the feudal structure. The idea of family links *padrone* and peasant as well as man and woman. The master-father and the peasant-child are as natural as the community's relationship to the land. The Duke, like an irresponsible parent, abandons his children, and by abandoning his children abandons his own heritage. His relationship to Daisy, like his relationship to the city and to modern life, thus appears an adulterous transgression that must be expiated. The near-death of the peasant family restores Marco to his domestic, economic, and social position of leadership. His unnatural behavior is atoned through nature, which is the mystical power that guides him and his dependents.

As in so many of Blasetti's films, the central conflict involves the oppression of the masses, but, while often utilizing the language of Soviet montage, he does not treat the masses as heroic. Rather, his emphasis on the role of the leader stresses authoritarianism, benevolent masters as the solution to social injustice. The peasants' submissiveness, suffering, and helplessness, call forth the best in the leader who realizes his power through their necessity.

Blasetti, in his portrayal of social class, maintains a consistent antibourgeois stance, presenting the bourgeoisie as vapid, indifferent, and decadent. His rural affinities lead him to idealize the peasants and to link them to the nobility who are the guarantors of harmony and fecundity.[11] Interestingly, the values revealed bear a resemblance to the bourgeois mythology of work, family, obedience to authority, harmonious class relations, reproduction, and productivity. His films are a good example of the way in which populist discourse was used in Italian politics and film as a way of both affirming the needs and struggles of the peasants and workers and also as a means of directing those struggles away from the objectives of revolutionary class struggle and toward a goal of class reconciliation.[12]

Blasetti's rhetorical style draws on images of mass suffering and oppression directly attributed to the landowning class. By means of the defense of patriarchal authority, family, and property the film reconstructs old forms of domination through new images of a cooperative and collective ideology. The montage in the film develops strategies of pacification and co-optation. The film language of revolutionary struggle is voided of its conflictual dimensions, particularly of the conflict between the peasant and landlord, locked in a struggle for power. The political differences are resolved through the idealization of the humble people and a strong, benevolent authority.

By way of contrast with the heroism of the adventure film

[11] Adriano Aprà and Patrizia Pistagnesi, *I favolosi anni trenta 1929-1944* (Milan: electa, 1979), pp. 76-77.

[12] Ernesto Laclau, *Politics and Ideology in Marxist Theory* (London: NLB, 1977), p. 115. As Ernesto Laclau asserts, "Fascism arose from a dual crisis: (1) a crisis of the power bloc which was unable to absorb and neutralize its contradictions with the popular sectors through traditional channels; (2) a crisis of the working class, which was unable to hegemonize popular struggles and fuse popular-democratic ideology and its revolutionary class objectives into a coherent political and ideological practice."

and melodrama, Brignone's 1931 *Rubacuori* (Stealer of Hearts)
plays in comic fashion with the Don Juan figure. The film is
like the "white telephone" films in its emphasis on light entertainment, on escapism, and on its settings and characters
in the world of the wealthy. The central figure is a restless
banker (Armando Falconi) who cannot resist an attractive
woman. His seductions are exposed but legitimized as merely
playful. Shown at work, where he disciplines his female workers for their frivolousness in listening to a radio broadcast of
the arrival of Joe Smith, a prizefighter, he spends his time
planning a liaison with a dancer. The nightclub performer
(Grazia del Rio) has planned a jewel theft and intends to use
the banker as a foil. He escapes from under the suspicious
eyes of his wife (Mary Kid) and mother-in-law on the pretext
that he has an evening appointment with a business colleague. At the nightclub, a necklace that belongs to Ilke, the
prizefighter's female friend, is planted on Giovanni. When
he returns home, he finds the necklace in his pocket and is
confronted with having to return it to Ilke without being exposed. He goes to Ilke's apartment and gives her the necklace.
When she embraces him in gratitude, it sticks to his jacket.
Furthermore, the fighter arrives, sees Giovanni, and begins
to chase him. Giovanni escapes, jumping into his chauffeur-
driven car for a classic chase scene. Unknown to him, the
necklace falls to the floor of the car as he exits for work.

At home, his wife and a friend order the car to go shopping.
They find the telltale jewelled "heart." The wife decides to
confront her husband with it, but the friend insists that she
should assume that the necklace is for her. The entertainer
arrives at the bank and demands the necklace from Giovanni.
They are interrupted by his wife who is wearing the necklace.
The entertainer threatens Giovanni. Desperate, he telephones
Ilke, and arranges to meet her at the fight, where he intends
to return the necklace. He finally manages to get the necklace
from his wife's neck, but she discovers its absence and loudly
shouts, "Theft!" The couple is escorted to the police station,
and in a confusing scene the commissioner fails to understand
whether or not a theft has actually taken place. The furious

wife and the penitent husband are reconciled, and a new day begins with a chastened Giovanni leaving for work as his mother-in-law admonishes him to be good. He exits from the house, sees a pair of woman's legs, and follows in the same direction.

*Rubacuori*, an early sound film, is modeled on Hungarian films—the roving husband-banker, the treacherous entertainer, the long-suffering wife, and the shrewish mother-in-law. The film feverishly piles on sound and movement: singing, dancing, chase scenes, and prizefighting. The element of performance in the film complements the position of the external spectator. Though the film seems to fulfill the classic requirements of light entertainment—diversion, voyeurism, and spectacle—certain elements invite analysis as they offer possible clues to the ways such films work to "entertain." For example, the presentation of the banker as a basically benevolent chaser of women and an honest restitutor of property allows for a laugh at his expense, while ignoring his actual activities as banker. Moreover, he provides the access into the world of the rich who are only different from everyone else in their being foolish.

The motif of theft and dishonesty, while not attributed to the banker's real occupation, is apparent. By focusing on the criminals who steal the necklace and on the banker who becomes the restorer of property, the film both associates him with and exonerates him from theft. The film even allows for satirizing his treatment of his employees when they are shown comically regimented under his command. The role of fighting in the film is linked to domestic discord, for the marriage, too, is a boxing match in which Giovanni emerges as the victor. The sparring before going to bed between the slippers ends with the male slippers victorious. In the antagonism between Giovanni and the prizefighter, Giovanni emerges victorious, too. Giovanni's intelligence and honesty triumph over physical force. His incorrigible Don Juanism serves as a revenge against a possessive wife and a nagging mother and, while momentarily curbed, returns at the end, thus insuring that comfortable repetition rather than rupture is a mark of this kind of entertainment. Thus, the film moves in two different directions: it presents repetition; it also represents change. The film confirms the idea that the appearance of conformity is all that is required.

Films like *Rubacuori* present conflict with the reassurance of resolution. The film draws on domestic dissatisfaction to play on the audience's awareness of its own dissatisfactions and on the potential of spectacle to provide compensation. These early escapist films make no pretense, according to the fascist rubric, of educating, but they are political. In the ways that they appease the spectator, in their construction of self-contained motifs and images, and in their providing entertainment within entertainment, they seek to create a hermetically sealed world. Class conflict, sexual conflict, and the struggle for economic survival are nonexistent. Everything is humorously sexualized, including the act of looking.

A related film, made in the same year (1931) but superior in form and content to many of the "white telephone" films, is Mario Camerini's *Figaro e la sua gran giornata* (Figaro's Big Day). This film also concerns domestic conflict, and involves spectacle and entertainment, in this case opera. The idea of performance is central to the film, using it to comment on the domestic drama and to situate the spectator in relation to the action. Basoto (Gianfranco Giachetti), the central figure, provides an image of the chastened rake. Like a character in a fable, he becomes the exemplum of the overreacher who is brought back to a sense of his limits.

The film, set at the turn of the century, begins on a festive note with a group of town notables awaiting the arrival of an opera troupe that is to perform Rossini's *Barber of Seville*. Basoto, one of the townsmen, is among the group and boasts of his own past operatic triumphs. The opera company arrives and Rantolini (Ugo Ceseri), the theater manager, introduces the players, whose only concern is for food. Basoto, smitten with jealousy when he meets the singer who is to play Figaro, sings in order to demonstrate his own superior talents, basking in the enthusiastic applause of his colleagues.

At home, Basoto is not a star. His wife, Costanza (Gemma

Schirato), keeps a jealous eye on his movements. She is not pleased with his involvement in the opera and particularly with his commitment to greet the prima donna at the train station. Unfortunately, the opera singer does not appear, and Basoto asks Nina (Leda Gloria), a young opera singer, to play the role.

Nina is doubly constrained. Her father has forbidden her to see Chiodini (Maurizio d'Ancora) because his poor job prospects disqualify him as a proper suitor, and Chiodini seeks to dissuade her from singing in the opera. She ignores Chiodini's pleas and decides to play the role. Basoto seeks to pass Nina off as the sister of the prima donna. Chiodini, passing himself off as a journalist, tries to subvert Nina's plans, but angrily she refuses his advice. In revenge, Nina introduces him coyly to the tenor, and he becomes jealous. He writes a note to Nina's father, informing him that his daughter has left home and is about to become a "music hall comedian" and urging the father to intervene immediately. He signs the note, "a watchful heart."

In exasperation, Rantolini fires his Figaro and replaces him with Basoto. The film develops the motifs of competition, competence and incompetence and, above all, the confusion between art and life. Costanza arrives at the rehearsal and becomes angry when she learns that Basoto intends to sign. Chiodini ingratiates himself with Costanza in an effort to make Nina jealous. Basoto, having antagonized the baritone, is warned by him that there will be trouble at the performance if he sings. As the audience arrives, Chiodini is seen in the dark plotting with the dismissed baritone. He also makes one more attempt to dissuade Nina from singing.

The curtain opens on the performance as a discomfited tenor and soprano sing. Basoto enters and begins to sing, but the former baritone interrupts the performance. Rantolini comes out and tries to restrain the audience from leaving, but the crowd exits nonetheless. Nina's father arrives and angrily denounces Basoto for abducting his daughter. He orders him arrested, and carries Nina away. The opera performance is totally ruined, and the "performances" of the actors offstage become considerably more dramatic than the formal theatrical production: Basoto arrested, Nina abducted, Costanza humiliated, Rantolini's performance ruined, the town officials infuriated, and the passions of revenge, jealousy, injured vanity, and pride running rampant. Basoto is taken to the police station where the baritone has been taken, but he is not significant enough to be incarcerated. He leaves the station and returns home. The chiaroscuro lighting reveals Basoto's shadow as he walks slowly along the street, then vanishes into total darkness. Finally, he and Costanza, Nina and Chiodini are reconciled.

*Figaro e la sua gran giornata* is representative of Camerini's films: the puncturing of grandiose pretensions, romantic complications, and the comic treatment of conflict and resolution. Particularly, this film plays with elements of self-reflexivity, which serve to comment on the nature of "performance." Melodramatic aspects of relationships are often more theatrical than theater. By contrasting the operatic performance and the offstage "opera," Camerini seems to be saying something about cinema, too, that its strengths lie in the low style, the nontragic mode. The comedy of reconciliation is based on a traditional acceptance of limits, on the curbing of aspirations. This form of entertainment deals with archetypal comic issues: sparring lovers, wayward daughters, irate fathers, jealous spouses, and manipulative intermediaries. Through the reflexive elements, Camerini suggests that cinema, more than opera, provides gratification in its ability to generate involvement by bringing the audience in close touch with the actors, and in its ability to regenerate the old forms of entertainment in a new medium.

The role of the central character, Basoto, is interesting in this context. As a major "organizer" of the operatic entertainment, he fails. The "big day" results in his transformation from an esteemed amateur singer to a "madman" repudiated by the audience, to a released felon, and then to a proper husband. His career as a singer and organizer of entertainment is over but his failure has been instructive. He is now restored, chastened, to his wife and the two of them can live

in domestic harmony. Nina and Chiodini are also reconciled
to each other and to Nina's father. The "big day" turns out
to be a *felix culpa* as the disaster of the ruined performance
becomes the basis for Basoto's discovery "that aspiring beyond one's social means inevitably leads to disappointments."[13] Basoto, like so many male characters in Camerini
films, learns that there's no place like home. The escapism is
thus not of the spectacular variety but is much more subtle.
The external audience promised one kind of performance at
the outset of the film gets another: the domestic drama as the
retreat from public failure.

The majority of Camerini's comedies have been described
as apolitical, but they cannot be said to be non-ideological.
Comedy is a means for sorting out and reconciling class and
sexual conflicts. The film's self-consciousness as entertainment is geared toward minimizing the issues it dramatizes.
The deflation of conflict has its counterpart in the film's thematic emphasis on the efficacy of reduced expectations, which
would appear to address an audience seeking such reassur-
ances. Tannenbaum validates that: "The bulk of the movie
audience in those days was young and lower middle class
with limited experience and limited horizons."[14]

In 1935, Camerini made *Il cappello a tre punte* (The Three-
Cornered Hat), a film that, according to Camerini, infuriated
Mussolini.[15] After seeing the film, Mussolini threw a chair
across the room, shouting his disbelief that such a work could
be created after thirteen years of the fascist regime. An admirer of Camerini's work, Mussolini felt that with this film,
Camerini had strayed from his usual concerns. Yet, an examination of *Il cappello* reveals it to be very similar to his other
films: the "little people" are present here, workers and peasants, and a clear dichotomy exists between them and the
rapacious and manipulative upper classes. *Il cappello* also satirizes overreachers and pretenders, revealing an antipathy to

[13] Tannenbaum, *Fascism in Italy*, p. 272.
[14] Ibid., p. 280.
[15] Savio, *Cinecittà anni trenta*, 1:211-12.

upwardly mobile aspirations. The resolution settles men in their own milieu, and identifies women as the vehicles for their chastisement and domestication.

Where was the offense in any of these elements? The answer must be the governor, the overbearing authority figure in the film who abuses his public role for personal, sexual motives. The film portrays a man who has no respect for other people's rights or "property." He abuses the power of his office to gratify personal desires, surrounding himself with shady figures.

The film in its treatment of family, sexual conflict, and class antagonism does not seem at all at odds with other films of the time or with fascist ideology. Yet it does reveal, as Mussolini recognized, glaring contradictions that comedy cannot camouflage. Camerini's timing was significant, producing a film that criticized authority at the outbreak of the Ethiopian war, and making the dominant figure a governor.

The film, which takes place in July 1716, opens with a rustic image of a cart moving along the road, driven by Luca, a miller (Peppino de Filippo). Luca and his wife Carmela (Leda Gloria) are bringing sacks of flour into town. The editing in its cross-cutting from high- and low-angle positions emphasizes Carmela's desirability, and this introduces a major problem, namely, Carmela as the object of desire, especially for men above her class, and Luca's uneasiness about her fidelity. As they ride, Luca teases her about how her beauty creates problems. Confusion follows as the wife of the customs inspector tells her husband that he had better count the flour sacks to ensure that there are as many as Luca asserts there are. Carmela overhears the woman making innuendos about her virtue. When the woman calls her abusive names, Carmela strikes her and the two begin to scuffle. Others join the fray. The bishop arrives and breaks up the fight. Luca explains to him how the woman, jealous of Carmela, had goaded her. The bishop, also smitten by Carmela's beauty, reprimands the woman, admonishing her to put aside her jealousy.

In the countryside, Carmela is shown at an outdoor table, singing while her husband plays the flute. Their audience is

the lawyer, the bishop, the governor, and the governor's aide
who are charmed by Carmela. The bishop praises her voice,
but Luca laments that Carmela's beauty is a source of difficulty, engendering gossip and jealousy. Carmela herself is
associated with nature and abundance, with streams and wa-
terfalls, the bountiful table, artistic talent, beauty, and virtue.

The company breaks for vespers, but the governor (Edoardo
de Felippo) follows Carmela. Now alone, she removes clothes
from a line. The shadow of a three-cornered hat on a sheet
exposes him, ogling Carmela. He joins her and repeats a
previous offer to help her brother. Suddenly, overcome by
passion, he blurts out that he is like a thirsty man within
reach of water that he cannot taste. He reaches for her, but
she pushes him down. His aide, Garmigna, rescues him, con-
soling him with a plan to seduce Carmela.

At a street fair, Carmela and Luca listen to a man sing a
tale of an unfaithful wife. The singer has a chart with illus-
trations that look as if they are from some old emblem books.
As he sings, he points to the image of a woman in bed with
a man, to a group of judges, and then to the man himself,
who points to a picture of a hanged woman. The self-reflexive
sequence develops the theme of justice and women's chastity.
An old man greets Luca with the complaint that he cannot
sell his wares because he is denied a permit. The man works
himself into a rage, attacks his enemy, and a street fight follows. In the skirmish, Luca is arrested by the governor's men.
Garmigna, discovering that Luca is among the men detained,
explains to the governor that now he has an opportunity to
be with Carmela. The governor's wife (Dina Perbellini) is annoyed about the highhanded way the people are treated, but
the governor tells her not to interfere.

Free now to pursue Carmela, he prepares for his big night.
At the jail, Luca is told by the captain that he need only be
incarcerated this one night, and Luca pretends to receive this
news with equanimity. The governor and Garmigna ride off
to Carmela. In the dark, the governor falls into a stream. At
Luca's house, Garmigna suggests to Carmela that the governor needs dry clothes and to be put to bed before he catches

cold. Carmela takes the governor to the bedroom where she gives him Luca's nightshirt. Once in bed, he tries to seduce her, but she steals the statement of release she had extorted from him and slips away to free Luca, unaware that he has escaped from jail and is on the premises.

Luca goes to his bedroom, looks through the keyhole, and spies the governor. As he goes to get his gun, the image of a hanged man appears and sobers him. Seeing the governor's clothes drying by the fire, he puts them on and returns to town. The governor's soldiers come to Luca's house to capture him, and instead, they seize the governor, dressed in Luca's nightshirt. At the governor's house, Luca is admitted because he is wearing the governor's clothes, while the governor, in Luca's clothes, rides to the palace.

In the palace, Luca finds the governor's wife who is getting ready for bed. In the dim light, she thinks that he is her husband and berates him for his behavior. He identifies himself and describes the jailing, his escape, and the seduction of Carmela, vowing revenge. When the governor arrives, the guards will not let him in. Finally his wife gives the order to admit him but withholds recognition. She further humiliates her husband by having him stand on the stairs, looking ridiculous in Luca's nightshirt. Carmela, who has gained entry, is exonerated by a captain who explains to the governor's wife that Carmela was not unfaithful, but has been trying to free Luca. The irate Luca is mollified, and the two are reconciled. They bow and thank the governor's wife, but the chastisement of the governor is not over. In the palace, Luca stands on the landing, posturing in imitation of the governor in gestures reminiscent of Mussolini. The governor, now chastised, confronts his wife who scolds him, tells him to get properly dressed, and try to be worthy of his office. He pleads with her to tell him if anything transpired between her and Luca, but she responds that she will never tell. The repentant governor asks for his children and sits demurely, holding a ball of yarn for his wife.

Thus, this film equates the desire for appropriation with the abuse of power. The plot hinges on the governor's neglect of his proper duties at the instigation of an unscrupulous aide. The governor's behavior is not presented as evil but as stemming from incompetence, suggestibility, vanity, and lechery. Camerini develops class conflict in the film as the opposition between the industrious country and townspeople and the greedy merchants, bureaucrats, and governor. In short, political rather than direct economic conflict is identified as the source of discord, though the politics does have economic implications. The hard-working people are presented as attractive, while the bishop, lawyer, governor, and aide are caricatured.

Originally, the film had included a section that overtly treated economic issues, by showing the people's rebellion against unjust taxes, but this section was deleted on account of censorship. The politics thus reside in the attempted seduction of Carmela, the unjust incarceration of Luca, the arbitrary inspectors who exploit the people, and the aides of the governor who are false counselors. The comic resolution is effected by the governor's wife in the interests of domestic harmony. The public order is restored in the name of family and sexual morality.

The film satirizes the use of power for personal gain, not the idea of leadership. The duplicity and hypocrisy of leaders is unmasked and chastised. The victims of oppression are presented in Camerini's film as active in their own behalf, unlike Blasetti's *Terra madre*. Carmela and the governor's wife are energetic in maintaining their respectability, virtuous in their wifely roles. Role reversals serve to dramatize the "unnatural" course that events have taken: Luca and the governor exchange positions and the governor's wife assumes her husband's authority in order to humble him. The governor is defrocked, loses his identity, and only assumes it again when he adopts a proper familial and penitent role as paterfamilias and husband. The imagery of laundry and of clothing enhances the motifs of hypocrisy and recovered identity.

The singer's tale, the most obvious self-reflexive element in the film along with the emphasis on exchange of roles and role-playing, situates the film as a parable. The element of performance serves to identify the wife's fidelity as natural and infidelity as unnatural transgression. It also serves to develop the underlying potential of violence. Contrary to the singer's tale, the female's departure from virtue is never the issue. The issue is the father-husband's potential transgression, which is averted by the women who ameliorate the threatening disorder and civil strife. Carmela and Luca are innocent but vulnerable spectators within the film. The external audience's position as a witness to the same filmic events creates a bond between them and Carmela and Luca. The pedagogical elements in the song, as in the film narrative, both satiric, function as in a parable to instruct, to chastise, and to point to the necessary conclusions: the restitution of the "natural" order of things whereby proper authority prevails.

As in so many of these films' treatment of men, the exploration of their place within the domestic and public spheres, the opposition between the libertine and the responsible paterfamilias, asserts itself. The woman continues to serve as the object of seduction and the intermediary who helps to restore a proper sense of authority and manliness. She is a threat and also the means of salvation, the source of disorder and the instrument of restitution. The libertine, again an aristocrat, is pardoned. The governor is disciplined to domestic respectability, aligned finally with the values represented by Luca, Carmela, and his other hard-working subjects. Conflict appears to be resolved in the fusion of the chastened authority figure with the people. Yet, at the same time, the wish-fulfilling, magical aspect of the mediation is also evident, providing an insight into the ways in which the film works on its audiences to overwhelm contradictions.

The chastening of the male figure is recapitulated in Amleto Palermi's 1938 *Napoli d'altri tempi* (Naples of Other Times) in the context of the conflict between artistic creativity and romantic fulfillment. The film portrays class differences as the familiar obstacle to a successful merging of love and career. *Napoli d'altri tempi* depends on the ambiance of the city and the inhabitants of Naples to render a more "realistic" presentation of economic and social struggle. The central character in the film, played by Vittorio De Sica, is a poor composer, struggling to support himself and struggling for recognition. He works as a house painter, later as a grocery clerk, prior to being discovered.

In the context of a celebration of men going off to fight in Africa in 1891, we learn that Maddalena's (Emma Gramatica) sister's fiancé was killed during an earlier war of conquest, leaving a child who had disappeared after the death of the mother. Maddalena is determined to find the child, now twenty-five years old. She traces him to a grocery store where she learns that he is a composer. She doesn't tell him of her relationship to him, but she offers to get him a piano so that he can compose at home. Proudly, Mario refuses until she offers him a business arrangement. Maddalena applies for work as a maid at the house of a wealthy family whose daughter Maria (Elisa Cegani) is interested in music, while Mario begins in earnest to visit music publishers, only to be treated indifferently. Learning from Ninetta, a young woman of his own class who is devoted to him, of Mario's discouragement, Maddalena arranges with Ninetta to take some of his music to Maria in order to enlist her help, and Mario agrees to attend a party at Maria's house where he will perform his music.

On the evening of the performance, Mario almost sabotages his chances by playing the music of other composers to which the audience is indifferent. Urged by Maria, he plays his own compositions and the audience is wildly enthusiastic. Mario's fortunes change. His music is played everywhere. When he meets Maria again, he assumes the role of a suitor. The young people begin to see each other often, to the consternation of her family. Maddalena, too, is uneasy about the developing love affair. His relationship with Ninetta begins to deteriorate and Maddalena tries to convince him that a marriage between him and Maria is out of the question. He stops seeing Maria, but by chance they meet in a music store and arrange to see each other by the seaside at Posillipo. This encounter is disrupted by the arrival of her fiancé, who takes her away. He rudely pushes some money as compensation into Mario's hand, but Mario throws it into the sea. Mario immerses himself in his work. Maddalena reveals that Maria's mother is his own mother's sister. The film ends on a note of celebration at a Neapolitan festival with Mario and Ninetta reconciled and walking arm in arm with Maddalena among the happy and singing crowd.

*Napoli d'altri tempi* has elements in common with *Carnevale di Venezia*. Both films feature musical creativity; both depend on a mother figure who makes success possible. Both films are heavily dependent on images of cities, Venice and Naples, and particularly on public celebrations and entertainment. In both texts, devotion to work, ties to family, and dedication to service are central. The idea of life as spectacle is dominant in each, as is the abolition of personal desire. The Palermi film, however, treats the class issues differently. Mario, unlike the heroine of *Carnevale*, does not marry into wealth but remains within his own class, with Ninetta, with his mother surrogate Maddalena, and with his music. His relationship to Ninetta is asexual as they work and play together. Sexual romantic elements are subordinated. Renunciation becomes a central feature in his emergence into creativity and responsibility.

Although Mario is deprived of the consummation of his romantic love, he is compensated through his reconciliation with family and community, which is based on his acceptance of social differences. He is the obedient son who learns to recognize the source of his creativity in his own social milieu. Each of the women serve him and help him to be creative. Maddalena provides him with a musical instrument and paves the way for his first performance, and Ninetta serves as his critic and a puncturer of his unrealistic desires. Maria, in her own way, by being the unrealized object of his desire, becomes the impetus for his continued creativity.

The man is thus again portrayed as the center of interest, and his transformation the object of others' efforts. The women's service enables him to achieve success and a sense of his identity. His musical success is identified, however, not with personal achievement but with "Napoli d'altri tempi," with the city and its achievements, and ultimately with the public good. The film develops the importance of personal sacrifice. Mario is not a dashing romantic hero. He is associated with more commonplace virtues: loyalty to your own kind, respect for work, a sense of difference from the upper classes, a "realistic" awareness of circumstances, and an identification with place.

## The New Man

The conversion narrative has a long history in confessional literature, spiritual autobiography, the folk tale, the novel, the popular romances, and, of course, the cinema.[16] Most often associated with the male subject, the "story" concerns his psychological and social transformation. The experience can be doctrinally religious but more often it is exemplified by the identification of concrete action with spiritual, even missionary objectives. Moreover, the experience of conversion translates individual behavior into collective action. The hero is "reborn" into "right thinking" and right courses of action.

Conversion narratives draw on basic archetypal characters, narrative patterns, and images. The reassuring presence of a hero, his quest for self-knowledge, his initiation into correct forms of action that will purify him and the community, the presence of agents working for or against the hero's evolution, and his overcoming of natural and cultural restraints symbolized in acts of physical endurance, intellectual cunning, and liberation are characteristic of the genre practices, creating a sense of *déjà vu*, identification, and the suppression of critical opposition.

The contemporary versions of the conversion narrative are not mere replications of earlier forms such as Augustine's *Confessions* or Dante's *Divine Comedy*. In their modern desacralized versions, they can be found in historical fiction, melodrama, and comedy. The primary strategy of the narrative

[16] A version of this section appears in the *Journal of Film and Video* 37 (Spring 1985).

involves a reevaluation of the hero's sense of self and his relation to the community. The hero begins in obscure circumstances, experiences forms of psychic and social oppression, confronts authority figures and nurturant figures, and experiences a "rebirth" into action most frequently associated with the regeneration of the community. His rebirth may entail his death or his appropriation of a new identity that confirms his authority. Susan Rubin Suleiman identifies such a narrative as a "story of apprenticeship" and describes its structures as follows:

Syntagmatically, we may define a story of apprenticeship (*Bildung*) as two parallel transformations undergone by the protagonist: first, a transformation from *ignorance* (of self) to *knowledge* (of self); second, a transformation from passivity to action.[17]

The threat of emasculation at the hands of either a man or woman, the constant threat of loss of life, of self, of "purpose," the threat of unbridled or undifferentiated sexuality, the possibility of exclusion and isolation from the community are neutralized by a series of successful trials that result in the hero's assumption of a new identity, if not a new name. Disguises, name changes, symbolic death and rebirth, or actual death and apotheosis are common features of the narrative of conversion. The convert becomes the "new man," and revenge and retaliation against his detractors is fully legitimated on the basis of the hero's past suffering. If he becomes linked to the "new woman," the relationship is domesticated, not sexualized.

An examination of the Italian films in this context helps to expose the constructed nature of male power and its roots in an ideological discourse of male virility, power, productivity, commitment, and discipline. The Italian films that present the male figure in the context of the conversion narrative appear to cluster in the middle to late thirties, which may in part be accounted for by the war in Ethiopia and the Italian intervention in Spain. Moreover, the vision of male leadership they

[17] Susan Rubin Suleiman, *Authoritarian Fictions: The Ideological Novel as a Literary Genre* (New York: Columbia University Press, 1983), p. 65.

portray does not seem unique to Italy but is duplicated in both the Soviet and American cinema of the era. The vision of heroic and rejuvenated male leadership and the regenerated community was endemic to the political conflicts of the thirties as well as characteristic of the Italian cinema's efforts to create a popular cinema, one that draws on old stereotypes clothed in contemporary images.

*Passaporto rosso* (Red Passport), directed by Brignone in 1935, is an overtly political film. The red passport was a document given to political agitators who were expelled from Italy and forced to go abroad in the last years of the nineteenth century. The film opens on a scene of political demonstration where different speakers are delivering speeches for and against government policies. Dr. Casati, one of the last speakers, is told that he will have to leave the country, since he stands accused by the authorities of fomenting rebellion. He is given a red passport, which will enable him to go to Argentina, serving as the ship's doctor on the ocean passage. Aboard ship, he meets an old friend, Antonio, and makes the acquaintance of Maria Brunetta and her father, also immigrants to Argentina. Aboard ship there is oppression—overcrowding, mismanagement, ill-treatment of the passengers, shortages of food—and Casati's role, along with the Brunettas' and Antonio's, is portrayed as altruistic. These events prefigure the struggles to come in Argentina.

The film's form seems to share elements with the American western. The people are headed for a new frontier that they must tame in order to create a new community, but not without conflict. The camera work employs much panning, mobile perspectives, extensive alteration of low- and high-angle shots and medium and long shots. The film's editing is dependent on affective strategies in its use of dissolves, superimpositions, and clear contrasts developed through strategic juxtaposition. The characters are juxtaposed: Easterners versus Westerners, speculators and land-grabbers versus exploited, but well-meaning railroad workers, heroic and intrepid male figures versus corrupt vested interests. The frontier landscape is evident in the crude buildings, the general store, the bar, the dance hall, the school, and the modest homes. The motifs of the film involve the disintegrative forces in the form of greedy exploitation, the legitimation of honest expansionism, and the idea of national pride.

Maria (Isa Miranda), the central female figure in the film, is a model of service. Aboard ship, she becomes a ministering angel to the suffering children. She is also marked out by the corrupt Don Pancho as a potential entertainer in his dance hall. He owns a good part of the town, including the general store, and thus wields power over the workers. Maria also gets to know Casati who tries to prepare her realistically for the hardships she will confront in America.

Brignone shows the arrival of the immigrants and also shots of the rugged terrain and of the workers at their heavy labor. Thus, opposition between economic profiteers and the oppression of the workers is heavily underscored in the first half of the film. The film highlights class differences, as in a Blasetti film. The company manager and Don Pancho are pitted against the impoverished workers. Casati, not a worker himself, is presented as the enlightened hero, situated outside a class identity in his commitment to morality, service, and heroic action. These qualities are linked to economic growth and nationalism. Moreover, the populist discourse here as in American films tends to single out the difference between legitimate and illegitimate notions of wealth and power, between moral and immoral acquisition of these. The workers do not object to unequal distribution of wealth or to the notion of being directed by leaders, but to their oppressive working conditions enforced by irresponsible, greedy leaders. The idea of national identity is introduced early in the film as Antonio presents Casati with a bag of soil from Italy, and the motif of nationalism intensifies as the film progresses.

The film's garnering of support for the oppressed Italian immigrant develops in several directions. The men are shown at work, hauling heavy carts of stone as they are goaded to produce at backbreaking speed. The women are shown at the company store, where Don Pancho turns away women whose credit he claims is overdrawn and who are, therefore, not entitled to buy necessities. An epidemic breaks out among the workers, tainted water being identified as the carrier. Soon many men begin to drop with the disease and die. In an elaborate montage sequence, the progress from disease to death, the superimposition of gravedigging, burning of contaminated objects, and burials is portrayed. Maria's father becomes a victim. Don Pancho, taking advantage of her now-impoverished condition, refuses to give her credit any longer, insisting that she must pay her debts by working for him as an entertainer in the dance hall. At this point the film shifts from its focus on the plight of the workers to a more melodramatic vein involving the evil seducer and subverter of women, the plight of the helpless female victim, and the heroic protectors of chastity and honor. The family romance comes into greater prominence, now fusing with the film's more overt political and social concerns.

Maria is forced to sing before an audience that ogles her lecherously. Don Pancho berates her for being uncooperative, but Antonio and Casati arrive and "buy" Maria from Don Pancho by paying her debt. The final sequence in the film's first section shows the defeat of Don Pancho and the company officials at the hands of the workers. Maria and Lorenzo and the new settlers stage a festival to inaugurate the new railroad and a new era of Italian-American unity. Lorenzo presents his plans for the creation of a model city to be built by the immigrants. As he talks, images are superimposed of the sea, flashbacks of the ship that brought them to America, and then of people working.

The film time changes to 1914. Gianni Casati, the son of Maria and Lorenzo, receives a diploma in engineering as jarring images of a battlefield and of men looking at a map of Europe and talking of the war intervene. Gianni, in opposition to his father, sees himself as American, not Italian, and as modern rather than traditional. The war in Europe is of no concern to him but Lorenzo broods on it, eager for Italy to participate, and concerned for Italian honor. The news is brought that Italy has declared war against Germany. Shouts of "Viva Italia" are heard as an image of the Italian flag is superimposed on the scene. Lorenzo serves as a recruiter for the Italian army, and he is pained because his own son does not volunteer. Maria learns that in his frustration he has enlisted, and she informs Gianni, who tries to dissuade his father without success. At a train station where Italian flags are waving, young men take leave from their families. True to his promise to his mother, Gianni will not allow his father to go to war. In a tearful scene, the father and son embrace as Maria looks on, weeping. The film ends at a grave with the awarding of a medal, a fascist medal. The "victory" of the Italians is, finally, the victory of fascism.

The son's transformation is consistent with the idea of the "new man," and the entry into a new life, which is associated with Italian nationalism, conquest of nature, family honor, militarism, work, the will of the father, and the sacrifice of youth. The history of Italian emigration is developed so as to elevate the idea that political destiny realizes itself in fascism. The shame of the "red passport" and the hardships of the immigrant experience are cancelled by the image of a new order. The role of the family, especially the role of generational conflict, takes precedence over the earlier class struggles. Once the immigrants "solve" their class oppression, their unity is sealed in their devotion to their place of origin. The new order and the new men who comprise it transcend familial and economic conflict through the heroic devotion to Italy that is, in Gianni's words, "in their blood." The violence, which was earlier an aspect of the struggle for survival, is now transmitted into the arena of politics. The family is the locus for the production of these new values, and Lorenzo, the father, is the progenitor of the new heroism, goading his son to great actions.

The film stresses the conversion of the community as well as of select individuals within that community. A dominant agent of change is a physician, a familiar hero figure in the films of the era. Images of disease are associated with the corruption of family, workers, and national identity, whereas the rebuilding of these institutions is a source of health. In this respect, the film seems to capture the pseudo–progressive discourse of early fascism, its emphasis on the need for change, its appeal to workers and peasants, its classic conciliatory strategies, revealing a dominant aspect about the ways in which fascism sought consensus.

*Passaporto rosso* rewrites the history of the pre-fascist years, the struggles of the workers, and the internal political struggles in Italy. Like a *Pilgrim's Progress*, the film creates a vision of a new heaven and earth, the defeat of greedy and irresponsible leaders, the building of new cities, the conquest over adversity as symbolized in the overcoming of the hardships on the "wilderness," the creation of a unified society, and the emergence of a sense of national honor upheld by idealistic young men, willing to sacrifice themselves for their homeland.

In contrast to the "epic" style of *Passaporto rosso*, Goffredo Alessandrini's 1936 film, *Cavalleria* (Cavalry), develops the motif of conversion through romantic melodrama. The film idol Amedeo Nazzari is the dashing Captain Solaro, a cavalry officer who falls in love with a young noblewoman. The film exploits the images of the horse shows, cavalry exercises, and the elegant people who inhabit this world. The world of the aristocracy is displayed as glamorous: sumptuous houses, salons, ballrooms, and bejewelled women exquisitely costumed.

Speranza (Elisa Cegani) believes that her arranged marriage to the Baron can be broken. However, her mother is adamant, for reasons of status and money. The conflicts multiply. Speranza is torn between her loyalty to her family and her love for Solaro. Her father is conflicted between the desire to see his daughter happy and his loyalty to his wife; Solaro is torn between duty and love, learning with the help of Ponza to accept the former. Ponza belives that his men, particularly brilliant officers like Solaro, must learn to accept the seriousness of their military commitments. In structure, the film juxtaposes the world of wealth, luxury, and status to the world of discipline, heroism, and service. The scenes alternate between the home and the cavalry school. For example, the father's physical collapse so crucial to Speranza's decision to

Luciano De Ambrosis (Prico) in *I bambini ci guardano*, Vittorio De Sica, 1944
(Museum of Modern Art, Stills Archive)

Maria Denis (Dorina) and Adriano Rimoldi (Mario) in *Addio giovinezza*, Ferdinando Maria Poggioli, 1940 (*Antologia del cinema italiano, il film sonoro, dal 1929 al 1943*)

Isa Miranda (Gaby) in *La signora di tutti*, Max Ophuls, 1934 (*Antologia del cinema italiano, il film sonoro, dal 1929 al 1943*)

Assia Noris (Arlette) in *Batticuore*, Mario Camerini, 1939 (Museum of Modern Art, Stills Archive)

Annibale Ninchi (Scipio) in *Scipione l'Africano*, Carmine Gallone, 1937 (Museum of Modern Art, Stills Archive)

Giuseppe Gulino (Carmeliddu) in *1860*, Alessandro Blasetti, 1934 (Museum of Modern Art, Stills Archive)

Vittorio De Sica (Gianni-Max) in *Il signor Max*, Mario Camerini, 1937
(Museum of Modern Art, Stills Archive)

Edoardo De Filippo (Thé Governor) and Leda Gloria (Carmela) in *Il
cappello a tre punte*, Mario Camerini, 1935 (*Antologia del cinema italiano,
il film sonoro, dal 1929 al 1943*)

Isa Miranda (Marina) in *Malombra*, Mario Soldati, 1942 (Museum of
Modern Art, Stills Archive)

Adriana Benetti (Maria) and Gino Cervi (Paolo) in *Quattro passi fra le
nuvole*, Alessandro Blasetti, 1942 (Museum of Modern Art, Stills Archive)

Clara Calamai (Giovanna) and Massimo Girotti (Gino) in *Ossessione*, Luchino Visconti, 1943 (Museum of Modern Art, Stills Archive)

marry the Baron is framed by sequences of Solaro performing cavalry exercises.

At the academy, Ponza lectures Solaro on the importance of duty and the necessity of renunciation. Resigned to his loss of Speranza, Solaro goes to the Pinaro Academy where he is an officer in the mold of Ponza. Speranza's brother arrives as one of the new students, and Solaro, greeting him along with the other new students, lectures the men on the importance of discipline, honor, and courage. The young man is wounded during maneuvers in a ravine where Solaro had been putting his men through extremely torturous exercises, and Speranza comes to the academy to visit him. Solaro, learning of her presence, intercepts her and arranges to meet her in the park on the following day. He presses her further to see her again. Unable to resist, she begins to meet him clandestinely, though gossip develops about their relationship. As a consequence, the brother feels compelled to defend his sister's honor. At the start of an important competition, Solaro learns about the duel and Speranza's return to her husband, and goes through his paces in a daze. His thoroughbred horse is wounded, and he decides to resign from the cavalry to become an aviator. The final sequences of the film are of combat (World War I). Solaro's plane is hit and plunges to the ground. The cavalrymen can be seen, Speranza's brother among them, carrying Solaro's body away from the wreckage. An image of flowers in a field precedes an image of the officers playing taps for Solaro as the shot tilts to the sky.

The film glorifies unfulfilled love; Solaro's heroism is intimately tied to his passion for Speranza. The striking aspect of Solaro's character is his lack of rebelliousness. His willingness to accept his superior officer's orders, his acceptance of the need to renounce Speranza, his discipline and self-control are offered as a model of heroism. His conversion to and immersion in duty and service are eroticized. Though Elisa Cegani plays the role of the beautiful Speranza, the object of Solaro's desire, her presence in the film is subordinated to the focus on Solaro. In most sequences he is the object of desire: while dressing, on horseback, as a leader of men, as a lover, as dashing aviator, and as doomed hero. The audience is snared by him.

The figure of Captain Ponza can be likened to the stern father surrogate who initiates the hero into the higher rewards of dedicated service and commitment to a cause. Speranza is a more contradictory figure. She is the object of Solaro's desire; she is also a figure of transgression who ultimately becomes the agent of his death and then of his transfiguration. Through her agency, the film reverses the usual polarity between life and death, identifying death as life. The stages of the hero's conversion are marked by stages of separation from the female. His crisis entails his final separation from her and from the life of the cavalry associated with the past. His new life is associated with the isolated life of the flier. He is no longer passive, chained to the past and to his desire, but a liberated man of action. His education in renunciation and discipline has schooled him to duty. The airplane sets him apart from others, above the earth like a god.

The film develops the equation of sexual deprivation and productivity. Erotic desire is transformed into action. Heroism, duty, and sacrifice are offered as compensatory actions, but the film, consciously, reveals that aggression and death are, in fact, the products of repression. The film also emphasizes male comradeship; Solaro's actions are understood and admired by the other men. The cavalry exercises and the competitions are set in the context of theatricality, highlighting spectatorship and performance. The transformation of life into melodrama and spectacle offers itself as a means of legitimizing death and aggression. The most telling image in the film is the image of flowers. Solaro's relationship to Speranza is symbolized by an exchange of flowers culminating in the image of a field of flowers where Solaro is buried. The image works in several contradictory directions. On the one hand it signifies passion, life, and hope, like Speranza's name; on the other hand, it signifies indifference to life. Solaro's burial in the field of flowers naturalizes the fusion of love, war, and heroism. His conversion to manhood lies in his acceptance of deprivation that translates into a worship of death. His death is considered a creative act, an insemination of the land.

Alessandrini's film was praised by a contemporary critic for its evocative atmosphere, its fidelity to an epoch, and its "masculine" style, compared by some critics to American films.[18] Like so many American melodramas, the film is able to fuse spectacle with psychological conflict. The opulent costumes and sets, the dashing image of Solaro as cavalry officer and modern aviator (a favorite image in Italy at this time), glamorize and romanticize the negative aspects of sexual repression, renunciation, suffering, and sacrifice.

The year 1936 saw the appearance of Genina's *Squadrone bianco* (The White Squadron), filmed on location in the Libyan desert. The film is a good example of the male conversion drama linked to the thematics of war and imperialism. It begins in the mode of a *film noir*, in darkness, illuminated only by the headlights of a car speeding through the night, with Ludovici (Antonio Centa) racing to see Cristina (Fulvia Lanzi), a fashionable socialite, who is indifferent to his attentions. The opening sequences develop one of the major issues and images of the film: the life of the bored, idle, decadent bourgeoisie and the screen darkness associated with their cruel and aimless existence. In sharp contrast, the film moves to the brightness of the Libyan desert, with shots of the desert, of natives working, and of Italians supervising the natives. A few individuals are singled out sympathetically, the old veteran Captain Donati and Dr. Fabrizi. Through them a picture of the struggles of the Italians in Africa emerges. Captain Santelia (Fosco Giachetti) is introduced as a man totally dedicated to his work. He is shot from a low angle as he postures before the men. His sentiments are those of an antique Roman: "Death is the most glorious end of a true soldier." The film emphasizes paternalism and discipline.

Lieutenant Ludovici, who has joined the squadron, arrives at the base and an antagonism develops between the lieuten-

---

[18] Francesco Savio, *Ma l'amore no* (Milan: Sonzogno, 1975), pp. 74-75.

ant and the captain, who describes Ludovici as a playboy and
voices doubts about his commitment. He lectures the lieutenant on the bravery of his predecessor's death in battle. In
these sequences, Genina establishes the classic conflict characteristic of many Hollywood films, an early antagonism between men to be overcome. The neophyte, in particular, must
undergo trials and prove himself worthy of esteem and comradeship. The shifting between the Italian and African setting
reinforces the juxtaposition between a parasitic existence and
the world of war and heroism. The squadron has been ordered
to battle in the desert, and scenes of mobilization follow.
Before setting out on the mission, Santelia reviews his men,
giving them personal encouragement. In his room, Ludovici
tries to write a letter to Cristina, but tears up the paper, a
sign of his initial break with his past. The troops leave with
Santelia and Ludovici at their head. The men on camels are
photographed from various angles and directions as they
move into the desert. A long shot dramatically reveals the
men against the background of the sky. As they disappear,
the natives who remain behind are shown looking at the
receding line of troops. The film has few shots of battle; its
main military shots are focused rather on the reviewing of
the troops and on ritualized processions across the desert.
Spectatorship is reinforced by keyhole-type shots of the action
through binoculars, favoring the external audience with a
select view of events.

The progress of the men through the desert is long, and
each step of the trek charts another stage in the conversion
of the hero and his relationship to the captain. At first, he is
reprimanded for not being cautious in his drinking of the
precious water, but he is determined to prove his competence
to Ludovici. Santelia leads the men to the grave of the dead
lieutenant as he pays his respects to the hero, while Ludovici
looks on curiously. The lieutenant becomes ill with fever. At
this point he throws away a cigarette case given to him by
Cristina, signifying his rejection of his past. The journey
through the desert is complicated by a sandstorm. The swirl-
ing sand becomes a correlative for the turmoil within him.

Still he refuses to stop. The sandstorm becomes blinding, and he finally falls from his camel. Santelia tenderly nurses Ludovici like a parent, and Ludovici learns that he has earned the captain's respect. Now, the two men work together to help the others. They locate the enemy and in a brief skirmish, one of them is shot, although it is not clear which.

Cristina, now concerned for Ludovici, waits at the headquarters impatiently for the news of his fate. One of her friends comments, "This is like a novel." The music is martial as the procession of men approaches. Donati, thinking he sees Santelia, calls out to him, only to discover that it is Ludovici who has survived. Ludovici now inhabits Santelia's office, reading the mail, issuing orders, and comforting Donati. He communicates Santelia's last words to Donati as light can be seen breaking through the window. Ludovici learns that Cristina wants to see him, and he agrees to meet her. Upon seeing him, she tells him, "You have changed." He agrees that he is no longer the same person she knew, and they part.

The film is highly stylized. The scenes are developed so as to create parallelism and contrast. The film opens on the road with Ludovici in his car and ends with Cristina driving away in her car. The image of processional movement persists throughout the film, marking Ludovici's progression from a romantic young man to a man of iron, from a plaything in the hands of a woman to a renouncer of women, from a youth to a man, from a son to a father, taking the place of the dead father figure. Scenes of battle, elaboration of the specific sources of the conflict, portrayals of the enemy, are minimal, for the film single-mindedly portrays conflict and reconciliation between Ludovici and Santelia, and Ludovici's assumption of Santelia's position.

The deflection from the concrete reality of war and imperialism onto the personal drama of conversion, the reincarnation of the hero in the image of the father, the negation or destruction of the woman, seems another variant of the films of war and imperialism of the era, in part traceable to the fascist celebration of leadership, male collectivity, and committed youth. However, these motifs are not unique to these films. These attitudes are also present in the Hollywood films, as are the motifs involving the devotion to work and of earned merit for competence.

*Lo squadrone bianco* was not designed solely for Italian audiences but was produced with an eye for foreign distribution. Gian Piero Brunetta notes that the film had a great success in England.[19] The politics of domination, portrayed in the relations between Italy and Africa, is conceived in the mold of British-Indian relations, as a tacit acceptance of the willingness of the natives to serve the white man. Santelia's benevolent leadership is sufficient rationalization for his control of native troops. The loyal service of the natives as portrayed through El Fennek is presented as a natural outgrowth of the native's admiration for the white man's power and wisdom. The central issue here is not the struggle for control of the native's hearts and minds, but the need to insure that the enterprise of conquest be understood as requiring a certain type of personal and public commitment on the part of Italians. Thus, this drama of conversion reactivates traditional conceptions of male heroism.

Also set in Africa, Guido Brignone's 1938 film, *Sotto la croce del sud* (Under the Southern Cross) dramatizes the conflict between debased heterosexuality and the ideals of male comradeship. Moreover, Brignone celebrates imperialism as the bringing of order and productivity to a primitive and dangerous corner of the world. Throughout the film, landscape itself will become an important signifier of the epic dimensions of the Italian conquest of Africa. Moreover, these landscape scenes serve, in Walter Benjamin's terms, to aestheticize the politics. They stress the exotic and the spectacular. Set within this exotic landscape is the native woman, Mailù (played by Doris Duranti) who is equally exotic and mysterious. Mailù lives with Simone, an Italian adventurer bent on exploiting the natives and the natural resources of Africa. He

[19] Gian Piero Brunetta, *Storia del cinema italiano 1895-1945* (Rome: Riuniti, 1979), p. 292.

treats her roughly and condescendingly. In contrast to Simone, the film elevates Marco, "Lord of the First World War" as he is called by the adoring natives. Marco's assistant is Paolo, a young, clean-cut engineer who has come to Africa to help with developing the land. Simone symbolizes the old form of colonialism, whereas Marco and Paolo are portrayed as representatives of a new, more humane system of administration and economic production.

The film is punctuated with scenes of the natives working and singing, unloading materials, chopping trees, and willingly serving the Italians. The Italian workers are presented as having come to Africa with zeal and dedication. They are also presented as virile, as brimming with sexuality about which they joke, but which they appear to sublimate in work and play.

Paolo meets Mailù and is attracted to her. Simone coerces Mailù into seducing Paolo as a way of subverting the work of the Italians. Marco, aware of Paolo's growing interest in Mailù, tries in a paternal way to discourage any further contact. Marco is the model leader of men, the good father and good leader. His age, his experience, his pragmatism, his concern for his men and the natives reinforces his exemplariness. Soon after his arrival, he announces that there will no longer be slavery. Henceforth, the natives will be paid for their work and will be treated humanely. Simone, on the other hand, brutalizes the natives, pays them with whiskey, not money. The natives themselves are often photographed against the landscape as they work, as if their work for the Italians emanates benevolently from nature.

Mailù and Paolo's relationship quickly reaches the point of his declaring his love for her, but love comes abruptly to an end when Paolo overhears a conversation between Mailù and Simone that reveals that Simone has manipulated her to seduce Paolo. Frantic to make his profit and leave Africa, Simone becomes more aggressive. He attacks Mario, almost succeeding in killing him. He also sets fire to the Italian warehouses, causing extensive damage to the property and materials. Without Mailù, he attempts to escape with his loot.

The dramatically shot scenes of the raging fire and the men working together heroically to bring the fire under control are juxtaposed against the natives' remorseless hunting down of Simone as he abandons his truck and seeks to escape on foot through the jungle. Simone finds himself in quicksand. Unable to pull himself out, he slowly slides under as the natives look on impassively, refusing to give him the assistance for which he desperately calls. Marco, the benevolent leader of men and Paolo, the engineer, are now in control of a community purged of irresponsible and obstructive elements.

*Sotto la croce del sud* romanticizes colonialism as an altruistic enterprise. The new order of work and economic production is the self–effacing creation of men who are motivated solely by a concern to ameliorate the exploitation of the natives by rapacious colonialists and economic mismanagement, and to develop proper uses of the land and a new ethos of moral and sexual rectitude. The conflict between the old and new order is portrayed in the opposition between degenerate sexuality, potential miscegenation, physical brutality, self-interest; and healthy collective contact among men, self-restraint, hard work, and concern for the underdog (the natives). The "fire" started by Simone is a dominant image in the film and reinforces the theme of the death of the old degenerate way of life and the emergent new order embodied in heroes such as Marco and Paolo. Simone's submergence in the quicksand, too, reinforces the disappearance of the destructive forces and the negative values associated with them.

The role of Mailù in the film, as she is associated with both Simone, the exploiter, and Paolo, the regenerate and committed young man, is important for the way it situates her as an intermediary in the conversion from the private world of desire to the public world of collective action and imperial destiny. Though she is physically attractive and presented as a solitary and subjected person, she is associated in her victimage with Simone's destructiveness. She is especially dangerous to the ideal of the male community, threatening to woo Paolo away from the ideals of authority and action associated with Marco. She seems, like the natives, to symbolize

Africa, its seductiveness, sensuality, physical weakness, and emotional dependency, that aspect of native life that needs to be eliminated. Unlike the other natives, who are associated with productive work, she is associated with idleness and dissension. In his portrayal of the natives, in the scenes of work, dancing, singing, and even in their hunting of Simone, Brignone fuses them with nature and with activity. They appear naturally positioned in work and ritual. They, like the natural resources being mined, seem to exist to be developed and controlled.

The film in many ways utilizes film language not dissimilar to the Hollywood and British films of the era, such films as *Beau Geste* (1926), *Under Two Flags* (1936), *Sanders of the River* (1935), or *Four Feathers* (1939), which celebrate territorial expansion, presenting nonwhites as the focal point of the conflict, agents to be acted upon, who in their dependency legitimize domination. The exotic landscape, and the exotic aspects of nonwhite individuals, especially Mailù, provide the necessary element of spectacle. She and Simone are the negative forces in Paolo's conversion, while Marco is the positive agent.

An ironic drama of conversion, completely different in style from the films of male heroism, is *Il fu Mattia Pascal* (The Former Mattia Pascal), made in 1937 and directed by Pierre Chenal, a French director.[20] Based on a work of Luigi Pirandello's, the film is a compendium of types, figures, motifs, and images that are archetypal conversion strategies.[21] Rich in visual experimentation as well as intricacy of character construction, plot, and narrative structure, the work is built around the principle of doubling, including the intermingling of fantasy and quotidian experience. *Mattia Pascal* begins deceptively as a pastoral idyll. The appearance of harmony is shattered by the harsh realities of money and family aggression. In order to marry Romilda (Nella Maria Bonora), Mattia

[20] Marco Pannunzio, "Chenal di fronte a Pirandello," *Cinema* 1 (10 November 1936), p. 391.

[21] Tzvetan Todorov, *The Poetics of Prose* (Ithaca: Cornell University Press, 1977).

(Pierre Blanchar) must find 50,000 lire to satisfy Romilda's grasping mother (Irma Gramatica). But his only possible source is his mother who has no money either. She borrows the money for him and stifles her uneasiness about the demands of his future mother-in-law.

The wedding begins on a festive note but this idyll is quickly shattered by a merchant who comes to collect unpaid bills for the party. Romilda's mother refuses to pay in spite of her receipt of money from Mattia. Mattia's mother mortgages everything she owns in order to pay. What emerges is a contrast between the two mothers; the tyrannical mother of the bride, and the submissive, self-sacrificing mother of the groom. Significantly, neither of the women has a husband. The absence of the paternal figure is paralleled by the submissiveness of Mattia, unable to extricate himself and to assert authority in any way.

Having lost everything, Mattia's mother has had to move in with her son and subject herself to the domineering Signora Pescatore. Helpless, Mattia sits by and watches Signora Pescatore insult his mother. His impotence, frustration, and exploitation are further dramatized when he tries to find work. He goes to the mayor's office where he is offered a position as librarian for a mere 60 lire a week. Mattia meekly accepts the terms of employment, while the mayor, behind Mattia's back, celebrates his cleverness in withholding part of the mandated salary. The concept of withholding sex and money is central to the development of the narrative. The highly stylized presentation of character as in a fairy tale highlights oppositions between oppressor and victim, aggression and passivity.

At the library, Mattia does menial work, oppressed now by an elderly deaf employer. He learns from a child that his mother is dying and he tells the child to inform Romilda to come immediately to his mother's bedside. Signora Pescatore forbids her daughter to go. In a sentimental scene at Signora Pascal's bedside, the son mourns his mother's death. He returns home to learn that Romilda's mother is insisting that

Mattia go to the mayor to arrange for a pauper's funeral for his mother.

Mattia wanders off like a somnambulist. Deciding to go to America, he boards a train where he meets a man who urges him instead to go to Monte Carlo where he can get rich quickly. At Monte Carlo, Mattia wins enormous amounts at the gambling tables. He returns home to discover a grave-digger digging a new grave. The body of a dead man was unrecognizable, and the corpse was identified as Mattia. Mattia asks his informant, who recognizes him, not to give him away, and he hides as he sees his wife and her mother dressed in black and weeping copiously. Now he is dead to this life. He has no identity. Again on a train, he throws his wedding ring out of the window. In Rome, he throws his identity papers away. At the Hotel Luxor, he signs the register as Adriano Meis of Milan.

After several months, he meets a woman in the park who is a spiritualist. She tells him that he is in need of rest and solace and she recommends a boarding house where he can find peace. Luisa, played by Isa Miranda, lives at the boarding house and offers to take Adriano there. At the boarding house he meets other unusual inhabitants: Luisa's tutor who is a surrogate father to her, Count Papiano (Enrico Glori) who supports himself by illegal means, and Miss Caporale (Olga Solbelli), the spiritualist from the park. The Count, interested in Luisa, takes a dislike to Adriano and when he sees his money, begins to scheme against him. Adriano's vulnerability is his lack of identity papers, and the Count sets about to expose him. Finding himself at a seance, Adriano is confronted by the Count, who asks him about his history and place of origin. Adriano responds that he is an American. Tension between the tutor and the Count over Luisa and over money continues to build. The element of spiritualism is consonant with the film's use of mythic characters and situations, with the religious and psychological emphasis on conversion and transformation, and with the use of Mattia's death and spiritual rebirth.

Adriano, aware that he must produce some mail in order

to quell suspicion, mails a blank letter to himself that is intercepted by the Count. The Count confronts him with the blank paper and, furious, Adriano decides to leave the pension. Luisa agrees to accompany him. On the following morning, he discovers that all his money has been stolen. The Count, knowing that Adriano cannot call the police, has taken the money. Adriano goes to the Count's room and recovers it, while the Count threatens to call the police.

Mattia decides to "kill" Adriano and go home. His new identity has brought him to the same place as the old one; again he is under another's intimidation and control. He goes to the river and drops in his jacket and hat in order to give the appearance of drowning. For a second time, he has given up his identity. He returns to the country to find that Romilda has remarried. He forces Romilda's husband, who is a clerk at the City Hall, to forge new identity papers in the name of Adriano Meis. In Rome, he and Luisa are reunited. (The Count, who brings the police to the house, is thwarted when Adriano produces his identification papers.) Adriano now confesses to Luisa that he was the former Mattia Pascal and that they will have a lifetime together for him to explain his story.

He has finally emerged as a "new man," confident, legitimate, financially comfortable, and in possession of the right woman. He triumphs over the weak and absent father figures by becoming a strong figure himself. In order to do this, he sheds his old submissive self. He has asserted himself over the tyrannical mother-in-law and established his dominance over the females in his life. He has also asserted himself over the decadent aristocrat. The film ends like a fairy tale with the acquisition of wealth and an identity. Not only has Adriano's money been restored to him, but he has been given legal legitimacy, albeit illegally.

His conversion is dependent on place. His first "death" takes place in the country and his rebirth is associated with Monte Carlo and Rome. His second death in the city is only provisional since, after his return to the country to legitimize his new identity, he appropriates his role more fully. Significantly, he does not remain in the country, but returns to Rome. Unlike Blasetti's *Terra madre* or Palermi's *La peccatrice*, Chenal's film does not idealize the country but presents the city rather as the locus of change.

The female characters, especially those associated with the village, are domineering and exploitative, and Mattia is a victim of role-reversal. Identified with his self-sacrificing mother, he is passive and unable to combat the aggressiveness of his mother-in-law, his wife, and the mayor. In the city, his only obstacle to his success is the Count. The other boarders in the pension are all presented as benevolent. Women in the film are either aggressive or self-negating; with the exception of the Count, the men are victims like Mattia. Mattia's conversion into manhood is dependent on his mother's death, his "escape," his acquisition of money, his removal to the city, and his attainment of legitimacy by forcing a public official to forge identity papers. The keystone of the film's structure is money, which is the dominant vehicle of his oppression, the means whereby Mattia is controlled and also the means whereby he is liberated. Sexuality also plays an important role in Mattia's conversion. His absent father, his domineering mother-in-law, his wife totally dominated by her mother, his self-sacrificing and dependent mother are the means of keeping him impotent. Only when he can compete with and defeat the powerful Count Papiano can he become legitimate. In his new sense of self, he can subordinate the two women from his past, overcome the village bureaucrat who is Romilda's husband, and "march" on Rome. The "new man" is aggressive, capable of holding his own in a world of exploiters. In spite of the "happy ending," there is no sense that the world around him is transformed.

The film seems an ironic dissection of the conversion narrative with its implications of personal and social transformation. Everything is included: archetypal situations, characters, and images. The stages of Mattia's "conversion" involve youthful naiveté and oppression, a journey to enlightenment, the "death" of his old life, the struggle to obliterate the past, and his rebirth. The figures whom he confronts are equally archetypal: good and evil mother figures, tyrannical male authority figures, cruel and benign women who alternately oppress or save him. The symbolism of the journey and of water are also typical of such narratives. Yet the fairy-tale quality of the film serves to make the exposure of the decadent environment more pointed and Mattia's conversion more important as a vehicle for the exposure of corruption than relevant in itself.

## Tyrants and Gigolos

Increasingly, the films from 1938 to 1943 are preoccupied with violence, deceit, and marginality. The characters' disguises and pretensions are no longer regarded as a necessary performance. Though the films may present the familiar conflicts of love and duty, productivity as opposed to idleness, authenticity as opposed to role-playing, they treat the conflicts differently. Confession and exposure are more obvious than suppression. The men portrayed are neither innocent nor benign; they are themselves manipulative. They live off women or by their wits. They are beset by economic limitation, internal psychological pressures, and the malevolence of others, which blocks their entry into proper domesticity and public service. Moreover, if they are able to overcome these obstacles, their transformation is the result of "authentic" confrontation with others and not of behaving properly.

The style of Poggioli's and Soldati's films differ markedly from the comedies of the early thirties and from the dramas of conversion and commitment. Not only are the characters flawed, but the world they inhabit is portrayed as dark and ominous, contributing to a sense of the claustrophobia. The threat of exposure and blackmail is omnipresent. The comic figures of Don Juan, the serious figures of the young apprentice or journeyman become the figures of the tyrant and the gigolo.

Even in Blasetti's *Corona di ferro* (Crown of Iron), the young hero's portrayal is subordinated to the portrayal of the tyrant-king who is wantonly cruel to his children, power-hungry, arbitrary and unjust to his subjects, and unrestrainedly violent. In Soldati's *Quartieri alti* (High Quarters), the young gigolo may decide to reform and become a respectable member of society but that society is exposed as totally corrupt. The emphasis on these unheroic figures would seem to converge with the increasing disaffection toward the regime, revealing a critique of power in both the public and the private worlds.

Blasetti's 1941 *Corona di ferro* explores the issue of legitimate and illegitimate authority. In the tradition of the Hollywood costume adventure, the film's politics are conveyed through its fairy tale and mythic framework. The pedagogical dimension of the film is transmitted through the film's use of allegory and parable. In many ways, the film is more subversive than Camerini's *Il cappello*, though *Corona*, too, naturalizes the conflicts.

King Sedemondo has ravaged his brother's kingdom and killed his brother, Licinio. Both his wife and his brother's give birth to children who are destined to play an important role in the future of the kingdom. Sedemondo is intent on destroying the iron crown that has been sent by the Emperor of Byzantium to the Pope in Rome. He attempts to bury it forever in a huge gorge at Natersea, but it becomes embedded in the stone. Forced to abandon it, he places the gorge in the care of a giant who is ordered to kill interlopers attempting to enter. Moreover, seeking to solidify his rule, he banishes the young Arminio who is destined to overthrow Sedemondo. Earlier, his wife and Licinio's had arranged to deceive Sedemondo, making him believe that Arminio, Licinio's son, was really his. Enraged when he learns of the deception, Sedemondo banishes the child, telling a slave to take him to the Valley of the Lions where Sedemondo expects him to perish. The slave is killed by the giant's arrow and thus no one can report to Sedemondo about Arminio's fate. In order to protect himself from the return of Arminio and the fulfillment of the prophecy, which also predicts that Arminio and his daughter Elsa will marry, Sedemondo locks Elsa up in a palace behind three impenetrable iron gates.

The film moves ahead twenty years, showing Arminio

(Massimo Girotti), now fully grown. He has learned to survive in this wild environment, where his companions are the animals. This pastoral idyll is interrupted, however, by the appearance of a young woman, Tundra (Luisa Ferida), who is the sworn enemy of Sedemondo. She is a young amazon who enlists Arminio to fight with her against King Sedemondo in a tournament to be held at Kindaor, the capital. The prize of the tournament is Elsa (Elisa Cegani). Sedemondo receives news that the Valley of the Lions has collapsed as a result of an earthquake and, relieved that Arminio is finally destroyed, calls for all the gates to be opened.

Taking advantage of this opportunity, Elsa slips away from the palace and meets Arminio, and they fall in love. Arminio participates in the tournament, which is presented as a lavish spectacle with processions, flags, beautiful costumes, ornate armor, and gaudy helmets. Long shots of the field of combat, low- and high-angle shots of victors and vanquished, and dynamic editing characterize these episodes. After severe trials in which he is almost overcome, Arminio wins against the superior weapons of his experienced opponents. He wins Elsa but refuses to accept his prize, asking rather that Elsa herself be free to choose her husband. She chooses Arminio, and Sedemondo, unaware of his identity, is delighted.

The question of identity surfaces when Arminio and Elsa discover similar scars from being whipped as children. They believe they are brother and sister. Driven almost to madness by this thought, Elsa flees to the gorge where she is mortally wounded. Sedemondo, who has learned the truth about Arminio, becomes insane but, over the body of the dead Elsa, a reconciliation takes place between the warring groups. At that moment, the iron crown appears. As the prophecy ordained, Arminio is decreed the new king. Tundra, now chastened, stands by his side, and the epilogue reads, "And thus the iron crown could take up its journey to Rome once more."

The motifs in the film are drawn from romance and fairy tale: the sundering of siblings, the abducted child, the prophetic old woman, the feral child, the sleeping beauty, the young Amazonian warrior, mistaken identity, the magical crown, the conflict between rival kings, the mystical bond between animals and humans, giants, the tournament and trials of identity, the competition of suitors for the princess' hand, and the wasteland regenerated by the potency of the young hero. The style of the film with its fusion of myth and history, the Byzantine and Roman past with the mythical kingdom of Kindaor, is heavily dependent on the visual spectacle richly evoked by Blasetti, on the exoticism of setting, costume, and character. Like the fairy tale, too, the parabolic elements of responsible and irresponsible authority make themselves felt. Interspersed throughout the film is the text from the ancient "legend" of the iron crown, acting as a choric commentator on the action. The editing of the film depends on parallelism, balance, contrast, and comparison. The opening and closing of the film are contrasted; the gorge is shown three times; the number of gates enclosing the palace are three, the old woman's prophecies are tripled and evenly interspersed through the film; the shots of the tournament are balanced in such a way as to convey the sense of ceremony.

The role of the men within the film is schematic. Rather than portraying the conversion of the erring authority figure, Blasetti uses a scheme that balances the tyrant against the natural leader, the older man against the young man. Sedemondo's crimes are multiple: fratricide, attempted infanticide, misappropriation of the land, repression of his people, oppression of his daughter, and desecration of the sacred unity of Church and state. The illegitimacy of his rule is conveyed through the symbol of the iron crown and his attempt to destroy it. In its reappearance, concomitant with Elsa's martyrdom and the designation of Arminio as successor, legitimate authority is restored. The film thus seems to offer a strong critique of the abuse of power, using the elements of spectacle so often associated with the fascist cinema to criticize that power. Yet consonant with Blasetti's earlier films is the film's magical belief in beneficent leadership, tempered by adversity, rooted in nature, chivalry, and altruism. This form of leadership, similar to the Duke's in *Terra madre*, is responsive to the people and the means of deliverance from tyranny.

Thus, at the same time that the film offers a critique of power, it safely stays within the orbit of accepted values, offering little offense to the censor. The fairy-tale, mythic quality helps to conceal any specific allusions, allowing the film to be read on face value as a timeless protest against tyranny. The film's trappings of ceremony function in an equally ambiguous manner. Ceremony functions in the film in conjunction with Sedemondo's reign of terror and is contrasted to the natural environment associated with Arminio and Tundra. On the level of form, it is possible to see the film acting as a critique of the ceremonies and rituals used to maintain public power. By 1941, Blasetti had become disillusioned with fascism and it would seem that *Corona di ferro* tentatively and cautiously inscribes his disaffection.[22]

Mario Soldati's *Quartieri alti* also appears critical of existing social relations, but this dour comedy focuses more narrowly on the domestic sphere and on the protagonist's change of heart. The central figure, Giorgio (Massimo Serato), is the familiar libertine who, with his family, lives off the income of the rich, avoiding any productive work and seeking only to gratify personal desire. Giorgio is led to confront his opportunism, lack of commitment, and irresponsibility. As in so many films of the era, the element of disguise is important. The role of the impostor and a preoccupation with inauthenticity seems to gain in importance in the films of the early forties. Visually the film conveys enclosed quarters, cramped rooms, and framed perspectives. The characters are involved in spying on each other. The central image of the film, the revolving doors of the hotel, is like a coda for the film's movement, conveying desperation, loss of direction, and circularity.

Giorgio rents a house in order to impress a young woman, Isabella, with his respectability. He also hires a butler, a catering service, and two actors to play his mother and father. Giorgio coaches them in their parts, directing them to avoid extravagant behavior and to present themselves as calm, pro-

---

[22] Savio, *Cinecittà anni trenta*, 1:45.

vincial, and domesticated. The woman must be a "good, devoted mother" and the father properly stuffy. However, before the young woman arrives, Giorgio is called away to the
telephone at the tobacconist's. He learns that he must return
to his hotel immediately or his relationship (and his parents')
with Lina, a wealthy older woman who supports Giorgio and
his family, will be jeopardized. He rushes to his car, thinking
to make it to the hotel and back in time. At the hotel, hysteria
prevails. Lina is about to go out with another man, while
Giorgio's mother and father and the other sycophants in the
household who depend on the continuance of Giorgio's relationship with Lina are frantic that she will abandon them
and find a new lover. If Giorgio does not return soon, they
will all be penniless. Lina's entourage lounges about discon-
solately, complaining about their fate: they are less protected,
they assert, than workers who have been fired. The father is
annoyed, inconvenienced, since he had wanted to go to the
opera. Giorgio finds Lina and pacifies her momentarily. They
quarrel again over Giorgio's inattentiveness. A shot is heard
by the others and Lina is found by a resident nurse. Giorgio
has left her to return to Isabella.

In Giorgio's absence, the "parents" entertain Isabella, who
learns by eavesdropping that the hospitality has been a performance. Isabella offers to pay the staff for their efforts. She
gives them money and they leave. Roberto, Giorgio's brother,
arrives and tells her that this episode is typical of Giorgio,
hoping to discourage her. Roberto roughly pushes the rocking
chair that Giorgio had earlier identified as the proper symbol
of calmness and domesticity.

The family arrives and Isabella is again told, this time by
Barbara, Roberto's wife, that it would be better if she left. But
Isabella is not easily dissuaded. Giorgio enters, wounded, and
asks to speak to Isabella alone. Unaware that Barbara is
trapped and unable to exit from the room without revealing
himself, Giorgio confesses to his relationship with Lina. He
tells her that he invented the story of a happy home life, but
that his life is marginal. He and his parents lead a life of
dependency and contingency. In contrast, her life is respect-

able, and a marriage between them would not work. She insists, however, that their relationship can work if there is love, but he, wishing to protect her, says he does not love her and advises her to leave.

Barbara, who has heard the conversation, tells him afterward that the bourgeois life he described sounded good, and she urges him to get away. At the hotel, Lina, unscathed, tells Giorgio's parents that she wants to marry him. Roberto informs Giorgio of the marriage offer, and the men quarrel over Giorgio's refusal to marry Lina. He plans instead to marry Isabella and begin a new life.

Soldati's film exhibits the same bias as many of Camerini's against the aristocracy and *haut monde* who are portrayed as manipulative, self-aggrandizing, decadent, and even violent. Soldati does nothing to make them appear attractive or to encourage a sense of voyeurism about the glamor of wealth and status. Opposing the vision of decadence are other, bourgeois values embodied in Isabella, namely, monogamy, security, and work. Giorgio is situated between those opposing attitudes, and he finally exposes the latter. The equation between sex and money is clear as the parents coerce their son into male prostitution.

The familiar motif of disguise, of imposture, is repeated in Soldati's film, Giorgio's life being presented at first as an exercise in role-playing and hypocrisy. His struggle involves the quest for legitimacy and authenticity. His real family represents the actual relations of economic exploitation and control as his parents use their son to enhance their own interests. The mythical family that Giorgio constructs for himself in order to "entertain" Isabella is, like the film, a fiction, and the film's reflexivity serves to underscore the idea that idyllic family life is fictional.

The narrative structure is developed through oppositions between characters such as Roberto and Giorgio, Isabella and Lina, and the real parents and the paid actor-parents, through settings such as between the hotel and the villa; and through thematic oppositions between the idea of playacting and of social realities. None of these oppositions is reconciled; the polarities remain intact. The narrative energy is devoted rather to exposing the economic underbelly of the family, the exploitation and violence that are part of domestic relations. Within this context, Giorgio's conversion can be read as a gesture of capitulation. His wound, created by Lina, the representative of the unscrupulous upper class, is a symbolic wound. The Don Juan is tamed and disciplined into bourgeois responsibility, and the women, Isabella and Barbara, are placed in the familiar positions of nurses and guardians. The male learns the safety of the home, but the conversion looks less like romantic transcendence and more like a retreat from conflict.

Giorgio's transformation bears few of the signs of the other dramas of conversion that emphasize heroic commitment, asceticism, or public leadership. The film's "reconciliation" has none of the playful features exhibited in Camerini's films as they evolve their communities of people with like-minded histories and interests. In this respect, Soldati's film seems to be closer to the concerns of a film like Visconti's *Ossessione*, where the main characters' struggles for legitimacy, and to escape the entrapments of economic and psychic dependence are, within the context of the claustrophobic world presented, doomed to failure. The conflict in Soldati's film arises from a character's desire to be extricated from exploitation and oppression. Giorgio's movement toward respectability constitutes a frail and insufficient gesture when measured against the decadence represented by his parents and by Lina. Moreover, his retreat to a modest position of work and respectability represents, on the one hand, a form of nostalgia; on the other hand, a critique of the status quo.

If the films of conversion chart the rejuvenation of a male figure who undergoes a series of transformations that provide him with a sense of identity and purpose, enable him to enter the world of other men, and reconcile him to the demands of domestic life, Poggioli's *Il cappello del prete* (The Priest's Hat), like Soldati's film, operates in a reverse direction. The dark world portrayed in this 1943 film is far removed from the conventional expectations of marriage, family, respect for tradition, work, and collective effort. This film dissects forms of obsessional behavior. The characters are acquisitive, dishonest, and aggressive. The tone of the film is grimly humorous, a satire that attacks individuals and institutions. A nobleman and a priest are the dominant players in this film based on a novel by Emilio di Marchi. Poggioli's penchant for drawing on literary works is again validated by *Il cappello*.

The Marquis, played by Luigi Almirante, lives a dissolute life devoted to gambling. His addiction to the casino keeps him in debt and forces him into conflict with creditors and with an unscrupulous priest. The priest is portrayed as sinister and avaricious, eager to get every cent he can. He visits the Marquis's family home, which is bereft of furniture or ornament, everything having been sold to pay for the nobleman's habits. The priest's visit is for the purpose of appraising the house, which he has sold for the Marquis. While in the courtyard, the Marquis pushes the priest into a well and takes the money from the sale of the house. He embarks again on his pastimes, going to the theater, entertaining women, and gambling. The priest is discovered by the nephew of the old family retainer who takes him to his quarters where Don Cirillo dies. The nephew also retrieves the priest's hat. News of the priest's death spreads, and the nephew is wrongly accused of killing the priest. The Marquis does not confess his crime, but is willing to let the innocent man be prosecuted. The priest's hat becomes the means of detecting the actual culprit, and the Marquis is arrested as he is about to take a trip with a woman.

The film's opening scenes, of a hand holding cards and then of the Marquis with the other men displaying his bravado in the face of losing, foreshadows the film's preoccupation with money and with a society that is addicted to commercial transactions. The image of gambling applies not only to the nobleman but to the other figures in the film, including the priest. Poggioli even includes a public raffle where a poor man and his children suffer as he waits for the announcement of the winning number.

The use of shadows conveys the sinister sense of the environment and the individuals who inhabit it. In the earliest sequence in the Marquis's room, the shadow of the window blinds on the floor creates the effect of bars and is visually linked to the playing cards that lay scattered about. The arrival of Don Cirillo is announced by the shadow of his head with his broad-brimmed priest's hat, and this image is repeated later in the film with another priest. The hat not only signifies the priest's office, but associates that office with the idea of stalking, of hunting, and becomes the symbol of retribution. An ambiguous symbol at that, it is associated with the avaricious priest but also with the detection of the crime and justice.

The image of concealing and withholding is equally important. The priest withholds money from the nobleman. Don Cirillo's papers and money are concealed under his bed. The Marquis seeks to hide a portrait of his mother from the acquisitive priest. He also seeks to hide the body and to conceal the priest's hat by throwing it in the river. And, of course, he seeks to hide his complicity in the crime. Like *film noir*, *Il cappello* plays with chiaroscuro light, with tight framing of characters, with claustrophobic settings, and with shadows, portraits, and reflections in order to visualize a world that is comprised of hunters and hunted, in fact, in which all the people are hunters who prey on each other, a world where guilt and innocence is unclear and where it is only by accident that misdeeds are uncovered.

*Il cappello* identifies the source of corruption as the dissolute upper classes and ineffectual, if not malevolent, clergy. The Marquis has gambled away his patrimony and there is no longer any sense of tradition and continuity. His house is empty of contents and even the money for the sale of the house is squandered. The old retainer and his nephew are presented as the innocent victims of the Marquis's indifference and decadence. The nephew is almost destroyed by the nobleman's lack of moral fiber. Although justice is ultimately effected, the world is not rejuvenated. One crime may be detected but the corruption seems uncontained. The only hope resides in the workings of coincidence or chance. The

truth surfaces not because of the heroic efforts of any individual, but because it is impossible to conceal everything.

The motif of conversion, so dependent on the elevation of
exceptional individuals and on the idea of a world where
social and political values can be clearly assigned and validated, is alien to this film. The central figure is locked into
his obsession and incapable and unwilling to find alternatives.
His world is also intractable, a relentless and inhumane environment, mirroring his own obsessions. Like so many other
films of 1943, *Il cappello del prete* portrays a deformed world
deprived of humanity, of understanding, and of feeling.[23]
While the film seems to take a strong moral stance as do other
Poggioli films, pointing a finger at contemporary abuses, it
also seems to communicate its own form of nostalgia and its
entrapment in a hopeless and fantastic environment.

## Summary

The representations of men are evidence of changing forms
of narrativization and of ideological shifts. The films of the
thirties are the closest to traditional images, archetypes, and
plots. Nonetheless, these films are not mere escapist vehicles.
In their very uses and abuses of tradition, they provide a way
of identifying an uneasy balance between tradition, resistance
to change, and flirtation with modernization. They provide
insight into the contradictory relations between men and
women and involve an excessive attention to the appearance
of conformity, if not actual conformity. The male protagonist
is a renegade, the female, the agent of discipline. Though
these films resolve their conflicts through the restoration of
domestic peace, they also expose how the domestic sphere is
an important arena of conflict.

The conversion narratives also highlight sexual conflict,
and, more often than not, the female's position is subordinated. She is excluded, desexualized, and confined to the
domestic sphere. Images of desire associated with females are
transferred to nature or to the machine. Love between men

---

[23] Brunetta, *Storia del cinema*, p. 508.

and women is transferred to male attachments, and the "new" relationships involve variations of the relations between father and son. The equation between sexual deprivation and aggression could not be more evident. These narratives reveal that the new world is only a variation of the old, and the "new man" like the machines he employs is an instrument for familiar forms of exploitation and even destruction.

The films of the early forties are different. They appear to challenge the forms and attitudes represented in the images of men and their world. Though highly stylized, at a great remove from the realist aesthetic, these films, least of all the films produced during the decade, can be considered escapist. For example, Aprà and Pistagnesi redeem Soldati's work from the charges of mere formalism. By reading his films in a metaphoric vein, they find "the dissolution of all values, . . . the explosion of passions that lead to death."[24] Moreover, such concerns are not unique to Soldati's work but are also evident in the films of Poggioli, Palermi, and, of course, Visconti. Their creation of character and setting, especially of male character, seems to be engaged in dialogue with the obvious ideology of the conversion dramas and the comedies. Certainly, these films are juxtaposed to the familialism of fascist ideology and its elevation of heroic sacrifice. In these later films, men are not heroes; the world is not so easily amenable to change. The films aggressively portray the resurgence of sexuality. Money is important enough to cause men to commit murder, and violence is not easily channelled into the heroic enterprise of war. In short, the style and the tone of the films appears to have much in common with the French *films noirs* of Carné and Duvivier.

[24] Aprà and Pistagnesi, *I favolosi anni trenta*, p. 10.

# Genres

# CHAPTER FOUR

# The Forms of History

U NDER fascism the role of the past and tradition was fundamental, not only for the fascist party and the regime, but for Italian educational and cultural institutions as well. Yet, as George Mosse queries: "Was the fascist man then tied to the past or was he the creator of new values?"[1] The answer to the question is, however, neither simple nor unambiguous. Mosse asserts that

the new fascist man in Italy ignored history no more than his Nazi counterpart. . . . this past remained, at least until the final years of the regime, a jumping-off point for the ideal fascist man of the future. Tradition informed his consciousness, but he himself had to rise beyond it without losing sight of his starting point. Such a flexible attitude toward the ideal reflected the greater openness of Italian fascism to the new in both art and literature.[2]

"Tradition" acted as a brake on the dangerous elements linking fascism to ideas of revolutionary struggle and to revolutionary rhetoric. One had to be a revolutionary and a traditionalist at the same time. The important objective was to separate ideas of revolutionary change from their specifically Marxian grounding. This separation was most obvious in the sloughing off of concepts of class consciousness and class conflict, elevating instead the idea of "the people." Past history thus served to create a sense of destiny, of common purpose, aimed toward the future and producing the "new man" whose life was consecrated to the service of the harmonious community and reborn in a struggle for national glory. This community was at first defined by the regime in

[1] George L. Mosse, *Masses and Man: Nationalist and Fascist Perceptions of Reality* (New York: Howard Fertig, 1980), p. 186.

[2] Ibid., p. 187.

terms of the struggle for economic and political renewal, later in terms of expansionism and war.

As part of its effort to achieve consensus, fascist ideology suppressed working-class opposition, discredited liberal institutions, invoked anticapitalist, populist rhetoric, and sought to merge working class and petty bourgeoisie in the common goals of hard work, increased productivity, the subordination of private and class interest to the public interest, submission to authority and loyalty to the nation. Toward these ends, the "lessons of history" were to be applied. Mosse argues that in this respect, Italian fascism was not a unique phenomenon:

> The frequent contention that fascism diverged from the mainstream of European culture cannot be upheld; on the contrary, it absorbed most of what had (or proved to have) the greatest mass appeal in the past. In fact, it positioned itself much more in this mainstream than socialism which tried to educate and elevate the tastes of the worker. Fascism made no such attempt: it accepted the common man's references and went on to direct them to its own ends.[3]

Mosse indicates that fascist ideology was rooted in a conception of "the people" rather than in the concept of class, using populist notions for nationalist, capitalist, and imperialist purposes.

The historical films provide corroboration for this point of view. Their themes and treatments involve uses of the past to inscribe generational conflict, expansionism, fusion of the exceptional individual with the people, questions of legitimate and illegitimate authority. Through the recuperation of history these films attempt to create a sense of the naturalness, appropriateness, and inevitability of fascism. As Jean Gili notes, "Against particularism, provincialism, dialects, fascism wanted a people originated from the same land, the same history, who speak the same language, under the proud eyes

[3] Ibid., p. 183.

of a single father, the ultimate incarnation of all tutelary fathers in Italian history, of all national heroes."[4]

In assessing the historical eras represented in these films, Gili notes that in spite of Mussolini's preference for antiquity and the reflection of this predilection in education and in contemporary architecture, the films on antiquity were few.[5] The most well-known of these films are *Nero* (1930), *The Birth of Salome* (1940), *The Trial and Death of Socrates* (1940), and, of course, *Scipio Africanus*. Films on the Middle Ages were rare, while films on the Renaissance were abundant, the Renaissance era being portrayed as the period of Italy's intellectual, artistic, and political supremacy. Films on the nineteenth century were also quite abundant, stressing the Risorgimento and *la belle époque*, nationalism and the struggle for the unification of Italy. Unlike the films on the Renaissance, which lend themselves to heroic achievements and opulent spectacle, the films on the Risorgimento present their history in dynamic fashion, stressing the overcoming of class struggle, the forging of a popular movement, the participation of the masses, and the continuity of change. Thus, the aims of fascism and these earlier struggles could be blended.

After examining these historical and costume productions, it is possible to differentiate objectives. For some films, the overriding concern is the transmission of propaganda through creating historical parallels between past and present; others use their subject matter as a way of escaping from the present into the past; and still others use past history as an indirect vehicle for criticizing contemporary Italian society and politics. The existence of such different treatments poses the following questions, articulated by Gian Piero Brunetta: "Where does propaganda leave off and pure spectacle begin? Where does the fascist production end and the antifascist or non-

---

[4] Jean A. Gili, "Film storico e film in costume," in *Cinema italiano sotto il fascismo*, ed. Riccardo Redi (Venice: Marsilio, 1979), p. 143.

[5] Ibid., p. 134.

fascist production begin?"[6] An analysis of these films may help to answer these questions.

In reopening the question of the relationship between the historical films and fascist ideology, I want to emphasize that I am not reading these films as mere exemplars of fascist propaganda. The relationship between ideology and history is not unique to the cinema produced under fascism. The popular cinema of all countries is closely linked to national history and mythology, and the Italian films of the thirties and forties are no exception. An interrogation of the films' uses of history should illuminate not only what is endemic to fascism but should also reveal where and how the discourse of fascism converges with, even grows from, already existing and even dominant ideological discourse.

The historical film was not invented by the cinema but has roots in nineteenth-century prose narratives, folklore, theater, and painting. John Fell, in *Film and the Narrative Tradition*, commenting on the eclecticism of the cinema, says that "the movies, free to prance in youthful spirits on the playgrounds of time and space . . . only needed to appropriate from everybody else's game and then to evolve a consistent set of ground rules."[7] The free "play" alluded to by Fell is not to be construed as an abandonment of history. The cinema as a popular folk art is, in fact, history. Like other genre films, the historical film is most revealing as a social text, a social text whose significance lies less in its fidelity to temporal events and more as a narrative enactment, for better or worse, of collective desire.

Fredric Jameson has urged that "genres are essentially lit-

---

[6] Gian Piero Brunetta, *Storia del cinema italiano 1895-1945* (Rome: Riuniti, 1979), p. 383.

[7] John L. Fell, *Film and the Narrative Tradition* (Norman: University of Oklahoma Press, 1974), xiii. Also according to Paul Monaco, "A body of motion pictures brings into the world a powerful enactment of collective psychic energy. It does so through its symbolic functions which mediate between the source of unconscious energy and the realities in which that energy is discovered." "Movies and National Consciousness," in *Feature Film as History*, ed. K.R.M. Short (Knoxville: University of Tennessee Press, 1981), p. 66.

eracy institutions, or social contracts between a writer and a specific public, whose function is to specify the proper use of a cultural artifact." Jameson seeks to historicize genre practices, "to use the narrative raw material shared by myth and 'historical' literatures to sharpen our sense of historical difference, and to stimulate an increasingly vivid apprehension of what happens when a plot enters into history, so to speak, and enters the force field of modern societies."[8] Genre practices arise from history and remain continuously sensitive to historical change in spite of the seeming "universality" of their narrative forms. For example, in his study of Hollywood genres, Thomas Schatz comments that "the earliest westerns (many of which actually depicted then-current events) obviously were based on historical and social reality. But as the genre developed, it gradually took on its own reality."[9]

Historical situations, personages, and settings are, moreover, a powerful means for creating audience identification, drawing on common sources of knowledge. The popularity in Italy of such writers of historical fiction as Massimo D'Azeglio, Francesco Guerrazzi, Tommasso Grossi, and Alessandro Manzoni and of their subjects was amply exploited in the cinema.[10] The accessibility of historical material, its familiarity, was an important tool in the creation of broader audience participation. Equally important are the ways in which the history is presented. Not all historical films are epics. Not all costume films are historical films. In short, the uses of history in the films represent different treatments and different points of view.

In discussing the uses of history in the films of the fascist era, Jean Gili proposes that a distinction be made between the uses of the more or less distant past and contemporary history. Moreover, he distinguishes between historical and

[8] Fredric Jameson, *The Political Unconscious: Narrative as a Socially Symbolic Act* (Ithaca: Cornell University Press, 1981), p. 130.

[9] Thomas Schatz, *Hollywood Genres: Formulas, Filmmaking, and the Studio System* (New York: Random House, 1981), p. 36.

[10] Richard Gamett, *A History of Italian Literature* (Port Washington, N.Y.: Kennikat Press, 1970), p. 349.

costume dramas. The former category refers to those films that treat precise historical situations: war, biographies of famous persons, and important moments from political history. The latter is based more often on novelistic materials that do not require the creator to adhere faithfully to a particular period. The characters are fictional, and the necessity for remaining strictly within the historical context is not mandatory. Gili asserts, too, that historical and costume dramas are not restricted to one genre but cut across genres such as musicals, melodramas, comedies, adventure films, and so on. Gili's comments and taxonomic distinctions serve as a reminder of the numerous ways history is inscribed in the Italian cinema.

Prior to the fascist era, the Italian film industry had specialized in historical films, the most notable being *The Taking of Rome, Cabiria,* and *The Last Days of Pompeii.* The production of such films during the twenties and thirties remained modest but in 1941-42, the number increased dramatically until Pavolini, the minister of culture, had to curb the production and to insist on films with a modern context.[11] The historical and costume films can be subdivided into the following categories: 1) those films that deal with the lives of illustrious historical figures; 2) those films that focus on individual figures but within the broader context of significant historical events, linking the individual actions to general political problems in which the focus is on the socialization of the individual, the insertion of the individual in the collectivity as represented in the personal and public spheres; and 3) those costume films where there is no absolute connection between the plot and the history but there is a tie in different ways and for different reasons to accessory facts.[12]

The increase in historical films prompted Pavolini to say that Italians had history in their blood, but the actual reasons for the rise in production of such films was, in fact, more practical and more ideologically complex.

Embedded in the traditions of Italian cinema, the historical

[11] Gili, "Film storico e film in costume," p. 131.
[12] Ibid., pp. 130-131.

film was a guarantor of economic success. Moreover, since a technology had been developed over the years at such studios as Cines and Tirrenia, along with professional set designers, costuming specialists, and cinematographers, it was easy to produce these films. Yet the more fundamental reasons for the growth of these films can be located in the politics of the form. These films enabled filmmakers to treat issues of an ideological nature and most particularly issues concerning contemporary events, either as they legitimate the dominant ideological direction or as they subtly erode prevailing attitudes.[13]

An historical film that develops the role of tradition as a source of cultural identity is Alessandro Blasetti's *Palio* (1931). The film is a celebration of men in groups, of sport as a test of manliness and physical prowess, and of the vitality of Italian regional traditions. The ancient horserace around which the narrative is organized serves a dual purpose of experimenting with a different kind of historical film and of linking that experimentation to new forms of political discourse. The film is a blend of fiction and documentary, spectacle and indirect polemic. Past and present are fused in the film's insistence on the continuity of the event.

The film reenacts the traditional ceremony of the Palio, the ancient race that takes place in Siena, because as the prologue reads, it is "typical of the combatative spirit of our people." At the time of the Palio, "the same burning passion unites all [classes] in work." In order to lend drama to the spectacle, Blasetti attaches a plot of romance and intrigue. The hero, Zarre (Guido Celano), one of the major contenders, has a falling-out with his fiancée, Fiora (Leda Gloria). Jealous and angry, he flirts with another woman who is a decoy for unscrupulous elements who want Zarre out of the race. He is kidnapped during the night on his way to a clandestine meeting with the woman and injured. He is hospitalized and it looks as if he will be unable to take his place at the race.

---

[13] James Hay, *Popular Film Culture in Fascist Italy* (Bloomington: Indiana University Press, 1986), p. 186.

Distraught upon learning what has happened to her lover, Fiora tries unsuccessfully to see him. Zarre, now conscious, struggles to get out of bed and take his place at the event. With the help of a sympathetic doctor, Zarre dresses himself and goes to the piazza, where he is victorious in the race. He and Fiora are reunited amidst a scene of jubilant celebration.

The film divides its interest between the ceremony and the straightforward narrative. The processions, the ritual of the flags, the drum-playing, the chants, and the traditional uniforms are in the forefront, reminding the viewer of the past and of the continuity of the event. The spectacle romanticizes past tradition and custom, competition, and male prowess. The event becomes a symbol of a way of life. The aura of excitement and festivity enhances daily life. The contemporary world is rooted in the past and in collectivity. The event unites aristocrat and workers in a common purpose. Class differences are a source of conflict between Zarre and Fiora. His jealousy is aroused by attentions paid to her by one of the upper-class guests, but these conflicts are overcome in the lovers' dedication to the event. As in so many Blasetti films, class and sexual differences are stressed merely to portray them as surmountable through adherence to a larger purpose.

*Palio* seems consonant with the aims of the Dopolavoro, the hybrid organization, sponsored by the Fascist party, the state, and private initiative, which sought to direct after-work, mass cultural activities, at least as applied to men, in its celebration of sports, and spectatorship. *Palio* also reveals a basic contradiction of fascism. On the one hand, through emphasis on the idea of "many participants and few spectators . . . Dopolavoro sports were not to encourage the ethos of aggressive individuality" but a sense of "team spirit" and collectivity.[14] Moreover, the object of public entertainment and recreation as articulated by fascist functionaries was "the formation of a new national culture that would transcend class

[14] Victoria de Grazia, *The Culture of Consent: Mass Organization of Leisure in Fascist Italy* (Cambridge: Cambridge University Press, 1981), p. 165.

and regional boundaries."[15] Yet, as the content and the style of Blasetti's film indicates, many were called but few were chosen. The unity emphasized in the film's narrative is undercut by the spectacle that divides the exceptional heroic individual from the crowd. The crowd scenes within the film and the treatment of the external audience emphasize mass forms of entertainment through spectacle.

Blasetti's montage treatment of the preparations, the processions, the ritual, the race itself, creates a sense of intensity and visual splendor, reinforcing further the idea of spectatorship as opposed to participation. The film's diversionary dimension can be traced to another form of entertainment under fascism, namely the Dopolavoro emphasis on tourism. Like so many other films of the era, the film's re-creation of the sense of place enhances the idea of spectatorship. The audience not only is a spectator at the Palio but a visitor to Siena as all the familiar landmarks are shown, and the external audience, like the audience within the film, are united in this summer tour of the town of Siena.

In this film, which purports to dramatize a significant Italian sports event, the filmmaker conveyed a number of messages familiar to the historical epic: the greatness of Italy, the role of tradition, the value of physical strength and skill, the need to root out dissident and disruptive elements, the desirability of transcending social differences, and the role of the masses as spectators in witnessing the continuity of the past and the celebration of greatness.

*1860*, directed by Blasetti in 1934, draws on popular history. Set during the Risorgimento and focusing on the struggle for national unity, *1860* depends on familiar Blasetti techniques to involve the audience in its portraits of exceptional individuals and heroic action. More than his later film *Ettore Fieramosca*, *1860* emphasizes the role of the peasants and common people in Italian history. The film also highlights the importance of mass action over individual heroic effort. Because of its Risorgimento context and because of its emphasis on col-

---

[15] Ibid., p. 165.

lective struggle, *1860* gives the illusion of being a revolutionary film.

The editing in the film is dynamic and enhances the film's ostensible "revolutionary" point of view. The indebtedness to Soviet montage reveals the Italian cinema's openness to other filmic techniques, thus suggesting the eclectic approach of filmmakers of the period. Most significantly, the argument that fascist ideology was often populist in origin can be supported through an examination of Blasetti's film. While the film satirizes bourgeois intellectuals, its emphasis on national unity, on consensus, on interclass unity differentiates it from Soviet models. The Marxist emphasis on class consciousness and class struggle is absent, revealing that the filmmaker's use of montage is directed rather toward portraying undifferentiated collective political action. Blasetti's use of Soviet montage reveals, however, that it was possible to experiment with this form of filmmaking. The film's style, sitting as it does alongside the use of American, German, and Hungarian models, documents a certain degree of diversity in Italian filmmaking practices.

The film uses history to draw parallels between the political struggles of the Risorgimento and the fascist nationalist enterprise, stressing continuity with the earlier historical era. Blasetti embeds political elements in spectacle and action. *1860* is like a vast, moving version of a nineteenth-century heroic painting.[16] The actors are portrayed as heroes, shot from low angles in diagonal compositions, looking upward, arms often upraised. Group compositions are choreographed, moving in diagonal lines toward a common objective. The camera seeks out the major figures who are part of the larger collectivity. The film begins with intercut scenes of riders, flames, ruins, soldiers, and peasants, and takes advantage of different planes of action and varying camera angles to present abundant images of sky and earth. Images of the peasants and of the priest reveal close-knit and affectionate relationships. In

---

[16] Angela Dalle Vacche, "Blasetti's *1860*" (paper presented at a meeting of the American Association of Italian Studies, Bloomington, Ind. April 1984).

spite of the hardships sustained, the peasants hold to the hope that Garibaldi will come to their aid, news having arrived that he has returned to Italy and is shortly expected in Sicily. With his arrival, the foreigners, the Bourbons, will be driven out.

Before his arrival, however, the peasants are shown being rounded up and tortured by the Bourbons. Carmeliddu (Giuseppe Gulino) avoids the mass roundup and escapes to secure aid in bringing Garibaldi to Italy. At the village, the peasants are mourning a dead child, when the soldiers break in and interrogate the priest who ministers to the dead child.

In a scene that marks a thematic transition from country to town, Carmeliddu arrives in Civitavecchia. Blasetti focuses on the street and on an outdoor café where groups of men sit discussing politics. He develops a contrast between Southern and Northern Italians as well as between peasants and townspeople. The film favors the peasant Carmeliddu over the more sophisticated people in the town. The men he makes contact with are better educated and more stylishly dressed in contrast to his rustic outfit and manners but are made to appear foppish and even a bit foolish by contrast.

Italian songs are interspersed throughout the film, especially nationalist songs, to enhance the film's patriotic themes, and to create identification with the action. By way of contrast to the urban scene, the action returns to the Sicilian village where the peasant men are lined up to be shot. Finally, the news is brought that Garibaldi has arrived, and the scene changes to the mobilization of his army, the thousand men that will go to Sicily to fight with him. A mother is shown kissing her young son farewell, as Carmeliddu observes them. The return journey to Sicily, associated earlier with Carmeliddu's isolated journey to the North, is now associated with collective action and with the unity of North and South as the boat carries the soldiers across the water to fulfill their heroic destiny.

Blasetti further intensifies the film's momentum as the villagers gather en masse, armed with sticks and farm implements, to fight the enemy. The soldiers attack the people and a battle ensues. Carmeliddu and the other men arrive in time to defend the beleaguered peasants. He and Gesuzza (Aida Bellia) are reunited. In a pastoral setting, abundant with flowers, Carmeliddu informs her of the impending battle and of the arrival of Garibaldi. Blasetti focuses on the supporters of Garibaldi who are portrayed as lighthearted and eagerly anticipating the battle.

The battle scene at Catalafimi is portrayed through images of Italian flags, sounds of martial music, and alternating shots between the opposing factions, replete with smoke and images of men in small groups as they fight. Gesuzza, an observer of the fighting, stops to tend a wounded man who dies in her arms. The news of Garibaldi's arrival is signalled by the waving of an Italian flag that had earlier fallen. Garibaldi himself is not shown, but his presence is conveyed through the responses of the men, the radiant image of one man with the Italian flag, and the facial expressions of his troops.

The foreigners are driven out by the united action of people from different parts of Italy, and Garibaldi, the leader, is the focal point of the action in the film's last moments. Blasetti has orchestrated a number of issues in the film that serve as analogies to the political situation in 1934: the role of "the people" in the glorious history of Italy and its heroic attempts to forge national unity, a unification effected through the collaboration of worker, peasant, and bourgeois, the idea that the rural element was the main force for Italian unity and the most militant nationalist element, the elevation of war and sacrifice as the essential component of national unity, the important motivating dimension of the leadership principle as supported by mass consensus, and a legitimation of basic social institutions, namely the family and the clergy. The film's idealizing of rural elements is conveyed in several ways: the dramatic landscape shots, the central role of Carmeliddu and Gesuzza who are not played by stars, but, as in neorealism, are meant to be typical. Their physical appearance is calculated to create audience identification. Their rugged plainness distinguishes them from the more sophisticated characters in the film who appear by contrast to be effete.

The film's rhetorical strategies are intense. The music by Nino Medin appears calculated to arouse patriotic and sentimental responses from the viewer. The uses of posters, of a poster-style of composition, the uses of banners and flags, the use of the *mise-en-scène* to emulate painting, are some of the more obvious rhetorical ploys. The use of women as observers, as bereft but proud wives and mothers, and the use of young children and young men as willing defenders of the cause, as sacrificial victims, helps create an emotional bond, too. The spectacle itself with its choreographed battle scenes and dynamic movement, endows the history with a sense of grandeur.

Allegory is an important device for veiling political attitudes, and many of the films achieve the linkage between past and present in this manner. Moreover, the situating of the narrative in the context of earlier periods and the emphasis on the spectacular dimensions of that history serve the interests of indirect politicizing and of creating a community of spectators. *Lorenzino de' Medici* (1935), directed by Guido Brignone, is set in the Renaissance and based on actual historical events. The film focuses on political corruption and on the individuals who exemplify the forces of corruption as well as those who are responsible for eliminating social injustice and restoring order to Florentine society. The film exploits intrigue, violence, romance, and spectacle in its reconstruction of the Renaissance era. The issue of legitimate and illegitimate power, legitimate and illegitimate strategies of control, is embodied in the opposition between Lorenzino (Alexander Moisse) and Duke Alessandro (Camillo Pilotto).

Spies lurk in the recesses and shadows of the Florentine Piazza della Signoria. The head intriguer is Duke Alessandro, a vain, sensual, and opportunistic aristocrat who is supported by vicious, greedy, and self-serving men such as Francesco Guicciardini (Sandro Salvini). The oppositional forces, fomenting a conspiracy to overthrow the Duke, are headed by Paolo Strozzi (Uberto Palmarini). He and his supporters confront a formidable opponent who has at his disposal all the powers of the state. Lorenzino, an aide of the Duke and considered by Alessandro to be his most trusted counselor and friend, is secretly an ally of the Strozzi faction, in addition to being a suitor of Strozzi's daughter, Bianca (Germana Paolieri).

The rule of Duke Alessandro is portrayed as utterly corrupt. He is callous to the people who come to the court for justice and economic relief. Totally indifferent to the Church, openly defying a papal condemnation of his actions, he extorts wealth from his political opponents and uses torture to intimidate and suppress opposition to his tyranny. His lavish style of living is demonstrated in a banquet scene when Brignone exploits visual spectacle to portray the decadent life of the court.

Lorenzino continues to pretend to be the Duke's esteemed advisor though Bianca urges him to rebel against the Duke. He tells her, as he tells Strozzi and his men too, that he considers open rebellion at this point impossible. He considers the Duke's power greater than theirs. Strozzi is arrested and brought before Alessandro but refuses to subject himself to the Duke's power and judgment, preferring prison instead. Bianca comes to Lorenzino to plead for her father's release, and he counsels her to be patient. Alone, he examines a page from Machiavelli's *Prince*, which reveals the following words: "It is advantageous to bring on what may be cruel if in the interests of the subjects." Bianca arrives and Lorenzino repeats the words to her, informing her that he has a plan in mind that is devious but will be of assistance to her and her father.

He plans to decoy Alessandro to his house on the pretext that Bianca will be there and willing to submit to the Duke. The final segments of the film are introduced with images of a festival. The nighttime streets are filled with marching people, carrying torches and singing. Lorenzino, in his house, coaches Bianca in the plan for entrapping the Duke. As planned, the Duke gets a brief distant view of Bianca through a door left open intentionally by Lorenzino to whet the Duke's appetite. Alessandro lusts to consummate his desire for her. Before Lorenzino kills him, he coerces the Duke to sign a release for Strozzi. The sounds of the dying duke can be heard from the darkened room but they are drowned out by the sounds of the crowd. On a balcony at the Signoria, a proclamation is read, announcing the election of Cosimo as the head of the republic.

Historically, Cosimo was reputed to have extended the power and influence of Florence, territorially and commercially. He was also credited with having drained the marshes as Mussolini drained the Pontine marshes, and with introducing new forms of agriculture. In addition, he was the patron of such artists as Cellini and Bronzino. (Cellini is one of the Strozzi supporters in the film.) The implied connection between Mussolini's assumption of power and Cosimo's, between the accomplishments of the Renaissance leader and *il Duce*, are the nexus in the accommodation of past to present.

The character of Lorenzino is played by Alexander Moisse, an Austrian actor, while the Duke is played by Camillo Pilotto, an actor associated with historical and epic films. After Lorenzino, Pilotto was to play Hannibal in *Scipione l'Africano*. Maria Denis, who was to become a major star in the late thirties and early forties, plays Nella, the young peasant woman, and Bianca is played by Germana Paolieri. The acting in the film, as commented on by contemporary critics, is theatrical, and Moisse, in particular, seems to be acting for the stage rather than cinema. The narrative is structured rigidly and programmatically to develop the dominant themes, the character oppositions, and the historical "lessons."

*Lorenzino* blatantly uses its history for political purposes. The film is transparent as allegory in which the Renaissance events are to be read in terms of contemporary political parallels. The Florentine court under Alessandro represents, on the one hand, the prefascist era, and Alessandro, the corrupt, decadent, and tyrannical rule of that time. His arbitrary and cruel actions create political divisiveness and, most significantly, he does not rule in the best interests of the people. His wastefulness, inefficiency, and neglect of government for personal ends are highlighted.

Lorenzino, on the other hand, the student of Machiavelli,

relies on his wit, his knowledge of *Realpolitik*, his flair for
planning and executing successful strategies. He is an opportunist who takes advantage of events. His betrayal and
cruelty toward the Duke is exonerated in his destruction of a
tyrant. He is portrayed as striking a blow for justice. He elevates his commitment to the state, to family, and to comrades
above personal desire and conventional morality. In his person he symbolizes the proper nature of the leader, legitimating coercion, intrigue, and violence in the name of the people.
Lorenzino's role as midwife to Cosimo de' Medici and hence
the splendor of Tuscany serves as a parable for the historical
Italian quest for the development of economic, artistic, and
political superiority.

Though the film can be read as a revelation of the strategies
of fascism, revealing its opportunism, its elevation of individual subversion over collective resistance, its attempt to
legitimize personal violence in the interest of the state, ironically, to the present spectator, the character the most representative of Mussolini is not Lorenzino, though his character appears to compliment Mussolini's political acumen, but
Duke Alessandro. With his corrupt advisors, his use of the
resources of the state for his own ends, his disregard for the
needs of his subjects, his employment of force, Alessandro
seems most to embody the reality of fascism. The portrayal
of the enemies of the state appears more nearly an approximation of fascist strategies, whereas Lorenzino presents the
official image of its political strategies. Moreover, the film
seems to abandon one of the dominant myths of the left
fascists, that fascism was a mass movement, revealing instead
what was becoming more apparent by the mid-thirties, that
personal intrigue and select leadership were preferable to images of collectivity and consensus as represented by the
Strozzi faction.

Brignone's film uses past history to dramatize political intrigue. Alessandro Blasetti's *Ettore Fieramosca* (1938) is similarly preoccupied with political treachery and its eradication,
but celebrates military heroism in dramatic scenes of combat
and chivalric romance. The film, like *Lorenzino de' Medici*, is

set in the Renaissance. A contemporary critic described the film in the following manner: "The myth of *Ettore Fieramosca* is a total vindication of our national honor,"[17] and Edward R. Tannenbaum states:

> At the beginning of the film, Ettore is the cocky, aggressive 'Great Captain,' an Italian mercenary soldier of the Renaissance. Little by little, however, he becomes 'patriotic', and in a chivalric tournament his group of thirteen Italian mercenaries defeat thirteen French knights at Barletta, in Apulia, in 1503; as a result he also wins the Duchess of Monreale. Ettore and his mercenaries were a small part of the Spanish force fighting the French, but the film glorifies the Italian victory at Barletta.[18]

The film opens on a scene of two French aristocrats discussing the fate of the Duchy of Monreale and their contempt for Italian culture and especially the Italian language, which they disparage. Blasetti satirizes the French as effete, given over to pretentiousness, luxury, and viciousness. The main motif, however, developed through this interaction is the legitimacy of the Italian defense against such hostile forces. Significantly, the setting for this sequence is the city. As in so many Blasetti films, the city is the symbol of decadence, whereas the country, the pastoral landscape of the Duchy of Monreale, is the source of regeneration.

The initial images of the countryside show the routed populace, particularly the peasants, forced to evacuate their homes as a consequence of the military defeat of the Italians, as if to accentuate the contrast between the human devastation and the purity of the natural setting. Blasetti films this scene of war against the background of sky and clouds. The castle of Monreale is shown from different perspectives, accentuating its architectural beauty. Inside the fortress, the people are mobilizing. Giovanna (Elisa Cegani), the lady of Monreale, is photographed as she will be throughout the film, in low angle and extreme close-up. Her appearance conveys

[17] Francesco Savio, *Ma l'amore no* (Milan: Sonzogno, 1975), pp. 128-29.
[18] Edward R. Tannenbaum, *Fascism in Italy: Society and Culture 1922-1945* (London: Allen Lane, 1972), p. 275.

spirituality and nobility, her only concern the defense of her lands and people.

In the photography of the castle, its battlements, drawbridge, rooms, and subterranean passages, and in the emphasis on ceremony, Blasetti seeks to create a sense of splendor and expansiveness. The scenes of military preparations and battle are interwoven with scenes portraying the romantic attachment between Giovanna and Fieramosca in the vein of courtly love. Ettore's growing conversion from self-aggrandizement to heroic commitment is in part effected by his deepening attachment to the noblewoman. Enraged by Giovanna's commitment to marry the nobleman Graiano d'Asti, in spite of her love for Fieramosca, Fieramosca becomes even more headstrong and militant in his contacts with the French and Spanish. Blasetti focuses on the glamor of the fighting Italians, stressing their courage, their good humor, and their mutual support of each other. The scenes of combat are developed through varied camera angles and distances. Images of hand-to-hand combat are shown, with an emphasis on the role of spectators, particularly women, observing the skirmishes from the battlements. Fieramosca is grudgingly admired by his French opponents for his skill, virility, and heroism. He is also portrayed as the teacher and benefactor of youth.

Fieramosca's archenemy is the French knight, Guy de la Motte (Osvaldo Valenti). In the fighting, Fieramosca is wounded. Though he has fought courageously, the battle ends in defeat for the Italians. Recovered and on the field again, Fieramosca, flamboyantly seated on a white horse, calls for revenge and the eradication of all traitors. The battle is drawn on the scale of *Birth of a Nation* and Soviet cinema. Fieramosca is again wounded and the rumor spreads that he is dead, while the French and Spaniards celebrate their successes.

Finally, Fieramosca challenges the French forces to combat in a tournament. At the lists, the Spaniards ally themselves with the Italians. Amid shots of banners, armored men on horseback, heraldic insignias, and formal introductions of combatants, the tournament begins. Blasetti lingers on processions, shots of face-to-face combat, and cries of Italian revenge, nobility, and honor. Fieramosca is dressed in black because, he asserts, he is commemorating his fallen comrades. The fighting sequences are shot from within the arena of combat and also from the perspective of the spectators in the grandstand. One after another Frenchman is unhorsed and demolished until finally the ultimate combat takes place between Fieramosca and de la Motte. The Frenchman is defeated. After the battle, Fieramosca returns to Giovanna. The last shot of the film is of raised swords, accompanied by the sound of intense martial music.

The style of the film is epic, containing numerous examples of parallel and contrasting montage, rhythmic editing, scenes of collective action, panoramic shots of nature and of combat. The alternation of long, medium, and close shots develops the contrast between historical context and individual action, between the heroic and the romantic, and between the public and private arenas of action. The film's rhetorical stance is heavily dependent on the iconography of the major characters, which provides an index to their roles, positions, attitudes, and values. The stirring musical score by Alessandro Cicognini, linked to the images of place, aristocratic symbols, and ritualistic actions, lends an aura of almost religious mysticism.

The conjunction of the motifs of love and combat, reaching back the conventions of the romance, helps to fuse sex and politics. The erotic elements serve to provide the rationale for action. The service of the lady, as in the romance, legitimates military conflict. The lady is both the motivation and the reward for heroic effort. The scenes of conflict and reconciliation between Giovanna and Fieramosca deflect from the scenes of death and violence. Moreover, when Blasetti presents scenes of destruction, he places them within the context of sympathy for the vilified Italians whose honor must be salvaged, reinforcing the idea that military conflict is generated by the quest for honor.

Blasetti's use of the women as spectators and choric commentators also serves the rhetorical function of enhancing sympathy for the fighting. They are surrogates for the external audience whose sympathies are also enlisted in the cause of national honor. The element of spectatorship in the film, as in *Scipione l'Africano*, situating the audience as it does within the action and creating identification with the protagonists, works in the direction of bonding the audience to the values presented.

The film invites an allegorical reading. Linking past historical events to the contemporary situation, Blasetti stresses the idea of the occupation of Italian soil by foreigners. The Italian alliance with the Spaniards suggests the contemporary Italian alliance with the Spaniards and involvement in the Spanish Civil War. The emphasis on the collective struggle of the Italians, their pursuit for national honor, the necessity of revenge for insults to the Italian nation, the emphasis on preparedness, military conflict, and courageous leadership, the superiority of the Italians over other nationalities, the necessity and beauty of military action and the rewards of war, all seem to have their contemporary equivalents in the thirties. Emphasizing women and young people as spectators, the film seems to suggest that the heroic actions portrayed are for their benefit. Through the use of history, the film glamorizes nationalism and war.

In the middle thirties, a number of films were set in Africa, films dealing specifically with colonialism and war. *Lo squadrone bianco, Sotto la croce del sud, Sentinelle di bronzo,* and *Il grande appello* are set in a contemporary context, but, according to Vernon Jarratt, "the major effort of the Italian film industry in the immediately pre-war years was *Scipione l'Africano* (1937), which was intended to remind the latter-day Italians of the glories of their past in the period of imperial Rome, and, once again, to repeat the theme of empire."[19]

*Scipione l'Africano*, directed by Carmine Gallone, one of the major productions of the fascist era, is a thinly veiled allegory. According to Susan Sontag's criteria for fascist art, the film displays the "tastes for the monumental and for mass obei-

[19] Vernon Jarratt, *The Italian Cinema* (New York: Macmillan, 1951), p. 48.

sance to the hero . . . The rendering of movement in grandiose and rigid patterns . . . a choreography and display of bodies, . . . the ideal of life as art, the cult of beauty, the fetishism of courage, the dissolution of alienation in ecstatic feelings of community; the repudiation of the intellect; the family of man (under the parenthood of leaders)."[20] Here Sontag outlines in broad strokes her view of the art of fascism, but a film like *Scipione*, while closer to her thesis on fascist art than the comedies and melodramas of the era, also has its parallels in the Hollywood cinema. *Scipione*, made on a grand scale, with a cast of thousands, lavish costumes and sets, properties, prominent actors, is in the tradition of the early silent Italian epics like *Quo vadis* and has affinities with the films of D. W. Griffith and Cecil B. De Mille.

A credit states that the film was made with the assistance of the Armed Forces, and a prologue locates the events in the film in the Second Punic War:

At the end of the Third Century B.C., the situation came to a head. It looked like Hannibal would triumph. Rome was helpless. On August 2, 216 B.C., fifty thousand Romans were massacred on the plain of Cannae.

The first images of the film are of a smoking field and a view of Roman state buildings. A group of Romans discuss a meeting of the Senate which will decide for or against another offensive against Carthage, and of Scipio's urging of aggressive action. The masses seem to be more sympathetic to him than they are to the jaded senators. Gradually this scene builds up to different perspectives of the masses and also of the massive Roman architecture. Intercut with the mass shots are shots of individuals in close-up, surrogate spectators for the film's external audience as well as humorous and humanizing commentators on the action.

Inside the Senate, an ineffectual debate rages over the war. Scipio (Annibale Ninchi) is accused of personal ambition and of disregarding the interests of Rome. His rhetoric is sono-

---

[20] Susan Sontag, "Fascinating Fascism," in *Movies and Methods*, ed. Bill Nichols (Berkeley: University of California Press, 1976), pp. 40, 43.

rous, his subject, Italian honor. The crowds outside call his name, demanding support for his policies, thus reinforcing the bond between him and the masses. The vote in the Senate is taken and Scipio's militant position is affirmed. The film adopts a condescending strategy toward the senatorial debate so representative of fascist antiparliamentary attitudes, and affirms the importance of spectacle in political life and the effectiveness of a powerful leader. The implied associations with Mussolini could not have gone unnoticed by the audiences of the time.

Following the public ceremonials where the masses are shown like the Red Sea parting for their hero and saluting him in a scene reminiscent of Mussolini's relationship to the masses, the film turns to the domestic arena where Scipio's wife is selflessly removing her jewelry and putting it in a box to offer to the state (another allusion to a fascist practice, the women's offering of their wedding rings to the state). Scipio is thus shown as a public figure and as a family man but the two merge as his private life feeds his sense of patriotic duty. The wife, too, subordinates herself to her husband's destiny.

The following scene shows the Carthaginians fighting as another man on horseback, Scipio's major antagonist, Hannibal (Camillo Pilotto), directs his men to slaughter Romans. Arunte (Marcello Spada) tears himself away from his fiancée, Velia (Isa Miranda) to join the Roman legions, and she is attacked and violently herded away with other Roman women and children. The general effect of the scene is to highlight the brutality of the enemy and thus portray the Roman war effort as a defensive gesture against barbarians who would violate innocent women and children.

By way of contrast, the Romans are shown as kind and industrious. Scipio learns of a shortage of grain for the troops and immediately orders grain to be delivered. Scenes of work follow, dramatizing the energetic support of the workers for the war. Scipio himself arrives to inspect the work and to encourage the workers. The bond between the leader and his men is emphasized here. He is greeted with wild enthusiasm and the choreography stresses the fusion of Scipio, his troops, the farmers, and the shepherds. On horseback amid Roman banners and insignias and cheering crowds, Scipio is shown orating on the need to fight for a safe homeland and a just peace.

Before the ships ready to take the troops to Africa, Scipio delivers another speech of encouragement. The departure ceremony is drawn out, showing the masses in orderly formation, singing and cheering. The image of multiple oars of a ship moving through the water leads to a panoramic view of the classical Roman buildings with the unified masses in the foreground. Paralleling the introductory scenes in the Roman Senate, the Carthaginians are shown in their Senate where men are debating the feasibility of Hannibal's return to Carthage as well as an ending to the war. The film makes an attempt to "humanize" the Carthaginian leaders. While it shows them in error, disorganized, and lacking in proper leadership, it also shows them as weary of the war. Queen Sofonisba (Francesca Braggiotti), however, resists the Romans. Massinissa (Fosco Giachetti), a Roman officer, urges her to join Scipio to avert the destruction of Carthage but she refuses. For her, there will never be peace until the Romans are obliterated. Her make-up, her clinging garments, her sensual movements, her passion, identify her as a descendant of the 1920s film, and of the dangerous, destructive, but fascinating female, a relative too of the *femme fatale* in a De Mille epic. The intensity of her passion is conveyed in fire imagery. An image of Carthage in flames is superimposed on a close-up of her face indicating her prescience, her capacity to intuit events, and prefiguring her own tragic fate. Scipio orders the march on Carthage. The city burns as horsemen ride through the flames and the people flee.

After the battle, Massinissa is brought to Scipio. Unlike Scipio, he has been unable to resist Sofonisba and, though an admirable man, is shown to be the victim of sexuality. He agrees, however, to urge Sofonisba to relent in her opposition to the Romans. In an operatic scene, she begs him to kill her rather than force her to surrender to Scipio. Scipio, however, urges Massinissa to abandon Sofonisba and reminds him of his true political objectives, which are to enhance the honor of Rome.

An image of a cup of poison with long, tapering fingers wrapped around it is followed by a close-up of Sofonisba's face as she commits suicide. She drinks slowly as the music rises in intensity. The Carthaginians are ready to sue for peace on the condition that Carthage will remain independent. Scipio announces that his terms are now unconditional surrender and gives the enemy three days to decide on peace or war. Scipio will accept no compromises. The final moments of the film are extravagant battle scenes. The combat is accompanied by heavy orchestral music. The Roman victors are shown marching to their ships, the victorious fascist march on Rome reenacted. The final image portrays Scipio, his child at his side, informing his wife that he will now work on the farm. With his wife and child, he walks toward a wheatfield.

The film won the Mussolini Cup at the Venice Festival in 1937 as the best Italian film of the year. As might be apparent from the description of the film, *Scipione* contains those qualities ascribed by Sontag to the fascist film: a charismatic leader, adoring and submissive masses, a glorification of sacrifice, an emphasis on ceremonial, a heightened use of image, music, and language. The film is operatic, especially in its presentation of the passionate actions of Sophonisba, in Velia's struggles with Hannibal, and in the death of both women. The music by Ildebrando Pizzetti is an important aspect of the film's epic nature, as exemplified in the mass choruses, and in the lush orchestral music that accompanies scenes of battle and of personal conflict. The settings, too, are reminiscent of grand opera and the choreography of the action, of movement within the shot, and the forward movement of the narrative, contribute to the power of spectacle. The operatic quality overwhelms the history.

Other aspects of *Scipione* help to create spectator identification. The emphasis on familial relations, dramatized particularly through assaults on the family, serves the important function of legitimizing the more spectacular dimensions of public action and combat. The presence of the Roman women in the film, the obedient and loyal wife of Scipio, the violated but defiant Velia, the innocent women and children torn from their homes, identifies the war as a defensive gesture, drawing on traditional values to rationalize aggression. Sofonisba serves, in contrast to other women, to personify the destructive aspects of the enemy. She is the personification of passion and death. Associated with fire and with the destruction of Carthage, she embodies the idea of African sensuality and its self-destructive aspects, which are finally controlled and contained by the more pragmatic values of the Romans.

The scenes of work exploit the familiar values of industrial and social unity. Apart from the Carthaginians who are presented either as impotent or destructive aristocrats or disorderly masses, the benevolent and dynamic image of the Roman masses in the film exploits a populism more relevant to the 1930s than to the earlier historical era presented. The Romans are dedicated to their nation. They are outraged by the brutal treatment of innocent victims, and are above all virtuous. The visual images contrasting order and disorder merge with the contrasting images of burning Carthage and of the massive Roman architecture and fertile countryside to exploit fears about chaos and loss of control and to minimize danger by portraying the restoration of order and unity.

The use of history in the film, the emphasis on the grandeur and power of Rome, the thinly muted allegory linking the Punic War to the war in Ethiopia rationalize the present. The idealized image of the historical past conflated with present history serves the function of negating historical differences. Not only is there a fusion of private and public life but of past and present.

*Scipione* orchestrates different responses: entertainment, escape into the exotic, nostalgia, and retreat into the past, a structure of reassurance against any threat to the status quo. The film is a parable and a prescription panacea elevating consensus and eliminating complexity. Above all, the film is geared rhetorically to reinforcing the values of family, work, self-control, and self-preservation and of making these values applicable to all classes. Albeit the film is built on a grandiose and expensive scale, evoking an heroic period, it also seeks to engender domestic attitudes, to personalize conflict.

Although Louis Trenker's *I condottieri* (1937), a German-Italian production, is constructed along the epic lines of *Scipione l'Africano*, it evokes a different atmosphere and ideological context. The film similarly glorifies the leader, the adherence of the masses to his authority, and national destiny, but Trenker's film also inscribes racism, a rare element in the other Italian films of the period. Moreover, the presentation of character and situation is monumental, not dynamic. Historical events are portrayed as on a large painting or tapestry. The viewer's position can be likened to that of an observer at a church service, and the film depends heavily on a merging of Christian and Germanic myth to present its allegory of history.

The film opens in epic fashion with images of military men, flags, and a background of clouds. A title announces that the film was made with the assistance of the Armed Forces, and a prologue reads, "This film is a re-creation of the times of the Italian adventurers who, in the spirited context of the Renaissance, for the first time led the civil militia of the people that rose against the mercenaries with the common purpose of unifying the Italian people." A statue of a horseman appears set against a sky of clouds. In the midst of the raging battle, two children are brought to a chapel, one of whom is Giovanni de' Medici and the other a young girl, Maria, who will later be his wife. In this battle Giovanni's father is killed. The boy is taken into exile but a title announces that "he will return from exile when he had made a name for himself." He is now shown as the man on horseback, looking like the statue in the earlier sequence. Trenker plays the title role. The music is Wagnerian and, in the background, mountains and clouds are visible. Giovanni rides to the fortress on the hill where Malatesta (Loris Gizzi) has control, makes his way to the camp, and joins the men.

After a "trial" in which he establishes his credentials, the young man is invited to join Malatesta's band. The men plan to go to Florence to rid the state of its French element. In a

series of victories Giovanni consolidates his reputation. He
also meets again with Maria, and he tells her he will return
to claim her. Giovanni and his men march to Florence, singing
patriotic songs. The film stresses his affinity with the common
people, though the aristocracy is suspicious of him. The Florentine nobles call him mad and accuse him of being a vision-
ary. Defiant, Giovanni gathers his men and asks them to
swear an oath of fidelity, to serve their leader and the cause
of unity to the last drop of their blood. But Giovanni is tried
by the council in Florence and declared a traitor. He is placed
on the rack, but saved by his men who spirit him away. As
he escapes, a proclamation is read declaring his excommuni-
cation.

His second exile is spent in the mountains, where he again
sees Maria (Carla Sveva). He proposes marriage to her against
a background of sky and mountains. Maria is blonde and
light-skinned, the ideal image of German, not Italian, culture.
She is presented as pure and virginal, like the natural context
with which she is associated, the opposite of Tullia della Gra-
zie (Laura Nucci), the dark-haired courtesan at Malatesta's
court, who is enamoured of Giovanni but whom he rejects.
According to James Hay, Giovanni's "eventual preference for
the more pure ideal of women occurs as he realizes where
his political allegiances lie. Italy must be identified in his and
the audience's minds with an ideal, something to be protected; and in order to realize this, he must reject the image
of Italy as courtesan—one who, while alluring as a result of
her outward trappings, has been defiled by foreigners."[21]

Maria and Giovanni return secretly to France where they
now confront Malatesta whom he fights and overcomes. After
his victory another scene of processions, flags, statues, and
gathering masses is shown as the crowds shout, "To Rome,"
thus signalling the obvious parallel with the fascist march to
Rome.

In Rome, the Pope blesses Giovanni and, following this
scene of reconciliation, Giovanni and Maria are married in a

---

[21] Hay, *Popular Film Culture in Fascist Italy*, p. 198.

service that seems more military than religious in spite of its taking place in the church. Giovanni and Maria return to the country and to a pastoral setting of flowers, rippling wheat-fields, and domestic serenity. The dramatic cloud-filled sky is always evident in the background. The pastoral idyll is broken, however, by renewed political conflict announced by the now-familiar image of the statue of the man on horseback and images of marching men with banners and weapons. Giovanni leaves Maria with the vow to return again when the battle is over, joining the enthusiastic throngs on their way to fight. On the battlefield, Giovanni is wounded. The enemy is routed and the dead Giovanni is carried into his tent and laid out with his sword at his side. The music is elegiac. The final image of the film is of Giovanni's sculpture on his tomb in the cathedral. The organ music and the image of the tomb reinforces the film's religious aura.

Julian Petley, in his study of the Nazi cinema, identifies the components of the film's ideology, stressing particularly the film's presentation of Giovanni as "the 'born' charismatic leader . . . a 'man of the people' " who is also "represented as a quasi-mystical, superhuman figure."[22] The mystical dimension is represented in the "recurrent apotheosized 'ascension' scenes in the mountains." Giovanni, according to Petley, "metamorphoses from an ordinary child into an heroic figure in imagery reminiscent of *Die Nibelungen*." The religious element is also apparent in parallels between Giovanni and Christ: the trials, temptations, and sacrifice. Giovanni is also portrayed as a peacemaker in contrast to the nobles of Florence and the adventurers who seek to undermine him. The inclusion of the scenes of reconciliation with the Pope are a specific reference to Mussolini's role in creating the Lateran Concordat in 1929.[23]

Although Petley correctly identifies the film's insistence on

[22] Julian Petley, *Capital and Culture: German Cinema 1933-1945* (London: British Film Institute, 1979), p. 122.

[23] Brunetta, *Storia del cinema*, p. 398.

the mystical power of the leader and the strange fusion of populism and authoritarianism, he underestimates the way the film looks, and the way it works on the spectator. The Wagerian elements to which he refers and which others have noted are indeed apparent in the music, the uses of myth, and the emphasis on heroic combat, but an important ingredient of Wagnerian dramaturgy is missing. The film does not contain the dynamic conflict so central to Wagnerian art. The scenes of combat seem to arrest action rather than advance it and the presentation of character is as immobile as the statuary to which it is likened. The film reveals itself in its recurrent use of the image of the man on horseback, and in the final scene where we see Giovanni transformed from flesh into a sculpture. At times during the course of the film it is difficult to discern whether the image is of Giovanni or his statue. Thus, the film both seeks to celebrate his superhuman qualities and at the same time reveals the inhumanity of the figure. The human figure has been metamorphosed into stone. The freezing of the figure and actions can be read back into the narrative as an ultimate image of control that immobilizes everything around it.

Moreover, the emphasis on nature in the film, the countryside, the identification of Maria with animals and fertility, which seem intended to create an aura of innocence and to overcome any opposition between nature and culture, is also undermined by the images of statuary that are based on the transformation of living things into dead objects. The blatant ruralism to which the film appeals is also undercut in this fashion. Petley has noted that the film makes an especial bid for the attention of the rural classes, particularly the rural proletariat to which

fascism presented a demagogic face . . . making false promises of "colonisation" and land distribution. But there was more to it. Fascism thoroughly exploited both the particular forms assumed by petty bourgeois rebel ideology in the countryside, and the ideological theme of solidarity and community of the soil. . . . Like the emphasis of ties of blood and ties of the soil, on personal loyalty . . . this aspect linked up with the survival of feudal ideology in "rural fascism."[24]

These contradictions are apparent in the film's imagery but also in its coercing of the spectator into an attitude of awe and worship.

The film's allegorical project of linking Giovanni and Mussolini are developed beyond the relations between Church and state to include a history of Italian fascism: the identification of Giovanni's men with the Black Shirts, the emphasis on the rituals of oath-taking, the battles for power, and the March on Rome. The film, which fuses the history of fascism and Nazism, is an encomium to the German leader as well as the Italian. Giovanni's struggles can also be read in relation to Hitler's rise to power: his conflicts with authorities, his reliance on the bands of Brown Shirts, his arrest, and his wooing of rural elements. Thus, the specific motif of nationalism is transformed and undercut like everything else in the film. Unlike the other historical films that celebrate nationalism, this film universalizes fascist ideology and reduces it to violence and death. Moreover, the romantic elements in many of the other historical films serve to create a form of spectacle that eroticizes the action, but this film desexualizes the relationship between the man and woman and substitutes religion and art in its place.

The treatment of history in the Italian films of the 1930s reveals, as James Hay indicates, a "capacity to displace current ideological conflict to a mythical setting, and, in turn, to reduce History to a diegetic world where the present suddenly becomes charged with value."[25] The images and symbols in the films reach deep into cultural mythology, tapping the elementary roots of kinship, the sanctity of the family and of the land, and sacrificial rituals that regenerate the culture and insure its continuity.

[24] Petley, *Capital and Culture*, p. 122.
[25] Hay, *Popular Film Culture in Fascist Italy*, p. 186.

In discussing Nazism and war, Walter Benjamin had written that the language of war appears mystical, contributing to generally augmenting or impoverishing social life. In either case, the imagery and symbolism of war are crucial to sustaining ideology.[26] According to Benjamin, mystical images and symbols mask the commonplace reality that war is sustained in fact by the captains of finance and professional soldiers. In a strongly polemic passage, Benjamin attempts to describe this "mysticism" that

. . . crawls forth on its thousand unsightly conceptual feet. The war that this light exposes is so little the "eternal" one which Germans now worship as it is the "final" war the pacifists carry on about. In reality that war is only this: The one, fearful, last chance to correct the incapacity of peoples to order their relationships to one another in accord with the relationships they possess to nature through their technology.[27]

In effect, Benjamin's discussion of the mystico-religious symbolism of war reiterates his famous dictum that fascism aestheticizes politics, whereby history loses its specificity and becomes myth. In *Condottieri*, the verbal and visual language is inflated and Manichaean, and the events, characters, and conflicts portrayed assume an aura of determinism. The analogies presented between past and present serve to create the sense that repetition is inevitable, necessary, and desirable.

The Renaissance films appear to adopt highly stylized and stiffly formal treatments of tradition, history, and political struggle. The films of the Risorgimento, in contrast, seem less inclined toward the ritualistic and monumental. Their allegories are more designed toward developing notions of popular struggle, toward a transformism that seeks to unify divergent political groups. *Il dottor Antonio* (1937), directed by Enrico Guazzoni, is representative of many of the films that treat this period of Italian history.

[26] Walter Benjamin, "Theories of German Fascism," Translated by Jerolf Wikoff, *New German Critique*, no. 17 (Spring 1979), p. 123.

[27] Ibid., p. 128.

Based on a novel of the same name by Giovanni Ruffini, the film allegorically links the events of 1848 to the fascist struggles for national unity and consensus. The first image of the film is a prison, a prefiguration of the final scene where Doctor Antonio will be incarcerated for his political activities and from which he will be rescued. The romantic element is introduced early with the hectic carriage ride of Miss Lucy (Maria Gambarelli) and her father, Sir John Davenne (Lamberto Picasso). Miss Lucy is injured by the overturning of her carriage and requires the services of Dr. Antonio (Ennio Cerlesi). Antonio is a Sicilian exile who has been forced to leave his home as a consequence of his subversive political activities on behalf of the struggle for national unity.

His relationship with Miss Lucy is the means for grafting the romance to politics. The two fall in love but not without a series of conflicts that threaten to keep them apart. At first, Miss Lucy assumes that Antonio's earlier imprisonment and exile is the consequence of criminality, and he explains to her that if it is a crime to be patriotic, then he is glad to be a criminal. She involves herself more sympathetically in his situation when Antonio talks eloquently of revolutionary goals and particularly of the plight of the Southern Italians whom he feels must be freed from the yoke of foreign domination and oppression. He speaks with particular animus of the role of Ferdinand II, King of the two Sicilies, who attempted to suppress rebellion in Sicily and then later in Naples. On the evening of a celebration of Miss Lucy's departure for England, Antonio is called away. Miss Lucy returns to England where she can neither forget her love for the doctor nor her sympathies with the Italian struggle. In contrast to her brother, who sees Italy as a land of volcanoes, gondolas, scenic panoramas, and "primitive" Italians, she describes the Italians as a civilized people, "like the English."

Antonio and his fellow patriots leave for Naples, charged with excitement and patriotism. In Naples, a crowd gathers to read a proclamation stating: "Ferdinand II of Naples concedes a constitution to the people." The document is signed, "King of the Two Sicilies by the Grace of God, Duke of Parma, hereditary Prince of Tuscany." While the people, carrying an Italian flag, cheer the news, Ferdinand plots ways of containing political rebellion. Having decided to join Antonio in his struggles, Miss Lucy finds Antonio, who tells her that though he loves her, he has no time in his life for personal affairs until his country is free. Antonio and her family urge her to return home, because the urban situation is dangerous, but she refuses.

The action intensifies as crowds barricade sections of the city. The soldiers are filmed shooting into the crowd as the people disperse in all directions. Antonio encourages resistance. The men build a barricade with mattresses, chairs, beds, and other bits of furniture and utensils, and hand-to-hand combat with the soldiers ensues. The cheer can be heard, "This is a people's war, classes fighting side by side against royalty and privilege." In the battle, Antonio's comrade is mortally wounded and the soldiers who have broken through the barricade forcibly enter· the closed houses. Antonio's friend makes light of his wounds and dies, a willing martyr to the cause. The soldiers arrest Antonio.

Lucy, having learned of the arrest, goes to Ferdinand to plead for Antonio. He promises to help her, but fails to keep his word, and Antonio is sentenced to twenty-nine years in prison. In prison, the men plot an escape, but it becomes clear that only one of the men can go and the prisoners' decision is that it be Antonio. He is reluctant to leave but they dupe him into believing that they will accompany him. The men break the bars on the window. Antonio is reunited with Lucy, and the final scene portrays the prisoners' celebration of Antonio's escape by singing patriotic Italian songs.

The film emphasizes the unity of bourgeoisie, peasants, and workers against the foreign aristocrats as well as unity between English and Italian people, an alliance that still seemed possible in 1937 when the film was made. The "Southern question" serves, as in *1860*, as the rallying point in the struggle for unification. Nationalism is couched in revolutionary rhetoric.

The link between the film's events and the contemporary

situation seem clear, involving the idea of a leader who is a man of the people. That he is a physician enhances the idea that he is a healer of a diseased state. He seeks to purge the destructive forces that have obstructed the well-being of the masses and have impeded Italy's heroic mission. Miss Lucy's role represents the link between English and Italian goals as well as identifying the Italian struggle with democratic values. The populist dimensions of the struggle are carefully choreographed through the scenes portraying political debate and the scenes of combat. The scenes in the prison portray Antonio as the prototype of the man of action and commitment, a man supported by the people and one who speaks for the oppressed, who is not afraid of imprisonment or death and whose presence commands the respect, loyalty, and sacrifice of others. His relationship to Miss Lucy also serves to illuminate the connection between the public and private spheres, the submergence of personal desire in the interests of political objectives. Her subordination to Antonio becomes emblematic of the idea of total devotion to the cause. Erotic energy is transformed into selfless political action.

The film's treatment of Risorgimento history situates Italian politics in a broader context than fascism and addresses contemporary issues by indirection. The emphasis on the revolutionary aspects of the nineteenth-century movement makes the political issues more accessible than the more remote and monumental *Condottieri* or the epic *Scipione*. The romantic treatment of Lucy and Antonio is also differently portrayed. Guazzoni's film presents the man and woman as partners in an adventurous and heroic struggle rather than in the context of courtly love where the woman is merely a source of inspiration. Love and politics are presented as mutually reinforcing, and their combination serves to humanize and sentimentalize the politics.

In the film, the portrayal of the oppression of the Neapolitan people serves also to produce identification. The people are presented as innocent women, children, and elderly citizens pitted against the impersonal power of the soldiers. The ruling class is the major object for attack as the suffering Neapolitans are the focal point of sympathy and solidarity. Following its symbolic use of a physician as the central character and hero, the film itself is prescription, a panacea for suffering and oppression, which offers the promise of eventual solution to political conflict through historical examples.

A film like *Il dottor Antonio* portrays real and fictional political figures in the context of national struggles. The element of biography is subordinated to the political action. However, there are films of the period that present history through biography, and the biography of the artist was a common form of historical film. Though these films may share similar objectives with the films celebrating war, empire, and national unity, they utilize different techniques. Most particularly, they offer entertainment as spectacle, entertainment within entertainment, and they celebrate creativity as a source of national honor. By highlighting personal failure and eventual triumph, they capitalize on voyeurism, curiosity about the personal lives of the great, but through the pattern of adversity and transcendence, they create a means for audience identification.

Carmine Gallone's film, *Verdi* (1938), is less a biography of the composer than it is an historical spectacle. Giuseppe Verdi becomes the excuse for dramatizing motifs of nationalism and heroic effort. According to Brunetta, this film, like Blasetti's *1860*, Guazzoni's *Il dottor Antonio*, and the films of directors like Soldati and Alessandrini, constitutes an attempt to recuperate traditional culture in order to reinforce the conservation of traditional values.[28]

In the history of Verdi, the composer, the association between art and politics had been forged in the nineteenth century. Luigi Barzini notes how "Verdi's heroic music accompanied a vast moral and political upheaval, the revolution of the Risorgimento,"[29] and, according to Edward R. Tannenbaum and Emiliana P. Noether, "during much of the nineteenth century, Giuseppe Verdi tried to be a symbol of Italian

[28] Brunetta, *Storia del cinema*, p. 386.
[29] Luigi Barzini, *The Italians* (New York: Atheneum, 1964), p. 174.

patriotism, but his image hardly reached the masses."[30] The Gallone film capitalizes on this image of Verdi and rewrites the extent of Verdi's popularity, identifying the composer as a favorite of the masses.

The film opens with a domestic scene, with Verdi at the piano and Margherita, his fiancée, singing. He is on the brink of leaving for the conservatory in Milan. The sequence stresses his conjugal and filial piety as well as his humble origins. In Milan, he encounters difficulty as the maestro at the conservatory rejects his work. There he meets a young opera singer, Giuseppina Strepponi, who will become his second wife. At La Scala, Verdi is asked to direct the orchestra and the sequence emphasizes the artist's control and artistry. Giuseppina urges him to present his first opera to the public and he agrees. While Verdi is working on a new opera, his child becomes ill and dies. After having experienced the humiliation of the audience's negative response to his work, he suffers his wife's illness. Her death is set to the strains of *La traviata*. After his professional failure and Margherita's death, Verdi withdraws from society. Impoverished, he wanders the streets and frequents cafés, refusing the charity and recognition of others. He is reduced to eating chestnuts from an old female street vendor to whom he promises a shawl. Verdi is shown in his garret room, huddling in bed to stay warm.

Giuseppina again comes to Verdi's assistance, and he returns to the music world and to success. He brings the chestnut vendor the promised shawl. Verdi and Giuseppina now see each other regularly and she introduces him to other artists such as Balzac and runs interference for him with managers and representatives of the Church. This sequence affords an introduction to the film's treatment of politics through posterlike scenes of flags, statues, a statue of Garibaldi in particular, a notice about the "Battle of Legnano," and men chanting the Risorgimento slogan, "Viva Verdi" ("Verdi" is an acronym for Vittorio Emanuele, Re d'Italia).

[30] Edward R. Tannenbaum and Emiliana P. Noether, *Modern Italy: A Topical History Since 1861* (New York: New York University Press, 1974), xvii.

Verdi appears on his balcony as the crowd below cheers the composer. The allegorical linking of Verdi and Mussolini is unmistakable here.

The filmic biography is, as in Hollywood films of a similar genre, divided equally between the narrative elements and spectacle drawn from segments of the operas. Verdi's fame grows. Shifting to his personal life, the film reveals problems between Verdi and Giuseppina. She is jealous and complains that Verdi never really cared for her. She spies on Verdi rehearsing with Teresa, a young opera singer. Though Verdi gives no cause, as a matter of fact discourages Teresa, Giuseppina cannot relinquish her anxiety over losing him. Teresa, tired of Giuseppina's harassment, threatens to leave, but Giuseppina stops her and apoligizes for her behavior. Verdi's own awareness of aging and fear of the loss of his powers are also stressed in these sequences.

A segment of Act II of *Aida* follows as if to verify Verdi's continuing vitality. The performance is lavish, a spectacle within a spectacle. The audience is wild with enthusiasm. Verdi's international reputation grows. The film ends with music from *Aida* and an image of trumpets pointing toward the sky, accompanied by fanfare, calling attention to the spectacular properties of the film and of Verdi's music.

The film is planned on an epic scale—large cast, spectacular segments selected from the operas, and incidents from Verdi's life geared to reinforce the composer's struggles for recognition, his uncompromising commitment to his art, and his overcoming of extreme personal adversity and public rejection. The alternating patterns of adversity and productivity, the escalating movement from suffering and deprivation to achievement, are joined to the film's overt and covert political concern. Above all, Verdi's figure becomes synonymous with Risorgimento nationalist ideals, particularly the greatness of Italy's contributions to culture.

Geared to an international audience, the film singles out Verdi's relationship to foreign writers such as Balzac and Dumas, to English musical critics, and highlights spectacle more prominently than politics. The politics of the film reside in its self-referentiality, its energetic effort to present a benign and palatable image of itself, using the biography of the great composer in parabolic fashion as a symbol of Italian genius and cultural superiority and of the Italian capacity to over-come personal obstacles and social impediments to success. In particular, the film's emphasis on the trials of the aging composer, his fears of superannuation yet his continued pro-duction of masterpieces in spite of waning vitality, reinforces the parallel between personal renewal and renewed political life. The merging of the composer's personal life, his operatic works, and the political climate of his era provides multiple paths for spectator identification and also dissipates a solely political interpretation of the film.

By contrast, Blasetti's *Un' avventura di Salvator Rosa* (Salvator Rosa's Adventure, 1940), selects only one period in the life and times of the seventeenth-century Neapolitan painter and transforms his biography into a swashbuckling costume drama worthy of Hollywood. The film makes no pretense of specifically documenting the painter's achievements, loosely using Rosa's life, work, and politics as a general frame of reference for Blasetti's own political and aesthetic concerns. Rosa's earlier work was devoted to the painting of battle scenes but later he went on to develop the art of landscape painting so identified with his style, especially in his mixing of heroic and pastoral motifs. His life has been characterized by the concept of *sprezzatura*, the Renaissance notion of the universal man. Actor, painter, musician, poet, satirist, and soldier, Rosa provides a counterpart to Blasetti whose own work exemplifies a fusion of epic, pastoral, romantic, heroic, and pictorial elements. Blasetti's films place great value on heroism and on the exceptional individual who redeems a corrupt political situation. All of his films involve the twin motifs of love and combat, and use the countryside as the signifier of innocence corrupted and innocence restored. He uses action and spectacle to create audience involvement with political issues.

Blasetti's treatment of his patriotic themes, however, changes somewhat from his early films such as *Sole* and *1860* to his films of the 1940s. He has been quoted as saying that his enthusiasm for the fascist regime diminished by the late thirties and a close reading of his later films such as *Un' avventura di Salvator Rosa* and *Corona di ferro* corroborates changes in point of view.[31] While he maintains his epic stance, his later films can be seen to focus on the abuses of authority, the arbitrary and cruel uses of power.

*Un' avventura* appears to be a basic entertainment in the genre of the adventure film, heavily endowed with the properties and conventions of that genre: lavish sets and costumes, panoramic landscape shots, an emphasis on physical action, damsels in distress, and, above all, a swashbuckling hero who performs exceptional acts of courage in the interests of the lady and on behalf of the common people, combating the evil forces who seek to exploit the land and subjugate the people. The prologue to *Un' avventura* reads: "This is the story of Salvator Rosa, versatile artist, poet, painter of landscapes and battles. His romantic life is the inspiration of this fictional tale, a parable of the masked hero, 'The Ant,' Rosa's alter ego, a friend and defender of the people."

One of the motifs in the film is the torture and abuse of the common people. A humble fish vendor has been sentenced to death because he dared to attack the arbitrary power of the Neapolitan authorities. Masaniello and several other rebels are condemned to the dungeons where they are rescued by "The Ant." The masked hero, their avenger, leaves behind him a note that states that he is going on a vacation and therefore he ironically implores the rulers to cease all arrests until he returns. The villain of the piece is Count Lamberto D'Arco, played by Osvaldo Valenti. A nephew of the Viceroy of Naples, he is obsessed with consolidating his prestige and power.

The casting of characters for the film is along Hollywood lines. Gino Cervi, who plays Rosa, was identified with swashbuckling roles, often through his roles in Blasetti films. Valenti

---

[31] Francesco Savio, *Cinecittà anni trenta*. 3 vols. (Rome: Bulzoni, 1979), 1:143-49.

alternated roles between suave hero and treacherous villain. Paolo Stoppa, who plays the Ant's sidekick, a good-hearted, bluff, and loyal character. The Blasetti combination of action and romance, as Roberto Campari notes, is characteristic of Hollywood formulas.[32] The differences, however, are equally significant. Blasetti pays as much attention to the struggle of the oppressed populace as to the hero and villain. Their political struggle is intimately linked to the individual conflicts much more than in Hollywood costume dramas.

When the action shifts from Naples to the countryside at the Duchy of Torniano, Blasetti introduces the dominant image of the film. The countryside itself, with its parched fields, takes on the connotation of a wasteland. The blight of the land is directly linked to the human forces that produce evil and sterility. Specifically, the film hinges on the refusal of the Duchess of Torniano (Rina Morelli), at the instigation of Count Lamberto, to direct the water from her gardens to the fields of the peasants, who are experiencing a dreadful drought. Unrest among them grows as their suffering increases and as the Duchess's intractibility remains. The Ant, aware of the plight of the poor, decides to remain in the duchy to defend the people. The Duchess is portrayed as trivial, vain, impressionable, capricious, extravagant, and misguided. She is captivated by the idea of playing off Count Lamberto against The Ant, but she appears to have no substantial interest in the duchy. Count Lamberto, the "evil counselor,"plays on her vulnerability to seduction.

A dinner party, presented with the typical Blasetti flair for spectacle, is interrupted by a rock thrown through the window. The perpetrator is Lucrezia, a wild peasant woman, played by Luisa Ferida. Lucrezia is carried away to the dungeon but Salvator has her brought to his rooms for interrogation. He seduces her and she gives him information about how the peasants' plan to divert the water themselves. In order to conceal his identity, he returns her to jail without

[32] Roberto Campari, *Hollywood-Cinecittà: Il racconto che cambia* (Milan: Feltrinelli, 1980), pp. 128-65.

explanation, leaving her with the impression that he has betrayed her. Moreover, he tells Count Lamberto about the conspiracy, suggesting that the four men be paraded forth on the following day as examples to be used as public target practice for the archers.

The hapless men are rounded up for a public demonstration, replete with pomp and ritual. As the men are marched out and the archers line up ready to aim, the Duchess is occupied with Rosa, trying to seduce him. At the execution, the peasant crowd observes the impending fate of their countrymen. The scene is elaborately composed, with long shots of Lucrezia with the soldiers, shots of a young peasant boy plaintively calling to his father, of the condemned men, of the Duchess with Lamberto, and of the archers. In the midst of this rapidly edited and extended sequence, the masked avenger arrives and frees the four men. Moreover, Rosa gives the Duchess a note purported to be from The Ant that states that she must not marry Count Lamberto. He tells Count Lamberto, however, that this is only a ruse to force the Duchess to make up her mind, and the Duchess, in fact, defiantly decides to marry the Count.

Lucrezia goes secretly to Rosa's room to insist that she be part of the action to restore the water to the peasants' fields. She also implores him not to reveal to The Ant that she has been with Rosa. He insists that she stay home and when she angrily refuses, he has her arrested again. Throughout the narrative, Blasetti uses incremental repetition to enhance the stylization, comic treatment, and continuity. His use of parallelism and contrast helps to develop the momentum and sense of inevitability so important to the genre film. The patterning of conflict and resolution, of strategy and counterstrategy, is central to the narrative structure.

In a night scene, the Duchess comes stealthily to Lucrezia's cell, offering freedom if Lucrezia will give her the keys to her home where The Ant is reputed to be hiding. When Lamberto learns of the disappearance of both the Duchess and Lucrezia, he begins to get suspicious of Rosa. Rosa, stalling for time, tells Lamberto he will find the Duchess. Lamberto can then follow and seize The Ant. At the farmhouse, Lucrezia and the Duchess await The Ant's arrival. Rosa arrives and attempts to overcome the peasants' suspicions of his role in the conflict. He informs the Duchess that he will soon trap the masked man, and once again orders Lucrezia to be taken off to prison. He tells the peasants about the impending "invasion" by Lamberto.

The inevitable climax is a battle between the Count and his men and the peasants. The peasants gather, coming from all directions in the countryside to converge on the farmhouse. They are shown jumping from trees, climbing through the brush, and forming a large contingent. Unlike 1860, however, Blasetti treats these sequences in comic rather than heroic fashion. The peasants with their farm implements do not kill the opposition but only humiliate and rout them. They send the soldiers sprawling down the hillsides and into the water. The long-awaited confrontation between Lamberto and The Ant takes place in the water where The Ant does not engage in a duel with his opponent but only submerges him several times in the water as he informs him of the Duchess's decision to assist the peasants. The water scenes are related to the symbolic use of water throughout the film. The evil agents are trapped in the forces they sought to control, and Rosa emerges as the agent of fertility, the redeemer of the wasteland.

In a ceremonial scene at the castle, lavishly costumed and opulently set, the Duchess announces that bad health has forced Lamberto to return to Naples. The film ends "happily" with order restored to the duchy. The wasteland has been revitalized; the lovers are reconciled. The aristocracy and the peasants are united. The film contains both a critique of the abuse of power and authority as well as a corrective formula. Blasetti's use of the costume drama with its fairy-tale quality and spectacle allows him to develop the political issues surreptitiously and safely. The same system of parallels between past and present that characterizes the use of history in the film allows him to criticize that ideology. The costumes, architecture, landscape, and swashbuckling action provide the necessary entertainment and diversionary dimension that renders the text innocuous.

By selecting an artist as his central figure, an artist who is a man of action, Blasetti seems to be making a reflexive comment on the nature of his own role and on the role of film as political. Not only can Rosa be seen as a director-surrogate, but the paintings on the walls, Rosa's paintings on an easel, the pictorial texture of the film, call attention to the filmmaker who not only composes the scenes but directs the action. The artist is thus seen as historically playing a role in calling attention to injustice and assisting in its amelioration.

The characters in the film are set up so as to develop thematic oppositions, conflicts between aristocrats and peasants, good leaders and bad leaders, and sexual conflict between men and women. The oppositions are resolved hierarchically with the peasants subordinated to a redeemed aristocracy. The women are subordinated to a strong but responsible male authority figure. Neither the Duchess nor Lucrezia have any autonomous power. When they act unilaterally they only create further problems. The film's comic resolution reaffirms male authority by supplanting the vision of arbitrary and tyrannical power with a vision of humane leadership. The conventions of the costume drama and of traditional comedy dictate such a conservative solution. No doubt, the censorship restrictions under the regime are also responsible for tempered or covert political criticism. Yet, Blasetti's historical and costume dramas consistently stress melioration and fascination with the leadership principle.

In spite of his conventional treatment of heroism, Blasetti offers a critique of the misuse of power and its consequences for the people. Invoking the question of the *Mezzogiorno* through the figure of Salvator Rosa as a hero of the peasants, Blasetti portrays the miserable lot of the peasantry, their subjection to violence and economic control, their need of a defender to protect their rights. In retrospect, the parallels between that earlier history and the deteriorating economic and political situation in Italy in 1940 seem more obvious than they might have at the time of the film's release. Blasetti's

use of the "cloak and dagger" genre is sufficiently stylized
and conventionalized so as to make the film's politics ambiguous. The film might be read much like *Terra madre* as a
reaffirmation of fascist ideology but for the absence of patriotic
motifs and for the inordinate emphasis on the devastation of
the land and the sufferings of the people that, as in *Corona
di ferro*, are actually more central to the action than the magical
figures of rescue.

   Not all of the films of the period dealt with earlier historical
periods. The war in Ethiopia and in Spain generated a number
of films. Augusto Genina who in his 1936 *Lo squadrone bianco*
had portrayed the Italian presence in Ethiopia turned in 1940
to the Spanish Civil War in his *L'assedio dell' Alcazar*. The use
of contemporary history, other than affording a different and
more direct perspective on political struggle, also allowed for
the use of on-location shooting and the insertion of documentary footage. According to Peter Bondanella, this film
"combined interior sets designed by Cinecittà with on-location shooting among the ruins of Toledo's Alcazar, the citadel
which Franco's soldiers defended against an overwhelming
republican army."[33] Genina's film portrays the defense of the
Alcazar as a defense of the traditional values as laid forth in
the prologue:

> In Spain, Bolshevism threatened to sink the land into chaos. Then
> a small group of nationals gathered around General Francisco Franco
> to fight against the red peril. In the final hours the group was suc-
> cessful in saving Spain from certain destruction by the red hordes.
> The heroic defense of the Alcazar was symbolic of this fight for
> freedom when Colonel Moscardo and his men remained firm for
> two months against the Bolsheviks, who outnumbered them. This
> film portrays the heroic fight of these brave men. The reported events
> are treated with historical accuracy.

The film, unlike Brignone's, is not an overt portrait of Italian
expansionism, though the presentation of the Spanish Civil
War inscribes within it a legitimation of fascism in its most

[33] Peter Bondanella, *Italian Cinema: From Neorealism to the Present* (New York:
Frederick Ungar, 1983), p. 19.

militant aspects. *Alcazar* elevates the values of family and nation, linking these values to war as a defense of traditional attitudes. The "red hordes" are the embodiment of the decadent, aggressive, and destructive forces that would undermine the social order.

The location shots and the references to actual individuals and conflicts transform the fiction into "history." Moreover, the emphasis on militarism, the epic shots of military formations, the choreography of leaders and men, the dramatic perspectives of the Alcazar, stress the traditional, hierarchical, and paternalistic dimensions of Franco's forces. The choreography also stresses the beauty of the collective will and of obedience, as the men chant in unison: "The fatherland is fate." Aligned to the introductory sequences celebrating the spectacle of militarism are the sequences involving the presentation of family, especially women and children, for whom the war is being waged. Through the women characters, especially the key characters of Carmen (Mireille Balin) and Conchita (Maria Denis), public duty and private sacrifice fuse. The iconography of these women and of their lovers serves in itself to legitimize the struggle. Juxtaposed against the ugly and unkempt opposition, against the brutal images of the war, these characters exemplify the idealism of their cause. Moreover, situated in this context of collective struggle, these characters serve to personalize the issues. They represent the preservation of the family, the principle of continuity, the beauty of sacrifice, and the preservation of beauty itself.

The figure of Colonel Moscardo (Rafael Calvo) in the film epitomizes the virtues of authority. Colonel Moscardo holds this frail and heroic community together in the face of vicious opposition. His own heroism and sense of duty has no limits; he is willing to sacrifice his own son to the enemy before he would tarnish the family's honor. His son willingly complies. Moscardo holds the beleaguered forces at the Alcazar together until Franco arrives with arms and men to save them in an emotionally charged conclusion. In fact, Moscardo is Franco's surrogate.

Early in the film, Carmen and Conchita, along with other

women and children, are brought to the Alcazar by Pedro
(Andrea Checchi) and Francisco (Aldo Fiorelli) to protect them
from the bombardment of the city. The Alcazar becomes an
emblem, a microcosm of Spanish society, inhabited by soldiers, the elderly, women, and children who are bound together in a life-and-death struggle of resistance and survival.
Their enemy is portrayed as brutal, indifferent to life and
honor, willing to throw grenades at innocent women and
children. The Republicans are shown in their quarters as glut-
tonous, drinking and feasting while innocent and helpless
victims starve. Physically, they are dirty and unattractive,
basically uncouth peasants bent on the senseless murder of
families. They can look at the human suffering they cause
and celebrate, feeling no remorse. In the casting of the film,
the nationalists are shown as well-dressed bourgeoisie whereas
the opposition appears to represent the lower classes.

The film alternates between battle scenes and personal
drama, particularly dramas of heroic conversion. Carmen is
portrayed at first as concerned only for her own comfort,
obsessively occupied with her appearance and with a romantic longing for adventure and seduction. Through her involvement with Captain Vela (Fosco Giachetti) she is transformed.
At first he is indifferent to her but gradually she earns his
attention by becoming involved in nursing the wounded, including him. Conchita, on the other hand, is imbued with
love for Francisco and for the greatness of the struggle that
is being waged. Though Francisco becomes a martyr for the
cause, she remains unshaken in her devotion and faith to the
cause of defending the Alcazar. The beauty and nobility of
personal sacrifice becomes a dominant theme in the portrayal
of life within the Alcazar. Most of the characters exemplify
variations of personal sacrifice. Francisco sacrifices his life for
Spain; Conchita sacrifices personal desire to service; Pedro,
who loves Carmen, sacrifices himself so that she and Vela can
be united; Moscardo sacrifices his son; the son sacrifices himself for the father and his fatherland; and Moscardo is willing
to sacrifice everyone in the Alcazar rather than surrender. To
add to this portrait of domestic loyalty and devotion to honor,

the film includes a scene of childbirth, symbolizing continuity and hope in the future. Furthermore, the child's father dies heroically for his country on a spying mission, linking personal sacrifice to the defense of the family.

The film includes scenes of parliamentary debate that exemplify political disarray and the impotence of the government. Contrasted to these scenes are those of the fascists who are united in spite of the disorder and demoralization that surrounds them. As they mourn for the death of one of their comrades, they are united in their desire for revenge. The final sequences of the film are of heavy combat photographed from different perspectives, always with dramatically compelling shots of the Alcazar and of its defenders climbing upwards through the rubble, attacking the enemy, and keeping their flag aloft. Within the Alcazar, the women encourage, comfort, and nurse the inhabitants and the wounded. A newspaper clipping announces: "The red opposition is broken to pieces in the victorious march of Franco's troops." The elated people from the Alcazar run into the courtyard, embracing each other. The photography singles out women and children with their parents. The crowd's attention is riveted on the formal meeting between Moscardo and Franco (played by an actor). Carmen and Captain Vela look on benevolently as the unified mass of people salute Franco. The final image in the film is the ruins of the Alcazar.

The film debunks liberal institutions. Heroism is associated with militarism, with firm leadership, discipline, and personal sacrifice. The style of the film and the character types are carefully choreographed to portray the aesthetic values of hierarchy. *Alcazar* uses images of communication—the radio, newspapers, telephone, and telegraph—as symbols of depersonalization, in contrast to the images of immediate personal contact among the inhabitants of the Alcazar, thus reinforcing the value of tradition in opposition to contemporary political chaos. The romantic and familial scenes, spaced so as to punctuate the battle scenes and scenes of political conflict, personalize the conflict, and enhance the audience's affective involvement.

The German-Italian production was addressed to several audiences, to Spaniards as well as to Germans and Italians. Italians had, prior to this film, made and continued to make films in Spain. The subject matter of *Alcazar* linked the Falangist aims to those of fascism and the forms of fascist spectacle to the Falangist forms of organization. Antonioni, writing on the film in *Cinema* in 1940, discussed how the film merited the Mussolini Cup it received that year. *Alcazar* was, according to him, a film of commitment. He singles out its uses of heroic gesture, its historical elements, its use of the Alcazar to re-create the life of a small city, its epic sense, and its choralelike composition.[34]

The film seems to correspond to the official line of the Catholic hierarchy that supported fascism and encouraged anti-Communist attitudes. According to Tannenbaum:

All the prelates praised the anti-Communism of the Fascist regime with varying degrees of enthusiasm, but most of them persisted in seeing Fascism as authoritarian and pro-clerical, rather than totalitarian and anti-clerical. This view was expressed especially clearly by Padre Gemelli, who often burned his bit of incense for the regime as a means of safeguarding his university in Milan: 'Against Communism Fascism has opposed the concept of hierarchy, order, discipline, sacrifice . . . as embodied in the State, the family, and the Catholic religion.'[35]

Moreover, clergymen attacked the Spanish Republicans, blaming Communism for the Civil War. *Alcazar*'s use of contemporary history, its references to actual events, are geared toward legitimizing Italy's involvement in Spain and to exploiting anti-Communist motifs. The victory of Franco's forces was not only a victory for Spain but for fascism in general.

Like *Alcazar*, DeRobertis's 1941 *Uomini sul fondo* (Men under the Sea) uses contemporary history to portray men in wartime, but in a radically different manner than Genina's film. *Uomini* seems to corroborate Tannenbaum's comments on the Italian political situation in 1941. He states,

[34] Savio, *Ma l'amore no*, p. 30.
[35] Tannenbaum, *Fascism in Italy*, p. 231.

After 1939 the Fascist regime lost favour among most Italians but continued to have considerable influence on their lives. Even unpopular wars have a way of forcing people to work together, to hate the enemy and to believe that the government's actions are right. Only on 25 July 1943 after Italian soil had been invaded, did the majority of the Fascist Grand Council vote to dump Mussolini and to abandon the 'false myth' of a 'Fascist War,' which had 'accelerated the rupture between the Nation and Fascism'.[36]

Though the cinema of the era produced its share of epics stressing the virtues of nationalism, patriotic duty, collective effort, and the glories of war, there is subtle evidence in the war films of the early 1940s of the disenchantment to which Tannenbaum alludes.

*Uomini sul fondo* is a film that avoids the rhetoric associated with *Alcazar*. In many ways, this film can be compared to the war films produced in Hollywood and in England, and critics have also noted connections between DeRobertis's film and postwar neorealism. The film begins by crediting the cooperation of the Italian navy, of its torpedo squadrons, and of the ships *Titano* and *Cyclope*. It is dedicated "to the heroism of the men in the submarine crews in war and peace." *Uomini* tells the story of a damaged submarine and of the rescue efforts to save the men. Unlike Rossellini's *La nave bianca* (The White Ship), the film does not introduce romantic elements but moves in linear fashion through the stages of the rescue operation, highlighting the efficiency and elaborateness of the work, the hazards to which the men are exposed, the cooperative relationships of the men, the nature of their heroism, sense of collective responsibility, altruism, and the responses of their families to their plight.

The action alternates between the events at sea and on land. The emphasis is on those actions and behaviors that reveal the generosity, humanity, and dedication of the men, the attachment to family, to friends, to animals, the acts of courtesy and generosity under stress, the emphasis on horizontal rather than vertical relations. There are no waving banners,

[36] Ibid., p. 354.

fascist insignias, no charismatic leaders, no parades, no ceremonies of dedication, and the emphasis is on survival rather
than on heroic death and sacrifice. Even in the sequence
where rescue operations are led by individuals, the film does
not overplay the role of these men in relation to the vaster
network of people involved in the enterprise.

In the photography and editing of men and machinery, in
conjunction with the specific equipment that fails, the equipment used in locating the lost ship, and the equipment necessary for the rescue, the men are portrayed as in control of
the machinery. Unlike Ruttmann's *Acciaio* (Steel), where the
machinery seems to have an identity of its own and seems
to signify a dynamism of production independent of or even
hostile to the men who control it, in DeRobertis's film the
relationship between men and machines is central. Even
though the submarine is damaged as a result of a collision,
only minimal destruction ensues, and it is as the result of the
competent handling by the men of the rescue equipment that
the rescue is effected.

DeRobertis stresses, however, the dangers of the sea and
the precariousness of life aboard this sealed underwater ship
rather than idealizing the work and workers. The insertion
of scenes involving concerned families who listen to reports
on the radio of the rescue operation and individuals waiting
on shore for a return of the ships serves to personalize the
responses. Rather than presenting these characters as mar-
tyrs, as transfigured through suffering, the film presents them
within the context of their daily lives, as anxious but also
hopeful, as concerned but as confident, as being involved in
the fate of their family members rather than in military or
political motives. The epilogue of the film, dedicated "to those
who will not return so that the sea will be ours," seems to
contain the actual sense of loss, stripped of histrionics and
the idea that victory is based on inevitable loss without consolation and compensation.

In its unceremonious, anti-epic, basically medium-shot
photography, the film, while fulfilling its objectives of being
a war film in the interests of the Italian struggle, also visually

and thematically subverts certain important features associated with the representation of fascist ideology in both its overt and subtle forms. The film focuses on ordinary people. Their appearance, their dress, their actions are commonplace. The absence of military formations, regimental regalia, triumphal music, and rhetorical speeches, indicates that DeRobertis is primarily concerned with the issue of survival. While the film does emphasize the male group, male relationships do not emanate from an abstract ideal of collectivity but rather from the idea of cooperation engendered through the emergency.

DeRobertis's film is thus interesting for several reasons: its scaling down of war to human proportions, its subversion of the idea of leadership and dependence on a single authority, its focus on survival rather than combat, its focus on individuals and small groups rather than on the masses. While the film is obviously not a film of resistance to war, nor could it be, its filmic discourse seems to suggest a different direction in Italian genre practices.

DeRobertis's use of contemporary history in the context of the war film differs from the style and language associated with the traditional nationalist epics. Most particularly, the style of *Uomini*, like its British and American counterparts, portrays the men as "doing a job" and as cultivating the "stiff upper lip" in contrast to emotional excess. Moreover, the film does not allegorize its characters or events but addresses what it portrays. The film thus invites a reading of itself as a critique of existing political and aesthetic practices.

*La nave bianca* (The White Ship), directed by Roberto Rosellini in the same year that *Uomini* was made, 1941, takes place on an actual ship and features nonprofessional actors. The style and point of view of the film differs from those of DeRobertis, chiefly in the presentation of combat. Even more than *Uomini* the film plays with certain generic features of the war film: the classic departure for combat, the emphasis on the "stiff upper lip," joking and camaraderie in the face of danger, the uplifting presence of the women nurses and volunteers, the "madrina," who do their patriotic service for the war effort, the linking of romance and combat, and the presence, though diluted, of military ceremony.

The plot very simply involves the men aboard a combat ship. As a result of a dramatic encounter with the enemy, some of the men are wounded and transferred to a hospital ship where they are competently tended. Basso, the central character, had anticipated meeting a woman who, as her patriotic duty, had undertaken to write the men letters containing news of home and items of general encouragement. Unable to meet her because of the hasty departure for combat, he is disappointed and waits for further news from his correspondent. He is wounded, but the woman is assigned to the hospital ship. Basso's wounds at first are so extensive that he cannot recognize her, but with her gentle tending he is finally restored to consciousness. The two are united in a mutual declaration of affection as the ship returns to port.

Like DeRobertis, Rosellini attempts to humanize the men, to elevate rather than suppress the nature and effects of war.[37] The film does not glorify militarism. The characters, sailors and officers, do not orate, posture, or exalt the use of force. Here, too, the emphasis is on healing and survival rather than on heroic sacrifice. The rescue and care of the men occupies a larger proportion of the film than do the battle scenes, the battle scenes serving more as the motivation for the rescue by the hospital ship. The narrative focuses on an ordinary sailor rather than on a beleaguered officer. The film ends not with a dedication to the war or to the glory of the Italian heroes, but to the "stoic suffering and faith of the wounded."

The photography in the film is also used in ways not normally associated with the films that aestheticize war. The film opens, strangely, with an image of a cannon rising frontally, directed at the spectator. Throughout the film, Rossellini will use this shot of the cannon photographed from different angles (as in *Potemkin*), but especially with this intimidating

[37] Pio Baldelli, "Les débûts de Rossellini et le cinéma de Salo (1943-1944)," in *Fascisme et résistance dans le cinéma italien (1922-1968)*, ed. Jean A. Gili (Paris: Lettres Modernes Menard, 1970), pp. 41-43.

frontal shot. The montage editing of the cannons and of the battle scenes portrays the power, the destructive power, of the weapons, and this is linked to the effects of the armaments on human beings. Juxtaposed to those scenes are those that stress the camaraderie of the men and the role of those who sustain rather than destroy life. For example, Rossellini portrays the difficulties encountered by the physicians as they seek to tend their patients during the battle.

The film is thus a curious mixture of the familiar aspects of fascist epics and a subversion of their practices. Combat and male solidarity in the war effort are deemphasized. The character of the *madrina*, similar to the nurses in the Hollywood film, while providing a romantic element, does not idealize such notions as duty, renunciation of desire, or self-sacrifice. Nor do the romantic elements serve as a legitimation for war, nor the preservation of the family and the traditional values associated with it. The use of nonprofessional actors contributes to a less inflated view of the conflicts in the film. The people and the events are not treated in the conventional manner of the epic film that depends on the exceptional, the identification with the unattainable, and the spectacle so necessary to the mythologizing of experience. Instead, Rossellini's film, like DeRobertis's, aligns itself with a new trend in documentary filmmaking of the 1940s, a filmmaking that was less rhetorical and stridently militant, if not necessarily and overtly against war and imperialism.

## Summary

An examination of the historical films reveals stylistic diversity and a spectrum of ideological treatments within boundaries permissible for the times, given the strictures of censorship. Looking at the films chronologically reveals changes in perspective and style, ranging from the blatant celebrations of war and empire in the films of the early and middle thirties to the films of the early forties that focus on issues of survival rather than epic conquests. These changes can be accounted for as a consequence of the changing ideological climate as well as by the increased technical experimentation and expertise in production. Peter Bondanella has remarked on the "noticeable trend toward a realistic style during the years preceding the advent of the first neorealist works."[38]

However, the films of war and empire, like the later films to which Bondanella refers, are not markedly different from the Hollywood and British films that treat historical subjects and from the war films of the period. The Italian historical films, with some notable exceptions like *Condottieri*, share with the British films of empire and the Hollywood westerns their myths of manifest destiny. For the most part, the Italian films are nationalistic, drawing on familiar events from Roman, Renaissance, and Risorgimento history to portray the struggles for dominance and power. Like their American and British counterparts, the Italian films use the history in allegorical fashion in order to develop their political themes, and generally the politicizing is indirect rather than overt. Romance, adventure, intrigue, spectacle, and voyeurism take precedence over propagandizing. The films strive to offer their audiences entertainment and pleasure in much the same ways as the Hollywood films of that era did. Seduction of the audience is more common than coercion, though the films are not opaque, and the discerning viewer can detect the emphasis on certain recurring motifs: the importance of the powerful leader, the need for national unity, the supremacy of Italian culture, the legitimation of war in the name of the preservation of the values of family and civilization, and the necessary and willing cooperation of the masses in the enterprise of war and empire. But the films also reveal the ways in which they transform actual events into myth, the way in which they use their historical personages in order to legitimize the aims of nationalism if not fascism, or, as in Blasetti's *Un' avventura di Salvator Rosa* and the war films of Rossellini and DeRobertis, offer oblique critiques of power and of violence.

In short, the historical films of the era are not uniform and

<hr>

[38] Bondanella, *Italian Cinema*, p. 19.

monolithic. They differ in their subject matter, in their treatment, and in the degrees to which they adhere to the ideology of fascism, struggling at times consciously to expose exploitation and oppression, but, for the most part, yielding up through their historical subject matter, selection, and style, an insight into the eclectic ideology of fascism. The uses and abuses of history are an important element in what Gramsci calls "folklore," the mosaic of contradictory attitudes that constitute ideology.

# CHAPTER FIVE

# The Comic Vision of Work and Play

In 1977, Stuart Byron and Elisabeth Weis made the following assumption about the Italian comedies during the years of fascism: "Under fascism . . . it's well known that the film industry went through a 'white telephone era,' and apparently the comedies, like the other movies, were about the class of people who could afford white telephones. The neorealist movement, which stunned the world when it appeared after the fall of Mussolini, concerned itself with the kinds of people, urban and rural, who had black telephones, or, more likely, none at all."[1] An examination of the comedies produced during the era, along with the other films, reveals that such a perception of the Italian cinema cannot be documented. The subject of this chapter is the relationship between the comedies of the era and their treatment of class issues, most particularly their focus on work and workers.

The comedies are indeed a sore spot in any discussion of the film productions of the thirties and forties. More than the historical films, the melodramas, and the films that overtly celebrate the new fascist culture, the comedies are dismissed as escapist, apolitical, and trivial. The films are neither apolitical nor trivial. They are a rich resource for the politics of containment, the ways in which ideology is clothed in the language of myth, fantasy, and dream. If they are to be described as escapist, then the idea of escapism must be redefined. First of all, the films reckon with familial and sexual relationships; issues of power, dominance, and subordination; economic success and failure; and isolation and community, topics characteristic of the genre of comedy. Moreover, they treat these issues, as is also common, with irony,

---

[1] Stuart Byron and Elisabeth Weis, eds., *The National Society of Film Critics on Movie Comedy* (New York: Grossman, 1977), pp. 259-60.

detachment, exaggeration, and, in some instances, with self-consciousness. Their superficial appearance of conventionality, their use of types and stereotypes, and their forms of audience address conceal frightening and serious issues.

Film comedy was a popular genre in Italy during the thirties and forties.[2] One type of comedy, the "comedian film," was associated with Macario and with Totò, whose films were to become internationally known in the postwar era. Totò's style, according to Peter Bondanella, "combined elements from the classic silent cinema as well as the native Commedia dell'Arte and Neapolitan theatrical traditions."[3] In this type of comedy, the personality of the actor takes precedence over the narrative structure. The camera techniques and editing are static, and the comedian himself can be considered the film *auteur*. Eric Bentley attributes the success of this type of comedy to the comedian's ability to establish a bond with a wide audience. The low comedian is the "real, if unpolitical champion of the common man."[4] Totò's work is characterized by an unusual blending of the bawdy and the dignified, the common and the aristocratic. The comedian creates identification through levelling class distinctions and, in particular, dignifying the commonplace, the "little man."

Romantic and social comedies of the sort produced by such directors as Max Neufeld, Goffredo Alessandrini, Raffaello Matarazzo, and Vittorio De Sica were typical, if not more popular. By far, the most successful and representative director of romantic comedies was Mario Camerini. His films focus on what Steve Seidman has described as the "dialectic between ec-

[2] Ernesto G. Laura, "A proposito di generi: Il film comico," in *Cinema italiano sotto il fascismo*, ed. Riccardo Redi (Venice: Marsilio, 1979), pp. 117-27.

[3] See also Mira Liehm, *Passion and Defiance: Film in Italy from 1942 to the Present* (Berkeley and Los Angeles: University of California Press, 1984), pp. 11-12, 22. For a further discussion of the centrality of and the continuing predilection for comedy in the Italian cinema, see Gian Piero Brunetta, *Storia del cinema italiano 1895-1945* (Rome: Riuniti, 1979), pp. 490-99, and Peter Bondanella, *Italian Cinema: From Neorealism to the Present* (New York: Frederick Ungar, 1983), pp. 86-89.

[4] Eric Bentley, *In Search of Theater* (New York: Alfred A. Knopf, 1953), pp. 76-77.

centric behavior and social conformity at the level of sexual confrontation between male and female. The confrontation has several variations . . . but it ultimately reaffirms marriage as a culturally important institution."[5] These films are of two varieties, the family comedy and the sexual comedy, which both resolve their conflicts in a marriage or in the regeneration of a marriage. Marriage is a synecdoche for the social structure and for social institutions. The significant aspect of the films is not their resolution but their conflicts.

The Hungarian cinema provided models of sophisticated romantic comedy and, like the Hollywood films of Ernst Lubitsch and George Cukor, portrayed the sexual conflicts and escapades of the rich. The classic elements of this comedy include the domestication of the roving husband, the reaffirmation of the wife's chastity, and, above all, the regeneration of the marriage. Through the personal complications of the wealthy class, "the audience could be reassured that the filthy rich were, after all, folks like you and me, and that although money didn't necessarily buy happiness, it certainly generated some interesting social and sexual complications."[6] The tendency of the upper-crust film, therefore, is to level any distinction between the haves and the have-nots and to create a sense of community in the common quest for personal gratification.

A large number of films of this era reveal a populist inclination, and, as in Camerini films, focus on the world of workers: taxi drivers, newspaper vendors, department store clerks, factory workers, and the unemployed. Some of the romantic comedies portray peasants in collision with rapacious landlords and repressive authority figures. These films dramatize the struggles of the peasants to redeem their self-respect and

[5] Steve Seidman, *Comedian Comedy: A Tradition in Hollywood Film* (Ann Arbor: UMI Research Press, 1981), p. 62.

[6] Thomas Schatz, Hollywood Genres: *Formulas, Filmmaking, and the Studio System* (New York: Random House, 1981), p. 150. See also Stanley Cavell, *The World Viewed: Reflections on the Ontology of Film* (New York: Viking, 1971), pp. 47-50, and Robert Bechtold Heilman, *The Ways of the World: Comedy and Society* (Seattle: University of Washington Press, 1978), pp. 32-34, 58-59.

to live harmoniously in a potentially idyllic pastoral setting. Camerini's *Il cappello a tre punte* would be a characteristic film.

The comedies of urban life concentrate on the sights and sounds of the city and on the conflicts of young men and women as they confront urban complexity, seek financial betterment, and often a rise in status. Complicating these economic and social objectives is, of course, the hero or heroine's search for personal fulfillment in love. The desire for personal satisfaction collides with the desire for upward mobility. In a few of the films, the resolution allows the attainment of both economic and sexual desires. In Camerini's *Darò un milione* and *Batticuore*, the heroine achieves love and wealth. More frequently, the resolution favors a compromise. The attainment of modest economic rewards is compensated by romantic gratification after a cold and alienating encounter with the world of the rich. The satiric treatment of the rich and powerful is as important in the films as their "happy endings."

The comedies with a populist bent seem modelled more along the lines of the Hollywood cinema, especially the films of Frank Capra. According to Thomas Schatz, "In particular, Capra injected a sense of homespun populism and middle class ideology" into the "frantic, decadent world of the idle rich."[7] The same comments can be applied to the films of Camerini at their best. However, there are important differences between the Hollywood and Italian comedies. For example, the portrayal of individualism so congenial to the Hollywood hero is absent. The most important strategy in the Italian comedy is the assimilation of the worker into his or her milieu after a period of trial and temptation in the upper-crust wilderness. In the Hollywood romantic comedy, the union of the male and female is, as in traditional romantic comedy (New Comedy) tied to the regeneration of the community. In the preponderance of the Italian comedies, and, in Camerini's films in particular, the audience is given no vision of a transfigured society. The unregenerate world re-

[7] Ibid.

mains intact and the only real changes effected are in the personal relations of the lovers. The lovers create their own separate community through self-imposed withdrawal and isolation from the destructive world. In the film's portrayal of sexual conflict, both male and female figures are domesticated. Moreover, the partnership of male and female in love and work as a resolution to the sexual conflict is rare.

These points of difference are as instructive as the points of similarity between the American and Italian films. Antonio Gramsci had commented on the introduction of American culture into Europe in the following manner: "The elements of a 'new culture' and a 'new way of life' which are being spread under the American label are just tentative feelers. . . . It is an unconscious reaction on the part of those who are impotent to rebuild." And Gramsci asked "whether America through the implacable might of her economic production (and therefore indirectly) will compel or is compelling Europe to overturn its excessively antiquated economic and social base."[8]

The style and preoccupations of the Italian film comedy seem to corroborate Gramsci's identification of the presence of Americanization as well as its tentative nature. According to Victoria de Grazia, the attempt to create a popular culture in Italy was Janus-faced, looking backward to the "paternalistic schemes of an earlier era of capitalism" and forward "to those social welfare services of advanced capitalism."[9] The films look backward to more traditional ideas and motifs of paternalism, regionalism, and familialism, but they also inscribe new images of urban life, work, productivity, and reservations about authority. In the thirties, the "popular culture" did "appropriate petty bourgeois ideological motifs, popular ritual forms, and, if only momentarily during the mid-thirties, a populist language with potential appeal to in-

[8] Antonio Gramsci, *Selections from the Prison Notebooks*, ed. Quentin Hoare and Geoffrey Nowell-Smith (New York: International Publishers, 1978), p. 317.

[9] Victoria de Grazia, *The Culture of Consent: Mass Organization of Leisure in Fascist Italy* (Cambridge: Cambridge University Press, 1981), p. viii.

dustrial workers."[10] Through the efforts of the Dopolavoro
the organization developed to organize the leisure-time activities of workers, the regime attempted to use sports, popular festivals, radio, and the cinema to create consensus and
to develop appeals to the worker "on the basis of non-work-
place identities."[11] The attempt to woo the workers was slip-
pery, since the regime had to circumvent the development of
a Marxist class consciousness and class division, yet at the
same time create an incentive for production and collectivity
expunged of Marxian associations.

The many contradictions surrounding the treatment of
work and workers are apparent in the films. The social/ro-
mantic comedies are a particularly appropriate place to look
for attitudes toward work and play, and I have largely pre-
selected these comedies for discussion, since they seemed to
be most representative of the film comedies produced and
most congenial to a dicussion of social class. Their treatment
of the immediate environment, their focus on the nature of
everyday relations, stylized though the representations might
be, communicate subtle differences in attitude toward social
institutions and conceptions of class. Some of the films represent positive and celebratory images of work and collectivity; others seek to emphasize leisure by portraying festivals,
sports, and tourism; still others portray the workers' consolation in the family. Moreover, many of these films are not
silent about the tensions that exist between the sexes and
between social classes.

*La segretaria privata* (Private Secretary, 1931), a joint German-
Italian production, presents a version of the modern independent woman,[12] but, as in many of the films that focus on
women, her independence is short-lived. The modernity is
illusory, merely a vehicle to recuperate the female into the
domestic sphere, rewarding her with economic compensa-
tions through her marriage to a rich man. Her modern ap-

---

[10] Ibid., p. 223.
[11] Ibid., p. 5.
[12] Francesco Savio, *Ma l'amore no* (Milan: Sonzogno, 1975), p. 315.

pearance, is a superficial cloak, like the film itself, for the traditional notions of female chastity and respectability. The other females in the film are portrayed as failures, doomed, like the audience, to be voyeurs of the heroine's success and rewarded vicariously through the comic fantasy of success. Elsa, the central character, played by Elsa Merlini, is a young woman who comes alone to the big city to find work. She puts herself up in the Pensione Primavera, a residence for young working women. The women are shown seated at the dinner table, all complaining of the sameness of the food and the monotony and low pay of their jobs. Elsa is more idealistic than they. She is a typist and she has fantasies of finding success in spite of the women's efforts to convince her of the dreary and unromantic nature of life and work in the city.

At the bank where she seeks employment, she is told that there are no jobs available. Undaunted, Elsa flatters Otello, the porter, about his musical abilities. They discuss opera and Elsa presents herself as a great music lover. She reminds him that even her name is operatic, for Elsa is a character in *Lohengrin*. Won over, Otello goes to the chief of personnel and gains an interview for Elsa. The personnel chief tries to seduce her and offers her a position on a "trial" basis. Delighted at getting the job she sings, "Oh come sono felice" (How Happy I am), a song that became popular in the era. At work on the following day, she is seated among a row of typists as the head of personnel marches up and down the aisle like a schoolmaster or a military officer. In contrast to the other workers, Elsa sings as she works. The chief of personnel, annoyed at her spurning of his advances, begins to find fault with her work and to harass her. She complains to Otello and threatens to complain to the banker himself whom she has never met. Working overtime to complete her heavy burden of typing, she is discovered by Berri the banker (Nino Besozzi), who asks her why she is still in the office. Unaware of his identity, she informs him that she is struggling to meet the stringent demands of the personnel director. He offers to help her, thus discovering that the mistakes in the typing text are not hers at all, but the work of the personnel director. He invites her to join him for dinner at a restaurant. Berri is portrayed as egalitarian, benevolent, and capable of enjoying himself with his employees. After dinner, Berri wants to take her home but she refuses, informing him that she is waiting for the "right man."

Elsa finally learns Berri's identity when she marches into his office to complain about more tyranny at the hands of the director. Berri arranges to send his own secretary off on an errand and asks Elsa to come to his house to take dictation. When she arrives at Berri's house, she realizes that he is trying to seduce her, and she leaves angrily, quits her job, and decides to leave the city. Repentant, Berri confesses his love for Elsa and proposes marriage as Otello, at the keyhole, peers at the lovers.

The combination of comedy with certain musical elements serves to enhance the film's fantasy structures. With the typical motif of the working girl who marries her boss, the film is a classical romantic comedy. *Segretaria privata* uses Hollywood themes, conventions, and style, but, in particular, the fantasy of escaping the working class and thereby low wages, drudgery, and exploitation. In this respect, this film seems more consonant with Hollywood depression comedies than with the populist orientation of the Camerini and Blasetti comedies. Alessandrini's banker is not the butt of satire. He is basically good, in that he will marry out of his own class for love and adopt the more stringent work ethic and sexual morality of the worker. The real villain is the intermediary, the chief of personnel who tyrannizes the workers. The banker's only flaw, one that appears to be a convention in the portrayal of bankers in the Italian films of the era, is his promiscuity, from which he is "saved" by Elsa. The marriage between bourgeois and worker reinforces not only the image of class collaboration but of sexual compromise. In exchange for her elevated status, Elsa becomes the guardian of the banker's chastity. The personnel director is chastised for his sexual license.

Although the film makes Elsa "special" and removes her from the context of routinization, bureaucracy, and exploitation, it also emphasizes the constraints of working-class life through the conversations at the pension and the scenes at work. Elsa's specialness thus inscribes the myth of upward mobility while at the same time closing off that possibility to the majority.

Thus, Alessandrini gives a keyhole view of work as drudgery in order to offer the fantasy of being saved from it. The point is made several times, however, and in several ways that this "release" is not for everyone. Elsa's elevation is ascribed to her superior beauty, industriousness, competence, cheerful attitude, playfulness, and, above all, her moral superiority, which enables her to resist sexual exploitation. Moreover, as indicated in her dialogues with the other women, she sets her goals much higher and is, therefore, more enterprising than her fellow workers.

The film plays with specularity in a number of ways: in the way it makes Elsa the center of the internal audience's regard from the time she is observed at the train station, through her surveillance by the director of personnel, to her scrutinization by the other women. The element of voyeurism is particularly highlighted in the final scenes where Otello and the women take their positions at the keyhole to observe the reconciliation of Elsa and Berri. The voyeurism makes it possible for the audience to "get into the picture," to become involved and occupy a prominent position in relation to the action.[13]

Otello's role as conductor is a surrogate for the film director and enhances the idea of life as performance. He directs Elsa to her job, which makes it possible for her to marry the banker. At the end, he directs the surrogate audience of women who as a chorus happily end the film. Thus, the film plays with its uses of fantasy, seeking to bridge the dichotomy between fantasy and reality. These seemingly self-reflexive elements are not used, however, to create a distance between perform-

[13] Noël Burch, "Correction, Please, or, How We Got into Pictures" (Great Britain: Arts Council of Britain Production, 1979), 16 mm., 52 minutes, color, sound.

ance and spectators but rather to create a bond between film and audience, implicating the external audience with the internal audience in the fantasy elements, gratifying and legitimizing voyeurism. The woman, the object of the look, is the point of convergence, in particular upon her acquisition of the banker.

A different conception of romance and work is offered by Mario Camerini's *Rotaie* (Rails), also made in 1931. A transitional film from the silent to the sound cinema, *Rotaie* begins as a melodrama and ends as a comedy. In fact, the juxtaposition of comedy and melodrama reinforces other strategies in the film that work to transform the decadent community into the utopian world of work and marriage intrinsic to comedy. The film develops the opposition between productive work and social parasitism. The solidarity of the industrious workers is elevated and the alienation of easy wealth denigrated. Upward mobility is a trap, and young people must go through a series of trials and initiation rites, culminating with their entry into responsibility and compromise with their own social class. Along with their discovery of the virtues of work, the lovers also find their appropriate domestic positions.

The film opens at night on a darkened street. Inside, a man signs his name on a hotel register, later adding the words "and wife," and thus revealing the couple as newlyweds. The man, Giorgio, assures the clerk that he will pay for his room in the morning, though he has no money. In the room, the couple sit, depressed, and the young woman reads a letter from her mother and cries. An image of a glass of water with a dissolving pill reveals that the desperate couple is about to commit a double suicide. As they hold hands for the last time, a train passes and the vibrations cause the glass to topple to the floor. The couple decides to leave the hotel and the city. They go to the train station where they find a wallet filled with money. Unable to find the owner, Giorgio takes the money and buys train tickets.

The couple meets Mercier, a slick gambler, who becomes interested in Maria, and they decide to detrain with him to stay at a hotel called "Honeymoon" where Giorgio hopes to augment their money through gambling. He spends his time at the gaming tables, leaving Maria alone and at the mercy of Mercier. Recognizing that their relationship is deteriorating, she begs Giorgio to leave the hotel, but he refuses. Totally obsessed, indifferent even to the debts he is accumulating, Giorgio remains riveted to the roulette wheel until restrained by the establishment. As a way of furthering his designs on Maria, Mercier gives Giorgio money to pay his debts. The gambler invites Maria to his room. Giorgio awakens from his trance and saves Maria from the seducer's clutches.

Their exit from the "Honeymoon" parallels their earlier escape from their hotel after the abortive suicide attempt. They spend the night in the park. At sunrise, they awaken and go to the train station. Once again on a train, they share their compartment, but this time with working-class people. The image of train tracks dissolves to smokestacks and images of factory machinery and of factory workers leaving for lunch. Giorgio has now become a productive worker, supported and sustained by Maria.

The film builds to its celebration of working-class life by negation. Like a parable, leisured life is portrayed as evil and decadent, associated with exploitation, vulnerability to unscrupulous elements like Mercier, psychological degeneration, sexual conflict, and self-destructiveness. The young unemployed couple are, according to the film, not well served by having found the unearned wealth. The antidote to this destructive existence is productive labor and family affection.

Like the films of conversion, Giorgio moves through a pattern of transformation, a passage from despair, obsession-compulsion, contemplated suicide, to creative work and the sublimation of desire. The populist element in the film resides in the elevation of the common man, the worker, who is redeemed and redeems others. Maria becomes the agent of his redemption. Giorgio's salvation depends on his saving her from the clutches of the seducer and thereby expressing his concern for the sanctity of women and hence of the family.

The inexorable movement of the narrative toward its resolution and establishment of equilibrium is developed by means of the imagery of wheels, the conjunction of train wheels, roulette wheels, and the wheels of the factory machinery. The first phase of the narrative is marked by the image of train wheels and is associated with the aimless movement of the couple, penniless, without means to succeed, and without a goal. The second phase is marked by the image of the roulette wheel, which brackets their involvement in the world of easy gain, seduction, treachery, and humiliation. The final phase returns to the image of the moving train wheels and ends with the symbols of work. The film's association of leisure with decadence and with the upper classes seems to be linked to the Dopolavoro attitude toward the organizing of workers' lives around productivity. Legitimate leisure could, therefore, be connected only to organized activities, and not to individual indulgence. Even leisure takes on the character of performance. The value of work seems obviously to supersede pleasure.

If *Rotaie* veers toward melodrama before reversing its course and flowing into comedy, Camerini's 1932 film *Gli uomini, che mascalzoni* (Men, What Rascals) is more consistently satiric. The film seeks to evoke laughter in its ironic treatment of the workers as they stray from their appropriate positions and need to be reclaimed.

*Gli uomini* is one of a number of films Camerini made that address the fantasies and desires of workers.[14] In most of his comedies, he links variations on the family romance to economic issues of survival. The rich are, for the most part, satirized. Camerini's effectiveness as a filmmaker is accounted for in several ways: the choice of such excellent actors as Assia Noris, Vittorio De Sica, Lia Franca, and Luigi Almirante who are carried over from film to film; a high level of technical expertise; the effective use of certain basic myths and archetypes congenial to comedy such as mistaken identity, romantic complications, social disorder, and restabilization; and the

[14] Ted Perry, "Before Neorealism" (New York: Museum of Modern Art, 1978), mimeographed, p. 4.

creation of narratives and characters that are similar to the everyday conflicts experienced by the audiences. The conflict is often generated by the hero or heroine's confusion over the quest for wealth and status, or with some form of social pretension. Camerini's characters are drawn from a repertory of comic types: foolish rich men and women, fops, decadent aristocrats, naive and inexperienced young men, sparkling young heroines endowed with good sense, spirit, and independence, and a variety of lesser supporting characters whose wisdom or folly provides insights for the hero's education.

The narratives are developed by means of incremental repetition, the use of prolepsis, parallels, and contrasts, which are reiterated in different contexts, stated and restated so as to call attention to certain themes and attitudes. The action itself is focused on transformations in character, enhanced by means of music, dialogue, and abundant physical movement. The placing of the action in settings appropriate to the character's role and to the class milieu lends an aura of credibility to the events and social conflicts portrayed. An analysis of Camerini's films offers insight into the ways in which bourgeois ideology can be made to appear attractive. The fantasies in his films come closest to the Hollywood films of the era in their ability to make fantasy appear to speak to real needs and aspirations. Camerini's comedies address those banal aspects of life associated with the daily struggle for survival.

*Gli uomini, che mascalzoni* employs many images of work. The heroine's father is a taxi driver and he is shown on the job. Mariuccia (Lia Franca), his daughter, is a shopgirl, and the film lingers on the rhythms and commonplace routines of work. Bruno (Vittorio De Sica), a chauffeur, attempts to impress her with his importance, passing himself off as a man of means. He offers her a ride in his employer's car. He decides to take her for a ride in the country where the two stop at an inn for refreshment and relaxation. The pastoral scene provides a contrast to the city. The people at the inn are dancing and singing. Bruno's employer's wife and friends arrive and demand to be taken home. He slips away unnoticed so Mariuccia will not discover the truth about his work. As Bruno speeds back to the city, he damages the car.

Mariuccia sits at the inn alone, waiting. When all the customers have left, it becomes clear that Bruno will not return. The inn is ready to close and she is left with the bill for which she is somewhat short of money. The innkeeper, properly sympathetic, waives the balance and commiserates with her about what scoundrels men are. When Bruno tries to recontact her, she will have nothing to do with him. Out of work, he begins to seek another position. By means of a montage sequence built around a want ad and a hand opening a mailbox several times, the information is communicated that Bruno is having difficulty finding work. Finally, he finds another position as a chauffeur.

Coincidentally, Bruno's new employer goes to Mariuccia's shop. Bruno sees Mariuccia also leaving and he hides behind the car. The employer, however, invites her for a ride. She refuses until she spies Bruno. As Bruno drives, the man tries to seduce Mariuccia. Enraged, Bruno stops the car, gets out, and tells his employer to drive the car himself. Traffic becomes congested and a policeman, sympathetic to Bruno, tells the employer to remove his car. Bruno accuses Mariuccia of only being interested in rich men, and they quarrel.

From one of her co-workers whom he meets on the street, Bruno learns that Mariuccia has left the shop and is now working a stand at a trade exhibition. Bruno finds her and they reconcile. He takes a job conducting tours of a factory. After work, Bruno arrives at the fair only to learn from Mariuccia's fellow worker that Mariuccia has left on a date. The woman, herself interested in Bruno, omits to explain the reason that Mariuccia has gone to dinner with the man—in order to find employment for Bruno. Angrily, Bruno invites the woman out and the following sequences take place in a restaurant as Bruno scornfully ignores Mariuccia while she sits soulfully watching him.

The final reunion of the lovers takes place with the assistance of Mariuccia's father. Bruno leaves the other woman and confronts Mariuccia. He calls a taxi, and the cab driver turns out to be her father who, unrecognized by his daughter, eavesdrops on their quarreling. The lovers reconcile when Mariuccia explains the reason for the dinner. The father takes the two young people into a bar and orders drinks for them, delighted with the prospect of his daughter's marriage. A horn reminds him of his work. He takes Mariuccia to the door of their apartment and sends her in, locking the door behind her, and invites Bruno to accompany him on his job.

Camerini's film plays self-consciously with the idea of spectatorship. Throughout the film, he utilizes strategies that call attention to the idea of observation and surveillance. Bruno's ogling and pursuit of Mariuccia is only one instance of looking. Camerini develops several audience surrogates through the young women who observe and act as choric commentators on Bruno's behavior: the "audience" at the inn that witnesses Bruno's singing and applauds it, Bruno's surveillance of Mariuccia and his employer through the rear-view mirror, the jealous surveillance of Mariuccia's co-worker at the fair, and, finally, Mariuccia's father who also surveys his daughter and Bruno through his mirror. The forms of looking help to establish different themes and different responses to the action. Camerini's self-conscious highlighting of ways of looking contribute, it would seem, to bonding filmmaker and audience, creating a self-enclosed community parallel to the one created within the film. The director and audience are implicated in the fate of the main characters. The voyeurism offers a way of privileging the external audience, situating the spectator in the position of the director.

Though Camerini portrays the routinization of work, the arbitrariness of employers, the difficulty of finding employment, the real conflict is the romantic conflict. The other elements relating to work are relegated to the role of obstructions to the main task, lovers' reconciliation, marriage, and future domesticity. The father's role, which opens and closes the film, seems to indicate that such reconciliation is possible under the aegis of the father figure. The same pattern is repeated in *Il signor Max* where the guiding role is occupied by the uncle.

Camerini's treatment of class issues is predictable in this film. Members of the same class belong with one another—safety resides in such a union. The rich only create difficulties for workers and they are satirized. Each class is restored to its proper domain, and the workers are rewarded by the guarantee of personal happiness derived from the sharing of common feelings, values, and interests. The sense of social continuity is reinforced at the end of *Gli uomini, che mascalzoni* in the bonding between the father and the future son-in-law, the taxi driver and the chauffeur. Moreover, Camerini seems to imply a distinction between the role of taxi driver and chauffeur. Mariuccia's father's work is portrayed as self-sufficient whereas Bruno's is dependent on the rich, and the father's work is preferable. Bruno's emulation of the rich gets him into trouble in the first place, and in his work, he balks at the dependency of his role, finally preferring unemployment to being a passive observer to his employer's seduction of Mariuccia. Even his position as tour guide in the factory appears uncomfortable and ridiculous. Thus, the film portrays the populist attitudes of self-sufficiency, family harmony, class solidarity (without class consciousness), male comradeship, and benevolent patriarchal authority. These attitudes are offered as compensation for social and economic impotence, attitudes that are raised but never confronted directly or "resolved."

The sexual relations in the film follow the conventions of romantic comedy. The male or female pursues an unwilling object of desire who succumbs at first, is disillusioned, withdraws, must be pursued even more intensely, and is finally conquered. The language implies the not-so-pleasing image of the chase and the surrender of the "victim." In the Camerini film, the male begins as the hunter, but, though he succeeds in capturing the female, he retreats from the economic world. His impotence in the world of commerce is not overcome. The resolution to his dilemma is retreat into the family, where he not only gains a wife but a father. Camerini was not naive about the defeat of the workers.

Alessandro Blasetti, too, was not indifferent to the position of workers and the unemployed in his films. In *La tavola dei poveri* (The Table of the Poor, 1932), a satiric comedy, he exposes false philanthropy and antiquated conceptions of aristocracy. The focal point in the film is the poor, but the dramatic interest resides in the opposition between a penurious aristocrat and a productive businessman. The film has its romantic complications. Like Camerini's *Rotaie* and Ruttmann's *Acciaio*, the film fuses comedy and melodrama but less for utopian purposes and more for the intensification of the social satire.

*La tavola*, one of the director's less epic films, does not concern itself with the overt political struggle so characteristic of *Vecchia guardia*, nor does it play with history and myth as exemplified in such films as *1860*, *Corona di ferro*, or *Salvator Rosa*. Set in a contemporary context, *Tavola* points a finger at the opposition between giving "charity" and providing work as the vehicle for developing and then "resolving" class oppositions.

The solid citizens of the community are organizing a charity drive for the construction of an almshouse. Mrs. Valmadonna, a wealthy woman enthusiastic about the fund drive, announces a dinner for the poor that will be held at the Volterra estate to celebrate the successful completion of the charitable project. Only one person opposes the project on the grounds that it would be better to put the poor to work.

The Marquis, Fusaro (Raffaele Viviani), an impoverished nobleman, is a member of the committee, though ironically he cannot even pay his servants. The butler offers to work without pay, aware of his master's situation. Fusaro is reduced to pawning his belongings, especially his paintings. Volterra, a rich lawyer-industrialist (Mario Ferrari), arrives and admires Fusaro's painting. He offers to buy it, but Fusaro is reluctant to sell. Before he leaves, Volterra meets Giorgina and invites the father and daughter to a party at his house. A new arrival, Biase (Salvatore Costa), complicates Fusaro's financial affairs further. Although appearing destitute, Biase, in fact, has a considerable amount of money that he wants Fusaro to invest for him. Fusaro tells Biase that he is mad, but the beggar insists that he wants the Marquis to take care of the funds. Biase does not realize that the Marquis is more of a mendicant than he. A delegation from the Benevolence Committee arrives, sees the money on the desk and assumes that this is Fusaro's contribution to their fund drive. The delegation elects him president of the committee, and he, of course, accepts.

The Volterra house creates a contrast between authentic wealth and Fusaro's shabby genteel existence. The lawyer takes Fusaro's daughter Giorgina (Leda Gloria) and her father on a tour of his art collection and Fusaro, impressed, agrees to sell his painting. As the Marquis frequents pawnshops in order to generate funds, he is observed by Nello (Marcello Spada), an admirer of Giorgina's, who now understands that the father and daughter are in financial straits. He offers Giorgina money but she indignantly refuses.

The film expands on Fusaro's public image as benefactor and the sordid details of his actual financial situation. He is hounded by creditors. They want to know how Fusaro can be generous with money when he is so deeply in debt. Angrily, an irate crowd of the creditors gathers at his house and is only pacified when someone suggests that Giorgina is marrying into money and this is the source of Fusaro's generosity. By the time Fusaro himself arrives on the scene, he has become a hero. Pompously, he accepts the adulation of the people. When he enters the house, he receives a phone call from the police, describing to him the incredible story of a beggar who has lodged a complaint against him for misappropriating funds. Biase is treated unsympathetically by the police. They cannot believe that he is the possessor of so large an amount of money in view of Fusaro's disclaimer.

The Marquis goes to Volterra's factory seeking help. Volterra gives him a tour of the place as the camera pans workers at their tables. The shots are not studio shots but are, as in many films of the era, shots of workers in an actual factory. Volterra is presented as a successful industrialist in contrast to Fusaro who is a fraud, though an aristocrat by birth. He lives off the poor while Volterra is engaged in providing work for the unemployed.

The day of the dinner arrives as carriages and automobiles are shown wending their way to Volterra's estate. At the estate, Volterra is greeting the committee as Fusaro, exiting from his house, is greeted by the police seeking to extract a confession. Fusaro maintains his innocence. The crowds begin to gather at the estate and the poor are shown seated at long tables while the women, including Giorgina, prepare food. The poor are appropriately appreciative of this attention. Fusaro arrives and identifies himself self-importantly as the president. Biase observes Fusaro from his place at the table. Fusaro is pompously uttering high-sounding platitudes about aiding humanity. Biase becomes increasingly restless and disruptive. As Fusaro ends his speech, a sound like that of a gun going off is heard and the source is identified as a camera, not, as it might seem, a gun. This reflexive note anticipates his being "finished off" by the filmmaker.

Biase approaches Volterra and tells him his story. Covering up for the Marquis, Volterra asserts that the money in question was really that which Fusaro received for the painting. Volterra repays Biase from his own pocket, suggesting that there has been an unfortunate misunderstanding. Biase takes the money, satisfied. Giorgina and Nello are reconciled. They decide to marry and to work to repay Volterra's generosity. Fusaro, now alone, inhabits the streets, proudly refusing charity.

Blasetti's comedy touches a number of issues central to all of his films and characteristic of films of the era. The juxtaposition of fraudulent and benevolent authority figures in the characters of Fusaro and Volterra serves to develop the familiar comic motifs of hypocrisy as opposed to authenticity, exploitative treatment of the masses as opposed to responsible and productive treatment of them. The aristocrat is devoted to appearances, to bolstering a decadent and useless life, while the bourgeois is the source of generosity and employment. The use of the aristocrat as scapegoat and the bourgeois as hero is consonant with Blasetti's ongoing positive attitude toward the petty bourgeoisie, workers, and peasants in his films. The goal of his central figures is always directed toward an amelioration of the conditions of the oppressed. Self-interest is subordinated to altruism and disreputability to honor. The positive bourgeois attitudes toward work and socially constructive behavior are embodied in this film through the young people, Giorgina and Nello, as they redeem the lies of the father and align themselves with the ethos of self-help and industriousness.

The film's attitude toward work is that those who are capable of being productive should work, while those who are not should be the recipients of charity. Ostensibly challenging the notion of ill-gotten wealth, the film legitimizes working capital and the producers of wealth. The class conflict in the film thus resides in the oppositions among the masses, the bourgeoisie, and the parasitic aristocracy, identifying the bourgeoisie as the vehicle for resolving the problems of poverty and unemployment.

Giorgina and Nello's role within the film generates the romantic interest. Their relationship signifies redemption from the old order and transformation to the new. Giorgina, horrified by being an object of charity, separates herself from her father, aligning herself with Volterra and the forces for progress as charted in the film. Moreover, her castigation of Nello and his own philanthropic inclinations helps to convert him to the ethos of work. The film also develops generational conflicts. Not only do the young redeem the older generation, but Blasetti is able to develop a distinction between merited and unmerited philanthropy, the elderly poor being worthy objects of charity. Blasetti's treatment of the poor presents them as childlike and dependent, grateful for consideration and charity, not as disruptive or militant.

The treatment of Fusaro, his weakness, his ineffectuality, his pretentiousness, his indolence, his addiction to theatricality, is also interesting in relation to the film's resolution. He is not exposed publicly. Volterra and the young couple redeem him. His punishment is merely to live out his life in proud isolation. Thus the bourgeoisie save the honor of the aristocracy, establishing hegemony over it without destroying it completely. The cover-up serves to limit its power by literally buying it off, revealing a situation not far removed from what had in reality occurred. The final image of Fusaro against the Neapolitan background, ascending the stairs isolated and penurious, is juxtaposed to the image of the young people ascending the stairs. The aged aristocrat, Fusaro, is overtaken by energetic youth.

Blasetti's treatment of social class is more pronounced than Camerini's, while his treatment of romance seems slighter. As always in a Blasetti film, the male figure is the center of the action—both hero and antihero. The aging aristocrat Fusaro is the film's surrogate and scapegoat for the hypocrisy and parasitism of the upper classes, but he is redeemed by the wealthy Volterra who becomes the sheltering father figure for the young lovers and for the poor, as in classical comedy. The importance of work and proper dispensation of wealth is established through the couple's decision to work and repay their debt and through the return of Biase's money. The figure of Biase is ironic, since though he appears a beggar, he is not destitute. In this way, Blasetti establishes that the poor are robbed by the unscrupulous rich and then put in the position of requiring charity. Thus, Blasetti addresses the situation of the *lumpenproletariat*, the unemployed, though, in the final analysis, he subordinates the poor to the figure of power and authority.

In a different, more festive vein, Matarazzo focuses exclusively on the world of workers as a miscrocosm of society. *Treno popolare* (People's Train, 1933) celebrates workers at play, not at work. The film is structured around a one-day outing for workers on one of the trains designed for such occasions. The carnival atmosphere blatantly evokes the *cultura dopolavoristica*. Victoria de Grazia describes how "by organizing a vast program of outings and tourism, the OND (Opera Nazionale Dopolavoro) sought in the most tangible way possible to promote a new national identity."[15] The pop-

---

[15] De Grazia, *The Culture of Consent*, p. 179.

ular trains that took workers to the different parts of Italy were designed to impress them with the benevolence of the regime. The trip entailed traveling to another locale, in country or city, free lunch, singing and dancing, and public political rallies. Organized by the state on a mass scale, these trips, as de Grazia indicates, were "strictly plebeian affairs" and were generally avoided by the "individualistic upper classes."[16]

The first half of Matarazzo's film involves the gathering of the people at the station for the train trip. The characters are presented stereotypically: the stodgy spoilsport, the husband who cheats on his wife, the vain flirtatious young woman, the misunderstood young single woman abused by the jealous wife for flirting with her husband, and the triangle of the two young men competing for the attentions of a woman. The film lingers on their getting settled and finding appropriate companions. The second part of the film takes place in the town as the groups from the train walk about the streets admiring the cathedral, which is photographed so as to allow the internal and external audiences to admire the rose windows and the bas-reliefs. Other images of the church are accompanied by a guide's explanation of the history and architecture. Lunch time arrives and groups settle down to picnic, to sing, and finally to doze. The trio decides to rent bicycles and take a short trip. (Bicycling was a favorite pastime in the organized leisure activities.) Carlo and Lina ride ahead of Giovanni and eventually lose him. They go to the river where they find a boat and take it out on the water. As Lina rows, she loses an oar. In her attempt to recover it, she falls into the water. Carlo pulls her out and takes her ashore. Giovanni continues to struggle on his bike to locate them, but he has been "left behind" as Lina and Carlo grow increasingly more intimate. She hangs her stockings and dress to dry, putting on Carlo's shirt for cover.

Giovanni arrives and they hide from him. Seeing the abandoned boat and the hanging clothes, he grabs the dress and

---

[16] Ibid., p. 183.

rides away for help. He comes to the town where people are dancing and he tries to enlist the help of the men to save Lina. Carlo arrives and tries to get the dress from Giovanni so that he can extricate Lina from her predicament. He grabs the dress and rides away on his bike. He and Lina are shown riding side by side, arms about each other, as the scene returns again to the train. The other people are shown, sleepy and contented. Even the quarreling couple are now huddled together, though when the husband sees that his wife is asleep he tries to extricate himself. Giovanni has found another woman, the young woman who has been the object of contention for the married couple. The film ends with an image of the train tracks.

The presentation of the day's outing offers itself as an idealized microcosm of Italian working-class life with its emphasis on generational, sexual, and behavioral differences. The people are presented as slightly ridiculous but basically good. The festive air, the emphasis on historical sites, the bucolic landscape, seem designed to give an impression of a world where the only serious conflicts are romantic. The singing and dancing are designed to enhance the image of harmony and pleasurable activity. The train itself provides the appropriate image of a technology that facilitates pleasure. The visual style of the film emphasizes the touristic dimension providing a montage of place and activities, and playful visual jokes such as a yawn that becomes the black hole of the tunnel.

The loose structure of the film is a counterpart to the riotousness of the carnival atmosphere. However, the film does present problems and complications. Though the characters are freed from the rigors of work, they are not freed from domestic burdens: poor marital relations, the demands of children, and disappointments in love. The return trip thus reveals itself a prelude to work and to repetition. The mixture of documentary and fiction also serve to enhance the sense of the "real" burdens and demands and the transitoriness of the pleasures.

Walter Ruttmann's *Acciaio* also blends documentary and

fictional narrative. The film, which focuses on the lives of workers and on the work setting, uses avant-garde techniques in order to present a celebration of work and technology.[17] Moreover, the film fuses the conflicts of workers with a romantic melodramatic plot that resolves itself in a utopian vision of harmony between work and domestic relations. The individual worker is reintegrated into the family and the larger community.

A young worker, Mario (Piero Pastore), who is a successful bicycle racer, returns home and takes a position in a steel mill after having spent time traveling and participating in competitions. When he attempts to recapture his former life, he finds that his former fiancée, Gina (Isa Pola), is now engaged to Pietro, another mill worker. The conflict between the two men over the woman is set against tense scenes in the factory where images of the power and danger of the machinery serves to illustrate the necessity of eliminating competition among the workers and of establishing tranquil domestic relations.

Pietro dies in an accident in the factory after an unpleasant argument with Mario and the other workers blame Mario for his death, ostracizing him. Though the machinery has been portrayed as a dominant and threatening force in the worker's lives, the source of the tragedy is attributed to the carelessness of the worker. Moreover, the film makes little sense of the social relations of production, the relationship of the workers to their supervisors and employers, except for a brief scene where a benevolent manager informs an older man of his present unsuitability for the factory.

The romantic elements in the film are concentrated on the triangle. The woman's role is subordinated to the level of instrumentality for the men's competitiveness and conflict. Scenes between Mario and Gina, and Mario, Gina, and Pietro, are alternated with scenes of work in the steel mill, illustrating the various stages of steel production. These scenes are reminiscent of segments of Vertov's *Enthusiasm*, which also dram-

---

[17] Brunetta, *Storia del cinema italiano*, pp. 479-80.

atizes the specific nature of steel production but does not mystify the plight of workers. The sense of the portrayal of the dynamism of machinery and men working is, in the final analysis, closer to the Futurist celebration of technology than the Vertov treatment, which celebrates revolutionary changes and the role of production in the creation of a new society. A contemporary critic in 1933 described Ruttmann's film as having "the form and movement of a poem. Against the background of the vast opposition between water and the machines, he [Ruttmann] has thematically inserted the song of love and of life."[18]

Thus, the struggle of the workers is dwarfed by the images of nature on the one hand, and the images of the mill and machinery on the other. The opposition between nature and technology is reproduced in the opposition between the men and their work. The resolution of the film brings Gina and Mario together once again and reconciles him to the townspeople and to his co-workers. The portrayal of the powerful passions of the central characters is conveyed by means of an expressionist use of lighting, composition, dramatic camera angles, and design, highlighting the jealousy, aggressiveness, and self-destructiveness of the relationships. The film's use of imagery suggests that the reconciliation between nature and technology, between workers, and between male and female is dependent on a recognition of subordination. Just as nature is harnessed to produce the power for technology, so the workers are harnessed to the machines, and the personal passions to work. The film is a poem to power. The power of nature and industrial production overwhelms and subdues the lives of the workers. Mario is made to realize that he is in the control of forces greater than himself.

The celebration of work and machinery in Ruttmann's film is allied to positive images of modernization and industrialization. Its use of avant-garde techniques similar to Vertov's revolutionary celebration of industrial productivity is different from the more conventional treatments of work and workers

---

[18] Savio, *Ma l'amore no*, p. 3.

characteristic of the other directors of the era. For example, while Max Neufeld's *Mille lire al mese* (1,000 Lire a Month, 1939) combines the struggle for gainful employment, the role of technology in modern life, and romantic complications, the film adopts the familiar conventions of romantic comedy reminiscent of *La segretaria privata*. The stern but ultimately benevolent father figure finally restores social equilibrium. The lovers experience vicissitudes but are ultimately rewarded for their competence and perseverance. A close reading of the film reveals that its treatment of work, upward mobility, and sexual conflict are, like the film's self-reflexive use of entertainment, a comment on the fusion of social and domestic relations and on the central role of the media in positioning individuals in society. Like *Segretaria privata* a German-Italian production, the film is even more self-conscious than Alessandrini's about the role of entertainment.

Magda, an enterprising and ambitious young woman, berates her fiancé, an engineer, for not finding a job. He is unable to marry her until he does. She decides to help him find a position and calls a friend in Budapest to assist her. Her friend, Theo, a pharmacist, agrees to get information about an available position as a television engineer. Magda arrives in Budapest and goes to visit Theo at the pharmacy. Unfortunately, her presence creates difficulties for Theo. Lili, his fiancée, observing him with Magda, becomes jealous and scolds him mercilessly, threatening to drop him. Between the two women, the film establishes the proper sphere for women as the guardians of the man's sexual morality and the director of his productive energy.

The film hinges on a series of disguises and misrecognitions. Magda, upon learning of the job opening for Gabriele, sets out for the station, unaware of the identity of the station director with whom she shares a cab. After arguing over its occupancy, she argues with him yet again when he pays her a compliment on her appearance. When she is finally ushered into his office, she realizes her error and works energetically to enlist his sympathies in behalf of her fiancé. He is interested in her and, though he tells her he has no opening, he takes information about Gabriele and promises to contact her if a position becomes available.

During an important preview of programming for some dignitaries, a performance is sabotaged. The dignified shots of a ship's christening are interrupted by frivolous images of female dancers. Finally, the equipment explodes. Unimpressed, the dignitaries leave the studio. The engineer responsible for the performance cannot repair the damage, because he must rush to his wife, who has just given birth. The director asks the porter to bring Magda to him. Again misunderstanding the director's motives, Magda puts up a fight about seeing him. When she finally learns what he wants of her, she is overjoyed at the idea of Gabriele's finding work.

Gabriele arrives in Budapest but he manages to get into a fight with the director, unaware, as Magda had been earlier, of his identity. The argument is serious and the director challenges him to a duel. When Gabriele shows up for work and discovers the director's identity surreptitiously, he realizes that he cannot face him. Magda again comes to the rescue and asks Theo to substitute for Gabriele during the job interview with the director while Gabriele will do the actual work in the sound booth. Inevitably, difficulties arise as Gabriele tries to gain entry to work on the equipment. Theo is forced to pretend that he can handle the equipment. Moreover, the director invites Magda and Gabriele to dinner where Theo must again substitute. Theo takes Lili to the restaurant in order to allay any suspicions and the familiar comic scene ensues of the character who tries to be in two places at once. When the director discovers Theo-Gabriele at the table with Lili, he assumes that the frequent absences from his table are due to "Gabriele's" unfaithfulness. He berates Theo and tells him that he must choose between Lili and Magda. Lili, of course, is also enraged. The final sequences of the film involve the unravelling of the misunderstandings. Gabriele is offered the job at 1,000 lire a month, and he and Magda are now able to marry with the blessings of the director. Lili and Theo are reconciled, and the film ends with the two couples linked arm in arm, singing the title song of the film.

Magda, played by Alida Valli, is both the source of the film's confusion as well as the intermediary for the resolution of the conflict. Her dominance is enhanced by contrast with her passive fiancé, and she is associated with the director, though his interest in her is thwarted by her involvement with Gabriele. Neither her wit nor her cleverness are responsible for Gabriele's acquisition of the job. Her intervention only complicates the situation. The director's efforts hinge on his admiration for Magda as he receives confirmation of her devotion to her fiancé. His behavior shifts from interest in Magda as an object of seduction, to a potential wife, and, finally, ends in his assuming a paternal role in relation to the couple. The potential mistress-wife becomes the dutiful daughter as the director takes the role of the good father who blesses her marriage and guarantees her economic survival.

One of the dominant motifs in the film involves incompetence; incompetence on the job and incompetence in handling personal relationships. The scenes at work are chaotic as seen in the disrupted programs, the mishandling of equipment, the temperamental singer who refuses to perform and, therefore, fulfill her obligations, and the misunderstandings arising from the confusion of identity. The comic attempts on Theo's part to cover up lack of expertise also highlight the idea of incompetence. The role of the station director serves as a rewarder of competence, and the specific rewards are monetary.

The notion of work is linked to the idea of entertainment. The film's situating of the conflict in a television station reinforces this conjunction. The director at the station, like the director of the film, is involved in the business of creating and selling information and entertainment and the engineer's role involves realizing that objective.

Therefore, to read the film's attitude toward work is also to read its attitudes toward itself as an entertainment production. Production is viewed in several ways: as entertainment for and involvement with the masses, as diversion and employment, as depending on notions of competence and merit, and as generating personal gratification. The title of the film speaks to its economic preoccupations, defining success in monetary terms and in terms of gainful employment. As in many other such films of the era, the heroine does not marry upward. Though this alternative is suggested, it is rejected. The film defines success in the more modest terms of employment, steady income, and marriage. Its objectives seems geared to an audience that defines success in modest rather than grandiose terms of power and status. Not everyone wants to become the director. The director's role is therefore not marked as an object of acquisition or emulation but as a vehicle of facilitation, the hinge on which the more modest desires of work and family turn. Thus, the forces of production can be seen, after the confusion is cleared away, as working for the benefit of the competent worker, just as the production of entertainment can be seen to articulate and exemplify these objectives.

This comedy is quite self-conscious and instructive about attitudes toward work, failure, and success, and the role of "entertainment" in managing collective fantasies. Camerini's comedies also confront the issue of social failure and are quite self-reflexive in their treatment. They differ, however, in significant ways from Neufeld's formulas in their greater cynicism about the value of and potential for upward mobility, though Camerini does not totally reject the Cinderella myth. A film like *Darò un milione* draws on many archetypes of comedy, most particularly the comic image of the carnival as a microcosm of the social world and a means of turning conventional relationships inside out in order to dissect them.

Cesare Zavattini, who later became De Sica's scriptwriter and film collaborator, worked on the film, which won a prize at the Venice Film Festival. Widely reviewed, the film was considered by critics to be highly successful. *Darò un milione* (1937) begins with a beggar, Blim, tying weights on his legs, preparatory to committing suicide, in a scene reminiscent of Chaplin's *City Lights* (1931) and of Renoir's *Bondu Saved from Drowning* (1932). Aboard a pleasure yacht, Gold, a rich man, played by Vittorio De Sica, jumps off his boat and swims off to save the tramp. The two men ashore strike up an acquaintance as they hang their wet clothing up to dry, and Gold complains about his meaningless life. The two men decide to sleep on the ground, and before going to sleep, Gold tells Blim that he would like to meet one person in the world who was not after his money but wanted to perform an altruistic act independent of the profit motive. The men go to sleep. Blim awakens to discover that Gold and his clothing are gone, though money hangs on the clothesline. Another image of a clothesline with sheets announces a new setting, the carnival. If the dominant and incremental image in *Gli uomini, che mascalzoni* is the car, in *Darò un milione* it is clothes and a clothesline which take on the signficance of barriers between people, identifying their roles and class characteristics, presenting disguises, confusion, and hypocrisy.

At a carnival, Gold is asleep on the ground but is awakened by a dog. He gets up, notices the sheets, and detects the shadow of a woman through the sheet. Hearing a woman calling a dog, he follows the figure of the woman's shadow along the sheets until Anna, played by Assia Noris, emerges. Her dog has run off after a cyclist, and Gold helps Anna find him.

Blim tries to explain to reporters what has happened to him with Gold in a scene similar to Capra's *Meet John Doe* (1941), and the editor decides Blim's story is worthy of journalistic exploitation. In a typical montage scene of printing presses, bread lines, people reading newspapers, the word spreads about the millionaire's offer of a million lire to a truly charitable person. Not only is the newspaper presented as greedy for profit by headlining the story, but people are shown in a series of vignettes as frantic to get the money. Camerini shows two men pressing money onto a bewildered tramp, a portly woman offering to aid another confused beggar, and a sign being removed that states the property was off limits to beggars.

The film has created at this point a topsy-turvy world in which roles of rich and poor are reversed, and commonly held attitudes are also reversed. The rich man becomes a beggar and the beggar rich. Now beggars are in demand. The

locus of the saturnalia becomes the carnival where Anna and
Gold become friends. Gold has saved Bob, the dog, who was
about to be carted away by the dogcatcher. As a consequence
for his good deed, he is arrested for obstructing the law. The
carnival manager, learning of the millionaire's offer and, after
the grand march of the performers, announces a free meal
and entertainment and a lottery for the beggars to demonstrate his own generosity. At the police station where Gold
has been taken, Gold, too, is the recipient of his own offer,
because the officer releases him, wanting to perform his own
act of generosity for the poor. He returns to the carnival where
Anna gives him the news of the manager's intentions.

In a scene reminiscent of Blasetti's *La tavola dei poveri*, the
poor people are gathered for their free banquet. The scenes
of philanthropy in the film have multiple significance. Camerini is, of course, satirizing the bad faith and greediness
of the bourgeoisie, who will exploit the unemployed and pro-
letarians for profit. The beggars, like the workers, are presented sympathetically, as superior to the bourgeoisie. Camerini exploits the stereotypes of the bourgeoisie as portly
and unattractive. The carnival setting serves to enhance the
comic reversals that characterize the topsy-turvy nature of the
themes, including the comic confusion between theatrical performance and social performance. The image of carnival also
creates the distancing necessary for satire.

Blim finally manages to escape from the editor's house but
not before a frantic chase scene occurs in which he exposes
the editor's wife in bed with a beggar, her way of offering
"charity." The editor pursues him as he tries to leave. At the
carnival, the big show and lottery for the beggars is about to
begin with the spotlighting of an oversized "million lire" bill-
board carried out by attendants. At the lottery, Anna draws
the winning number, which happens to be held by Gold. The
manager finds him at the water fountain where Gold douses
him with water and gets drenched himself. Angrily, the manager orders Gold off the premises. Anna steps in to assist
Gold, offering to help him dry his clothing. She takes him to
her dressing room and he disrobes, the imagery of clothing

again assuming importance in the film. Outside everyone appears to be going mad. Blim is chased by the editor and the police are trying to restore order. In the tent, Anna irons the clothes while Gold sits in her robe smoking. He lays out Anna's slip next to him as if to anticipate union.

Anna, in ironing Gold's clothes, finds a diamond ring in a pocket. Thinking that he has ulterior motives for offering it to her, she angrily returns the ring to him. The manager enters and again throws Gold out. As Gold leaves, he hears the manager talking to Anna and assumes that she is involved in a conspiracy to get the money. Disconsolate, he turns to leave, when he meets Blim who wants to return his money to him. The millionaire has done him a disservice by giving it to him. "I understand," says Gold sadly.

In the arena, the manager promises to announce the identity of the millionaire, and Blim, desirous of ridding himself of his pursuers, says that he will reveal the millionaire. He selects one of the beggars and the once-philanthropic bourgeoisie turn against the remaining beggars. Confusion and chaos break out. Gold breaks some dishes, and Anna pays for the damage. Concerned for Gold, she gives him ten lire to tide him over. Elated, he kisses her, telling her that he has finally found a generous person. He proposes marriage and takes her to his yacht. The beggars, however, have become *personae non grata* again. No one is interested in offering them charity, but Blim still has the money from Gold, and he offers the beggars rides at the carnival. In a rapidly edited sequence, the camera captures the happy faces of the beggars cavorting on the rides.

The film focuses on different class strata, the rich and benevolent bourgeoisie, the hyocritical petty bourgeoisie, and the happy-go-lucky *lumpenproletariat* who are much better off with their own kind than with the hypocritical favors of their philanthropist oppressors. Iconography in the film favors the rich man, Gold, the working-class heroine, Anna, and the poor beggars, who are made to appear childlike. As in *Gli uomini, che mascalzoni*, each group tends to find its own level. Camerini satirizes social institutions, the press, the police, the radio, and charitable institutions. Anna is the recipient of wealth and status as a consequence of her generosity. She is exempted along with the beggars from the grasping and exploitative world and rewarded with love and economic benefits. Camerini, however, minimizes the importance of money, concentrating on the liberatory aspects of play, freedom from working-class constraints, and romance.

Anna gets taken away by her millionaire to Utopia, a nowhere place at sea, where Gold need no longer be weary of life since he has proved to himself that money is not everything, that he can be loved for himself. As for the beggars, the pleasures of the carnival are preferable to the oppression of being dependent, taken care of by people who are manipulative. Entertainment is liberating; regimentation, even when it involves free meals, is stultifying. Escape from the burdens of materialism seems to be the motive force of the work and the experiences of this topsy-turvy world set in motion by Blim and Gold serve to legitimize the idea that love and personal freedom are superior goals.

The idea of escape, so central to the film, is linked to images of concealment. The carnival becomes a microcosm of the world and the role of performance or entertainment takes on the connotation of role-playing, posturing, and counterfeiting. The idea of a quest for authenticity is played out in the realization that honest people are indeed rewarded as Blim treats the beggars to a "real" entertainment and as Anna gets her millionaire. The notion of escape, however, seems to contain contradictions. On the one hand, escape in the film is associated with fantasy, with turning one's back on the unpleasant features of the world and saving oneself. On the other hand, it seems to serve a subversive role. It appears to make fun of spectacles, of pompous posturing, of work, of prevailing institutions, of mass organizing and, in general, of projects to help the poor and unemployed. Unlike the usual comic social vision, the world is not transformed, but divided between the regenerate and unregenerate, the "solution" being to avoid rather than confront and change the corrupt practices and practitioners. But this, in itself, seems to imply the hopelessness of the situation.

*Il signor Max* (1937) is less encyclopedic than *Darò un milione*, concerned primarily with the question of the identity of the title character. Through the devices of doubling, disguises, and name changes, Camerini portrays the plight of the workers in comic fashion, deflating grandiose pretensions to wealth and status. A young newspaper vendor, Gianni, played by Vittorio De Sica, leads a double life; his other identity is as the foppish Mr. Max. Scheduled to take a cruise to Greece paid for by a wealthy customer, he sees a beautiful Englishwoman and learns that she is on her way to San Remo. He changes his destination. Gianni's uncle, a bus conductor, comes with his wife to give Gianni a proper send-off. An unpretentious fellow, gruff and fatherly, he gives Gianni minute directions for taking care of himself. Aboard the ship, Gianni meets the Englishwoman again. He offers her lavish gifts and insinuates himself into her select company. Having run out of money, he appears at his uncle's modest apartment. The uncle is furious with him, calls him an imbecile for becoming involved with wealthy people, and angrily and ironically offers him his life savings so that he can keep up with the rich.

Not cured of his fascination for the rich, Gianni teaches himself English and tennis in preparation for a new encounter. Lauretta, the nursemaid for Lady Paola's daughter, played by Assia Noris, comes to the newsstand and identifies Gianni as "Max" when she sees him. He denies that he knows any Mr. Max, but she is overwhelmed by the resemblance. His different way of speaking, which he points out to her, convinces her finally that he is Gianni. Through her, he learns of Lady Paola's whereabouts.

Gianni returns to playing at being Mr. Max. Dressed elegantly, he enters the Grand Hotel, smoking affectedly and adjusting his tie. He greets his shipboard friends and dances with Lady Paola again who wants to know why he left them abruptly and without explanation. His response is that he was jealous of her admirers and she responds, "How bour-

geois!'' Lauretta goes again to the newsstand to see Gianni
and meets his uncle. Impressed with her, the uncle invites
her to a local celebration with him and Gianni, where the
entertainments of the rich are contrasted to those of working
people. The singers comprise an actual group, not a group
of actors, which enhances the authenticity of this scene. After
the concert, Lauretta tells Gianni that he is different from Lady
Paola's friends and asks him to come to the train station with
her, since she must take a trip with her employers. "Max" is
also supposed to be on the train. Again Gianni enlists his
newsvendor friend to help him over this obstacle, where he
must be two people at the same time. At the station, his friend
puts on Max's clothes and stands with his back to the platform
as Gianni says goodbye to Lauretta, thus allaying any suspicion she might have.

On the trip, Gianni finds himself in the dining car with
Lady Paola and company. The conversation turns into a mum-
ble of inanities as Gianni says,"Yes, yes" to everything. He
exposes his ignorance of bridge, to the scorn and disgust of
the players. He excuses himself to get a drink. Finding Lauretta in tears as he comes through the corridor, "Max" asks
her what the problem is and she blurts out that she had
originally taken the job to be in the world of rich and elegant
people, but she has learned that she lives in a different world.
She has nothing in common with them, and she talks to
"Max" about her love for Gianni. Impetuously, "Max" grabs
her and reveals his identity but she refuses to believe him.
The conductor appears and tells her that Lady Paola is looking
for her. Her child is screaming that Lauretta has slapped her.
Lauretta tries to explain the child's antics but only Max will
defend her. She resigns her post.

Gianni and Lauretta race to the newsstand. Gianni arrives
first, goes in and changes clothes as she appears and tells him
that she has resigned her job. They go for a carriage ride and
Gianni proposes marriage. When the uncle learns of Gianni's
impending marriage with Lauretta, he is overjoyed. Gianni
asks him to reveal nothing about his earlier escapades. As the
uncle brings Lauretta into the apartment, the door closes on

them, and from behind the closed door the uncle can be heard saying that he will never reveal anything.

The main target of the satire is the pretensions of the rich, their vanity, their aimless existence, their tyrannical and arbitrary behavior and their banality. The hero and the heroine are little people like Gianni, Lauretta, and the uncle, who are reliable, truthful, industrious, good-hearted, and who are capable of seeing beneath the entertainments of the rich to see that too much money destroys character. By playing with the motif of double identity, disguises, and role-playing, the film presents class and sexual oppositions, resolving them through the rejection of the rags-to-riches myth in favor of class solidarity. The little man's satisfaction is not in upward mobility but in domesticity as the last images in the film reveal when the door closes on the family.

The film is built around numerous oppositions: the references to exotic places such as Greece, San Remo, Sofia, London, and New York versus the down-to-earth reality of Naples; the lavish shipboard settings, the ballroom, the Grand Hotel, the elegant railroad car, versus the uncle's modest apartment, the club where the people gather to sing, drink, and talk, and the newsstand; the work world versus the world of play; the contrast between Lady Paola's narcissism and Lauretta's concern for Gianni, which reveals differences between female dominance and female subordination, modern and traditional female roles. Above all, the opposition between the escapist fantasies projected by the fiction and the grim realities of mundane social practices and institutions remains bifurcated and, like the other oppositions, impossible to mediate.

The most satiric of Camerini's social/romantic comedies, *Batticuore* (Heartbeats, 1939) equates economic relations with theft. From top to bottom, institutions are portrayed as corrupt, and the survival of the workers is dependent on their learning how to profit from that corruption. The specific form of "work"shown is literal thievery, and the characters apply themselves diligently to this work. Structured around class oppositions, *Batticuore* portrays the hypocrisy of the world of diplomacy and wealth. The external audience is invited to become voyeurs in this world of intrigue, adultery, and luxury. The film's particular trope of the school of thieves as proper preparation for acquiring the skills necessary to social and economic survival can hardly be considered as a celebration of the regime or of the status quo. Like the melodramas of the early forties, the film is unrelenting in its exposure of social hypocrisy, misappropriation of property, and collective complicity.

Early in the film, Camerini establishes the role of the spectator as voyeur as he plays with gratifying the desire to see while inhibiting sight. Through-the-window shots of a school situate the spectator outside the building as a professor of sorts can be seen lecturing to a group of attentive students. The professor moves toward the window and draws the blinds, thus shutting out part of the scene. He moves to the other window, does the same, and thus, again, obstructs the spectator's vision. The students are being lectured on their "profession." The following sequence reveals two students plying their trade in the streets. Arlette, played by Assia Noris, is a star pupil, whereas her male colleague is less clever and experienced. He appears to have difficulty in putting theory into practice. He bumbles incompetently through his work, forcing Arlette to rescue him.

At the school, the professor, like an officer reviewing his troops, puts them through the exercise of pickpocketing a mannequin. He checks their agility and timing. He also has them pretend that they are aboard a crowded tram, designated by benches, where they are to pick the pockets of the passengers. The students pass their examinations and the professor invites them to a celebration marking their graduation. Arlette is honored as the top of her class.

Arlette's first job involves the deft removal of a man's pearl tiepin on a crowded elevator. The man, noticing the absence of the pin, pursues her as she, seeking to avoid him, steps into a movie theater where a poster advertises a Fred Astaire and Ginger Rogers film. Arlette enters, finds a seat, but the man sits next to her and points to the empty place on his tie.

At first, she recites all of the dialogue learned at the school to avert arrest. She "confesses" that this is her first offense and gives a pitiful story of her desperation. On the movie screen, the actress is repeating the same speech. Unmoved, the man orders her to come with him, but instead of taking her to jail, he brings her to the Embassy of Stivonia, telling her that he has an assignment for her.

The Count suspects his wife of adultery with a British lord, Lord Jerry Salisbury, and he needs Arlette to pilfer the evidence. She is properly outfitted with clothing and brought to a lavish ball where she is to do her job. She dances with Lord Jerry and stealthily removes his pocketwatch, which contains a picture of the Countess. Arlette gives the watch to the Count who verifies his suspicions. Her job is then to return the watch to Lord Jerry's pocket without incident. After the ball, Lord Jerry convinces her to join him at a café. On their way, they stop at a photomat where they take a picture of themselves. The photo will become important in the film's resolution.

Arlette cannot extricate herself from Lord Jerry, because he insists on accompanying her to the expensive hotel where she has claimed to be staying. After several attempts to escape only to find Lord Jerry outside, she decides to spend the night. She awakens in a luxurious room, surrounded by attendants, bellboys with flowers, a maid with breakfast, and room service with a large trunk, containing elegant clothes for her. Lord Jerry calls on the phone, and it becomes clear that he is aware of her ruse and intends to teach her a lesson. He plans to indulge her and then to expose her, though not without some regret, since he finds her beautiful and entertaining.

The professor, however, is overjoyed at her progress, offering to pay for the room. Lord Jerry arrives to visit Arlette only to have his watch stolen again by the student who brushes against him as they pass each other in the lobby. At first, Jerry suspects Arlette when he discovers the theft, but with the help of the police, the real thief is apprehended. At the hearing to which the young man is taken, Arlette attempts to confess her criminality, but Lord Jerry disclaims her story. The officer of the court attempts to verify her confession, but the Count disclaims the theft of his pin, indicating that he is in possession of it. As for the stealing of the watch, he "confesses" that he did ask for it to be stolen but that this is a delicate political matter that cannot be divulged publicly. In a private antechamber, the telltale watch is finally opened, but the Countess's picture has been replaced by the photo of Lord Jerry and Arlette. Lord Jerry and Arlette are married as the professor, his wife, and their students observe them admiringly.

More than Camerini's other romantic comedies, *Batticuore* is cynical about the world it portrays. The conventional romance elements, the resolution of conflict, and the symbolic wedding at the end do not mitigate the sense that theft, incompetence, and hypocrisy are essential to social life. That crime does pay and is amply rewarded is dramatized in Arlette's union with Lord Jerry. Her "work" provides her the entree into the upper echelons of society. The idea of treating theft as gainful employment with its own hierarchy of skills and rewards seems to parody prevailing attitudes toward work. Arlette's conspiracy with the Count and her marriage to Lord Jerry seems to suggest that the lower classes and the upper classes are, indeed, united as partners in criminality. The lower-class thieves steal material goods; the upper classes are engaged in stealing each other's wives. Though Arlette seeks to confess her crimes and abandons petty crime when she marries Lord Jerry, she links herself to a class that by its own admission at the end is engaged in "conspiracy and espionage," based on hypocrisy, manipulation, and intrigue. No one in the film is exempt from complicity.

The self-conscious element of voyeurism and self-reflexivity in the film, with its emphasis on spying and forms of visual entertainment such as films and photography, gives the viewer the familiar sense of doubling, of implicating the audience in the action so central to comic forms. The idea of spectatorship takes on the connotation of exposure while at the same time equating that exposure with entertainment, thus minimizing the subversive elements. Moreover, the equation between the film-within-the-film and the film itself serves to fuse "reality" and fiction, creating an enclosed world around the events within the film that includes the spectator. Self-reflexivity works in *Batticuore* to reinforce the idea that life is like a film. The emphasis on the act of spectatorship, characteristic of comedy, enhances the film's satire by indicating that the bond among the observers is our shared knowledge of social corruption.

Critics have compared Camerini's work to René Clair's, which also satirizes greed, corruption, and exploitation. *Batticuore*, though it emulates Hollywood and French models, finally conveys a pessimistic and cynical attitude toward its subject matter. If Clair's films insist on the class conflict, Camerini's films work cleverly to divert the spectator from this idea, exposing the conflict but finally retreating into fantasy.

Not all of Camerini's films are set in the contemporary urban context. *I promessi sposi* (The Betrothed, 1941) is based on Alessandro Manzoni's classic novel. Camerini's concern for the common people is well served by his use of this literary text. The film appears to be yet another adaptation of a literary classic, yet another historical costume drama, yet another legitimation of traditional values. Its appearance in 1940, its particular treatment of the nineteenth-century novel, raises questions, however, about the film's ideological concerns. The Manzoni text authorizes the director to treat contemporary issues in an oblique fashion much as in the other historical films. The film portrays existence as precarious. Innocent and vulnerable people fall prey to unscrupulous forces. The film dramatizes the disasters that befall the victims but also emphasizes the role of religion as an antidote to natural and social catastrophes. *I promessi sposi* uses religion in a conventional sense as the cosmic, and, hence, comic resolution to earthly corruption and conflict, but whether or not he endorses the religious sentiments from the original text is irrelevant. What is important is that Camerini's production of the literary text enables him to criticize the abuses of power.

In a seemingly benign pastoral setting, Don Abbondio (Armando Falconi) is accosted by brigands in the service of Rodrigo who warn the priest to postpone the wedding of Lucia

and Renzo. Unaware of these complications, the family prepares for the forthcoming marriage. Lucia (Dina Sassoli),
Agnese, her mother (Gilda Marchio), and Fra Cristoforo (Luis
Hurtado) supervise the arrangements, while the bridegroom,
Renzo (Gino Cervi), learns from Don Abbondio, the parish
priest, that the wedding must be postponed. The cowardly
priest gives no explanation for the delay, but Perpetua (Inez
Zacconi) reveals that Don Rodrigo is the source of the difficulty.

The casting and direction of the characters in the film is,
as critics of the time noted, designed to create a sense of their
approximation to the Manzoni figures. For example, Don Abbondio is plump, physically unattractive, and awkward. Perpetua is fat, secretive, and officious. Lucia, the ingénue, is
young, attractive, and shy. Agnese is the sweet, maternal
figure, while Don Rodrigo is the dark, mustachioed villain.
Fra Cristoforo is thin, tall, and ascetic-looking, while the cardinal is an imposing figure of stability. The peasants and
workers in the city are presented as innocent and good while
the aristocrats are often satirized, though the religious figures
are treated sympathetically. The costuming is designed to
create a sense of period authenticity. The juxtaposition of
scenes highlights the excesses of the aristocrats and the common bond between the people and the clergy. For example,
when Fra Cristoforo goes to Rodrigo to intercede for Lucia
and Renzo, he is treated insolently. His simplicity is contrasted with their cruelty and decadence.

At the instigation of Rodrigo (Enrico Glori), the brigands
go to the village to kidnap Lucia. Fra Cristoforo intervenes to
save Lucia and Agnese whom he sends to a convent at Monza,
while Renzo plans to go to Milan. Mayhem ensues as the
people seek to defend themselves from Don Rodrigo's men.
At Milan, Renzo finds himself in a bread riot. He speaks out
and is seized by the police, but he escapes. At the convent,
Lucia encounters "La Signora" (Evi Maltagliati), who attempts
to save her from Don Rodrigo. Nonetheless, Lucia is caught
by his men and taken off to the castle of the "Innominato"
(The Unnamed One), where she is imprisoned. These men

live by plunder and violence. Lucia confronts her captor and begs for mercy "in the name of God." Seemingly implacable, the man leaves her to suffer. Kneeling, she prays and vows to become a nun and dedicate herself to the Virgin if she escapes. Moved by Lucia, the man goes to the cardinal and seeks to be reconciled with the Church. Camerini dwells on the scene of his conversion. The Unnamed One returns home, begs Lucia's pardon, and releases her, chastising his men and ordering them to leave his castle.

Plague breaks out and people clog the roads, attempting to escape. Amid scenes of disaster, Renzo arrives looking for Lucia and Agnese, while the Duke of Milan and his council debate the efficacy of a request for a public celebrational mass. Some are opposed on the grounds that this would spread the disease; others argue that a ritual could only help public morale, and this group prevails.

Rodrigo, struck down by the plague, seeks help from one of his men, but the man betrays him and turns him over to the authorities who have quarantined the plague victims. Renzo encounters Fra Cristoforo to whom he vents his desire for revenge against Don Rodrigo, but angrily the priest lectures him that this is not the time for revenge but for compassion. Finally, Renzo finds Lucia who greets him strangely, explaining her vow to the Virgin. He is shocked and angry, but Fra Cristoforo explains to her that God does not demand this kind of personal sacrifice. He urges the couple to go home and to get married. The film ends on a vision of rain, washing away the corruption of a plague.

While not faithful to every detail in the Manzoni work, especially in omitting the conquering foreign hordes, the film selects those scenes that dramatize dominant incidents and motifs: thwarted love, the villainy of Don Rodrigo, the bread riots, the plight of Lucia, the conversion of The Unnamed One, the sickness and the death of Don Rodrigo, and the salvation from the plague. Spectacle and ritual are central; the motif of religion and religious piety is conveyed through the tableaulike scenes of ceremony and through the characters of Fra Cristoforo and the lovers. In the scenes of the plundering of the village, in the bread riots, and in the plague scenes, Camerini highlights the vulnerability, yet honest piety, of the peasants and workers in contrast to the cruel and sordid manipulations of the aristocracy. The conversion of The Unnamed One and the violent death of Don Rodrigo reinforce the idea of the triumph of justice. The final scenes incorporate the image of the ultimate benevolence of nature as the working out of divine wisdom and link this image to the reconciliation of the lovers. The linking of the priest with the couple identifies the film's fusion of the family and the Church.

This film recapitulates the familiar Camerini works concerned with the disruption of familial and class solidarity by the abuses of power, the malevolence of the upper classes as against a consistently sympathetic view of the peasants and workers. Most explicitly, in this film Camerini maintains the religious element derived from the novel to reinforce the idea that the sufferings of the oppressed will ultimately be relieved. Camerini elevates the simple virtues of familial love, religious reverence, modest aspirations, and adherence to your own kind. In this parable, the spectator is invited to become part of this idyllic community, to identify with its simple virtues and simple characters, and to worship along with the internal audience before the altar of the Virgin. The re-creation of the nineteenth-century milieu begins to look suspiciously as if it is to be read against the times in which the film was made, as a commentary on the final years of the fascist regime, by alluding obliquely to economic hardship, the sufferings of the war, and the general disaffection and demoralization of the populace. Though the film appears to be a divine comedy that justifies the ways of God, the film can be read as a critique of prevailing institutions, the exercise of naked power, and the absence of trust and benevolence.

## Summary

Contrary to the long-held view that the comedies of the era are "escapist," indicative of the regime's commitment to "dogma"or "drivel,"[19] the comedies, like the historical and adventure films and like the melodramas, reveal a self-conscious preoccupation with the positioning of work and workers in a number of different contexts: in the home, in the job world, in leisure, and in relation to the rich. The so-called "white telephone" films offer fascinating images of sexual politics, fantasies about men and women, about marriage, and about broader social relationships. While the narratives are not self-conscious about the role of social class, they do portray class conflicts, are aware of class difference, and often adopt a satiric attitude toward the upper classes. The concern with class issues and the positioning of workers can be accounted for in several ways. Most obviously, the issue of work and class, while potentially disruptive, was inescapable in the creation of narratives with a popular appeal. The Italian film industry, conscious of successful Hollywood practices and particularly of Frank Capra's work, emulated the populist comedies with their emphasis on the "little people." The efforts of the regime itself, as it sought to create a popular culture, were directed toward the seduction and pacification of workers.

The comedies are, moreover, not the only films to feature workers and peasants and to show them in a work environment. In the epic *Scipione l'africano*, peasants are portrayed as the sustainers of the economy of Rome. *Terra madre* treats peasant life as wholesome in contrast to the decadence of the city. The same is true of *La peccatrice* where the scenes of work are fused with images of nature. *Un'avventura di Salvator Rosa* actually has the peasants rebelling against their ruler and her unscrupulous counselor, though their ultimate salvation is dependent on the exceptional hero, Rosa.

In general, the narrative structures and the iconography of the films is stylized. The workers are not differentiated and the individual conflicts are fused with broad oppositions between town and country, "natural" and "artificial" styles of

---

[19] Gerald Mast, *A Short History of the Movies* (Indianapolis: The Bobbs-Merrill Company, Inc., 1976), pp. 343-44.

life, and exceptional leaders and the masses. The style and thematics of the films are not static. They vary from the films of the early thirties to the films of the early forties. The mannered, playful, and celebrational stance of the thirties becomes subdued, if not satiric. The image of social solidarity disintegrates, and ever-widening images of conflict surface. The later films create a more active and conflict-laden sense of the characters' environment and their struggles to survive. If the resolution of the comedies is often utopian, the conflicts presented are related to everyday life. The films focus on problems of economic survival; tensions between men and women, workers and bosses, family members; frustration and the quest for gratification. The struggle for identity and involvement is often situated in a context of reduction of expectations, the restoration of the character to his/her "proper" class and familial position after the narrative establishes the attractiveness of such a choice. In creating this type of closure, the narratives also permit an insight into the strategies of reconciliation that can enable us today to understand better the ways the narratives speak to actual conflicts. Moreover, like the carnivals and festivals of the era, which allowed dissent within bounds, these films, often by using the image of the carnival, exercise a license to satirize certain social practices.

The "happy endings" of these films might seem to the casual observer to be one-dimensional and simplistic, presenting an image of an ideal society where problems are easily mitigated. In short, the films can be read for their surface content as mere reproductions of the dominant ideology. As in many classical comedies, the resolution is effected through romance and marriage, through the receipt of economic rewards, and through the elimination or conversion of authority figures who thwart the young people. Although it is the case that the narratives rely heavily on the conventions of comic form, these conventions are not univalent. They are, in fact, as Schatz has suggested, an outgrowth of basic cultural oppositions that are "unresolvable." "The conflict is simply recast into an emotional context where it can be expeditiously, if not always logically, resolved."[20] The "resolution" becomes the index to the film's transformational strategies and exposes the unresolved and unresolvable situations.

Furthermore, no audience, and this would apply to the Italian audiences of the era, totally confuses the distinction between the filmic event and life. For the audience there is a world beyond the film. The film texts themselves are often self-conscious about their status as "entertainment." Their self-reflexivity, however, is two-edged. On the one hand, the "real" world is effaced in the triumph of spectacle; on the other hand, the entertainment calls attention to itself in contrast to externally "real" events. The films cannot and often do not totally obliterate their self-construction. They highlight the disparity between the conflicts they present and their resolutions. For example, while Camerini's comedies resolve the sexual and class conflicts of the central figures, resolution is effected by providing psychological compensation for material injustices. In his *Il signor Max*, he provides the viewer with an interesting self-conscious image of the nature of comic closure. Max goes into the house with his uncle, and the final image of the film is of the slamming of a door on the viewer. It signals closure, but not mitigation of conflict. It also sharply divides the text from the viewer and creates a final opposition between text and audience.

Finally, the comedies become ever more insistent, like the melodramas, on the inabilities of the texts to sustain a positive and affirmational resolution to the sexual and class conflicts portrayed.

[20] Schatz, *Hollywood Genres*, pp. 31-32.

# CHAPTER SIX

# The Family Melodrama

IN discussing the new industrialism, Antonio Gramsci asserted that "the new industrialism wants monogamy: it
wants man as worker not to squander his nervous energies
in the disorderly and stimulating pursuit of occasional sexual
satisfaction."[1] Most of the films of the thirties, whether set in
the domestic or public spheres, emphasize a puritanical ethos
in greater or lesser degrees. The family appears as the source
of continuity, nurturance, social stability, and, as we have
seen in the films of Camerini, a haven from the conflicts in
the world of work. In this context, the woman serves as a
procreator, nurturer, disciplinarian of the husband, self-dis-
ciplinarian, and guarantor of the integrity of the family unit.
The male is the economic provider, the inseminator, the pro-
tector of the woman's honor and hence of his own honor, the
straying child who must be restrained, and the responsible
paterfamilias. The family is at the intersection of economic,
political, and social conflict.[2] The most ideologically challenging and aesthetically superior films of the Ventennio are the
melodramas of the early 1940s that focus on the family.

Many of the melodramas are the work of a group of filmmakers identified as "calligraphers." Such directors as Mario
Soldati, Luigi Chiarini, Ferdinando Maria Poggioli, and Renato Castellani were associated with this type of production.
The works are characterized by a high degree of formalism,
a dependence on narratives derived from earlier literary
works, especially of the nineteenth century, and by a seeming
retreat from overt political issues. As such, the films were

[1] Antonio Gramsci, *Selections from the Prison Notebooks*, ed. Quentin Hoare
and Geoffrey Nowell-Smith (New York: International Publishers, 1978), pp.
304-305.
[2] Patrizia Pistagnesi, "La scena famigliare nel cinema fascista," in *Cinema
italiano sotto il fascismo*, ed. Riccardo Redi (Venice: Marsilio, 1979), p. 101.

criticized by such writers as Giuseppe De Santis in the journal *Cinema*, the forum for new directions in Italian film. While it was generally recognized that the calligraphers were attempting to experiment with film form, moving narratives in a more psychological direction and using authentic settings, it was not acknowledged that these films, because of their stylized and heavily coded forms of representation, contained a powerful political critique of existing social conditions.

Melodrama was not a genre new to Italian culture. Gramsci traces its origins to the sixteenth century whence the genre maintains a consistent course into the twentieth century.[3] Most significantly, the genre is identified with the steady growth of forms of popular culture. An examination of the sources of the film melodrama reveals their dependence on popular Italian and foreign novels. For example, Visconti used James M. Cain's best-selling *The Postman Always Rings Twice* for *Ossessione*; Poggioli used Aldo Palazzeschi's novel for his *Sorelle Materassi*, and Chiarini used a tale by Matilde Serao for his *Via delle cinque lune*.

Melodrama, more than any other form of traditional narrative, seems to be an appropriate vehicle to explore and to criticize prevailing social attitudes. In his "Tales of Sound and Fury: Observations on the Family Melodrama," Thomas Elsaesser finds that

the family melodrama . . . more often records the failure of the protagonist to act in a way that could shape the events and influence the emotional environment, let alone change the social milieu. The world is closed and the actors are acted upon. Melodrama confers on them a negative identity through suffering, and the progressive self-immolation and disillusionment gradually ends in resignation.[4]

Elsaesser explores the forms and language of melodrama, identifying the stylistic and structural operations that characterize it. The use of strong psychological effects, the em-

---

[3] Antonio Gramsci, *Letteratura e vita nazionale* (Rome: Riuniti, 1979), pp. 94-96.

[4] Thomas Elsaesser, "Tales of Sound and Fury: Observations on the Family Melodrama," *Monogram* 4 (1973), pp. 2-15.

phasis on emotional crises, the exploration of failure are embedded in a style that makes it possible to identify ideological operations. For example, the sexual conflict, the presence of ruptures and discontinuities, the stylized and figurative treatment, the transformation of conflict from the social into the psychic area are keys to unlocking the ideological and political impact of the genre.[5] Moreover, the subversions of melodrama are discernible not only in the narratives but also in an examination of the historical context. In the case of the Hollywood cinema, critics have focused on the popularity of melodrama in periods of intense social or ideological crisis.[6] Relative to the historical context, melodrama can function either subversively or as escapist entertainment according to ideological necessity.[7]

An examination of the Italian melodramas of the late thirties and early forties reveals the potential of the genre as an instrument for exposing social conflict. The films explore the breakdown of social relations, using the family romance to encode the weakness of authority, the dominance of obsessional behavior, competition, the manipulative aspects of petty bourgeois life, the decadence of the upper classes, and the flimsiness and hypocrisy of male relationships. Visconti's

[5] David N. Rodowick, "Madness, Authority, and Ideology in the Domestic Melodrama of the 1950's," *The Velvet Light Trap*, no. 19 (1982), pp. 40-45; Sandy Flitterman, "*Guest in the House*: Rupture and Reconstitution of the Bourgeois Nuclear Family," *Wide Angle* 4 (1980), pp. 18-27.

[6] See E. Ann Kaplan, *Woman and Film: Both Sides of the Camera* (New York: Methuen, 1983), pp. 38-39; Peter Brooks, *The Melodramatic Imagination: Balzac, Henry James, Melodrama, and the Mode of Excess* (New York: Columbia University Press, 1984; Michael Renov, "*Leave Her to Heaven*: The Double Bind of the Post-War Woman," *Journal of the University Film and Video Association* 35 (Winter 1983), pp. 28-36; Russell Merritt, "Melodrama: Postmortem for a Phantom Genre," *Wide Angle* 5 (1983) pp. 24-32; Christian Viviani, "Who Is without Sin? The Maternal Melodrama in American Film, 1930-39," *Wide Angle* 4 (1980), pp. 4-17; Jean Loup Bourget, "Faces of the American Melodrama: Joan Crawford," *Film Reader 3* (February 1978), pp. 24-34.

[7] Christopher Orr, "Closure and Containment: Marylee Hadley in *Written on the Wind*," *Wide Angle* 4 (1980) pp. 29-35. See also Bryan Crow, "The Cinematic and the Melodramatic in *A Woman of Affairs*," *Wide Angle* 4 (1980), pp. 44-51.

film, *Ossessione*, is only one of a number of texts that dramatize these conflicts. There was an increasing tendency to use film and film criticism for the purposes of challenging cultural and ideological practices. These critiques provide further insights into the contradictory practices of fascism.

Recent critical work on the Hollywood film has focused on melodrama as genre and style, and as a way of looking at social relations. The power of the Hollywood film, it was conceded even by the fascist regime, was its ability to use narrative forms that transmit ideology effortlessly; however, as Visconti discovered, and the French New Wave a decade later, there were ways to demystify the genre films, to see in them contradictions and areas of resistance to the dominant discourse. The critics saw the forms themselves as capable of subversion, of turning against themselves, and of exposing their secrets, and the power of melodrama would seem to reside in the ways in which the narratives utilize psychological structures as a commentary on social life. At their center are the ways in which desire and conflict are unleashed. Thomas Schatz has described how

The family unit seems to provide an ideal locus for the genre's principal characters and its milieu for two fundamental reasons. First, it is a preestablished constellation whose individual roles (mother, father, son, daughter; adult, adolescent, child, infant, and so on) carry with them large social significance. Second, it is bound to its community by social class. . . . Ideally, the family represents a "natural" as well as a social collective, a self-contained society in and of itself. But in the melodrama this ideal is undercut by the family's status within a highly structured socioeconomic milieu.[8]

Within the Italian cinema of the early 1940s the melodrama appears often to function in the manner described by Schatz. In the films of the thirties, whether domestic and romantic comedies, male conversion dramas, war and imperialist epics, or operatic films, the family played a major role as the guarantor of social stability, a symbol of continuity, a rationale for

---

[8] Thomas Schatz, *Hollywood Genres: Formulas, Filmmaking, and the Studio System* (New York: Random House, 1981), p. 227.

war, and a motivation for productivity. The only rival to the family was the public arena of heroic action, though here, too, the conflicts between fathers and sons and the subordination of women played important roles.

For example, in the 1936 *Cavalleria*, discussed in Chapter Three, the separation of the lovers is aestheticized. Suffering is made to appear ennobling. The camerawork and the editing ritualize events; the narrative builds inexorably in linear fashion around the inevitability of loss and its compensation in war, public service, creativity. While the Italian films of the 1930s reproduce, romanticize, and naturalize ideas of social order, the melodramas of the 1940s are dark, morally ambiguous, and preoccupied with disintegration. They are also closer to the neorealistic aesthetic in their treatment of conflict and setting.[9] If the earlier films reveal the projection of the family romance into the public arena, these later dramas seem to expose this strategy, using melodrama as the vehicle of demystification.

Psychological conflict is central to the Italian films of the 1940s, particularly the conflict generated by obsessional behavior: jealously, thwarted sexuality, fetishism, violence, and disintegrating identity. These obsessions (obsession is central to melodrama) are often tied to economic, class, and political conflicts, involving such issues as irresolvable class differences that thwart gratification, violent or manipulative responses to the confining world of work, or the desire to escape the restrictive demands of an authority figure—father, husband, mother, or wife. In all these films, one can find a desire for freedom that is distorted, misdirected, and frustrated.

The style of the films can vary from a naturalistic portrayal of milieu and social conflict to a highly stylized treatment.[10]

[9] Filippo Maria De Sanctis, "La rivolta dei formalisti," in *Il cinema italiano dal fascismo all'antifascismo: Testi e documenti dello spettacolo*, ed. Giorgio Tinazzi (Padua: Marsilio, 1966), p. 169. See also Franco Venturini, "Origins of Neorealism," in *Springtime in Italy: A Reader on Neorealism*, ed. David Overbey (Hamden, Conn.: Archon Books, 1978), pp. 171-75.

[10] Gian Piero Brunetta, *Storia del cinema italiano 1895-1945* (Rome: Riuniti, 1979), pp. 498-513.

The lighting, as in *film noir*, is expressive of ambiguity and the troubled psyche. Music is important in developing emotional intensity and tone. The iconography and gesture of the characters often provide clues to their struggles. As with the films of Douglas Sirk, the stylized treatment can serve as an alienation effect whereby the film provides a commentary on itself. In a few instances, more obvious forms of self-reflexivity invite awareness of a point of view. In most of these films, conventional virtues are inverted or destroyed.

The melodramas reveal, in spite of their different styles and narratives, the presence of opposition, if not resistance, to the prevailing trends in filmmaking as exemplified in the "escapist" film, the film of propaganda, the film of war and empire, the comic film—all the films that sought to emphasize the virtues of renunciation, service, loyalty, male camaraderie, and populism. If the group of critics gathered around the journal *Cinema*, with their predilection for French cinema and American cinema and literature, represented the most vocal forces seeking to institute different cultural and ideological practices, the melodramas of the early forties also seem to constitute a form of departure from previous practices. Though these films do not treat obvious political themes as is characteristic of the neorealist cinema, they do afford a different perspective not only on the final phase of the fascist Ventennio, but also on some of the major myths and strategies of fascist life as it was encoded in the cinema. Melodrama's preoccupation with sexual, psychological, and domestic aspects of life illuminates the forces that position individuals and classes in ideology.

Amleto Palermi's 1939 *Cavalleria rusticana* is a complex melodrama that involves the breakdown of parental and conjugal relations and the consequences of this familial discord for the entire community. Palermi introduces a "female sinner" in the figure of Lola, who is the destroyer of domestic unity. However, Turiddu's psyche is a battleground as the women compete for him. The film is based on the Verga story and not on the opera, though it contains operatic elements in abundance. Opera is, for the most part, a congenial vehicle for melodrama. Palermi's drama of renunciation, thwarted desire, revenge, fought on the terrain of sexual rivalry, is conveyed through a combination of aria, recitative, chorale, and spectacle. During the late thirties and early forties, the Italian film industry produced other operas, but Palermi's film is, like so many of his other works, not a mere transcription of novel or opera but a work that utilizes melodrama as a critique of social relations and as a critique on its own filmic practices.

Using a lush and authentic pastoral setting, Palermi introduces Verga's seemingly simple Sicilian peasant world which, it quickly turns out, is fraught with conflict, competition, and struggles for dominance. The return of Turiddu to the village becomes the vehicle for reintroducing discord that the families hoped had been laid to rest. As one of the characters comments, for Lola's sake she hopes that "what is past, is past." Upon Turiddu's arrival, and his discovery of Lola's marriage, it becomes clear that the past is very much alive. Though he attempts to divert himself with Santuzza, his consuming passion for Lola is irrepressible. Palermi sets the triangle of Lola, Santuzza, and Turiddu against the collective life of the villagers in their observance of religious rituals and local festivals marking the social continuity of the village. The personal lives, however, of the individuals, especially of the younger people as opposed to the older generation, are characterized by aimlessness and boredom, as in Lola's restlessness and playing with Turiddu, in Turiddu's inability to reassimilate into the traditional patterns of the family and community expressed through his unabated desire for the inaccessible Lola, and in Santuzza's jealousy, which drives her to become the vehicle of revenge and death. Her betrayal of Lola and Turiddu's liaison results in the death of Turiddu, her own anguish and loss, the suffering of Turiddu's mother, and the disruption of community life.

The operatic elements in the presentation are conveyed in the folk singing of the peasants, the choreographed dancing of the tarantellas with their accompaniment of pipes, Turiddu's serenading of Lola outside her house, the organ music in the church, and the processions of the peasants that serve to punctuate the stages of the personal drama of the major characters.

The role of Mama Nunzia is central. Like the mother in *La peccatrice*, her role heightens the affective dimensions of the film. Her anticipation, dread, and desire for her son also serve as choric commentary on the film's actions. The final sound in the film is of her scream as she learns of his death. The prior image of Santuzza prostrate on the church floor and the image of the hysterical mother, inconsolable, and surrounded by the villagers, is reminiscent of Agrippina's prostrate image at the end of *Gelosia* and provides a strong visual image of failure and impotence as a dramatic contrast to the pastoral scenes of nature and of collective rituals and actions in the early thirties films.

Palermi's film orchestrates a number of domestic conflicts: the conflict between mother and son as Nunzia seeks to divert Turiddu from his fateful pursuit of Lola, the conflict between Santuzza and her father as he senses difficulties in her relationship with Turiddu, the conflict between Lola and her husband, Alfio, as he seeks to satisfy her and to hold her interest, the conflict between Santuzza and Turiddu as he seeks to avoid her and as her jealousy mounts, and the ultimate conflict between Turiddu and Alfio that results in Turiddu's death. The return of Turiddu to the peasant environment after having lived outside it reveals another conflict, between the traditional values of the countryside and the more sophisticated world beyond. Thus the question of his "place" and his identity becomes important and also calls into question the stability of the village world. He is now an "outsider" and a disruptive force as such. His pursuit of Lola flies in the face of familial as well as communal values.

He spends his time seeking out Lola, observing her, serenading her, and finally visiting her clandestinely. His inability to conform to expectations takes the form of obsession in relation to his illicit passion for Lola. As in *La peccatrice*, Palermi seems to be exploring the contrast between town and country life, between traditional and unconventional behavior, and between submission and rebellion. The "sanctity" of church and family are destroyed here, though affirmed in *La peccatrice*. But in both films the countryside, religious practices, and the life of peasants seems to be idealized and nostalgic. Turiddu's return to the community and his struggles to assimilate into the community open the question, however, of the possibility of maintaining traditional ties. His absence only reinforces the sense in which he has always been an outsider. He cannot forget what is "past." More than ever, he seems to be drawn by forbidden desire.

The film stresses Turiddu's willful flouting of his mother's will; his refusal to conform to her wishes. Santuzza, the potential wife-mother, the alternative to Lola, is also unattractive to him. Her possessiveness and rage alienate him even more from her. Santuzza's jealousy of Lola, her constant surveillance of the two of them and of Lola individually, seems to put her in the position of a spy. In typical "vendetta" fashion, her rage and aggression exceed her desire for Turiddu. Lola, on the other hand, is described as the "queen"; she is waited on, showered with gifts, an object of everyone's gaze. Her typical stance is at the window or balcony, restless and bored, like Madame Bovary, her beauty a snare for others.

The conventional triangulation is augmented by the film's orchestration of the role of spectatorship. Palermi plays with the role of looking in several ways. First of all, the film creates a link between the groups of spectators within the film and the external audience that occupies the position of the internal spectators. There are abundant opportunities to self-consciously call into play the role of audience, at the public activities such as religious spectacles, feasts, reunions, processions, dances, and other activities in the village square. Moreover, the visual composition of the rural scenes as tableaus reinforces the sense of the film's opposition between a static, traditional environment and the unsettled, explosive quality of the lives of the inhabitants. Thus, the style of the film reproduces a central aspect of the film's thematics, a differentiation and examination of modes of perception. The film emphasizes forms of looking that produce both involvement and distancing. One form of looking is associated with unity, the other with fragmentation.

Individual characters in the film are implicated as voyeurs. Lola is associated with looking out beyond her house, beyond the village, with a look that does not differentiate. She is also associated with sitting at her mirror and looking at her own image. Alfio looks at her with the pride of possession, Turiddu with the look of desire, and Santuzza with the look of jealousy. The scenes of actual passion and violence are subordinated to those of spectatorship. The emphasis on looking also creates an effect of alienation, which brings out an opposition between the continuity and richness of tradition in Sicilian rural life and the disruptive forces at work that arouse repressed desires. This opposition signifies the misalignment between communal values and individual desire. The characters cannot contain the aggressive elements associated with sexuality. In short, the economy of the family based on the containment of desire in the interests of socially approved objectives is exposed in the characters' competitiveness, possessiveness, and violence. The looks directed toward the forbidden object of desire are translated into transgressive action and are the means of destroying community cohesiveness. Thus Palermi's film, with the assistance of Verga's text,[11] portrays the breakdown of consensus, tradition, the family, and social life. Jealousy and obsession are the signifiers of instability. If Palermi's film appears nostalgic about this precarious state of affairs, it nonetheless records and corroborates failure.

In contrast to Palermi's rural setting and preoccupation with the agrarian community, Franciolini's *Fari nella nebbia* (Headlights in the Fog, 1942) is located in an urban context. The film's style is *noir*, a characteristic of many of these melodramas of the early forties. *Fari* begins on the road, in the night fog, with two men driving a truck, and in an apartment house where a man, Cesare (Fosco Giachetti), and his wife,

[11] Mario Alicata and Giuseppe De Santis, "Ancora di Verga e del cinema italiano," in *Dai telefoni bianchi al neorealismo*, ed. Massimo Mida and Lorenzo Quaglietti (Rome-Bari: Laterza, 1980), pp. 209-212.

Anna (Mariella Loti), quarrel. He returns to the trucking company's headquarters, where the supervisor asks Cesare to
deliver an emergency cargo. The scenes on the road, the dark
and shabby interiors of the homes, the scenes in the workplace, provide an authentic working-class atmosphere.

Cesare and his colleague Gianni head toward Genoa but
Cesare suddenly decides to turn off the road toward home.
The fog is thick, and their truck collides with a farmer's truck,
but the damage is slight. Cesare arrives at a darkened apartment where he finds a note from Anna, informing him that
she has left. On the road again, Cesare and Gianni stop to
pick up a young woman with a broken bicycle. Cesare is
reluctant to do this but Gianni urges him to help the woman.
The woman, once in the truck, begins to seduce Cesare,
though he appears to have no interest in her. At the station,
the dispatcher confronts Cesare with his insubordination in
diverting the truck to his home before finishing his job. Angry, Cesare says that there is no reason to reprimand him.
He has worked for the company for ten years and has made
money for it. The dispatcher, however, lectures him on how
work should come first even before family. He does not dismiss Cesare but deducts the cost of the damages to the truck
from his salary. Cesare is bitter.

Anna is shown with her mother, preparing herself for a
date arranged by a friend at work. Her mother is anxious
about Anna's going out with a man other than her husband.
The evening ends disastrously, for Anna refuses to accede to
his sexual advances. At loose ends, Cesare goes to Gianni's
house for dinner and in a scene that seeks to evoke the atmosphere of working-class family relations, Gianni's wife,
Maria, complains about money and the burden of caring for
the children. The setting is somber and shabby.

Gianni tries unsuccessfully to reconcile Cesare and Anna.
Instead, Cesare accepts Piera's invitation to dinner. The setting of the restaurant is, like Gianni's house, unembellished.
Cesare invites Piera to his apartment where they make love,
talk, and where he recalls his past relations with Anna by
means of a flashback. The motives for their quarrel emerge

now. Anna resented visiting Gianni and Maria. She also resented Cesare's constant absence from home. He, in turn,
complained of her working and her neglect of domestic duties.

Cesare invites Piera to live with him and she accepts, but
complications emerge. He is uneasy, haunted by the past,
and fearful that if he and Piera spend more time together,
they too will quarrel. He returns to his former apartment to
retrieve some blankets only to find it dirty and unoccupied.
Anna, dissatisfied with her life, has quit her job and has
become more involved with Gianni and Maria, helping them
to nurse their sick child.

Cesare's relationship with Piera deteriorates. He is bored
and she accuses him of tiring of her. She now reiterates Anna's
former complaints about Cesare. Anna, however, has
changed and is totally involved with Maria's children, while
Piera has now begun to receive visits from Carlo (Antonio
Centa). Cesare learns that he and Carlo must go out on an
assignment together. A neighbor who has been friendly with
Piera greets Carlo familiarly, thus informing Cesare that Carlo
and Piera have been seeing each other. Cesare plans revenge.
He stops the truck at his home and goes to get a gun, but as
he is ready to leave the apartment, Anna enters. The two
reconcile. Cesare empties the bullets on the ground as he and
Carlo drive off together.

The film employs the classic reconciliation—between men
and between the married couple, restoring the status quo, so
that the film seems to compromise the problems it raises. Yet,
in its exploration of marital conflict, *Fari* reveals the discontents of working-class domestic relationships: that people tire
of each other, that life's banality overwhelms relationships,
that work is unsatisfactory, that financial hardship is a primary source of discontent, that the care of children is a burden, and that loyalty cannot be taken for granted. The conflicts in the film involve conflicts between married couples,
between workers, between workers and bosses, between
work and family, and between the fantasy of escape and the
reality of conflict. Though Anna and Cesare are "converted"

to the notion of fidelity and service to family, their transformation barely mitigates the conflicts presented. Moreover, the style of the film, its dark interiors, the night scenes, the tight framing of characters, the use of mirrors, the studied creation of grim and shabby interiors, the equally studied avoidance of romanticizing character and situation, suggest a world dominated by failure and resignation.

The Gothic costume drama is yet another form of melodrama, one of the most extreme and excessive expressions of violent contrasts between good and evil, "normality" and deviance, past and present history. The form thrives on the development of extreme sentiment—love, hate, treachery, shifting and arbitrary allegiances, and excruciating psychic pain that leads to madness and acts of aggression.[12] The pivotal point is power and its abuses, and here the genre makes most obvious its equations between the exercise of power in the public and private arena although it concentrates largely on intersubjective relations.

Mario Soldati's film, *Malombra* (1942), is a costume melodrama of madness and destruction. The film's central figure, Marina di Malombra, is played by Isa Miranda. Family intrigue is central to *Malombra's* development, themes, and style. It opens with the following statement:

Marina di Malombra, orphaned after a life of ease and luxury, is taken to live with her uncle, Count D'Ormengo, to a lonely villa on the lake. The uncle, a man of principles, sets one condition, that Marina cannot leave the villa until married.

The house is large, imposing, cold, and unfriendly as in American/English Gothic melodramas such as *Rebecca* (1940) and *Jane Eyre* (1944), where the woman is swallowed up by the large house. She occupies a room that had been her grandmother's. The woman had been imprisoned in the room and eventually became insane. Hidden in the grandmother's spinet Marina finds a packet containing a lock of hair, a pair of gloves, a brooch, and a note that says that whoever reads

[12] David Gerould, ed., *Melodrama* (New York: New York Literary Forum, 1980), pp. 141-59. Also see Brooks, *The Melodramatic Imagination*, pp. 17-20.

the note will be reborn as Cecilia and should wear the brooch. Moreover, the note talks of revenge on Count D'Ormengo, which will be effected by the arrival of "Renato of the black hair."

Marina begins to decline physically and her uncle calls in a physician, a familiar figure in melodrama. His professional judgment is that she should leave the house for reasons of health. The Count is adamant and refuses to let her leave. Marina's condition begins to worsen. She falls into a fever and begins to hallucinate. Her uncle finally agrees to let her depart, but she no longer wants to leave. She becomes more deeply involved in a book she finds, *Fantasms of the Past*, writing a note to the author in which she asks if it is possible to live a second life, and she signs the note, "Cecilia." The author, Corrado Silla, by coincidence and unknown to her, arrives at the villa as a guest of the Count.

Marina's character has undergone a radical transformation. She has become unstable, subject to rapid shifts in mood. Corrado, though fascinated by her, finds her irritable and uncommunicative. He decides to leave, but on his departure he sees Marina, alone in the storm, about to take a boat trip on the turbulent water. He jumps into the boat with her. The wild winds set them adrift, but eventually Corrado manages to return the boat to the pier. When they arrive and disembark, Marina throws her arms around him and identifies him as "Renato."

The Count, impatient with Marina's behavior, calls her to his study and informs her that she must marry Count Nepo without delay, and she acquiesces to his request. Edith, the daughter of Steinegge, an aide of the Count, arrives, and the father and daughter are united in an emotional scene. A contrast is set up between the devoted father-and-daughter relationship and the cold relations between uncle and niece, and between Count Nepo and his manipulative mother. The latter pair are fortune hunters, concerned only with the extent of Marina's future inheritance.

Corrado and Edith strike up a friendship under the aegis of her father. The three of them share happy evenings at

Steinegge's home. Edith begins to teach Corrado Hungarian and he looks as if he is beginning to forget Marina. Marina, meanwhile, has fallen even more deeply into her fantasies of the past. For a second time, she hears a voice telling her, "The moment of revenge has arrived. Count D'Ormengo is the murderer," and she goes at night to the Count's room. When he hears that Count D'Ormengo is fatally ill, Corrado decides to return to the villa. At the villa, the police, suspecting foul play, interrogate the inhabitants and visitors about the Count's condition. Count Nepo and his mother, however, are eager to effect a marriage with Marina as quickly as possible in order to avert the possibility that the Count's inheritance will go to Corrado. Edith, concerned for Corrado's safety, returns to the island and tries to enlist the priest's aid in extricating Corrado. Corrado and Marina have, however, been reunited, declaring their love for one another.

At the Count's deathbed where the inhabitants of the villa are gathered, Marina shrieks out, "Marina is here with her lover to see you die." She begins to laugh madly and has to be led away. Corrado remains at the villa and resumes work on the research he had abandoned earlier, but is uneasy about Marina. She plans a dinner party where she informs her guests, all men, of a long journey she is about to take, and then she shoots Corrado. Afterward she escapes, takes a boat, and disappears on the water. The final images in the film are of Edith and the priest, and of Corrado's grave as the priest expresses the hope that Corrado will finally rest peacefully.

In this film, which exploits classic Gothic elements—the imprisoned highborn woman, the tyrannical male authority figure, the obstacles confronting the young rescuer who seeks to extricate the endangered woman, the motif of mistaken identity, the isolated romantic setting, the demands of the past, the emphasis on madness, violence, and death—there is no salvation. The heroine is not saved, and the rescuer is destroyed. Based on Fogazzaro's novel, Soldati's film maintains its overwhelming emphasis on darkness, disorder, and unmitigated suffering. The film, like Blasetti's *Corona di ferro*, highlights the disastrous consequences of tyranny. Marina's

suffering stems from the repressive restriction of her aristocratic uncle who imprisons her as the king had imprisoned
the daughter in the Blasetti film. The folly of the older generation is visited on the younger, though in the Blasetti film,
the young revenge themselves on their elders. If in the earlier
films of the era, youth is celebrated as the hope of the future,
in these later films, the reverse is true. The death of young
people seems to signify sterility and breakdown. In spite of
the prayerful commentary by the priest and Edith at the end
of *Malombra*, their words and the final image of Corrado's
grave reinforces the vision of death governing the film.

Stylistically, *Malombra* plays with stark light-and-dark contrasts, highlighting oppositions, creating a sense of ambiguity
around events. The film's emphasis on the past, as conveyed
in the book title, *Fantasms of the Past*, introduces the problematic issue of repetition as does Palermi's *Cavalleria rusticana*,
but on a more complex note. Soldati's insertion of paintings,
photographs, research materials, the packet of mementoes,
books, references to the past, and the role of "voices" orchestrates the film's preoccupation with entrapment in the
past and the characters' obsessions with repetition.

Marina's reiterative question, "Can a person live twice?"is
central. On the surface, her question enhances the element
of supernaturalism so necessary to the Gothic melodrama,
but underlying the obvious and going beyond the game of
coincidence is the idea that life is mere repetition and that
entrapment in the past is inevitable. In Soldati's film there is,
however, nothing supernatural about Marina's situation. She
is, like her aunt, a victim of tyrannical authority. Both women
are driven mad, though Cecilia dies unavenged and Marina
dies an avenger. The particular form of her madness lies in
her identification with the dead woman. Her assumption of
Cecilia's identity forces her to destroy the Count. She com-
pletes the unfinished business from the past. Though the
specific cause of the Count's death is not explored, the information is provided that he held in his hand the brooch
belonging to Cecilia and worn by Marina and that his face
was disfigured by horror. The implication seems to be that

the fury of the avenging woman was sufficient to destroy him. Thus Marina settles her account with the past and avenges both her aunt and herself, though she destroys herself, too, in the process.

In its obsession with the past and with the destruction of the figure of oppression, *Malombra* explores the degree to which individuals are doomed to repeat history and the possibility of altering that history. Though it appears that Marina is driven mad by her victimization, madness enables her to confront and destroy her oppressor. In the process, she also destroys Corrado and Edith's hopes for happiness. The film constructs a dark world where subjugation, madness, and death prevail and, as such, seems to provide a nihilistic commentary on a world in which the obsession with the past destroys the present and future as well.

Renato Castellani's 1942 *Un colpo di pistolo* (A Pistol Shot), based on Pushkin's "Queen of Spades," replays many themes common to these other melodramas, particularly exploring and exploding the inadequacy and destructiveness of conventional values and attitudes. The film demystifies the elevation of male heroism and comradeship associated with the films of the thirties. Sexual conflict arising from competition between men is the vehicle for exposing the uneasy world inhabited by these characters. Castellani's films, like those of Poggioli and Chiarini, were labelled by the critics of *Cinema* as "calligraphic" because of their ornateness, like the beautiful handwriting to which the term refers. These films employ a highly stylized mode of representation, earlier literary and dramatic works as sources, an arch, self-enclosed treatment of the filmic events, a retreat into the past, and an emphasis on eroticism.

The film is situated in nineteenth-century Russia and opens on a sinister note with the attempted suicide of Count Andrea Anchikoff (Fosco Giachetti), who is saved by a writer, Di Valmont, as he observes Andrea walking on the thin ice. Andrea recounts his history to the writer, concerning his conflicts with Prince Sergio. By means of a flashback, Andrea's love affair with Mascia (Assia Noris), is introduced. Mascia plays with his affection, unwilling to give him any definite assurances about her own feelings. Andrea is a military officer with a promising career. He meets Prince Sergio and develops an immediate antagonism toward him that further complicates his life. Andrea, desperate for a response from Mascia, proposes marriage to her, inviting her to live with him in the country. On very flimsy encouragement from her he resigns his promising career in the army to the surprise and shock of his commanding officer and colleagues.

Andrea introduces Sergio to Mascia and he jealously watches as Sergio monopolizes her and she flirts outrageously with him. The setting is in the beautiful countryside where the leisured class is enjoying outdoor games and a lavish picnic. The lengthy sequence is elaborately composed, stressing the lush natural panorama, the elegant costumes, the fashionable people, and the playful pastimes of the aristocracy. As in an earlier scene of military maneuvers observed by the fashionable society, the spectacle of place and the choreographed movement of groups of people is emphasized. Situated in this environment but isolated as a morose and uneasy observer is Andrea himself.

Sergio taunts Andrea, revealing that he had informed Mascia of Andrea's resignation. Furious, Andrea challenges him to a duel. The duel scene is one of the most memorable in the film. Set in a field, on a foggy morning, Andrea and two seconds await Sergio, who arrives nonchalantly. He goes to a cherry tree and casually begins to eat the cherries, communicating his indifference to the proceedings. He flippantly takes his hat, fills it with cherries, and then offers them to the others. Sergio is designated as the first to shoot, and he aims his gun but intentionally misses Andrea. When it is Andrea's turn he aims his gun, sees Sergio eating cherries as his life hangs in the balance, and lowers his gun, saying that he will not shoot now but wait for a time when Sergio is happy and wants to live. The scene returns to the present with Andrea thanking Di Valmont for saving his life: "One must have the courage to live out his destiny."

A year later in the Romany countryside, Andrea and Di

Valmont meet again and Andrea informs the writer of further events during the past six months. Andrea learns that Mascia still loves him and awaits him in Kiev, and he goes to see her. In Kiev, Sergio proposes marriage to her. She accepts in spite of her initial refusal to see him and her avowed love for Andrea. At a ball celebrating the engagement, Andrea learns of the engagement and confronts Sergio, determined to have his revenge. He arranges to meet Sergio at dawn. Mascia, distraught, tries to find Andrea and dissuade him. She wanders through the dark, foggy streets until, exhausted, she enters a church. There she finds Andrea, and he informs her that he will not fight Sergio. A ray of light like a halo is shown illuminating the darkness of the church. Mascia and Andrea are finally reconciled.

The film is rich in visual detail, calling attention to itself in the opulent costumes and lavish interiors, rivalling Hollywood decor of the same era. The scenes not only serve to re-create the aura of nineteenth-century Russia, but the nature scenes serve as a correlative for the intense conflicts experienced by Andrea. The ice, fog, darkness, and storms are visible signs of his conflict, alienation, and pain. The image of Andrea as an outsider, a passive observer, pervades the film. The film, in part, seems constructed so as to generate the sense of life experienced from a distance. Events are recollected through flashback; Andrea narrates his story to Di Valmont, a writer; and the camerawork itself uses the long shot to convey the sense of place and of the social group as observed from afar. The distancing elements coupled with the psychological treatment of the main characters' conflicts produce an unsettling picture of social and personal relations. The social context and the psychological antagonisms are mutually dependent.

The role of the woman, Mascia, is important only insofar as she is the object of desire, the apparent source of the men's competition and struggle. Mascia is the figure at the piano, a signifier of a society, more particularly of a class, associated with performance, games, and also with deprivation.

*Un colpo* is a film that does not elevate the positive aspects of male camaraderie, nor are the conflicts between the men resolved in war or heroic action. The film juxtaposes two forms of male relationships: Andrea's relationship to Sergio is fraught with envy, obsession, while his relationship to Di Valmont is supportive and uncomplicated. Di Valmont saves Andrea's life. He is the sympathetic listener, an artist, not a military figure. Andrea renounces his military career, preferring a peaceful life in the country, and finally he also renounces his revenge on Sergio. In his character, he is represented as Sergio's polar opposite. Sergio is gregarious, dashing, energetic, and has a quick, even mordant, wit, whereas Andrea is shown as intense, introspective, awkward, morose, and even inarticulate. He does not represent the "virile" man.

The element of competition contains within it the ambiguous attraction of the men to each other, their common bond in their attraction for Mascia, the sadomasochistic terms of their interaction as Sergio capitalizes on Andrea's pain. Moreover, the film's focus on the men's competition subordinates the woman's role and deemphasizes any erotic connection to her. The element of family relations is also subordinated. Desire in the film is concentrated in the conflict between Andrea and Sergio, eroticized in their verbal and physical struggles, embodied in the dramatization of the ways in which Sergio seeks to taunt and humiliate Andrea, and in Andrea's impotent responses to Sergio's dominance.

The film presents the upper-class environment, the entertainments of the rich and their games with each other as empty and cruel. Even the scene in the church at the end appears to represent another claustrophobic dimension of this world. Thus, Castellani's film replays the fascination with obsession, jealousy, and the struggles for domination characteristic of other forties melodramas. Its aristocratic settings and characters present an external image of beauty but the analysis of their internal relationships reveals deadly flaws. In spite of the "reconciliation" at the end, the fundamental oppositions and conflicts remain. The film is far removed from a legitimation of conventional family romance, of public service, and of the redemptive aspects of physical action. The conversion here moves from notions of honor and revenge to renunciation and possibly even resignation as the alternative to conflict. The element of spectatorship in the film reverses the role of spectacle, calling it into question, alienating the audience from its power, and revealing instead the underlying psychological conflicts that create discomfort rather than gratification.

Another "calligraphic" film directed by Luigi Chiarini in 1942 is *Via delle cinque lune* (Street of the Five Moons). Based on a literary work by Matilde Serao, the film explores family conflict within a context of jealousy, acquisitiveness, and power plays. While the earlier *Carnevale di Venezia* celebrates the total subordination of the mother to her daughter, Chiarini's film grimly portrays the daughter's destruction at the hands of a domineering mother. The daughter is sacrificed to the older woman's desire. With the death of the husband early in the film, Ines (Luisella Beghi), the mother, is now unopposed in her management of Teta's (Olga Solbelli) life. The domestic conflict is played out in the Street of the Five Moons where people struggle, legally and illegally, to survive economically and emotionally. The inhabitants of the street provide a choric commentary on the life-and-death struggle of the mother and daughter.

Teta is in love with Checco (Andrea Checchi), an impoverished artist, who returns her affection. Ines, irrevocably opposed to the relationship, tries to keep Teta and Checco apart, forcing the lovers to meet clandestinely. The film's melodramatic elements are enhanced by the film's stylized settings, reminiscent of German films of the 1920s, and by the chiaroscuro lighting that enhances the dark and brooding themes. The film's use of classic melodramatic motifs include a controlling parental figure, a victimized young woman, illicit sexual relations, illegal and extortive financial machinations, and a dramatic suicide.

In addition to Ines's obsession with making money, she is also intent on gratifying her own desires at any cost. Checco, thinking to ingratiate himself with her, offers her a gold watch that he has acquired. Seeing the potential of having Checco as a collaborator, she draws him into the business. Gradually she begins to woo him away from Teta, as the daughter helplessly observes changes in her own relationship with Checco. At a dinner party in a restaurant, Ines flaunts her growing intimacy with Checco. The editing in this scene alternates between the merriment at the head of the table and Teta's position as an isolated observer. Slowly the camera retreats from the scene as the windows are closed and the spectator is excluded.

Checco begins to frequent Ines's house in order to help Ines with her business transactions, and Teta tells him that he has changed, that he is now more concerned with money than with her. Glibly, he tells her that he is only working with Ines in order to acquire money for himself and Teta. Finally, Ines seduces Checco. The final sequences of the film take place during a festival with crowds of people in the street among whom are Teta, Checco, and a sculptor friend. Checco leaves Teta with a friend and goes to Ines's house. Teta returns home and discovers her mother and Checco together. Exiting, she stops at the landing overlooking the street, then jumps.

Chiarini's three major films, *La via delle cinque lune*, *La bella addormentata* (Sleeping Beauty), and *La locandiera* (The Innkeeper), feature women. In the first two films, the women are victims driven to madness and death, or are victimizers like Ines. In the third film, the woman outsmarts sycophants and charlatans, exposing their machinations. In all three films, the men are portrayed as weaklings. In *Via*, Chiarini develops the motifs of familial conflict and economic greed. He portrays a dark, unpleasant world where obsession, fanaticism, and the struggle to dominate produces despair and suicide. By means of the triangulation of mother, daughter, and lover, Chiarini fuses the economic and domestic issues. Ines is presented unsympathetically. She is completely calculating and unscrupulous in her financial enterprises, profiting from the vulnerability of her customers, who are desperate for money. In her familial relations, she is equally unscrupulous. Her husband, who dies early in the film, was unable to restrain her or defend himself and Teta against her. With his death, Teta is completely subjected to Ines, and Ines is able to move unimpeded in a course of action that results in her daughter's suicide.

The film does not move to punish Ines or even to present her as experiencing remorse over her daughter's death. It ends starkly with the tragedy. Moreover, there is an absence of strong mediating figures in the film. The world seems divided into victims, aggressors, and ineffectual observers. Checco is unable to resist Ines's power. The compounding of his cupidity and sexual vulnerability place him within the sphere of aggressors. The visual effects in the film reinforce the sense of the entrapping nature of this environment. The hierarchical relations conveyed in Teta's relationship to her mother are reproduced in the convent where the girls are shown to be surveyed, supervised, and regimented. Ines's power over her customers is also reflected in her power over Checco. The narrow alleys, the tight framing of the courtyard where Ines and Teta live, the emphasis on enclosed rooms, convey drabness and claustrophobia.

The *mise-en-scène* conveys a self-conscious emphasis on design, calling attention to the film's concerns with control and surveillance. The stairs and alleys appear labyrinthine, representing the devious and complex relationships in the film. The camera in its stylized backward-forward movement also reinforces the highly choreographed dimension of the film's form and content.[13] The emphasis on windows and doors, and on placing characters and audience outside, sometimes as voyeurs, other times as deprived of participation, also calls attention to the issues of control and closure. The film is highly structured around parallelism and contrast which, like incremental repetition of the house setting, create a sense of inevitability. The movement in film involves a gradually increasing tempo that climaxes in Teta's suicide.

[13] See Chiarini's discussion of film form and techniques in *Cinque capitoli sul film* (Roma: Edizioni Italiani, 1941). Also Brunetta, *Storia del cinema italiano*, pp. 456-57.

Chiarini underscores the role of performance, including a scene at the theater where the camera studies the audience, highlighting individuals whose dramas are as intense as any theatrical performance. As in *La locandiera*, he develops the element of self-reflexivity to the end of creating an alienation-effect that calls attention to the disastrous consequences of domestic and social roles people play. *Via* is framed by death, the death of the father at the beginning and of the daughter at the end. The world of the film is one of disintegrating relationships, of treachery, and of destruction but also of terror and impotence.

*La bella addormentata* (Sleeping Beauty), also by Chiarini, was produced in 1942. Based on a work by Rosso di San Secondo, Chiarini explores many of the same themes as in *Via delle cinque lune,* but with greater emphasis on powerlessness through the dominant image of somnambulism. The setting is an Italian village of the nineteenth century. Carmela (Luisa Ferida), a young woman who has just arrived from the countryside, is observed by others as she walks, including Salvatore (Amedeo Nazzari). In the village square, a puppet show is performed in which the motifs of passion and revenge are enacted as a prefiguration of Carmela's drama. There Salvatore gives her a flower as a token of his esteem.

In the lawyer's house, two women and a man are seated at the kitchen table. The lawyer is berated by his mother for his bad habits, and the young woman, his sister, voices her own dissatisfactions. Carmela takes the position of servant in the house and is tyrannized by the older woman. The lawyer begins to harass Carmela, trying to seduce her. He offers to help her learn to read and write and to make a good marriage. He is impatient as he waits for his mother to go to bed so he can visit Carmela. Alone in her room, Carmela undresses and admires the flower given to her by Salvatore. Finally, the lawyer succeeds in entering Carmela's room. She backs away from him in fear, but he overpowers her. The scene cuts to the water tap, dripping in the kitchen.

The following morning Carmela leaves the house. As she walks into the marketplace with her bundle, she studies a statue of the Archangel Michael on the church steeple. Salvatore, in the country, is unaware of what has happened to Carmela and therefore unable to help her. She goes to stay with Concetta, who with her father runs a bordello. Concetta tries to awaken her, but she appears like a somnambulist. Outside a festival is going on in the village square. A crowd has gathered to watch a tightrope walker, while in Concetta's waiting room, men sit waiting impatiently for Carmela. Finally Carmela appears, still dazed. Salvatore, who has returned and heard about Carmela's new situation, angrily leads her out of the house. Concetta's father calls the police as Salvatore and she walk through the village where the statue of the archangel is prominently displayed.

The outraged contingent of men come to the lawyer's house to lodge a complaint and he agrees to assist them. Salvatore reveals to the mother what has happened to the young woman. The mother, at first indignant and later pleased, asserts that her son will marry Carmela. On the day of the wedding, Carmela, dressed in white, is led, still dazed, in a procession to the church. She faints and has to be carried back to the lawyer's house. Taken from the bed, she is set in a chair flanked by candles, like a corpse.

The film involves the classic melodramatic situation of the deflowering of an innocent young woman. The lawyer's rape of Carmela initiates the subsequent stages of her destruction as she passes from prostitution to madness, and then death. With the exception of Carmela and Salvatore, everyone in the village is grasping and exploitative. The images of family life as portrayed in the house of the lawyer are totally negative. The mother is a shrew, the son a bully and rapist, the daughter self-centered. Concetta's father is a brutal, violent man and together with his daughter is involved in prostitution and extortion. Violence permeates the film in the performance of the puppet show, in the rape itself, in the verbal violence of the mother, and the issue of avenging the crime is embedded in the image of the Archangel Michael. However, Carmela is not avenged.

*La bella addormentata* is hardly like its fairy-tale source. Sleeping Beauty is not awakened by the prince's kiss. The "kingdom" that has fallen into ruin is not regenerated. People do not live happily ever after. The young lovers are not united. Marriage is thwarted. Like *Via delle cinque lune*, the film is theatrical. It does not pretend to be realistic but depends on highly structured parallelisms and oppositions. The film begins with Carmela walking, proud and innocent in her youth, and ends with her degradation, paralysis, and death. Throughout, the film is punctuated by the image of her movement through the town, marking the stages of her demise. The film is also punctuated by public performances—the puppet show, the entertainers of the festival, and the wedding procession through the streets—marking the stages of Carmela's transformation as well as calling attention to the idea of spectacle itself. In its stylization, its use of lighting contrasts, its creation of a closed and threatening environment, in its incremental use of certain visual images such as the flowers, the statue of the Archangel Michael, the final image of Carmela herself propped in the chair, the film is reminiscent of the French films of the early forties with their aura of fatality.

Chiarini's films make no pretense of alluding to the contemporary situation and to historical or political events. The deteriorating social, economic, and political conditions in 1942—the problems of military losses, the deteriorating economic situation, Mussolini's sinking prestige, the scarcity of necessary commodities, the disparity between the propaganda machine and these realities, growing cynicism and criticism—cannot be read directly into *La bella addormentata*. For that matter, the work might be considered as totally divorced from a temporal context. Yet, like the other melodramas of the time, if only by virtue of its silences, the film responds to contemporary issues.

No vision of social solidarity or consensus is in any way dramatized. Public concern, the efficacy of and reward for work, the altruism of commercial interests, are undermined in the portrayal of sexual, legal, and commercial rapaciousness. Petty bourgeois values are exposed as mean, deforming, and hypocritical. Those who would seek to reassert justice, like Salvatore, are themselves arrested. Set into the context of the times, the film, removed as it seems from any political issues, situated as it is in an earlier period and based on a prior literary work, seems to reinforce the dark themes and treatments of the other melodramas that undermine contemporary reality.

In 1942, Luchino Visconti directed *Ossessione* (Obsession), based on James M. Cain's novel, *The Postman Always Rings Twice*. Although many of the films of the fascist era were later forgotten *Ossessione* was not. It was identified with the film style known as neorealism.[14] Not only did the film become incorporated into the canon of neorealism, but it was credited with being a major precursor of the movement and a significant antifascist film. In part, its reputation derives from a time when little was known about the other films of the era except the "white telephone" and propaganda films, in part because it was made by Luchino Visconti, who was identified with the resistance to fascism, and in large part because the film explores fascism, touching particularly on those aspects of ideology and practice that relate to the everyday mode of existence as opposed to its spectacular and public aspects. Self-reflexive, the film probes the immediate everyday practices that served to keep fascism in place.

A handsome stranger arrives by truck at a small gas station-restaurant owned by the fat and crude Bragana, a caricature of the petty bourgeois property-owner who sees himself as a patriarch over his small corner of the world. Gino, the young man (Massimo Girotti), enters the restaurant. He helps himself to some food as Giovanna (Clara Calamai) watches him. Bragana complains about freeloaders and berates his wife, telling her that strangers are dangerous. Gino exits but leaves money on the table for the food, which Giovanna pockets.

---

[14] Peter Bondanella, *Italian Cinema: From Neorealism to the Present* (New York: Frederick Ungar, 1983), pp. 24-25. See also Gaia Servadio, *Luchino Visconti: A Biography* (New York: Franklin Watts, 1983), pp. 80-82; Mira Liehm, *Passion and Defiance: Film in Italy from 1942 to the Present* (Berkeley and Los Angeles: University of California Press, 1984), pp. 51-59.

Bragana, thinking that Gino has not paid, rushes after him. Gino, understanding what Giovanna has done, agrees to come back and do a few odd jobs to pay for the meal. He will fix the truck and the water pump.

In examining the truck, which is reparable without new parts, Gino surreptitiously places a small piece of equipment in his pocket, forcing Bragana to leave the premises in order to get the part. When Bragana and the local priest ride off, Gino and Giovanna take advantage of his absence. After lovemaking, Giovanna complains to Gino of her husband, that he is disgusting and demanding, and he invites her to come away with him. She ominously hints that if Bragana were gone, she would be free.

Gino and Giovanna attempt to escape, but Giovanna cannot leave. He, however, boards a train, and a friendly passenger who introduces himself as "lo Spagnolo" (the Spaniard), offers to pay the fare. He is an artist, a traveling entertainer. That he is called the Spaniard is significant for several reasons. His role in the film is as an outsider, as someone enjoying a freer life. His specific association with the Republican cause in Spain was expunged by the censors. Nonetheless, his character stands in opposition to the obsessional world of most of the others. If Giovanna is associated with romanticized notions of respectability and security, he is associated with nonconformity and a mobile life. He directly confronts Gino with the idea of freedom. Like the young dancer, Anita, whom Gino meets later, Spagnolo poses an alternative to the dark, static life associated with the restaurant and with Giovanna's passionate but obsessional and distorted conception of freedom and with Gino's enslavement to her.

Spagnolo invites Gino to stay with him. At a performance, Gino sees Giovanna and Bragana in the audience. They invite him to join them for a drink. Gino struggles to escape, to extricate himself from the lure of Giovanna, but his struggle ends vainly. Bragana is unaware of this drama. Deeply involved in the singing competition, he performs an aria from *La traviata* to the acclaim of the audience. The romantic music of desire seems incongruous coming from Bragana, the coarse

and coercive figure of repression and conformity, but nonetheless provides a commentary on the motif of death and
thwarted sexuality. The young man who follows him to the
platform accompanied and supervised by his mother also reinforces the contrast between desire and denial, between the
repressive and ugly environment and the desire for escape.

The operatic arias and their performance further develop
the element of reflexivity introduced in the previous scene
with Spagnolo, inviting the audience to examine, not identify,
with the conflicts. The scene also provides a commentary on
Gino and Giovanna's entrapment in a romantic fantasy of
escape that is marked by possessiveness, violence, and denial.
The melodramatic aspects of opera are thus used by Visconti
to indicate not only that such art is linked to bourgeois as-
piration, but that romantic aspirations are a source of repression, not liberation.

Signor Bragana's victory in the singing contest leads him
to drink excessively until he is barely able to maneuver. He
struggles to his truck, followed by Gino and Giovanna. Out
of sight of her husband, she enlists Gino's cooperation in
killing Bragana. The murder scene is highly stylized: the headlights of the truck at night, the tight framing of the characters
within, the highlighting of contrasts. Gino and Giovanna insist
that Bragana cannot drive and they push him and the truck
off the road. The death introduces a new element into the
film, the role of police and of surveillance.

Gino and Giovanna are interrogated by the police at the
scene of the crime, then afterward at the police commissioner's office where Giovanna is asked to sign necessary papers
and collect her husband's belongings. The commissioner is
suspicious about this "accidental" death and warns Giovanna
that he may want to talk to her again. The return home provides a stark contrast between the brightness of the day and
the darkness into which Gino and Giovanna are plunged
within the *trattoria*. Giovanna begins to make plans for reopening the restaurant so that life will appear normal. Gino,
however, pleads unsuccessfully with Giovanna to abandon
this life. Life returns to the restaurant. Don Remigio, the

priest, is uncomfortable about Gino's continued presence, and Gino himself is eager to leave. He does not want money or security. In contrast to the image of Gino's isolation and alienation, the growing crowd within the restaurant is cheerful and loquacious, enjoying themselves in singing and dancing. Gino finds Bragana's watch, and contemplates his present life. The watch, the signifier of Bragana's continued presence, has been introduced several times, a reminder of Gino and Giovanna's continued enslavement to Bragana's world, to material objects, and to conformity.

Gino sees Spagnolo on the road. Overjoyed, Gino greets him. Spagnolo renews his invitation to travel, urging Gino, as Gino had urged Giovanna, to get away. Angrily, Gino tells him that he does not want to be a vagabond. Finally, he hits Spagnolo in an effort to silence him. Sadly, Spagnolo leaves, but he is stopped by a policeman who tries to ingratiate himself in order to get information about Gino. Spagnolo refuses to be an informer.

The following sequences in a garden at Ferrara highlight the contrast between the constraints of Gino and Giovanna's world, their alienation from each other, and the beauty and open spaces of the world beyond the *trattoria*. While sitting on a bench waiting for Giovanna, who is collecting her husband's insurance, Gino meets Anita, a dancer, who invites him to accompany her to the theater. He refuses at first. When Giovanna meets Gino in the garden, she ebulliently shares her plans with him to enlarge the business. Gino accuses Giovanna of murdering Bragana for the money, and defiantly he goes to Anita's apartment. When Gino and Anita emerge, Giovanna sees them and confronts Gino, but he coldly tells her to leave him, finally striking her as a crowd observes. Anita and Gino return to her room. He confesses to her that he is tied to Giovanna forever. Seeing a policeman, he suspects Giovanna of denouncing him. He escapes to the train station only to discover the police there. He finally flags down a ride in a truck and arrives at the *trattoria*, a much different person from his first arrival, also in a truck.

From Giovanna he learns that she is expecting a child. The

two reconcile and spend the night together on the beach. Gino tells her the following morning when they awaken that he feels liberated now. They decide to leave the place forever. As they return to the *trattoria* to pack, a child observes them. They drive away in the truck, hopeful and eager to escape, but Gino crashes into another truck and Giovanna is killed. Prostrate over Giovanna's body, Gino is arrested.

The film's self-conscious use of melodrama probes sexual conflict, the entrapment in romantic fantasy. Giovanna is obsessed with the banality and obstructiveness of Bragana, the father-husband who controls her life and whom she seeks to destroy. Bragana, indifferent to her, plays out his authority, expecting the world to conform to his petty bourgeois expectations. Gino, the young intruder, has his own romantic notions of escape to freedom, which are blocked by his desire for Giovanna. Giovanna's fantasy is to replace Bragana with the younger man but maintain, even improve, the style of family and business life she has known, while Gino is incapable of extricating himself, bound as he is first by passion but then later by having shared in the crime of destroying Bragana. Rather than bringing the two closer to liberating themselves, the crime mires them deeper in their own obsessions, she becoming enslaved to the business and accumulating money, he enslaved to sexual desire and to the notion of enslavement itself.

The images of inside and outside, represented by the enclosed world of the *trattoria* and the open road and movement seem to convey the unbridgeable gap between commitment and freedom, between the world of creativity and of accumulation, between the repression of the family and the liberation from its demands, between pleasure and profit. Giovanna's desire for security becomes a prison for her and for Gino. The film amply illustrates that the more she submerges herself in commerce, the less she derives personal gratification from her desire to replace Bragana and to assume his responsibilities. Visually, the images within the *trattoria* convey a sense of imprisonment corresponding to the confines of possessive love. In terms of character development, a role reversal takes place and Giovanna becomes the jailer to Gino that Bragana had earlier been to her. Thus the myth of the family and the ennobling aspects of romantic love are here dissected and revealed to be coercive, strangulating, and threatening.

The role of the police and of surveillance are intimately related to the maintenance of the family and the consequences of transgression. The police in the film function to raise consciousness on two levels, the symbolic and the historic. On the level of the symbolic the police represent the organized and coercive forces of society that punish violations of the Law and work to maintain the status quo. The role of the police develops further the disjunctions in the film between public and private spheres. Visconti thus explores the relationship between the internalization of family positions and the external social forces that ensure and maintain continuity. In a more specific historical fashion than is evident in other films of the early thirties, Visconti evokes an image of a society in which surveillance, informing, hunting, and punishment are central aspects of life.

Through Spagnolo, Visconti develops the motifs of resistance and freedom. Spagnolo constitutes an alternative to the image of the virile male so popular in the era, and his friendship with Gino is also an indirect commentary on more classical forms of male relationships. His slight figure, his nurturant role, his avoidance of forms of coercion and dominance, seem to offer a critique of male bonding. That he is an artist is also important; he "entertains" in order to provide for minimal necessity, not as Bragana, to compete with others. He is a man of the people, and his entertainment is a gift, part of the generosity that prompts him to befriend Gino, a generosity dramatically in contrast to Bragana's, which gives nothing away. Recognizing and exposing Gino's obsession, he does not use it as a means of control and manipulation but sees Gino's plight as an opportunity for friendship and support. Spagnolo is associated with travel and movement as Gino had been earlier; he is mainly seen out of doors.

Anita is a parallel character. She, too, is an entertainer, also single, and also itinerant. Like Spagnolo, she holds no veneration for the law and is not an informer, willing even to help Gino escape the police. She asks for nothing materially or emotionally from Gino. Unpossessive, she accepts transitoriness in contrast to Giovanna, who is obsessed with security and permanence. The conjunction of open sexuality, openness of encounter, an encumbered way of living, the antiromantic nature of Spagnolo's and Anita's attachments to Gino, contrasts sharply with the other characters' obsessional nature.

Giovanna's death at the end raises a number of issues. In designing her as a *femme fatale*, Visconti makes Giovanna a contradictory figure. On the one hand she resists subordination, on the other she is a total victim. The devouring destroyer, the instigator of transgression, is also destroyed and a victim. Giovanna's death at the end and Gino's imprisonment at the point where they finally feel unburdened is Visconti's way of subverting the happy ending and, more significantly, of underlining the precariousness of an easy alternative to the conflicts posed in the film. This ending also develops the sense of unnaturalness that Visconti has tried to stress throughout the film. The film has sought to denaturalize romance, the notion of the idealized family, and the idea of security. Through melodrama as a narrative form that can place these concepts into question, Visconti seems to be calling attention to the violence inherent in the commonplace in contradistinction to those films that make violence commonplace, glamorizing it, concealing it, and renaming it.

Blasetti's *Quattro passi fra le nuvole* (A Walk among the Clouds), is also a domestic drama but, unlike Visconti's film, blends melodrama and comedy. The film is framed in a closed, dark, and hostile environment similar to the other melodramas of the time. Moreover, Blasetti uses a contemporary setting rather than situating his narrative in the past, and in the central sections of the film he creates a realist *mise-en-scène*, quite different from films such as *Malombra* and *La bella addormentata*. Made in 1942, it, too, has often been cited as one of the precursors of neorealism. The central characters of the film, the traveling salesman, Paolo (Gino Cervi), and the young countrywoman in distress, Maria (Adriana Benetti), share a kinship with the workers and peasants in neorealist films. The settings are modest and the other characters are, for the most part, also workers. Significantly, the plight of both characters derives from their social and economic entrapment. The film does not end happily by resolving the obstacles in love. Maria is left with her illegitimate child to raise, dependent on the largesse of her family, and Paolo returns home to his confining existence with his shrewish wife. The style of the film, however, seems to mark it as being cast in the genre mold with certain affinities to other earlier films of the era and to the Hollywood cinema in the use of major stars such as Gino Cervi and Adriana Benetti, the stylized and stereotyped casting of the lesser characters, the choreographic and stylized editing, and the festive treatment of workers' lives. The film seems to begin with a "realist" treatment, veer to self-conscious illusionist techniques, and then return to the "realist" frame.

The first image in the film is clouds, followed by a view of a deserted street. An image of an apartment building dissolves to an apartment shuttered and in shadows. A man enters and turns on the light. A medium shot of him in the shadows as he goes into the bathroom is succeeded by the arrival of the milkman. The man opens the door, takes the milk, and trips. A woman emerges angrily, grabs the milk, and berates her husband, Paolo, for disturbing her sleep. As she complains and asks for money, the viewer sees a table in deep focus through the doorway piled with dirty dishes. Paolo takes his briefcase and leaves this dark and uncongenial environment, slamming the door behind him.

On the street, he hurries to the train station, buys a paper, then jumps on a crowded train. People are irritable as they elbow each other to get seats. Paolo finally finds a seat, places his briefcase on a rack, and goes into the corridor. He reveals to a fellow passenger that he is a candy salesman. When he returns to his seat, it is occupied by a young woman. He forces her out of the seat. He takes his paper out to read, but is guiltily distracted by her presence. He finally gets up and offers her the seat.

The conductor arrives to collect the tickets, and Maria cannot find her ticket. Paolo berates the conductor who is ready to give up on her just as she finds the ticket. Paolo then goes into the compartment to get his monthly pass, but finds that he has forgotten it. In a scene satirizing bureaucracy, Paolo waits in the office of the station as the officials take their time getting the necessary information while he is forced to wait at the risk of missing his bus connection. Finally, the long-awaited telephone call of verification is received and Paolo races off to his bus.

He arrives to discover that Maria is also aboard, though the driver has not arrived. When he finally comes and the bus sets out, the shout, "It's a boy," is heard. The bus turns back, much to the consternation of the passengers. The driver gets out and is congratulated. Even the passengers are mollified by the news, all except Maria, who becomes melancholy. The driver talks about the future of his baby, while Maria cries. Paolo tries ineptly to comfort her, offering her candy from his sample case. A contrast is set up between the gay passengers and Maria's suffering. Paolo learns that Maria is pregnant and she fears going home, since she is not married. She invites him to accompany her and pretend to be her husband for the day. Reluctant at first, Paolo finally agrees to take part in the subterfuge. Maria is greeted enthusiastically by her mother and grandfather. She introduces Paolo as her husband and, with the exception of her father, the family is overjoyed to meet him. Finally, he is mollified, though he insists that Paolo must stay for a proper celebration. Furthermore, the priest announces that the couple must get married again at home. Maria faints and thus the secret of her pregnancy is revealed. Everyone congratulates the "father." Paolo, however, is eager to leave, but he learns that there is no transportation available until morning. He will have to spend the night.

Maria and Paolo are in the awkward position now of having to pretend that they occupy the nuptial bed; when the parents retire, they argue about who will sleep in the bed. He leaves and goes to the barn to sleep. The pastoral setting contrasts to the dark and dingy images of the city. In the morning, Maria serves him fresh milk, in an ironic reminder of the bottled milk he brought into his apartment the previous morning. He takes a cart ride in the country with Maria in a scene that further highlights the natural setting. When they return to the house, Maria's father is in a rage, having found a picture of Paolo with his wife and children, and Paolo confesses. The father rants madly about his blighted honor, the ruination of his household, his ingrate daughter, but Paolo tells him that he should be proud of his fine family, and of his daughter. He urges the father to pardon her. The speech has the desired results, and the father relents. Paolo goes to Maria and tenderly says goodbye, takes his candy case, and exits. The film returns to the street shown at the beginning of the film, to the milkman and to Paolo taking the milk. His wife can be heard, scolding, as he takes the milk into the kitchen, lights the stove, and pours the milk into a pan. He drops the lid of the pot to the floor.

The film thus breaks into two segments: the urban sequences and a pastoral idyll. The beginning and ending with its repetition of images and actions portrays the drab urban petty bourgeois existence, its routinization, marital conflict, and squalid environment. By contrast, the country appears more authentic in its freshness, sense of community in spite of domestic conflicts, and beauty. Blasetti suggests, as in his other films, that the simple virtues are redemptive. In Paolo's speech to Maria's father, Blasetti urges an ethos of acceptance, capitalizing on simple virtues, taking advantage of your "blessings" because others are worse off than you. He also seems to be suggesting that in the pastoral environment problems can be more easily resolved, even the righteous rage of the father-authority figure. While the film critiques the father's virulent attitudes upholding honor and revenge, it also reveals his amenability to reason. Paolo thus serves as an important agent of service and transformation. His own suffering becomes the basis for his serving others and legitimizing the acceptance of the simple virtues of familial respect, work, nature, and nurture. The scenes of festivity on the bus involve the birth of a child and Paolo's act of service involves helping a pregnant woman, thus situating his actions within the context of nurture. His role in relation to his wife, contrasted to his relations with Maria, is of an unappreciated nurture figure. Like so many other Blasetti heroes from the thirties, Paolo represents an agent of continuity, life, and devoted service to others.

If Blasetti's 1943 film reveals the crowding and sordidness of urban life, the claustrophobia of domestic relations, routinization and bureaucracy, the impotence of the petty bourgeoisie, it offers as prescription a bond between city and country in the implied common fate of workers and peasants, as they confront and surmount conflict. The "natural" images of childbirth and country life serve as a compensation for alienation and indifference. Paolo's seemingly barren life has been transformed through his act of transforming others; however, the final image of the film of the lid coming off the pot seems to suggest the possibility of future conflict and change, that Paolo will no longer assume a submissive role in relation to his own situation as a consequence of his experience with Maria. Though the ending reproduces the same situation as at the beginning of the film, this slight variation in the routine vaguely promises something different in the future.

The role of women in the film deserves comment because it seems to circumscribe the film's critique and sense of alternatives. Women are procreators primarily, either serving to enhance the man's position, contributing to his sense of mission, or, like Paolo's wife, obstacles in the way of the man's self-realization. Paolo is enhanced by his service to Maria and her devotion to him, while his sterile family life seems to be attributed to a woman who expects herself to be served and does not fulfill her domestic and marital duties. Thus, it is not the economic and environmental pressure that burden the salesman, or the pressures of the urban setting, but marital discord. In its themes, if not in its style, Blasetti's film bears affinities to the other melodramas of the forties. In spite of its nostalgia and idealistic affirmation of authentic human relationships, it exposes domestic failure and social conflict.

In a darker vein, Castellani's 1943 film, *La donna della montagna* (The Woman of the Mountain) dissects sexual conflict. The film is based on a novel by Salvator Gotta. The original title was "The Shadow of the Mountain," and, like other Castellani films, it explores obsessional behavior. The melodrama opens with the death of the wife of the engineer, Rodolfo Morigi (Amedeo Nazzari). She has met with a fatal accident in the mountains. Mourning her loss, Rodolfo not only loses interest in people, but also in his work. Zosi (Marina Berti), a young woman totally devoted to him, is willing to accept a relationship with Rodolfo on any terms. He tells her that he can only think of his dead wife, that he wants to die himself, and that he asks only for tranquillity. Nonetheless, he marries her. From her chauffeur, Zosi learns that Rodolfo's obsessive attachment to Gabriella, which causes him to disregard her, is based on ignorance of Gabriella's marital infidelity.

Rodolfo treats Zosi badly. He ignores her, abuses her verbally when he does make contact with her, and relegates her to a life of household drudgery, leaving the more attractive domestic duties to the housekeeper. The housekeeper treats Zosi shabbily, and Rodolfo refuses to talk to her. One of the chores she is called upon to perform is the feeding of Rodolfo's dog. The snarling animal cannot be approached and, as she pushes the meat close to him, the dog menaces her. Castellani develops a parallel between the dog and Rodolfo in their hostility to the woman.

Zosi's cousin, Luca, comes to visit her and is shocked by her appearance. He buys her some decent clothes, only to have them ruined when she feeds the dog. She excuses Rodolfo's behavior to Luca, insisting that she is really happy. Luca urges her to confront Rodolfo with what she knows about Gabriella but she rejects this alternative. Leaving in haste in his car, Luca hits Rodolfo's dog by accident. Angrily, Rodolfo abuses Luca and Luca reveals Gabriella's escapades to him. Rodolfo returns home and burns a packet of letters from his wife. In the morning he gets up early and goes to the mountains. Zosi follows him. A storm is brewing. When Rodolfo sees her, he is angry with her for coming and insults her, but gradually his anger abates, and he begs her forgiveness. She looks at him and smiles, as he lays his head, like a child, on her bosom. The final image is Zosi's, looking up toward the sky.

The film appears to be closed and crepuscular, an exercise in decadency, in exploiting passion and suffering for its own sake. Reading the text more carefully, one discovers that Castellani, as in his other films, explores a male's obsessive attachment to a female as well as to the past. His exploration of a master-slave relationship is coupled to his emphasis on guilt and redemption. Zosi is the quintessential image of self-sacrifice, renunciation, and complete trust and dependency. She asks only to be near her husband and to serve him. He is also single-minded, but in his devotion to the dead woman, which impels him to treat Zosi with cruelty and indifference.

The women in the film, one present and one absent, seem to signify the traditional dichotomy between the whore and the Madonna, the destroyer and the life-giver, the seductress and the maternal figure. Zosi, as the nurture figure, is abused, maligned, and long-suffering, but in the long run she triumphs over the seducer, Gabriella, the unworthy object of devotion who, though dead, exerts her power from the grave, from the very fact of her death. The central object of concern in the film, however, is the male and the exploration of his paralysis. Gabriella's death renders him incapable of work or of attachments to others. He is portrayed as being totally dependent on the female for misery or relief.

The underlying sexual politics is conveyed not only in the ostensible subjugation of the male to the female, the portrayal of the woman as the other, but also in the equation of sexual relations with animality through the imagery of the dog. The dog, as a substitute for women, is the only living creature who can elicit affection from Rodolfo. Moreover, the dog's attachment to the master parallels Zosi's doglike attachment to her snarling master. The dog's death becomes the crucial incident in Rodolfo's acceptance of Zosi, for he substitutes her for the animal. The master-slave relations that are never resolved are most graphically played out by means of this imagery. Zosi's gaining of dominance becomes the means for curbing Rodolfo's aggressive behavior. The final sequences of the film assert a "natural" order to things, the female becomes the vehicle for neutralizing guilt, aggression, and for establishing continuity. The imagery of the mountains, of nature, serves to reinforce the inevitability of threatening and destructive forces and the naturalness of the woman as a benevolent force. The violence in nature is paralleled by the violence of social relationships. When the conflict ceases, so do the violent images of nature. The reinstatement of the dominance of the maternal-Madonna figure appears to appease nature.

Castellani's film thus portrays a fractured world, fraught with conflict, obsessive attachment to the past, violent social relations, domestic discord, unresolved male identity, and personal entrapment, but, as in Camerini's films, though much more darkly and schematically, the film falls back on a traditional resolution. However, the film language subverts the "resolution," revealing contradictions. The final image of the film with the isolated shot of Zosi looking at the sky, the disappearance of Rodolfo's image from the frame, has the curious effect of subverting the "reconciliation," serving to obliterate Rodolfo and to establish Zosi's dominance over him as if the power conflict has merely been reversed, not ameliorated.

Unlike *La donna della montagna, Gelosia* (Jealousy, 1943), directed by Ferdinando Maria Poggioli, is a stark melodrama, unrelieved by any resolution to the narrative conflicts. The film emphasizes crime and punishment and portrays hostile, competitive, and deteriorated social relations. In spite of the Christian symbolism, the film affords no spiritual compensation. The Christian symbolism functions more as an ironic commentary on the protagonist's exploitativeness as a way of marking the various stages of his dissolution and "damnation," than as a moral alternative. The film could be read as simple prescription film, proposing morality and charity as opposed to lecherousness and privilege. However, a close examination of the film's structure and style undercuts such a reductive analysis. Poggioli's exploration of the power of obsession and of its consequences makes the film less a narrative which legitimizes and more a narrative which demystifies existing social relations. The refusal of reconciliation, the final visual images of emptiness, the uncompensated victims, reinforces the sense of the complexity and depth of the conflicts presented.

In the middle of the night, a rider on horseback is shot. The police enter a house, and a woman within cries that he is innocent but the man is dragged from the house. At the home of Antonio, the Marquis of Rocca Verdena, a lawyer informs the nobleman that the man who was killed was Antonio's foreman, Rocco Curcione. The lawyer complains that the case is complicated by the absence of witnesses. A peasant, Neli, has been unjustly accused of the murder. Rocco, the victim, earlier known as a womanizer, had lately become domesticated. The murder appears unmotivated. Agrippina (Luisa Ferida), the widow of Rocco, comes to seek help from Antonio. He scolds her, saying that he is doing everything he can, and rudely asks her to leave. As she exits, she is stopped by the housekeeper who castigates her, charging that if Agrippina believes that Antonio still loves her, she is mistaken. Thus we learn of Antonio's former relationship with Agrippina.

The housekeeper is not the only one concerned to restrain Agrippina, but also the Baroness of Lagomorto, a relative of the Marquis who expresses her desire to circumvent any resumption of Antonio's affair with Agrippina. In talking with Don Silvio, the priest, the noblewoman expresses her fear that Antonio might marry Agrippina. She concocts a plan to arrange a marriage for Antonio with Zòsima Munoz, the daughter of an old friend. Poggioli portrays the Baroness as a spiteful, frivolous woman, rude in her treatment of subordinates though overly affectionate toward her dog.

At Antonio's estate, the lawyer, insisting on Neli's inno-cence, tries to enlist the nobleman's help for the unfortunate peasant. In the trial scene that follows, Neli is shown in the dock. Antonio observes the proceedings as Agata, Neli's wife, protests her husband's innocence, asserting that in the past Rocco and Neli had had problems but recently these had been set aright. The incriminating testimony hinges solely on the recollection of past quarrels. Neli is declared guilty as the camera singles out a motto on the wall (as in Pudovkin's *Mother*): "The Law Is Equal for All."

Agrippina comes again to see Antonio and reaffirm her love for him. At first, he orders her to leave, but then changes his mind. Equally abruptly, he sends her away, and goes to visit the priest. With a crucifix in the background, Antonio con-fesses to his relationship with Agrippina and how his relatives feared that he would marry her, how one night he ordered Rocco to marry Agrippina but not to consummate the mar-riage. His difficulties were not over, however, for he was tormented by jealousy, a jealousy so overpowering that he finally murdered Rocco. The priest tells Antonio that God will forgive him but Antonio must express deep contrition and make reparations by taking Neli's place. Mere charity would be insufficient.

Don Antonio's character reveals once again, as in the dinner party sequence and as in his encounter with Agrippina, a profound instability. His behavior is subject to rapid shifts from tenderness to cruelty, from remorse and guilt to rage. He taunts Don Silvio as he had taunted Agrippina, asserting that Don Silvio's vows as a priest enforce him to silence. He must respect the privacy of the confessional. Don Silvio's response is, "But *I* have not forgotten." In the following scene, Antonio is shown in the room with the statue of Christ. He moves closer to the statue and contemplates it, but he is interrupted in his meditation by the arrival of a group of priests who have come to remove the statue to the church at Don Silvio's request. They take the statue down and carry it as if it were the dead Christ taken down from the cross and they the mourners.

While Antonio contemplates confession and suicide, Zòsima arrives to solicit money for the poor. His act of charity
consoles him, and he destroys the note of confession. He is
frequently photographed with his back to the viewer as if to
stress his isolation and as if to intensify the secrecy and ambiguity of his motivation. His removal from the spectator provides a distancing device, inhibiting identification with the
character.

Antonio's decision to marry Zòsima is motivated, as he
informs the lawyer, by his desire to quell once and for all any
gossip about his relationship to Agrippina. On the day of his
marriage, Agrippina lurks in an alley to observe the wedding
party's procession through the streets. After the marriage,
Zòsima reveals that relations between her and her husband
are poor. Antonio is melancholy and disconsolate most of the
time. They sleep apart. Instead of remaining at home, he seeks
out Agrippina. He finds her working in the fields, dismounts,
and the two embrace passionately. His movements are concealed from Zòsima by the Baroness and housekeeper.

Agata, Neli's wife, arrives with her children and begs Zòsima to help her by taking the eldest son into service, and
Zòsima takes the entire family under her protection. Antonio
returns and learns what Zòsima has done and, enraged, he
begins loudly to berate her. That night, Antonio is disturbed
from sleep. The room is lit by candlelight. The play of shadows
on the wall is reinforced by the sound of horses' hooves, the
same sounds that accompanied the murder in the opening
scene. Antonio's mind is beginning to fail. Agitated, he goes
to Zòsima's room, but finds the door locked. He begs her to
talk to him, and she relents. He pleads with Zòsima that he
needs her, and they plan a trip together for the following day.

Poggioli presents an idealized picture of the countryside—
rich fields, harvest time, happy peasants at their work. However, this idyllic scene is interrupted by a peasant's confronting Antonio with a request for permission for his son to marry
Agrippina. Imperiously, Antonio refuses his petition. Zòsima
understands that Antonio cannot relinquish his obsessions.
Furthermore, Antonio learns from Zòsima that Neli has been

executed, and his sanity crumbles totally. He begins to hallucinate, complaining that he hears the sound of a horse's hooves as he screams, "They are persecuting me." Zòsima leaves Antonio, and Agrippina comes to visit her lover, but he does not recognize her. Alone in the large room where the statue of Christ had hung, she sits on the floor as a mournful procession of the choirboys passes, chanting *"miserere nobis."*

This Gothic melodrama depends heavily on religious symbolism to develop its critique of male dominance, coupled to class domination. Antonio's power over and exploitation of Agrippina and the peasants stems from the abuse of his privileged position. Poggioli stresses not only Antonio's destruction of others but his inevitable self-destruction. The world in which he functions is one of violence, sterility, and death. Wherever Poggioli situates Antonio, in his home, in the priest's room, in the countryside, there is conflict and violence. The film links Antonio's behavior to existing social institutions—the courts, the Church, and the family—revealing how he seems to place himself above these institutions while claiming to participate in them. Poggioli does not, however, seem to be criticizing the institutions themselves. He seems rather to be contrasting legitimate ideas of justice, morality, and charity to the illegitimate exploitation of power.

The issue of legitimacy is central: the legitimacy of sexual relations, of Church practices, and of the courts of law. Significantly, the issue of legitimacy is also central to films such as *Alcazar*, *Squadrone bianco*, *Camicia nera*, and *Sotto la croce del sud*. The films of war, imperialism, and heroism, however, stress the legitimacy of power, of leadership, and of control. In Poggioli's film, legitimacy resides in the institutions and in the individuals who restrain those who threaten their operations. Poggioli uses characters such as Don Silvio, Zòsima, and the lawyer to confront Antonio with his perversion of social relations. Unable to function according to his desire, Antonio, already unstable, is driven mad.

Antonio's jealousy is linked to his desire for power, and in particular his attempt to control the lives of those economically and sexually dependent on him. His desire to exact submission is traced in the film to several sources—psychological instability, alienation, subjection to class expectations as exemplified in the Baroness and, above all, in his need to legitimize his behavior to himself and others, to see himself as noble, pious, and charitable. He is, however, unable to control his desire, his rage, and his unrestrained guilt. He is surrounded by women, manipulated by one, the manipulator of another, and resisted by another. He exploits a woman of the lower classes while he is controlled by his own aristocratic relatives. His involvement with Agrippina, therefore, becomes a sign of his need to debase others and to feel debased himself, which he attempts to reproduce in different form with his bourgeois wife. Vulnerable, Agrippina cannot defend herself, whereas Zòsima can. Antonio's passion, which he asserts proceeds from jealousy, does not seem linked to romance but to his unrestrained contempt for others and to sexual impotence, expressed not only in his inability to consummate relations with his wife but in his need to experience passion with, what is for him, a degraded sexual object, a peasant woman.

Poggioli's *Sorelle Materassi* (The Materassi Sisters), released in 1943, hovers between melodrama and satire. As in so many of Poggioli's works, the film concerns compulsion and self-delusion. The two major female characters are oppressed and oppressive. The essential force that drives them is a fear of isolation. The sisters are locked into their sexual fantasies vainly waiting for someone to free them. Their desires for affection and recognition involve them in degradation, violence, manipulation, exploitation, which they refuse to acknowledge. Obsessively, they deceive themselves in their desire for self-enhancement and self-importance. Through the agency of the young opportunist, the gigolo, Remo (Massimo Serato), Poggioli exposes the destructive side of bourgeois attitudes toward work, family, and respectability.

The Materassi sisters, Carolina and Teresa (Irma and Emma Gramatica) are respectable manufacturers of lingerie and linen who are invited by the Pope to the Vatican to honor them for their excellent work. The sisters are shown in the Vatican, dressed for the occasion, walking in a long corridor filled with paintings. In contradistinction to this scene of dignity, virtue rewarded, and respectability, the next scene introduces Remo on a train, trying to pass off a third-class ticket in a first-class compartment. Unruffled by the conductor's insistence for a proper reckoning, Remo allows a woman in the compartment to pay the difference. Another passenger looks and shakes his head reproachfully at Remo's successful manipulation. At the Materassi house, the sisters return, elated and garrulous, describing to Laurina, one of their workers, and to Niobe, their cook, their visit to the Vatican as the happiest moment of their lives. Their pleasure is disrupted by Giselda, another sister, who can be heard crying loudly. The sisters go to her room where she often closets herself. When the sisters enter, her tears change to reproaches as she complains that her sisters have all the fun while she is excluded from pleasure. She taunts them with their ignorance of life and love. When they leave she picks up a photograph of her husband who has deserted her and kisses it.

Remo, it turns out, is the nephew of the Materassi sisters. He arrives at the house and immediately wins the affection of the sisters. He tells them a pathetic story about his home life and of being forced to work. The women surround him greedily, unable to keep their hands off him. They beg him to stay with them. The other sister, Giselda, is not at all receptive to his presence, but Carolina and Teresa insist that he stay. Realizing their susceptibility to seduction, Remo flatters them and attempts to fill the void identified by Giselda earlier: the absence of love in their lives. The sisters praise Remo's virtue (they call him "a perfect angel").

A mother accuses Remo of having taken advantage of her daughter, but the Materassi sisters refuse to believe her and angrily defend their nephew. Remo's ambitions steadily increase. He becomes involved with an older woman, and his desires for material acquisitions also increase. No longer satisfied with the simple bicycle given him by his aunts, he now wants a motorcycle at the cost of 4,000 lire, and he asks them for the money. At first, they refuse him with the well-worn

phrase, "What do you think we are, millionaires?" Remo
punishes them for this refusal by withdrawing affection. That
night, the sisters complain to each other sadly that Remo has
not kissed them good night and they determine to get the
money for him.

Niobe, the cook, is also drawn to him. She brings him the
money for the motorcycle. However, he is no longer conciliatory. He is indifferent to the aunts' pleas for information.
He even taunts them with his conquests, and he begins to
manipulate them for a car.

He invites the sisters out for dinner at a restaurant. Prior
to the dinner, he helps the excited sisters dress and he fixes
their hair. The sisters, ecstatic, are escorted by Remo to a
restaurant, a meeting-place for him and his shady friends.
During dinner he divides his time between his aunts and his
friends at another table from whom he borrows money. When
he returns to the aunts' table, he allows them to pay for the
dinner to which he had invited them. New evidence emerges
about Remo's unscrupulousness. Laurina, their young assistant, reveals, after being pressed, that she is pregnant with
Remo's child. Moreover, Remo now brings his friends to the
house to carouse as the sisters stand outside on the landing,
watching the merriment. Remo takes the opportunity to rid-
icule his aunts by holding up a pair of oversize underpants
that the aunts have sewn and laughs at them and their work.
The aunts, however, continue to indulge Remo. Although
they have scolded him for taking advantage of Laurina, they
agree to find her a suitable husband from her own class, since
they feel Remo must marry someone more highly placed.

Remo's financial troubles escalate as his colleagues press
him for the money he owes them. He tries to get the money
from his aunts but they inform him that their estate is fully
mortgaged. But Remo is adamant about getting the money.
He tells his aunts that they are his only resource now. For
once, they resist with firmness and they tell him to leave. He
escalates his strategies, moving now into violence as he locks
the sisters into a closet with the promissory note that he wants
them to sign, guaranteeing him the money he desires. The

aunts stand silently in the closet looking at the note as Remo nonchalantly goes to wait in the doorway to the courtyard.

Finally, Remo unlocks the door and the aunts come out with the signed note. The atmosphere in the neighborhood has changed. Neighbors and former clients mock and sneer as the sisters enter and exit from their house. Within the house things have reverted to their former condition with the aunts again waiting on Remo. He has taken a job as an automobile salesman. An American woman, Peggy (Clara Calamai), enters, looking for a car and willing to pay for it on the spot. Her only condition is that Remo drive it for her to demonstrate its condition. He wants to return to the city. She takes the wheel and races the car as they run out of gas. Remo is furious that they must spend the night in a guesthouse. They quarrel and he slaps her, but they are reconciled. The sisters, distraught over Remo's absence, receive a telegram that informs them that Remo is engaged. When Peggy arrives and descends from the car, the voyeuristic neighbors comment to each other favorably about her appearance. The sisters find her crude and vulgar, and are unwilling to believe that Remo will actually marry her. Their jealousy is virulent. Poggioli films the wedding day in highly stylized fashion. Crowds of people wait at the steps in the front of the church. A car stops, and Peggy emerges, radiant, as the crowds cheer. From a following car the aunts also emerge, each dressed in the same wedding dress as the bride, to the amusement of the crowd. The three "brides" go into the church with Remo.

After the wedding when Peggy and Remo are alone, she gaily throws him money to spend. He pretends reluctance, but finally sucumbs. Thus Peggy's dominance, financially and sexually, is established. The final sequences involve Remo's separation from his still-doting aunts. In an almost Buñuelian scene, the aunts are shown seated in their wedding finery, looking like deserted brides. Remo enters and informs them that he will repay them what he owes. They beg him to write to them. Pathetically, they weep, saying that they may never see him again. Remo kisses them and leaves. He goes to the kitchen where he finds Niobe also crying. He repays her, kisses her, and exits, leaving her in total dejection. The aunts are again at work in their workshop as at the beginning of the film.

Fabrizio Sarazini in 1945 in *Il tempo* criticized the film, affirming the superiority of the novel as more realistic than the film in its conjuration of the Florentine context, though he finds the film narrative to be told with "persuasive clarity."[15] This critique leveled at Poggioli reveals the new critical directions from 1943 into the postwar era, the predilection for psychological or social realism, as propounded by the writers for the journal *Cinema*. The comments indicate a distaste for the stylized representation that is characteristic of Poggioli's work. In *Sorelle*, external landscape is subordinated to the fantastic inner landscape. The ending of the film itself is a play on the fantasy of the happy ending involving economic and sexual fulfillment in a context where deprivation is ubiquitous. Most particularly, the film probes the scarcity of men and its psychosocial consequences. This is not surprising in the war society characteristic of 1943 with the men fighting in Greece, Russia, Africa, and even in Italy.

Moreover, Carolina and Teresa's degeneration cannot be reduced simply to sexual deprivation. The carefully wrought interactions with Remo suggest that Poggioli, as in his other films, is involved in exploring the issues of dominance and subordination, legitimacy and illegitimacy. The interaction between Remo and the sisters provides a critique of the ways in which people (women, in this case) are bound in desperation to a dominant figure, actually endowing that person with great power willing to go to any extent to maintain the illusion that the transaction is natural and inevitable. Carolina and Teresa are willing to accept any degrading and abusive treatment of them (including physical violence) in order to maintain their illusion of being cared for, needed, and useful. Giselda lives vicariously through her nursing of past grievances. Niobe's straightforward erotic interest in Remo makes her vulnerable to manipulation. In general, all the women in

---

[15] Francesco Savio, *Ma l'amore no* (Milan: Sonzogno, 1975), pp. 336-37.

the film, including Peggy, are willing to go to any length to maintain Remo, to give him what he emotionally and, more significantly, materially, demands.

The game of dominance and subordination is enacted on the turf of economics and sexuality (money, cars, and sex). The basic thematic ingredients of earlier films are here over-turned—the basic soundness of family relations, the elevation of industriousness, the notion of loyalty and service rather than opportunism. These attitudes are deconstructed in *Sorelle Materassi*. The two older women are the dominant carriers of the underlying psychological drama of conflict. The family conflicts are orchestrated in several ways: in the sisters' ag-gressive and competitive relationship with each other, in their "adoption" and conflict with Remo, and in their competition with Peggy over possession of Remo. The petty bourgeois world they inhabit can be read in the sisters' conspiracy with Remo to maintain the ideal of being "useful" even to the extent of tolerating verbal and physical debasement.

Like *Ossessione*, the film exposes thwarted desire, jealousy, desperation, and the unwillingness to confront the disjunc-tion between exploitation and its denial. Unlike Visconti's film, however, it is Remo, the male, who is the focal point, the agent of manipulation. He is the one who converts sexual desire into money. His primary motivation is to be supported and he has no difficulty exploiting women sexually in order to accomplish this end. The money, interestingly, is used primarily for vehicles of locomotion—bikes, motorcycles, and cars. The job he finally acquires is an automobile salesman, and his relationship to Peggy results from this employment. The vehicles become symbols for his sexuality. If he himself is for the women the object of desire, these locomotory objects are his fetishes, a corollary of his inability or unwillingness to confront human needs, his exploitation of people in ex-change for objects.

The women in the film express their desire through looking. The sisters are frequently shown as voyeurs, gratifying their desire through observing their nephew. Giselda lives through looking at a photograph of her deserting husband.

But in developing the vicarious act of looking, Poggioli also includes another viewer in the film; namely, the crowds on the street who accumulate in number as the film progresses, commenting scornfully on the folly of the Materassi sisters as they allow themselves to be manipulated by their nephew. They represent a surrogate for the external audience, a distancing device that permits sardonic laughter and commentary on the characters and events. The film opens itself to provide a view of a darker world, closer to the realities of 1943—of a view of opportunism, repression, false expectations, the folly of idealism, the inadequacy of simplistic notions of service, loyalty, and commitment.

The ending of the film, rather than serving to resolve the conflicts, only reinforces the sense that nothing is actually resolved. Remo's success in finding a rich woman and leaving the sisters' house puts the women in their original position, illusions intact, but the internal as well as the external audience has witnessed the consummate expression of exploitation, which has been exposed on the street to the eyes of the public.

The film is not contemptuous of the sisters. They are portrayed as pathetic, desperate, and fragile, the victims of their desire, but they are also culpable in their willingness to endow Remo with power over them. The imagery in the film, the lingerie and linen, the house, the objects of locomotion, the photograph, the clock that signifies Remo's absence and the sisters' longing, all testify to the fetishism of need. Everything and everyone in the film dramatizes the desire to possess, to manipulate, and to control: the desire for money and respectability, the desire for conventional domestic relations, the terrifying fear of isolation, characterizes this world. The audience within the film thus seems to be moved between scornful laughter and shock as it confronts the pain, waste, folly, and hypocrisy exposed.

## Summary

With the melodramas we come to the end of the long journey of the twenty-year rise and fall of the fascist regime and with the rise and development of the Italian film industry that would command world attention after the war. The melodramas provide a fitting sense of an ending. Signs of social and political disintegration are written in their narrative structures, iconography, and visual style. The films are, however, more than a critique of fascism. They offer a fascinating glimpse into the ideological structures that precede and underwrite fascism, touching such fundamental conceptions of the family, of men and women and the discourse of difference as inscribed in their representations. The films also contain attitudes toward history and the ways that history is interpreted and given authority. The conflict between past and present, between myth and concrete historical events, between traditional Italian-European culture and of American culture with its technological and cultural imperatives, the conflict between the myths of rural life and of urban existence, are all deeply embedded in these films. They are not unique to fascist discourse but can be found in the other world cinemas. Most especially, the melodramas expose tensions in relation to conceptions of power, authority, and legitimacy.

If the melodramas (and certain comedies) of the 1940s seem most congenial to us and artistically superior to the films of the 1930s, it is not because they introduce new issues or that they expose contradictions not evident to a critical viewer of the thirties films. The difference between the films of the two decades resides in the self-consciousness of the treatment and style of the latter films. They cover the same psychosocial terrain in familiar genres, with familiar conflicts, but with different critical and stylistic instruments. Their often extreme stylization, their *noir* quality, their revelation of the submerged eroticism at the basis of the earlier films, their exposure of the violence in seemingly "natural" personal relationships, and their ruthless identification of the psychologically oppressive strategies of conformity account in good measure for the critical acumen and aesthetic excellence of these films.

Examining the films in this context thus helps to make Lucchino Visconti's 1942 film, *Ossessione*, if not the immediate post-World War II cinema, more comprehensible. When *Ossessione* appeared, it was identified, as it continues to be, with the cinema of antifascism, with the movement known as neo-realism. *Ossessione* embodied many of the objectives of the *Cinema* group for a different type of film, but it also is fair to say that it was not the sole basis and paradigm for neorealism. As Ted Perry has indicated:

In the late 1930's and early 1940's, the films begin to go backwards, reflecting the same confusion, perplexity, and ambiguity from which the country was supposed to have been saved in 1922.
Neorealism was born then, not by some spontaneous generation as if by magic, but rather out of this pessimism, the effects of the war, and out of the rich cinematic tradition which had been advanced full speed in the 1930's.[16]

The Visconti style, so admired by viewers of *Ossessione* and his later films, is recognizable in the other melodramas. The form and content grow from the hybrid French-American *noir* style, which is an exemplary vehicle for psychological and social issues, thus permitting a rare insight into the complexity of social conformity and undercutting the assumption that conformity is merely a matter of social coercion.

*Ossessione* is better understood, then, without denigrating its achievements, as part of a continuum, an undercurrent of opposition that finally realized itself in the postwar era.[17] Elements of the realist aesthetic so lauded by André Bazin can also be identified in other films of the late fascist period. Moreover, the awareness that the Italian cinema of the thirties and forties was largely a cinema of genre tied to the classical rules of spectacle helps to account for the stylized elements in neorealism itself.

Many of the filmmakers, directors, writers, and actors associated with the postwar cinema learned their craft during the fascist era. While new names gradually became familiar and some old ones disappeared in the postwar period, there

[16] Ted Perry, "Before Neorealism" (New York: Museum of Modern Art, 1978), mimeographed, pp. 12-13.
[17] Venturini, "Origins of Neorealism: *Springtime in Italy*," pp. 177-79.

was also a continuity in personnel, facilities, and even themes. Rossellini had made films in the early forties as had De Sica. Visconti, Lattuada, Lizzani, Germi, Barbaro had already written, scripted, or directed films. Anna Magnani and Aldo Fabrizi had made films prior to Rossellini's postwar *Open City*. The attraction for American culture was also continuous. If the American film was the earlier locus for this attraction, American literature usurped its place. Moreover, a penchant for rhetorical and emotional filmmaking as well as for the existence of a political cinema was continuous, although the politics shifted and the rhetorical elements likewise in the postwar era. There is also a continuity, especially in De Sica's neorealist films, in the treatment of social class, where the line is hazy between working-class and bourgeois relations, and where class differences are also mystified, though the films continue to articulate an anti-bourgeois position. The use of women and children as the locus of conflict, as signifiers of oppression in the society, is continuous, as is the preoccupation with Italian history and the search for connections between past and present. The presentation of the family as the site of conflict and contradiction is also a consistent thread between the prewar and postwar Italian cinema. Therefore, a study of the film production under fascism clearly calls into question the neorealist myth of beginnings and restores many long-neglected films to their place in the history of Italian cinema.

It should be evident that the preoccupations of neorealism, the films of the postwar era, are not a dramatic rupture from the films of the Ventennio, but carry forward many of their concerns, if not their style. No study of the history of the Italian cinema and of the postwar cinema, in particular, need be embarrassed by a discussion of these films. While the melodramas provide a sense of an ending, they also point to beginnings.

Alicata, Mario, and Giuseppe De Santis. "Ancora di Verga e del cinema italiano." In *Dai telefoni bianchi al neorealismo*, edited by Massimo Mida and Lorenzo Quaglietti. Rome-Bari: Laterza, 1980.

Amingual, Barthélmy. "D'une résistance à l'autre." In *Fascisme et résistance dans le cinéma italien 1922-1968*, edited by Jean A. Gili. Paris: Lettres modernes Menards, 1970.

Aprà, Adriano. "Linee di politica cinematografica da Blasetti a Freddi." In *Cinema italiano sotto il fascismo*, edited by Riccardo Redi. Venice: Marsilio, 1979.

————, and Patrizia Pistagnesi. *I favolosi anni trenta 1929-1944*. Milan: Electa, 1979.

————. *Notes on the Unknown Italian Cinema*. New York: Museum of Modern Art, 1978.

Aristarco, Guido. "Le cinéma italien pendant le régime fasciste." In *Fascisme et résistance dans le cinéma italien 1922-1968*, edited by Jean A. Gili. Paris: Lettres modernes Menards, 1970.

Baldelli, Pio. "Les débuts de Rossellini et le cinéma de Salo (1943-1944)." In *Fascisme et résistance dans le cinéma italien 1922-1968*, edited by Jean A. Gili. Paris: Lettres modernes Menards, 1970.

Barbaro, Umberto. *Neorealismo e realismo*. Edited by Gian Piero Brunetta. Rome: Riuniti, 1976.

Barthes, Roland. *S/Z: An Essay*. Translated by Richard Miller. New York: Hill and Wang, 1974.

Barzini, Luigi. *The Italians*. New York: Atheneum, 1977.

Benjamin, Walter. "Theories of German Fascism." Translated by Jerolf Wikoff. *New German Critique*, no. 17 (Spring 1979).

Bentley, Eric. *In Search of Theatre*. New York: Alfred A. Knopf, 1953.

Berger, John. *Ways of Seeing* Harmondsworth: Penguin, 1977.

Bondanella, Peter. *Italian Cinema: From Neorealism to the Present*. New York: Frederick Ungar, 1983.

Bourget, Jean-Loup. "Faces of the American Melodrama: Joan Crawford." *Film Reader 3* (February 1978).

Bragaglia, Anton Giulio. "Avanguardisti." *Bianco e nero* 2 (February/March 1938).

Brooks, Peter. *The Melodramatic Imagination: Balzac, Henry James, Melodrama, and the Mode of Excess*. New York: Columbia University Press, 1984.

Brunetta, Gian Piero. *Cinema italiano tra le due guerre: Fascismo e politica cinematografia*. Milan: Mursia, 1975.

———. *Intellettuali, cinema e propaganda tra le due guerre*. Bologna: Patron, 1972.

———. *Storia del cinema italiano 1895-1945*. Rome: Riuniti, 1979.

Burch, Noël. "Correction Please, or, How We Got into Pictures." 16mm., 52 min., color, sound. Great Britain: The Arts Council of Britain, 1979.

Byron, Stuart, and Elisabeth Weis, eds. *The National Society of Film Critics on Movie Comedy*. New York: Grossman, 1977.

Caldiron, Orio, ed. *Il lungo viaggio del cinema italiano: Antologia di cinema*. Padua: Marsilio, 1965.

Campari, Roberto. *Hollywood-Cinecittà: Il racconto che cambia*. Milan: Feltrinelli, 1980.

Cannistraro, Philip V. *La fabbrica del consenso: Fascismo e mass media*. Rome-Bari: Laterza, 1975.

Cavell, Stanley. *The World Viewed: Reflections on the Ontology of Film*. New York: Viking, 1971.

Cecchi, Emilio. "Stanchezza del cinema americano." *Bianco e nero* 3 (March 1939).

Chiarini, Luigi. *Cinematografo*. Rome: Cremonese, 1935.

———. *Cinque capitoli sul film*. Rome: Italian Editions, 1941.

Cogni, Giulio. "L'anima razziale d'Italia e il suo cinema." *Bianco e nero* 3 (March 1939).

Cook, David A. *A History of the Narrative Film*. New York: W. W. Norton and Company, 1981.

Cook, Pam. "Melodrama and the Women's Picture." *Gainsborough Melodrama*, Dossier 18. London: British Film Institute, 1983.

Crow, Bryan. "The Cinematic and the Melodramatic in *A Woman of Affairs*." *Wide Angle*, 4 (1980).

Cunningham, Stuart. "The Force-Field of Melodrama."*Quarterly Review of Film Studies* 6 (Fall 1981).

Dalle Vacche, Angela. "Blasetti's *1860*." Paper presented at a meeting of the American Association of Italian Studies, Bloomington, Ind., April 1984.

Dalzell, Charles F., ed. *Mediterranean Fascism 1919-1945*. New York: Harper and Row, 1970.

De Felice, Renzo. *Fascism: An Informal Introduction to Its Theory and Practice*. Edited by Michael Ledeen. New Brunswick, N.J.: Transaction Books, 1976.

———. *Mussolini il fascista*. 3 vols. Turin: Einaudi, 1966-1970.

de Grazia, Victoria. *The Culture of Consent: Mass Organization of Leisure in Fascist Italy*. Cambridge: Cambridge University Press, 1981.

De Santis, Giuseppe. "Towards an Italian Landscape." In *Springtime in Italy: A Reader on Neorealism*, edited by David Overbey. Hamden, Conn.: Archon Books, 1978.

"Dive: Maschere e miti." *Cinema* 1 (10 September 1936).

Doane, Mary Ann. "Film and the Masquerade—Theorising the Female Spectator." *Screen* 23 (October 1982)

———. "The Voice in the Cinema: The Articulation of Body and Space."*Yale French Studies*, no. 60 (1980).

"Dossier on Melodrama, Contributions by Griselda Pollock, Geoffrey Nowell-Smith, and Stephen Heath." *Screen* 18 (Summer 1977).

Ellis, Jack C. *A History of Film*. Englewood Cliffs, N.J.: Prentice-Hall, Inc., 1979.

Ellis, John. *Visible Fictions: Cinema: Television: Video*. London: Routledge and Kegan Paul, 1982.

Elsaesser, Thomas. "Tales of Sound and Fury: Observations on the Family Melodrama." *Monogram* 4 (1973).

Erens, Patricia, ed. *Sexual Stratagems: The World of Women in Film*. New York: Horizon Press, 1979.

Fell, John L. *Film and the Narrative Tradition*. Norman: University of Oklahoma Press, 1974.

———. *A History of Films*. New York: Holt, Rinehart and Winston, 1979.

Fermi, Laura. *Mussolini*. Chicago: University of Chicago Press, 1961.

Feuer, Jane. *The Hollywood Musical*. London: British Film Institute, 1982.

Fischer, Lucy. "The Two-Faced Women: The 'Double' in Women's Melodrama of the 1940's." *Cinema Journal* 23 (Fall 1983).

Flitterman, Sandy. "*Guest in the House*: Rupture and Reconstitution of the Bourgeois Nuclear Family." *Wide Angle* 4 (1980).

Freddi, Luigi. *Il cinema*. Rome: L'Arnia, 1949.

Gamett, Richard. *A History of Italian Literature*. Port Washington, N.Y.: Kennikat Press, 1970.

Germani, Sergio Grmek. "Introduzione a una ricerca sui generi." In *Cinema italiano sotto il fascismo*, edited by Riccardo Redi. Venice: Marsilio, 1979.

Gerould, David. *Melodrama*. New York: New York Literary Forum, 1980.

Gili, Jean A. "De la résistance à l'anti-fascisme: La génération de

1960." In *Fascisme et résistance dans le cinéma italien 1922-1968*, edited by Jean A. Gili. Paris: Lettres modernes Menard, 1970.

———. "Film storico e film in costume." In *Cinema italiano sotto il fascismo*, edited by Riccardo Redi. Venice: Marsilio, 1979.

Gramsci, Antonio. *Letteratura e vita nazionale*. Rome: Riuniti, 1979.

———. *Selections from the Prison Notebooks*. Edited by Quentin Hoare and Geoffrey Nowell-Smith. New York: International Publishers, 1978.

Guichonnet, Paul. *Mussolini et le fascisme*. Paris: Presses Universitaires, 1971.

Harvey, Steven. "Teresa Venerdí." New York: Museum of Modern Art, 1978. Mimeographed.

Haskell, Molly. *From Reverence to Rape*. New York: Holt, Rinehart and Winston, 1973.

Hay, James. *Popular Film Culture in Fascist Italy*. Bloomington: Indiana University Press, 1986.

Heath, Stephen. *Questions of Cinema*. Bloomington: Indiana University Press, 1981.

Heilman, Robert Bechtold. *The Ways of the World: Comedy and Society*. Seattle: University of Washington Press, 1978.

Hughes, H. Stuart. *Prisoners of Hope: The Silver Age of the Italian Jews*. Cambridge: Harvard University Press, 1983.

Jameson, Fredric. *Marxism and Form: Twentieth-Century Dialectical Theories of Literature*. Princeton: Princeton University Press, 1971.

———. *The Political Unconscious: Narrative as a Socially Symbolic Act*. Ithaca: Cornell University Press, 1981.

———. *Aesthetics and Politics*. London: NLB, 1977.

Jarratt, Vernon. *The Italian Cinema*. New York: Macmillan, 1951.

Johnston, Claire. "Myths of Women in the Cinema." In *Women and the Cinema*, edited by Karyn Kay and Gerald Peary. New York: E. P. Dutton, 1977.

Kaplan, E. Ann. *Women and Film: Both Sides of the Camera*. New York: Methuen, 1983.

———, ed. *Women in Film Noir*. London: British Film Institute, 1980.

Kay, Karyn, and Gerald Peary, eds. *Women and the Cinema*. New York: E. P. Dutton, 1977.

Kedward, H. R. *Fascism in Western Europe 1900-1945*. New York: New York University Press, 1971.

Kolker, Robert Philip. *The Altering Eye: Contemporary International Cinema*. Oxford: Oxford University Press, 1983.

Kracauer, Siegfried. *From Caligari to Hitler: A Psychological History of the German Film*. Princeton: Princeton University Press, 1947.

Kuhn, Annette. *Women's Pictures: Feminism and the Cinema*. London: Routledge and Kegan Paul, 1982.

Laclau, Ernesto. *Politics and Ideology in Marxist Theory*. London: NLB, 1977.

Landy, Marcia. "The Narrative of Conversion and Representations of Men in the Prewar Italian Cinema." *Journal of Film and Video* 37 (Spring 1985).

Laura, Ernesto G. "A proposito di generi: Il film comico." In *Cinema italiano sotto il fascismo*, edited by Riccardo Redi. Venice: Marsilio, 1979.

Leiser, Erwin O. *Nazi Cinema*. New York: Collier Books, 1974.

Leprohon, Pierre. *The Italian Cinema*. New York: Praeger, 1972.

Lesage, Julia. "Feminist Film Criticism: Theory and Practice." *Women and Film* 1, nos. 5/6 (1974).

Liehm, Mira. *Passion and Defiance: Film in Italy from 1942 to the Present*. Berkeley and Los Angeles: University of California Press, 1984.

Lizzani, Carlo. *Il cinema italiano 1895-1979*. 2 vols. Rome: Riuniti, 1979.

Lyttelton, Adrian. *The Seizure of Power: Fascism in Italy 1919-1929*. New York: Charles Scribner's Sons, 1973.

Macciocchi, Maria-Antonietta. "Female Sexuality in Fascist Ideology." *Feminist Review* 1 (1979).

McLennan, Gregor. *Marxism and the Methodologies of History*. London: Verso, 1981.

Maggio, Raffaello. "Avanguardisti." *Bianco e nero* 2 (February/March 1938).

Mancini, Elaine. *The Free Years of the Italian Film Industry 1930-1935*. Ann Arbor, Mich.: University Microfilms, 1981.

Mast, Gerald. *A Short History of the Movies*. Indianapolis: The Bobbs-Merrill Company, Inc., 1976.

May, Renato. "Civiltà romana—LUCE—montaggio." *Bianco e nero* 4 (January 1940).

Mayne, Judith. "Visibility and Feminist Criticism." *Film Reader* 5 (1982).

Merritt, Russell. "Melodrama: Postmortem for a Phantom Genre." *Wide Angle* 5 (1983).

Micciché, Lino. "Il cadavere nell' armadio." In *Cinema italiano sotto il fascismo*, edited by Riccardo Redi. Venice: Marsilio, 1979.

Mida, Massimo, and Lorenzo Quaglietti. *Dai telefoni bianchi al neo-realismo*. Rome-Bari: Laterza, 1980.

Mira, Giovanni, and Luigi Salvatorelli. *Storia d'Italia nel periodo fascista*. 2 vols. Turin: Einaudi, 1970.

Modleski, Tania. *Loving with a Vengeance: Mass-Produced Fantasies for Women*. Hamden, Conn.: Shoestring Books, 1982.

————. " 'Never to Be Thirty-Six Years Old': *Rebecca* as Female Oedipal Drama." *Wide Angle* 5 (1982).

Monaco, Paul. "Movies and National Consciousness." In *Feature Film as History*, edited by K.R.M. Short. Knoxville: University of Tennessee Press, 1981.

Mosse, George L. *Masses and Man: Nationalist and Fascist Perceptions of Reality*. New York: Howard Fertig, 1980.

Mulvey, Laura. "Visual Pleasure and Narrative Cinema." *Screen* 16 (Autumn 1975).

Mussolini, Vittorio. "In cerca della formula." *Cinema* (10 February 1937).

*The New York Times Encyclopedia of Film*, vols. 2 and 3. New York: Times Press, 1984.

Nichols, Bill. *Ideology and the Image: Social Representation in the Cinema and the Other Media*. Bloomington: Indiana University Press, 1981.

Orr, Christopher. "Closure and Containment: Marylee Hadley in *Written on the Wind*." *Wide Angle* 4 (1980).

Overbey, David. *Springtime in Italy: A Reader on Neorealism*. Hamden, Conn.: Archon Books, 1978.

Panicali, Anna. "L'intellettuale fascista." In *Cinema italiano sotto il fascismo*. Venice: Marsilio, 1979.

Pannunzio, Marco. "Chenal di fronte a Pirandello." *Cinema* 1 (10 Nov. 1936).

Perry, Ted. "Before Neorealism." New York: Museum of Modern Art, 1978. Mimeographed.

————. "The Road to Neorealism." *Film Comment* 14 (November/December 1978).

Petley, Julian. *Capital and Culture: German Cinema 1933-1945*. London: British Film Institute, 1979.

Piccone, Paul. *Italian Marxism*. Berkeley: University of California Press, 1983.

Pistagnesi, Patrizia. "La scena famigliare nel cinema fascista." In *Cinema italiano sotto il fascismo*, edited by Riccardo Redi. Venice: Marsilio, 1979.

Place, Janey. "Women in *Film Noir*." In *Women in Film Noir*, edited by E. Ann Kaplan. London: British Film Institute, 1980.

————, and L. S. Petersen. "Some Visual Motifs in *Film Noir*." In *Movies and Methods*, edited by Bill Nichols. Berkeley: University of California Press, 1976.

Polan, Dana. "Above All Else to Make You See: Cinema and the Ideology of Spectacle." *Boundary 2*, 11 (Fall/Winter 1982/83).

————. "Brecht and the Politics of Self-Reflexive Cinema." *Jump Cut*, no. 17 (April 1978).

Poulantzas, Nicos. *Fascism and Dictatorship: The Third International and the Problem of Fascism*. London: NLB, 1974.

Powdermaker, Hortense. *Hollywood, The Dream Factory: An Anthropologist Looks at the Movie-Makers*. New York: Little, Brown, 1950.

Renov, Michael. "From Fetish to Subject. The Containment of Sexual Difference in Hollywood's Wartime Cinema." *Wide Angle* 5 (1982).

————. "*Leave Her to Heaven*: The Double Bind of the Post-War Woman," *The Journal of the Film and Video Association* 35 (Winter 1983).

Rodowick, David. N. "Madness, Authority, and Ideology in the Domestic Melodrama of the 1950's." *The Velvet Light Trap*, no. 19 (1982).

————. "The Difficulty of Difference," *Wide Angle* 5 (1982).

Rosen, Steve. "Difference and Displacement in Seventh Heaven." *Screen* 18 (Summer 1977).

Sadoul, George. *Histoire générale du cinema*. 2 vols. Paris: Denoel, 1951.

Salvemini, Gaetano. *The Origins of Fascism in Italy*. New York: Harper and Row, 1973.

Savio, Francesco. *Cinecittà anni trenta*. 3 vols. Rome: Bulzoni, 1979.

————. *Ma l'amore no*. Milan: Sonzogno, 1975.

Schatz, Thomas. *Hollywood Genres: Formulas, Filmmaking, and the Studio System*. New York: Random House, 1981.

Seidman, Steve. *Comedian Comedy: A Tradition in Hollywood Film*. Ann Arbor: UMI Research Press, 1981.

Servadio, Gaia. *Luchino Visconti: A Biography*. New York: Franklin Watts, 1983.

Short, K.R.M., ed. *Feature Film as History*. Knoxville: University of Tennessee Press, 1981.

Silverman, Kaja. *The Subject of Semiotics*. New York: Oxford University Press, 1983.

Sillani, Tomaso. *What is Fascism and Why*. London: Bern Limited, 1931.

Smith, Dennis Mack. *Italy: A Modern History*. Ann Arbor: Univrsity of Michigan Press, 1969.

Sontag, Susan. "Fascinating Fascism." In *Movies and Methods*, edited by Bill Nichols. Berkeley: University of California Press, 1976.

Suleiman, Susan Rubin. *Authoritarian Fictions: The Ideological Novel as a Literary Genre*. New York: Columbia University Press, 1983.

Tannenbaum, Edward R. *Fascism in Italy: Society and Culture 1922-1945*. London: Allen Lane, 1972.

———, and Emiliana P. Noether. *Modern Italy: A Topical History Since 1861*. New York: New York University Press, 1974.

Tasca, Angelo. *The Rise of Italian Fascism, 1919-1922*. New York: Howard Fertig, 1966.

Telotte, J. P. "The Doubles of Fantasy and the Space of Desire. "*Film Criticism* 6 (Fall 1982).

Tinazzi, Giorgio, ed. *Il cinema italiano dal fascismo all' antifascismo: Testi e documenti dello spettacolo*. Padua: Marsilio, 1966.

Todorov, Tzvetan. *The Poetics of Prose*. Translated by Richard Howard. Ithaca: Cornell University Press, 1977.

Togliatti, Palmiro. *Lectures on Fascism*. New York: International Publishers, 1973.

Vajda, Mihaly. *Fascism as a Mass Movement*, New York: St. Martin's Press, 1976.

Venturini, Franco. "Origins of Neo-Realism." In *Springtime in Italy: A Reader on Neo-Realism*, edited by David Overbey. Hamden, Conn.: Archon Books, 1978.

Viviani, Christian. "Who Is without Sin? The Maternal Melodrama in American Film 1930-39." *Wide Angle* 4 (1980).

Walker, Janet. "Feminist Critical Practice: Female Discourse in *Mildred Pierce*," *Film Reader* 5 (1982).

Williams, Linda. " 'Something Else Besides a Mother': *Stella Dallas* and the Maternal Melodrama." *Cinema Journal* 24 (Fall 1984).

Williams, Raymond. *Marxism and Literature*. Oxford: Oxford University Press, 1977.

Zagarrio, Vito. "Il modello sovietico: Tra piano culturale e piano economico." In *Cinema italiano sotto il fascismo*, edited by Riccardo Redi. Venice: Marsilio, 1979.

# INDEX

**Library of Congress Cataloging-in-Publication Data**

Landy, Marcia, 1931-
Fascism in film.

Bibliography: p.
Includes index.
1. Moving-pictures—Italy—History.   2. Fascism—Italy.   I. Title.

PN1993.5.I88L36  1986   791.43'0945   85-43296
ISBN 0-691-05471-1 (alk. paper)

Marcia Landy is Professor of English and Film Studies
at the University of Pittsburgh.